中国滑雪产业核心数据报告
（2015—2019）

伍 斌　李 宇　魏庆华 ◎著

REPORT ON KEY DATA OF
SKI INDUSTRY IN CHINA
2015-2019

WU Bin, LI Yu, WEI Qinghua

北京

图书在版编目（CIP）数据

中国滑雪产业核心数据报告.2015—2019：汉英对照／伍斌，李宇，魏庆华著.--北京：中国经济出版社，2020.9

ISBN 978-7-5136-6286-4

Ⅰ.①中… Ⅱ.①伍…②李…③魏… Ⅲ.①雪上运动—体育产业—产业发展—研究报告—中国—2015—2019—汉、英 Ⅳ.①G863.1

中国版本图书馆CIP数据核字（2020）第158176号

责任编辑	耿　园
责任印制	巢新强
封面设计	华子图文

出版发行	中国经济出版社
印 刷 者	北京九州迅驰传媒文化有限公司
经 销 者	各地新华书店
开　　本	787mm×1092mm　1/16
印　　张	22.75
字　　数	360千字
版　　次	2020年9月第1版
印　　次	2020年9月第1次
定　　价	98.00元

广告经营许可证　京西工商广字第8179号

中国经济出版社 网址 www.economyph.com　社址 北京市东城区安定门外大街58号　邮编 100011

本版图书如存在印装质量问题，请与本社销售中心联系调换（联系电话：010-57512564）

版权所有　盗版必究（举报电话：010-57512600）
国家版权局反盗版举报中心（举报电话：12390）　　服务热线：010-57512564

法　律　申　明

1. 本报告由伍斌、李宇、魏庆华主笔编撰，报告中所有的文字、图片、表格均受到中国法律知识产权相关条例的版权保护。欢迎业内人士及机构引用、传播，但必须注明出处：伍斌，李宇，魏庆华. 中国滑雪产业核心数据报告（2015—2019）[M]. 北京：中国经济出版社，2020。

2. 本报告中采集于公开信息部分的文字和数据，著作权为原著者所有。本报告中部分数据基于行业访谈、市场调查等获得的数据分析得出，受研究方法和数据采集样本选择范围的限制，部分数据不能够完全反映市场的真实情况，请斟酌使用。报告作者及作者所服务的工作单位对报告数据的准确性不承担任何法律责任。

3. 对违反上述声明者，报告作者将保留追究其相关法律责任的权利。

伍　斌　李　宇　魏庆华
2020 年 3 月 10 日

Legal Notice

1. The report was authored by Mr. WU Bin (Benny Wu) and Prof. LI Yu co-written by Mr. WEI Qinghua. All text, images, tables are protected by copyri-ght laws and Chinese regulations relating to intellectual property. These reports are free for the public, and all included information can be quoted with proper citation of source: WU Bin, LI Yu, WEI Qinghua. Report on Key Data of Ski Industry in China (2015-2019) . Beijing: China Economic Publishing House, 2020.

2. This report is compiled from public domain information with text and data, which copyrighted by the original publishers. In this report, part of the data was based on industry interviews, market surveys and other data were obtained from the analysis results, research methods and data collection since the limiting scope of the sample selection. This data can not fully reflect the real market situation. Please use discretion. The authors of the report and associates do not bear any legal responsibility for the accuracy of reported data.

3. If the above statement is violated, the authors will retain their rights to pursue the relevant legal liability.

WU Bin, LI Yu, WEI Qinghua

March 10th, 2020

前　言

2015年7月31日17:58，国际奥委会主席巴赫在国际奥委会第128次会议上正式宣布：北京获得2022年冬季奥林匹克运动会举办权！2015年由此载入了冬奥史册，中国冬季运动也在万众瞩目下迈上一个全新的高度。

五年弹指一挥间，回顾五年来中国滑雪产业发生的变化，不得不说让人心潮澎湃。从供给侧来看，截至2019年年底，全国滑雪场数量由2014年的460家增长到770家，累计增幅67.39%。其中，有架空索道的滑雪场数量由2014年的98家增长到155家，累计增幅58.16%；室内滑雪场的数量由2014年的7家增长到31家，累计增幅342.86%。从需求侧来看，滑雪场滑雪人次由2014年的1030万上升至2019年的2090万，累计增幅达到102.91%。如果将近几年蓬勃发展的旱雪场地以及室内滑雪模拟器的滑雪人次一并统计在内，那么2019年我国滑雪总人次已经达到2202万。

2020年年初，新冠疫情突然爆发，直接导致国内滑雪场全部在春节期间暂停营业。截至2020年7月，全球疫情仍然面临着巨大的不确定性。2022年北京冬奥会为中国滑雪产业创造了一个蓬勃向上的发展大背景，这次新冠肺炎疫情大流行却对整个行业发展造成了巨大的影响。一方面我们要更加坚定信心，相信市场自身的力量；另一方面我们也有了冷静反思的机会，要脚踏实地循序渐进。因为有五年来高速增长奠定的基础，我们相信，疫情不会改变滑雪市场长期增长的发展趋势。

本报告为中国科学院地理科学与资源研究所中国冰雪产业研究中心资助出版成果。"让数据说话"是本报告一直秉承的理念，五年来每年年初发布于网络上的《中国滑雪产业白皮书》是本报告研究的基础。在国内滑雪产业从业 20 多年的我们，为能参与并见证中国冬季运动的成长以及即将到来的北京 2022 冬奥会而感到庆幸，为能将多年的积累转化为眼前的《中国滑雪产业核心数据报告（2015—2019）》而感到骄傲，为能为我国滑雪产业持续发展提供系列基础科学数据参考和借鉴而感到欣慰。

我们由衷地感谢历年来参与研究的以下团队：中国科学院地理资源所区域生态经济研究团队、雪帮雪业、中雪众源、卡宾滑雪、《中国滑雪场大全》、雪族科技（iSNOW/滑雪族）、冷山、滑呗、美团门票、马蜂窝滑雪、携程旅游、尖锋旱雪、雪乐山、雪梦都、龙之讯、金雪花等。特别感谢长期支持本报告研究的 ISPO 北京"亚太雪地产业论坛"以及瑞士的 Laurent Vanat 先生。Laurent Vanat 先生每年发布的 *International Report on Snow & Mountain Tourism：Overview of the Key Industry Figures for Ski Resorts* 为本报告提供了很多方法论上的重要指引！中国科学院地理科学与资源研究所李雪老师、温雪颖硕士、叶海鹏硕士生为报告图表绘制和内容编导付出了辛勤工作，中国经济出版社余静宜主任、耿园责任编辑对本报告出版给予了大力支持，在此表示衷心的感谢。在本报告编制过程中，由于信息完整性和资料获取方面的原因，难免有疏漏和值得商榷的地方，恳请读者批评指正。

最后，向所有为本报告提供数据支持的业界同人致敬！分享创造价值！

伍　斌　李　宇　魏庆华

2020 年 7 月

Foreword

At 17:58 on July 31st, 2015, Mr. Thomas Bach, the President of International Olympic Committee (IOC), officially announced that Beijing is the winner of 2022 Winter Olympics during the 128th Session. 2015 was enshrined in the history of the Winter Olympics, and China's winter sports have taken to a whole new level in the limelight.

Time flies, looking back at the changes in China's skiing industry over the past five years, it has to be said that it is exciting. From the supply side, the number of ski resorts in China increased from 460 in 2014 to 770 in 2019, with an accumulated growth of 67.39%. The number of ski resorts equipped with the aerial lifts increased from 98 in 2014 to 155 in 2019, with a growth of 58.16%, and the number of indoor ski resorts increased from 7 in 2014 to 31 in 2019, with a growth of 342.86%. From the demand side, the number of ski visits increased from 10.30 million in 2014 to 20.90 million in 2019, with a growth of 102.91%. If the ski visits of dry ski resorts and indoor ski simulators which had developed rapidly in recent years were all taken into account, the total number of ski visits in China in 2019 had reached 22.02 million.

In early 2020, due to the COVID-19 crisis, all domestic ski resorts were shut down during the Spring Festival. By July 2020, the global epidemic still faced considerable uncertainties. The 2022 Beijing Winter Olympics created many opportunities for China's ski industry, while the COVID-19 brought grave damage for the entire ski industry. On one hand, we should be more confident in the market forces. On the other hand, we also obtained an opportunity for calm reflection that we should be down-to-earth and step-by-step. Because of the solid foundations laid by five-year rapid growth, we are confident that the epidemic cannot change the long-term growth trend of the ski market.

This report, funded by the China Ski Industry Research Center, Institute of Geographic Sciences and Natural Resources Research (IGSNRR), Chinese Academy of Sciences (CAS), has been persisting in the concept of "let the data speak". *White Paper on China's Ski Industry*, published on the Internet in the past five years are the foundation of this report. Since we have researched the domestic ski industry for more than 20 years, it is a great honor for us to participate in and witness the growth of winter sports in China and the upcoming 2022 Beijing Winter Olympics. And we are proud to turn our years accumulation into the *Report on Key Data of Ski Industry in China* (2015 – 2019), in order to provide a series of basic scientific data and reference for the sustainable development of China's ski industry.

Our sincere thanks to the following teams which have participated in the ski industry research over the years: Research Team of Regional Ecological Economy, IGSNRR, CAS, Xuebang Snow Enterprise, China Mountain Development, Carving Ski, *China Ski Resorts Encyclopedia*, iSNOW/HUAXUEZOO, Cold Mountain, Ski+, Meituan Tickets, Mafengwo Ski, Ctrip, Peak Dry Snow, SKINOW, Winter Wonderland, Longzhixun, Gold Snowflakes Ski Industry Alliance, and so on. Meanwhile, We deliver our gratitude to ISPO Beijing: Asia Pacific Snow Conference and Mr. Laurent Vanat of Switzerland for their long-term support to this report. *International Report on Snow & Mountain Tourism: Overview of the Key Industry Figures for Ski Resorts*, issued by Mr. Laurent Vanat every year, provided many important guidelines for this Report! We would like to express our sincere thanks to LI Xue, M. D. WEN Xueying and M. D. YE Haipeng from IGSNRR for paying hard work on report diagramming and content compilation, to Director YU Jingyi and editor GENG Yuan from Economic Press China for providing substantial support for the publication of this report. In the whole process of writing, due to the limitation of information and data, there are many inevitably omissions and deficiencies in this report. Your suggestions would be appreciated.

Finally, we would like to salute to all colleagues providing data and support for this report. Sharing creates value!

WU Bin, LI Yu, WEI Qinghua

July, 2020

目 录
Contents

中国滑雪产业核心数据报告（2015—2019）

总　论 3

第一篇　2015年度中国滑雪产业核心数据报告

第一章　2015年滑雪场情况 13
　　第一节　滑雪场数量及分布 13
　　第二节　滑雪场分类统计信息 17
　　第三节　滑雪场设施 20
　　第四节　主要滑雪场人力资源状况 27
　　第五节　四季滑雪场所 29

第二章　2015年滑雪者情况 32
　　第一节　滑雪者人次及分布 32
　　第二节　滑雪者客源地及特征 34
　　第三节　滑雪者装备市场 35

第三章	滑雪赛事	37
第一节	中国近代竞技滑雪历程	37
第二节	中国参加历届冬奥会情况	38
第三节	国内举办过的重要赛事	39
第四节	国内已建设的竞技滑雪场	40

第二篇　2016年度中国滑雪产业核心数据报告

第四章	2016年滑雪场情况	43
第一节	滑雪场数量及分布	43
第二节	滑雪场分类统计信息	46
第三节	滑雪场设施	49
第四节	滑雪教练统计数据	53
第五节	四季滑雪场所	54

第五章	2016年滑雪者情况	56
第一节	滑雪者人次及分布	56
第二节	滑雪者特征：移动互联网数据	58
第三节	滑雪者装备市场	65

第三篇　2017年度中国滑雪产业核心数据报告

第六章	2017年滑雪场情况	69
第一节	滑雪场数量及分布	69
第二节	滑雪场分类统计信息	73
第三节	滑雪场硬件设施	77
第四节	滑雪场软件设施	84
第五节	四季仿真滑雪场所	91

第七章　2017年滑雪者情况 ··· 93
第一节　滑雪者人次及分布 ··· 93
第二节　滑雪者特征：移动互联网数据 ··· 95
第三节　滑雪者装备市场 ··· 101

第四篇　2018年度中国滑雪产业核心数据报告

第八章　2018年滑雪场情况 ··· 105
第一节　滑雪场数量及分布 ··· 105
第二节　滑雪场分类统计信息 ··· 109
第三节　滑雪场硬件设施 ··· 113

第九章　2018年滑雪者情况 ··· 122
第一节　滑雪者人次及分布 ··· 122
第二节　滑雪者特征 ··· 125
第三节　滑雪者装备市场 ··· 136

第五篇　2019年度中国滑雪产业核心数据报告

第十章　2019年滑雪场与滑雪人次情况 ··· 141
第一节　滑雪场数量、滑雪人次以及滑雪者人数 ··· 141
第二节　滑雪场及滑雪人次分布 ··· 143
第三节　滑雪场分类统计信息 ··· 145
第四节　旱雪场地 ··· 150
第五节　滑雪模拟器 ··· 151
第六节　总滑雪人次 ··· 152

第十一章 滑雪场硬件设施 ··· 153
　第一节 滑雪场上行设施 ·· 153
　第二节 滑雪场场地设施 ·· 158
　第三节 滑雪场租赁设施 ·· 159

第十二章 滑雪者特征 ··· 161
　第一节 滑雪者的性别 ·· 161
　第二节 滑雪者的年龄 ·· 162
　第三节 滑雪者的其他特征 ·· 162

第十三章 滑雪者装备市场 ··· 166
　第一节 迪卡侬Wed'ze滑雪品牌中国报告 ······························ 166
　第二节 冷山GOSKI报告 ··· 166

Report on Key Data of Ski Industry in China (2015–2019)

General ·· 171

Part 1 2015 Report on Key Data of Ski Industry in China

Chapter 1 2015 Ski Resort ·· 183
　Ⅰ. Number & Distribution ·· 183
　Ⅱ. Classification Statistics ······································ 187
　Ⅲ. Facilities Statistics ·· 190

Ⅳ. Human Resources Statistics ··· 197

　　Ⅴ. Four Seasons Ski Resorts ··· 200

Chapter 2　2015 Skier ··· 202

　　Ⅰ. Visits & Distribution ··· 202

　　Ⅱ. Characteristics ··· 204

　　Ⅲ. Ski Equipment Market ··· 205

Chapter 3　Ski Competiton Development ··· 207

　　Ⅰ. The History of Ski Racing in Modern China ··· 207

　　Ⅱ. China's Participation in Previous Winter Olympic Games ··· 208

　　Ⅲ. Important Ski Competitions in China ··· 210

　　Ⅳ. Competitive Ski Resorts in China ··· 211

Part 2　2016 Report on Key Data of Ski Industry in China

Chapter 4　2016 Ski Resort ··· 215

　　Ⅰ. Number & Distribution ··· 215

　　Ⅱ. Classification Statistics ··· 218

　　Ⅲ. Facilities Statistics ··· 221

　　Ⅳ. Human Resources Statistics ··· 225

　　Ⅴ. Four Seasons Ski Resorts ··· 226

Chapter 5　2016 Skier ··· 228

　　Ⅰ. Visits & Distribution ··· 228

　　Ⅱ. Characteristics: Mobile Internet Data ··· 230

　　Ⅲ. Ski Equipment Market ··· 237

Part 3   2017 Report on Key Data of Ski Industry in China

Chapter 6   2017 Ski Resort ········ 241
   I. Number & Distribution ········ 241
   II. Classification Statistics ········ 245
   III. Hardware Facilities ········ 249
   IV. Software Facilities ········ 257
   V. Four Seasons Ski Resorts ········ 265

Chapter 7   2017 Skier ········ 267
   I. Visits & Distribution ········ 267
   II. Characteristics: Mobile Internet Data ········ 269
   III. Ski Equipment Market ········ 276

Part 4   2018 Report on Key Data of Ski Industry in China

Chapter 8   2018 Ski Resort ········ 279
   I. Number & Distribution ········ 279
   II. Classification Statistics ········ 283
   III. Facilities Statistics ········ 288

Chapter 9   2018 Skier ········ 297
   I. Visits & Distribution ········ 297
   II. Characteristics ········ 300
   III. Ski Equipment Market ········ 312

Part 5 2019 Report on Key Data of Ski Industry in China

Chapter 10 2019 Ski Resorts and Ski Visits ... 315
- I. Number of Ski Resorts, Ski Visits and Skiers ... 315
- II. Distribution of Ski Resorts and Ski Visits ... 317
- III. Classified Statistics of Ski Resorts ... 319
- IV. Dry Ski ... 325
- V. Ski Simulator ... 326
- VI. Total Ski Visits ... 327

Chapter 11 Facilities of Ski Resorts ... 328
- I. Lifts Facilities ... 328
- II. Grooming & Snowmaking Facilities ... 333
- III. Rental Skis ... 335

Chapter 12 Characteristics of Skiers ... 336
- I. Gender of Skiers ... 336
- II. Age of Skiers ... 337
- III. Other Characteristics ... 337

Chapter 13 Ski Equipment Market ... 342
- I. China Market Report from DECATHLON Wed'ze Ski ... 342
- II. Cold Mountain GOSKI Report ... 343

中国滑雪产业核心数据报告
（2015—2019）

伍 斌　李 宇　魏庆华　著

总　论

一、全国滑雪产业主要指标变化情况

2019 年，国内滑雪场与 2015 年相比新增 202 家，总数达到 770 家，累计增长 35.56%，但增长速度有所下降。截至 2019 年年底，全国 770 家滑雪场中，有架空索道的滑雪场达到 155 家，相比 2015 年的 122 家增长 27.05%。全国室内滑雪馆数量由 2015 年的 9 家上升至 2019 年的 31 家，累计增长 244.44%。国内滑雪场的滑雪人次由 2015 年的 1250 万上升到 2019 年的 2090 万，增幅为 67.2%。滑雪场数量、有架空索道的滑雪场数量、室内滑雪馆数量、滑雪场滑雪人次的变化如图 0-1 至图 0-4 所示。

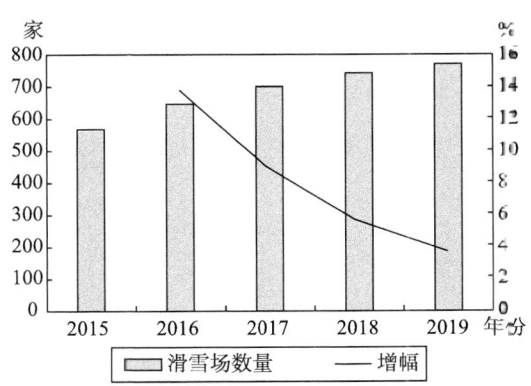

图 0-1　2015—2019 年全国滑雪场数量

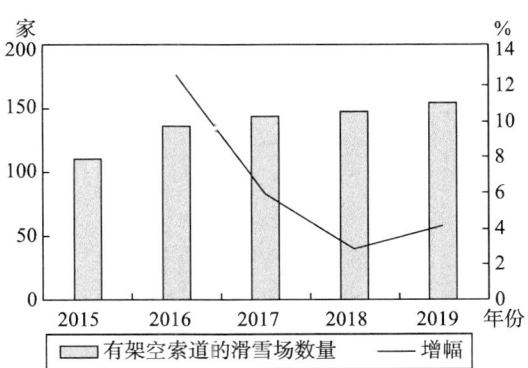

图 0-2　2015—2019 年全国有架空索道的滑雪场数量

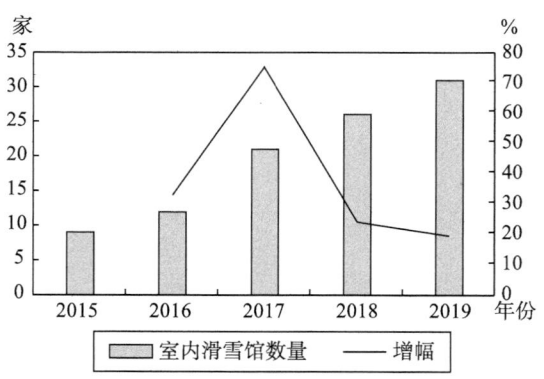

图 0-3　2015—2019 年全国室内滑雪馆数量

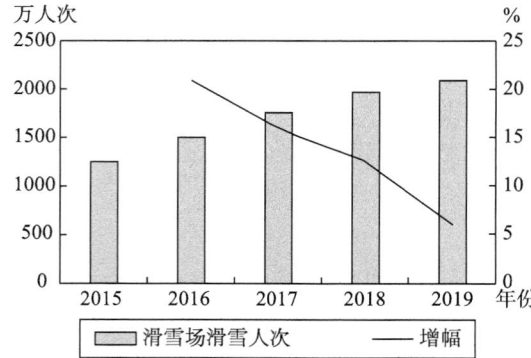

图 0-4　2015—2019 年全国滑雪场滑雪人次

雪道面积是衡量滑雪场大小的一个重要维度。2019 年，全国雪道面积超过 30 公顷的滑雪场共计 30 家，比 2015 年新增 13 家，占比上升了 1.6 个百分点（见表 0-1）。

表 0-1　2015 年、2019 年按雪道面积统计的滑雪场数据

雪道面积/公顷	2015 年数量/家	占比/%	2019 年数量/家	占比/%
>100	1	0.18	8	1.04
50~100	7	1.23	7	0.91
30~50	5	0.88	15	1.95
10~30	20	3.52	37	4.81
5~10	50	8.80	126	16.36
<5	485	85.39	577	74.94
合计	568	100.00	770	100.00

二、各省（区、市）滑雪产业主要指标变化情况

（一）滑雪场数量分析

2015—2019 年，全国新增滑雪场总数为 202 家。按滑雪场绝对数量排序，到 2019 年，排名前五的省份依次为黑龙江、山东、新疆、河北、山西。与 2015 年不同的是，山西超越吉林进入了前五。按 2019 年相比 2015 年新增加的滑雪场数量排序，河北增加 21 家，位居第一，随后是山西、山东和内蒙古，分别为 17 家、16 家及 16 家，此外，陕西、新疆、湖北等地也增加较多（见图 0-5）。

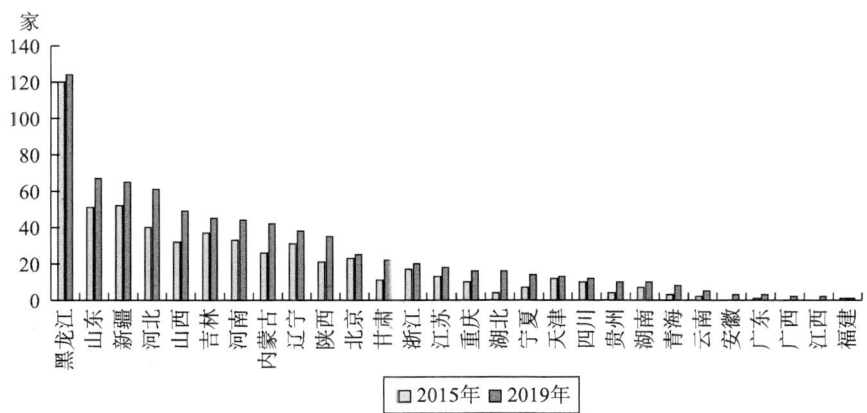

图0-5 2015—2019年全国各省（区、市）滑雪场数量变化

按滑雪场数量占全国比例排序，2019年排名前五的省份依次为黑龙江、山东、新疆、河北、山西，5省（区）滑雪场占全国滑雪场总数的47.5%。从2015—2019年年均增长率来看，湖北省滑雪场年均增长率居全国第一。其次是广东、青海、云南，增长率分别为31.61%、27.79%和25.74%，安徽、广西、江西等原来没有滑雪场的地区也开始逐渐发展起滑雪场。相反地，滑雪场基数较大的黑龙江、辽宁、山东等地年均增长率较小（见图0-6）。

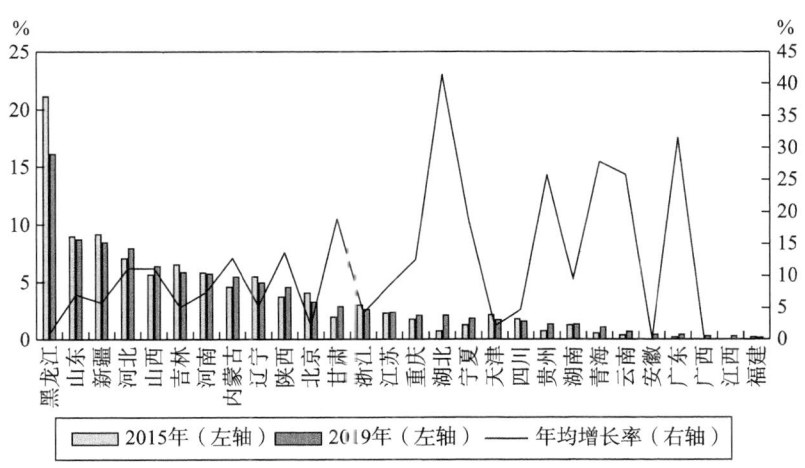

图0-6 2015—2019年全国各省（区、市）滑雪场数量占比及年均增长率变化

我国滑雪场的分布在整体上呈现出由北向南逐渐递减的趋势，集中分布于黑龙江、河北和山东等东北和华北地区，长江以南地区滑雪场分布较少，且数量变化不大。

为了更清晰地了解滑雪场在全国的分布状况,可将全国划分为东北、华北、西北、华东、华中、华南及西南 7 个大区。从大区的分布来看,滑雪场分布状况如图 0-7、图 0-8 所示。2015—2019 年滑雪场数量增长最多的是东北大区,五年间新增滑雪场 57 家,占比保持全国第一,但比例有所下降,从 33.1% 下降至 26.88%,下降速度较快。其次是华北地区,五年间新增雪场 50 家,所占比重增加了 2.15 个百分点。华中和华东地区五年间分别新增了 28 家、27 家。

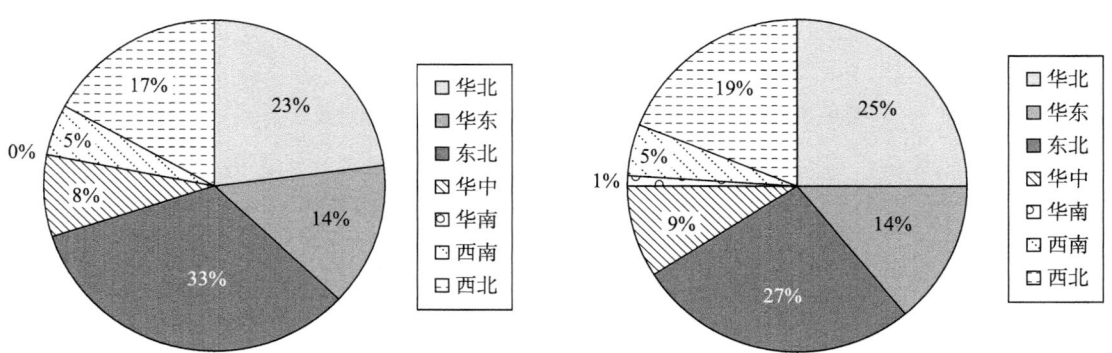

图 0-7　2015 年全国各大区滑雪场分布比例　　图 0-8　2019 年全国各大区滑雪场分布比例

各省(区、市)滑雪场数量的占比情况如图 0-9 所示。2015 年,黑龙江、新疆、山东是主要的高值区,值域范围为 9.2%~21.3%,长江以南的大部分区域为主要的低值区,值域范围为 0~0.7%。2019 年高值区与 2015 年基本保持一致,没有大范围的变动,但低值区范围明显缩小,湖北、贵州等长江以南的多个省份逐渐向中值区转化。

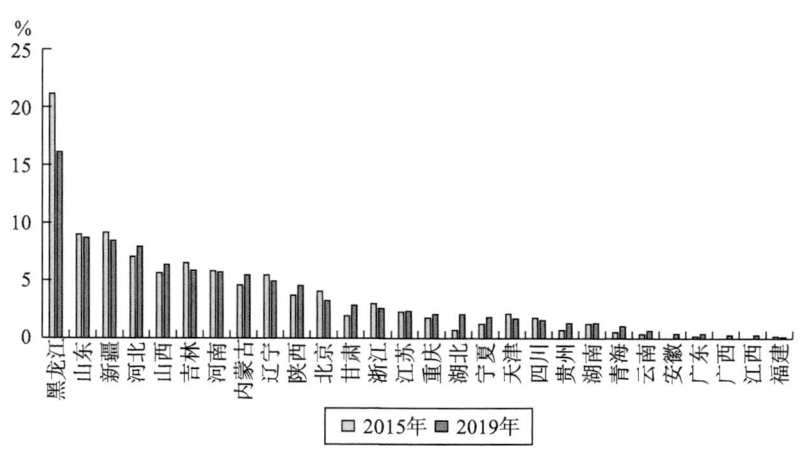

图 0-9　2015 年、2019 年各省(区、市)滑雪场数量占全国的比重

图 0-10 为 2015—2019 年全国各省（区、市）滑雪场数量的年均增长率变化。2015—2019 年，湖北、广东、青海、云南、贵州为主要的高值区，年均增长率较大，这些地区 2015 年滑雪场基数较小，之后迅速增加，因此增长速度较快。

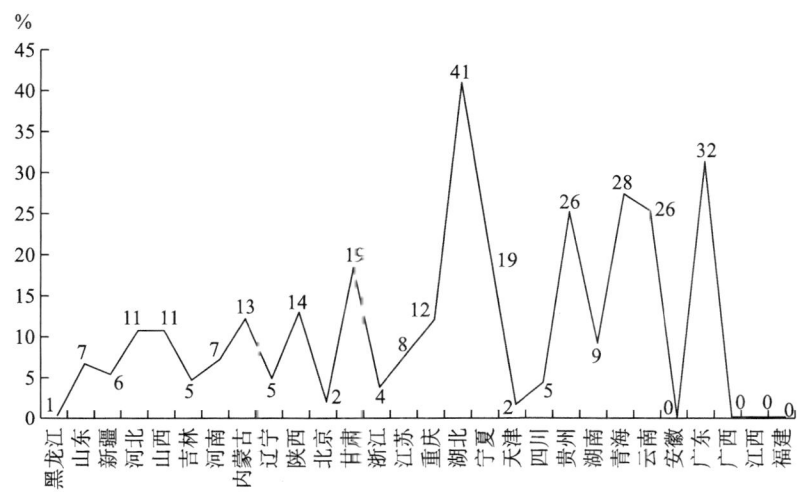

图 0-10　2015—2019 年全国各省（区、市）滑雪场的年均增长率

（二）滑雪人次变化分析

图 0-11 为 2015—2019 年全国各省（区、市）滑雪人次占全国的比重及年均增长率变化。按滑雪人次占比排序，2019 年排名前五的省份依次为河北、吉林、北京、黑龙江、新疆，河北地区滑雪人次占比由原来的第五攀升至第一，黑龙江、山东和北京占比有所下降。从 2015—2019 年的年均增长率来看，全国年均增长率为 13.77%。广东滑雪人次共增加了 63 万人次，年均增长率为 138.77%，位居全国第一。其次是贵州、青海、云南，其增长率分别为 59.05%、39.16% 和 31.61%。

2015—2019 年，全国滑雪人次的分布在整体上呈现出由北向南、由东向西逐渐递减的趋势，集中分布于东北及华北等具有滑雪优势的地区及东部发达地区。2019 年各省（区、市）滑雪人次都有了明显增加，以河北、吉林和广东表现最为突出。江西、广西和福建等华南和西南大部分地区滑雪人次较少，且没有明显变化。

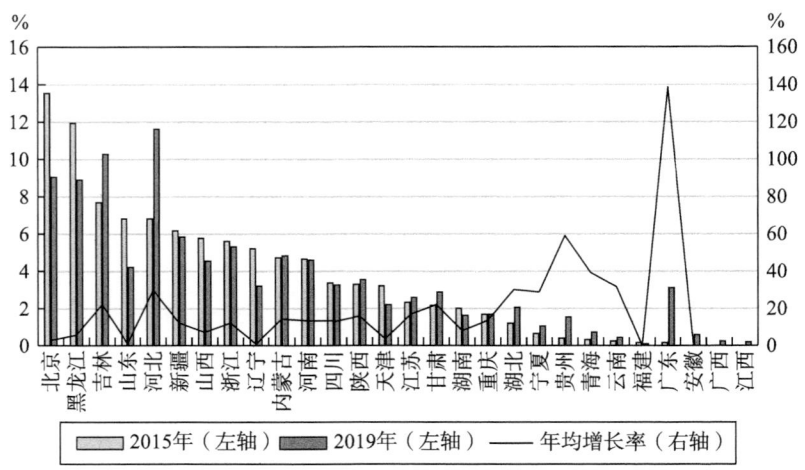

图 0-11 2015—2019 全国各省（区、市）滑雪人次占比及年均增长率变化

从滑雪人次占比上看，2015 年，北京、黑龙江和吉林为高值区，值域范围为 7.7%～13.5%；长江以南的大部分区域为主要的低值区，值域范围仅 0～0.6%。与 2015 年相比，2019 年高值区的范围更大，河北也进入了高值区。同时，低值区范围明显缩小，湖北、贵州等长江以南的多个省份逐渐向中值区转化。

图 0-12 为 2015—2019 年全国各省（区、市）滑雪人次的年均增长率变化。与滑雪人次分布不同，滑雪人次年均增长率高值区多分布于我国南部地区。2015—2019 年，广东、贵州等长江以南地区为高值区，值域范围在 59.0%～138.77%，年均增长率较高。辽宁、北京、山东等北部省份为主要的低值区，年均增长率较小。

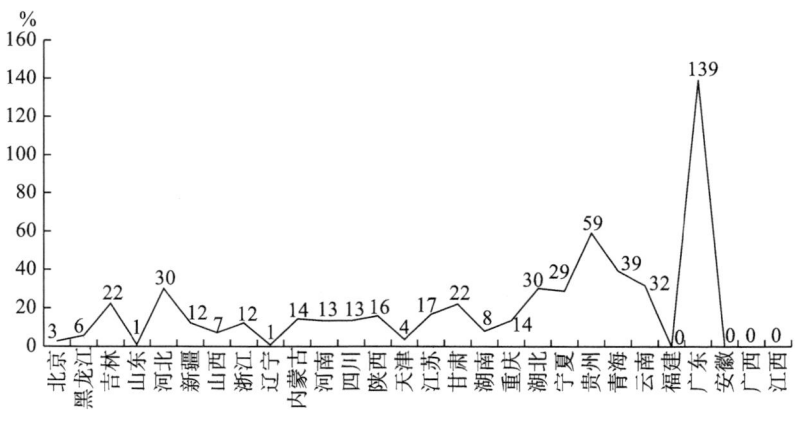

图 0-12 2015—2019 年全国各省（区、市）滑雪人次的年均增长率

（三）架空索道分析

2015年、2019年全国架空索道数量及有架空索道分布的滑雪场数量变化情况如图0-13、图0-14所示。与2015年相比，2019年全国架空索道共增加了64条，河北新增最多，增加了24条。其次为吉林、内蒙古。有架空索道分布的滑雪场数量从2015年的122家上升至2019年的155家，共增加33家。其中，河北新增最多，新增13家，占新增总数的39.4%。其次为吉林、黑龙江和内蒙古，分别增加了9家、6家、5家。

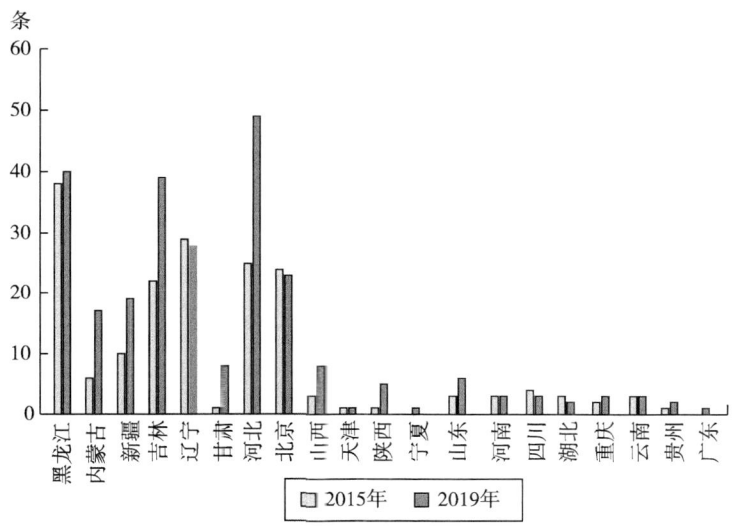

图0-13　2015年、2019年全国架空索道数量变化

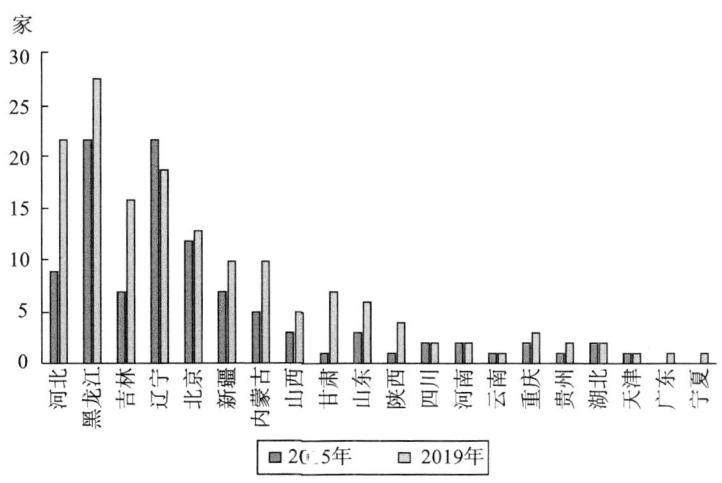

图0-14　2015年、2019年有架空索道分布的滑雪场数量变化

从全国架空索道数量来看，全国架空索道集中分布于东北、华北以及新疆等地区，其次为中部地区，西南以及东南沿海地区分布较少。有架空索道的滑雪场的分布与架空索道的分布具有极强的关联性，空间分布大致趋同。

图0-15为2015—2019年全国各省（区、市）有架空索道的滑雪场的年均增长率。各省（区、市）有架空索道的滑雪场的年均增长率以低值为主，高值区较少，主要分布于甘肃、陕西和河北，其次为吉林；而低值区广泛分布于长江以南的大部分区域，最低值为辽宁，年均增长率为负。

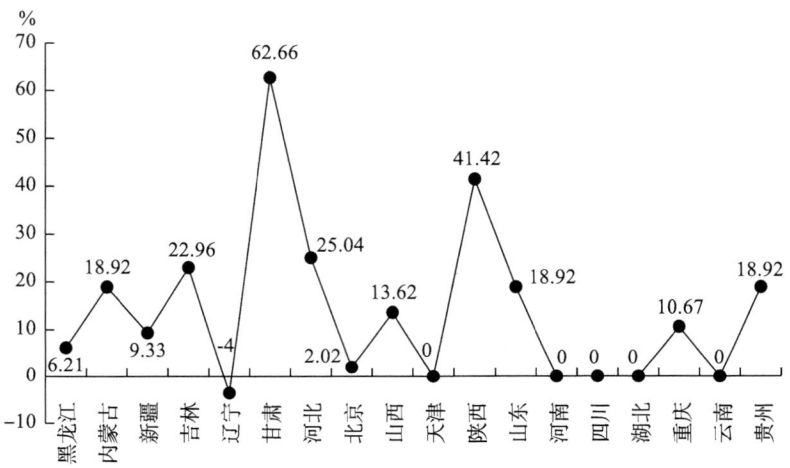

图0-15 2015—2019年全国有架空索道的滑雪场的年均增长率

第一篇

2015年度中国滑雪产业核心数据报告

第一章　2015年滑雪场情况

2015年，国内滑雪场数量同比增幅较大，比2014年增长23.48%。国内投入运营的滑雪场总数为568家，其中包括9家室内滑雪馆（不含各类户外及室内的戏雪娱雪乐园），相比2014年新增108家。

国内滑雪场投入设备设施情况统计如下：滑雪架空缆车合计198条，滑雪拖牵合计367条，滑雪魔毯合计618条；全部造雪机估算为4000台（含进口造雪机和国产造雪机），全部压雪车数量约为330台（其中进口压雪车300台、国产压雪车数量按10%的比例估计有30台）；滑雪场租赁双板总量估算为35万副，租赁单板总量估算为3万副，租赁雪服总量估算为10万套；国内用于滑雪者雪板维护的进口修板机数量合计为60台（包括滑雪场租赁和雪场外雪具服务店，不含雪板工厂购置数量）。

第一节　滑雪场数量及分布

1996—2015年20年间，国内滑雪场的数量增长状况见图1-1，其中1996—2011年的数据在中国滑雪协会公布的数据基础上结合从业经验修正而来，2012—2015年的数据依据《中国滑雪场大全》，剔除戏雪娱雪乐园的部分并根据实际调研的情况修正部分资料而来。

2015年，全国滑雪场数量达到568家，相比2014年新增108家，增幅为23.48%，相比2010年增加298家，增幅为110.37%。

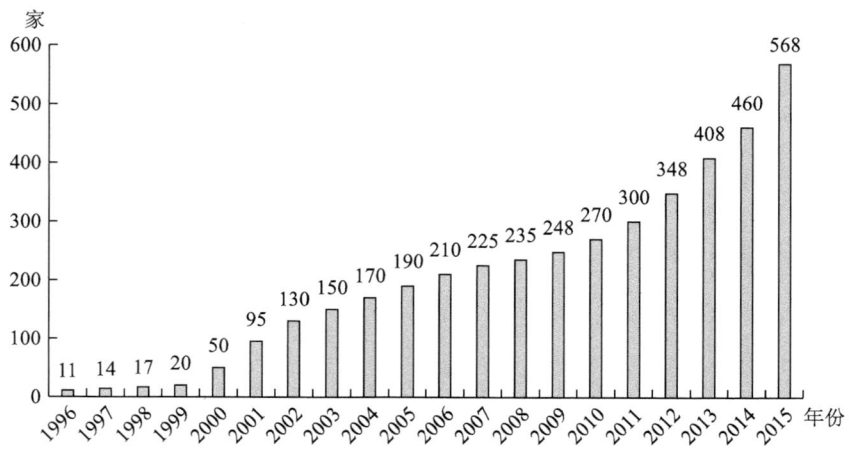

图 1-1　1996—2015 年全国滑雪场数量统计

568 家滑雪场分布于全国 25 个省（区、市），其中，黑龙江滑雪场数量为 120 家，为全国之冠（见图 1-2）。

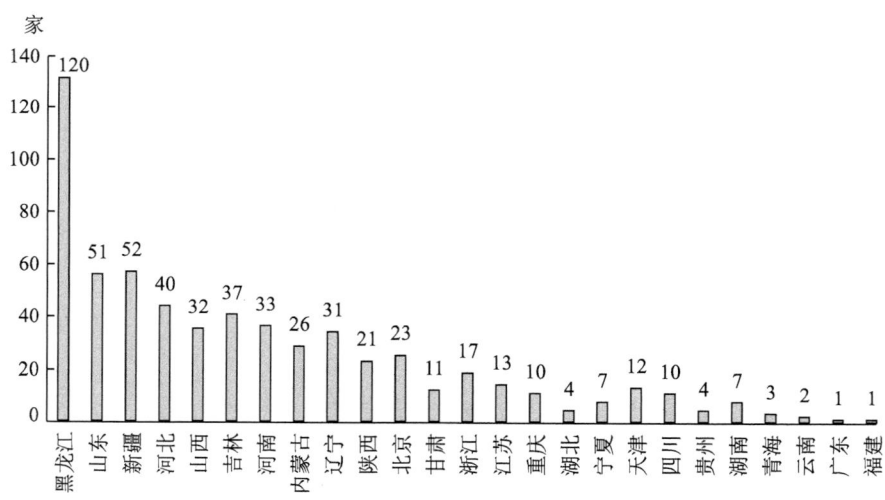

图 1-2　2015 年全国滑雪场分布

从东北、华北、西北、华东、华中、华南及西南的大区来看，滑雪场分布如图 1-3 所示。其中，东北区域雪场数量占比最大，为 33.10%，其次为华北区域，为 23.24%。

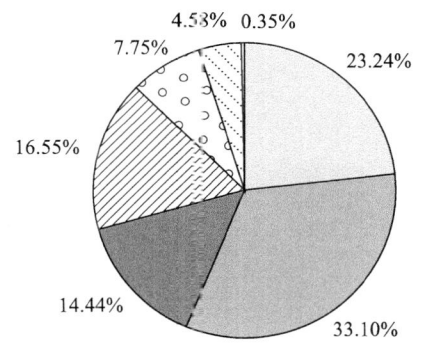

图 1-3 2015 年中国各大区滑雪场分布

2012—2015 年全国各地滑雪场数量变化如图 1-4 及图 1-5 所示。2015 年，全国新增滑雪场总数为 108 家。按滑雪场绝对数量排序，2015 年排名前五的省份依次为黑龙江、新疆、山东、河北、吉林；按 2015 年相比 2014 年新增加的滑雪场数量排序，山东增加 22 家，位居第一，随后是河南、山西、陕西，分别新增 14 家、11 家及 9 家，浙江、江苏和吉林各新增 7 家滑雪场。

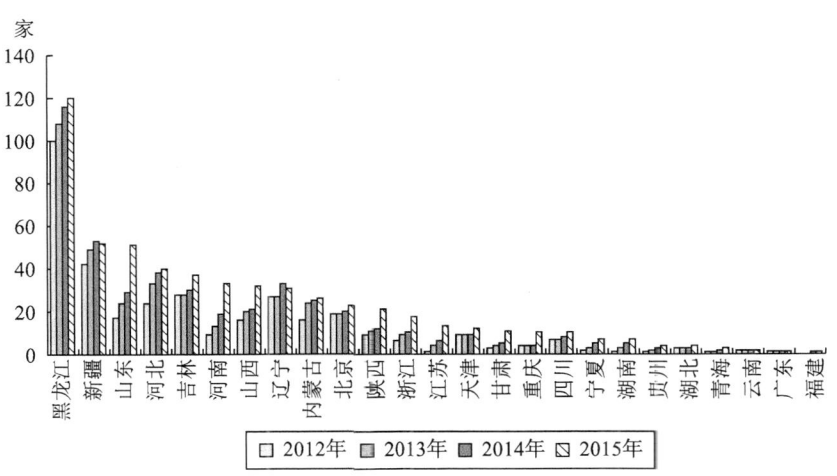

图 1-4 2012—2015 年全国各省（区、市）滑雪场数量变化 A

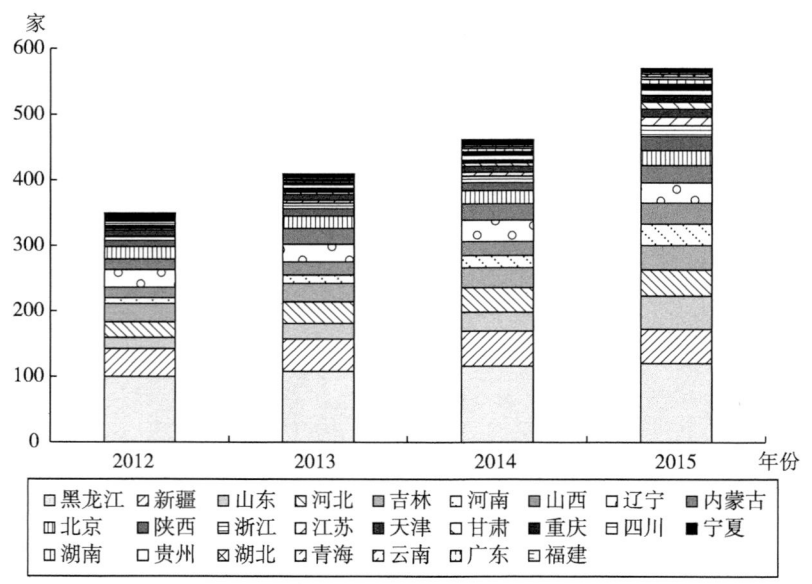

图 1-5　2012—2015 年全国各省（区、市）滑雪场数量变化 B

从全国七大区域来看，与 2014 年相比，2015 年滑雪场数量增长最多的是华东区域，新增滑雪场 36 家；其次是华北区域，新增滑雪场 20 家。与 2012 年相比，同样是华东及华北两个区域新增滑雪场数量排在前列，华东地区共计新增 58 家滑雪场，华北地区共计新增 49 家滑雪场（见图 1-6）。

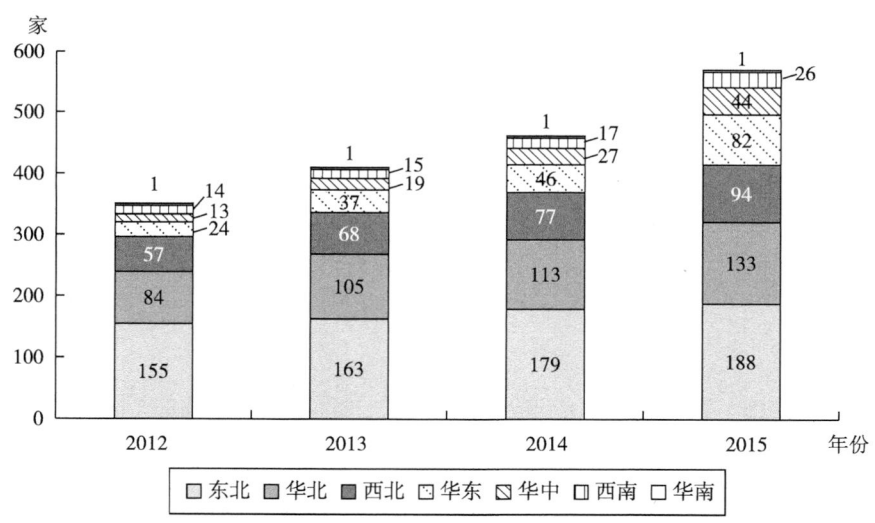

图 1-6　2012—2015 年全国各大区域滑雪场数量变化

第二节　滑雪场分类统计信息

为更清晰地呈现国内滑雪场的现状，本节从核心目标客群、垂直落差、雪道面积以及滑雪人次4个不同的角度出发，对滑雪场进行分类统计。

一、按核心目标客群分类

按滑雪场核心目标客群的差异，国内滑雪场可以分为三类：旅游体验型、城郊学习型以及目的地度假型。此三类滑雪场占比分别为75%、22%及3%（详细特征见表1-1）。

表1-1　2015年国内滑雪场按核心目标客群分类

滑雪场类型	数量占比	客群定位	主要体现滑雪属性	滑雪场特征	客群特征	典型案例
旅游体验型	75%	旅游观光客	旅游属性	设施简单，只有初级道。位置一般在旅游景区或城郊	90%以上为一次性体验客户，客人平均停留时间2小时	雪世界、鸟巢
城郊学习型	22%	本地居民	运动属性、旅游属性	山体落差不大，位于城市郊区，开发有初级、中级、高级雪道	本地自驾客人占比很大，平均停留时间为3~4小时	南山、军都山、怪坡
目的地度假型	3%	度假人群	度假属性、运动属性、旅游属性	山体有一定规模，除有齐全的雪道产品外，还有住宿等设施的配套	过夜消费占比较大，客人平均停留时间在1天以上	万科松花湖、万达长白山、北大壶、亚布力、万龙、云顶

二、按垂直落差统计

滑雪场的垂直落差是衡量滑雪场所在山地的资源规模的一个重要指标。按滑雪场实际开发雪道的垂直落差，国内滑雪场可以按以下三类统计：垂直落差超过300米的滑雪场19家（见表1-2）、垂直落差在100~300米的滑雪场103家以及垂直落差小于100米的滑雪场446家。按垂直落差分类的滑雪场占比如图1-7所示。

表 1-2 2015 年国内垂直落差超过 300 米的滑雪场

排序	滑雪场名称	已开发垂直落差/米	山顶海拔/米	山脚海拔/米	所在省份
1	长白山天池雪	950	2600	1650	吉林
2	亚布力体委	885	1360	475	黑龙江
3	北大壶	870	1404	534	吉林
4	云南香格里拉	662	3980	3318	云南
5	万科松花湖	600	935	335	吉林
6	万龙	580.3	2110.3	1530	河北
7	新疆丝绸之路	580	2440	1860	新疆
8	亚布力阳光	540	995	455	黑龙江
9	太舞	510	2062	1552	河北
10	美林谷	480	1660	1180	内蒙古
11	云顶	420	2100	1680	河北
12	阿勒泰将军山	405	1320	915	新疆
13	伏牛山	400	1931	1565	河南
14	丹东天桥沟	392	878	486	辽宁
15	万达长白山	380	1200	820	吉林
16	多乐美地	323	1963	1640	河北
17	石京龙	310	836	526	北京
18	帽儿山	308	626	318	黑龙江
19	长城岭	300	2060	1760	河北

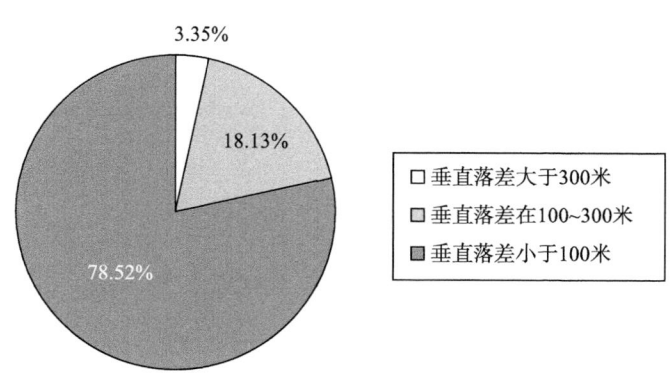

图 1-7 2015 年国内滑雪场按垂直落差统计占比

如表 1-2 所示，垂直落差超过 300 米的 19 家滑雪场中，有 5 家位于河北（全部落户崇礼），4家位于吉林，3家位于黑龙江，此外，新疆有2家，内蒙古、辽宁、河南、云南、北京各1家。需要说明的是，长白山天池雪滑雪场开发的雪道垂直落差居于全国之首，但提升设施依赖于压雪车和雪地摩托；北京延庆的石京龙滑雪场垂直落差达到310米，是全北京落差最大的滑雪场，在其他统计资料中经常被遗漏。

三、按雪道面积统计

雪道面积是衡量滑雪场大小的另一个重要维度。截至2015年，"三万"（万科松花湖、万达长白山、万龙）的雪道面积位列国内滑雪场的前三。其中，万科松花湖是目前国内唯一一家雪道面积突破100公顷的滑雪场，万达长白山和万龙两家滑雪场的雪道面积分别为96公顷及97公顷（见表1-3）（亚布力如果按三山联网的范围来计算，雪道面积也在100公顷以上）。

表1-3 2015年国内滑雪场数量按雪道面积统计

雪道面积/公顷	滑雪场数量/家
>100	1
50~100	7
30~50	5
10~30	20
5~10	50
<5	485
合计	568

四、按滑雪人次统计

根据初步统计资料估算，国内2013—2014年雪季、2014—2015年雪季、2015—2016年雪季3个雪季滑雪人次曾达到或将达到15万的滑雪场约为12家，其中万达长白山、万科松花湖、万龙、南山4家滑雪场已确定会率先突破20万滑雪人次大关，而万达长白山滑雪场即将成为国内首家突破30万滑雪人次的滑雪场。此3个雪季滑雪人次曾达到过5万但少于15万的滑雪场约为69家。另外487家滑雪场滑雪人次在5万以下，其中至少有超过半数的滑雪场，全年滑雪人次不超过2万（见图1-8）。

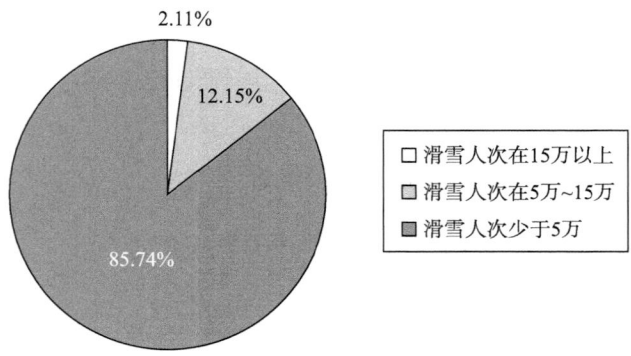

图 1-8 2015 年国内滑雪场按滑雪人次统计占比

第三节 滑雪场设施

一、滑雪场上行设施

高山滑雪离不开上行设施。过去 20 年来，国内滑雪场陆续使用过越野吉普车（1996 年崇礼塞北）、拖牵、魔毯、固定抱索器架空索道、高速脱挂式架空索道、雪地摩托和雪猫滑雪（长白山天池雪）、直升机滑雪等上行设施。随着滑雪市场的发展，国内滑雪场上行设施演化过程主要的特点如下：

第一，滑雪场初级雪道区域对魔毯的需求越来越大，运用范围越来越广泛，国产魔毯的长度已突破 400 米；早期被滑雪场初级雪道区域广泛使用的拖牵类上行设备因运力不足，需求大幅度缩减，逐渐被运用到教学区和训练区。

第二，高速脱挂式架空索道基本集中在垂直落差超过 300 米的滑雪场中，近两年新开发和新扩建的部分目的地度假类滑雪场甚至完全放弃了固定抱索器架空索道。

各类统计数据综合显示，截至 2015 年，全国滑雪场投入运营的架空索道合计 198 条（其中包括按 10%估算的统计遗漏项），分别分布于 122 家滑雪场；全国滑雪场中投入使用的拖牵类上行设施合计 367 条；全国滑雪场投入运营的魔毯总数为 618 条。

（一）滑雪场架空索道

黑龙江、辽宁、河北、北京及吉林占据了全国滑雪架空索道数量的前五位（见表 1-4）。

表1-4　2015年全国滑雪场架空索道分布

排序	省份	架空索道数量/条	有架空索道的滑雪场数量/家
1	黑龙江	38	22
2	辽宁	29	22
3	河北	25	9
4	北京	24	12
5	吉林	22	7
6	新疆	10	7
7	内蒙古	6	5
8	四川	4	2
9	河南	3	2
10	湖北	3	2
11	山东	3	3
12	云南	3	1
13	山西	3	3
14	重庆	2	2
15	天津	1	1
16	贵州	1	1
17	陕西	1	1
18	甘肃	1	1
按10%估算的统计遗漏数量		19	19
合计		198	122

截至2015年，滑雪场架空索道中，脱挂式架空索道合计有26条投入运营，其中，吉林省13条、河北省9条、黑龙江省4条（见表1-5）。

表1-5　2015年全国滑雪场脱挂式架空索道分布　　　　　　　　　　单位：条

雪场	数量
万科松花湖	6
万达长白山	5
云顶	3
太舞	3
亚布力阳光	2
北大壶	2

续表

雪场	数量
万龙	2
多乐美地	1
帽儿山	1
亚布力体委	1
合计	26

根据统计数据，全国滑雪场投入运营的国产固定抱索器架空索道合计153条（不含10%遗漏项），索道长度合计116938米，平均每条索道的长度为764.30米。据业内专业人士测算，目前国内每年新增的滑雪场架空索道数量约为30条。

（二）滑雪场魔毯

根据道沃机电官方网站公布的数据，结合对业内相关人士的访谈，我国自2007年开始至2015年投入运营的魔毯总数为618条，累计总长度为92062米，平均每条魔毯的长度为149米。2015年新增魔毯164条，总长度超过2万米（见表1-6、图1-9）（鉴于2007年之前滑雪魔毯总体投入量很小，本报告忽略不计）。

表1-6 2007—2015年全国滑雪场魔毯情况

年份	新增魔毯数量/条	新增魔毯长度/米	平均每条魔毯长度/米
2007	37	5131.58	139.29
2008	56	6292.59	113.27
2009	51	9030.23	176.50
2010	30	5381.82	177.60
2011	48	7547.54	158.76
2012	57	8666.67	153.33
2013	59	10285.51	173.10
2014	117	17941.00	153.15
2015	164	21785.07	133.02
合计	618	92062.01	148.91

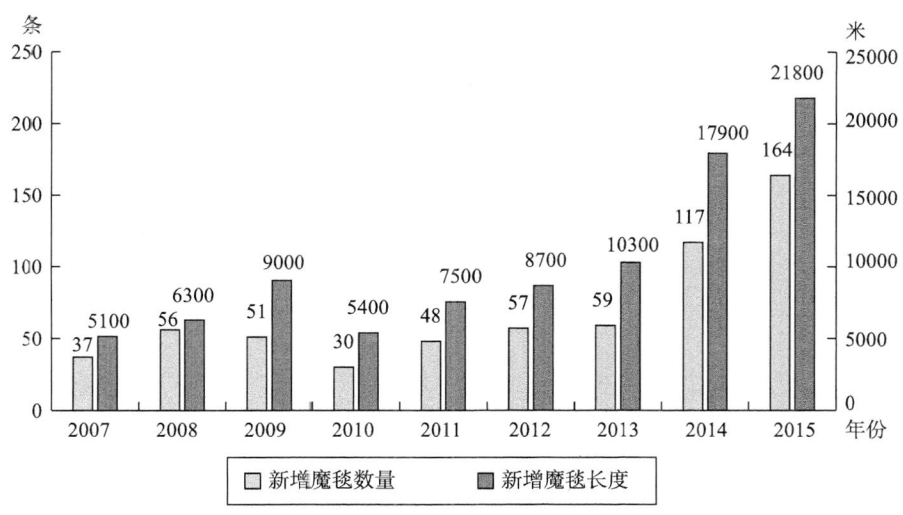

图 1-9　2007—2015 年全国滑雪场新增魔毯情况

根据已投入运营的滑雪场魔毯在全国七大区的分布情况，华北区域占据了绝对优势，占全国滑雪场魔毯总数的 36.98%，其次是东北区域，占 21.60%（见图 1-10）。

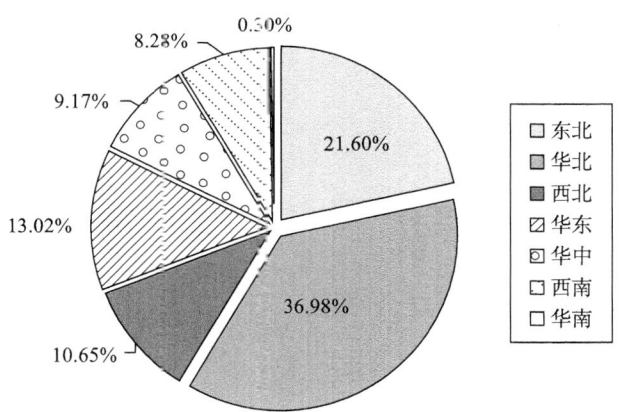

图 1-10　2015 年全国各区域滑雪场魔毯分布比例

二、滑雪场造雪压雪设施

根据统计数据初步测算，国内滑雪场整体雪道面积约为 3080 公顷，人工造雪面积及压雪面积约占总雪道面积的 99%。

（一）造雪系统工程

通过承接国内滑雪场人工造雪系统工程最多的硕华基公司提供的数据，可以大体了解国内部分主要雪场造雪系统的基本状况（见表1-7）。

表1-7 硕华基公司造雪系统工程信息

排序	项目名称	建设规模/公顷	雪道总长度/千米	建设时间
1	万科松花湖	152	31	2014年
2	万达长白山	100	34	2010年
3	万龙（1~5期）	100	35	2004—2014年
4	崇礼密苑云顶	80	30	2010年
5	崇礼太舞	72	26	2014年
6	亚布力阳光	55	16	2008年
7	吉林北大壶（1~2期）	50	37	2005年、2009年
8	新疆丝绸之路（2~3期）	50	8	2009年、2010年
9	牙克石凤冠山滑雪场	42	5.8	2008—2009年
10	牙克石凤凰山滑雪场	20	5.8	2010年
11	辽宁丹东天桥沟滑雪场	20	6	2012年
12	乌兰巴托滑雪场	17	7.1	2008年
13	崇礼长城岭（1~2期）	16	5	2006年、2013年
14	吉林市莲花山滑雪场	14	6	2003年
15	云南香格里拉滑雪场	12	5.5	2007年
16	沈阳棋盘山滑雪场	10	3	2009年
17	杭州大明山滑雪场	10	2	2010年
18	河北玉田玉龙湾滑雪场	8.5	4.5	2012年
19	成都西岭雪山滑雪场（2~3期）	8	8	2009年
20	国际体育场（鸟巢）	5.7	0.8	2009年
21	北京奥林匹克公园雪场	2	—	2013年
22	北京温都水城	0.6	0.5	2009年
	合计	867.8	277	

（二）造雪机

根据各大造雪机供应商提供的信息测算，国内滑雪场全部造雪机总数约为4000台，其中进口造雪机约3500台、国产造雪机约500台。2015年新增造雪机数量在700台左右。

（三）压雪车

国内雪场全部压雪车数量约为330台，其中进口压雪车300台，国产压雪车数量按10%估计为30台。2015年，国内新增进口压雪车61台。根据意大利Prinoth公司提供的资料，2011—2015年我国每年新增进口压雪车数量如图1-11所示。

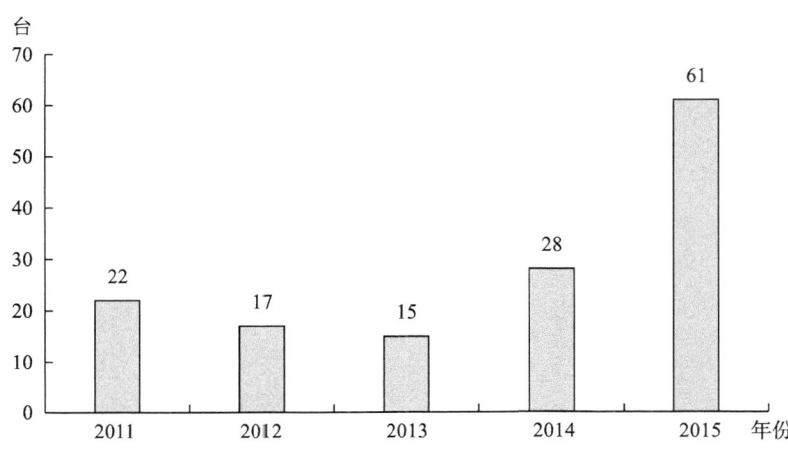

图1-11 2011—2015年我国每年新增进口压雪车数量

三、滑雪场主要租赁装备

根据主要雪板供应商提供的信息，2014年、2015年，国内滑雪场每年新增租赁双板的总量已接近或达到10万副的数量级。2015年，滑雪场新增租赁双板12.27万副，相比2014年增长24.65%（见表1-8、图1-12）。

表1-8 2014年、2015年国内滑雪场新增租赁双板数量

类别	2014年数量/副	2015年数量/副	年增长率/%
进口租赁双板	30936	43200	39.64
国产租赁双板	56000	63000	12.50
二手租赁双板	11500	16500	43.48
合计	98436	122700	24.65

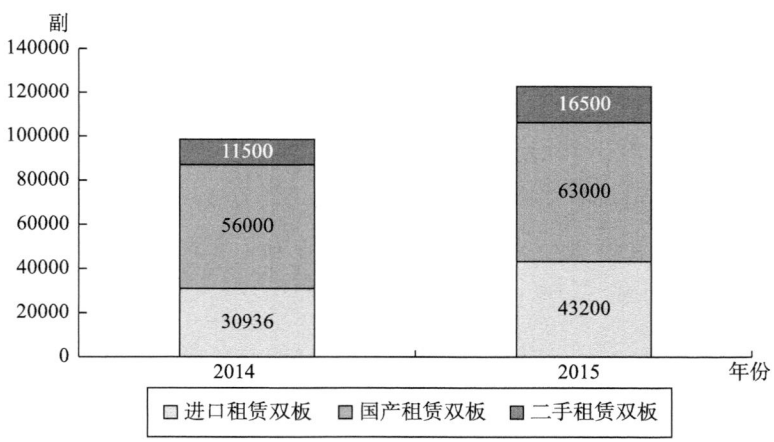

图1-12　2014年、2015年国内滑雪场新增租赁双板数量

2015年，新增进口租赁双板以及二手租赁双板的比例有所上升，国产租赁双板所占比例有所下降（见图1-13）。

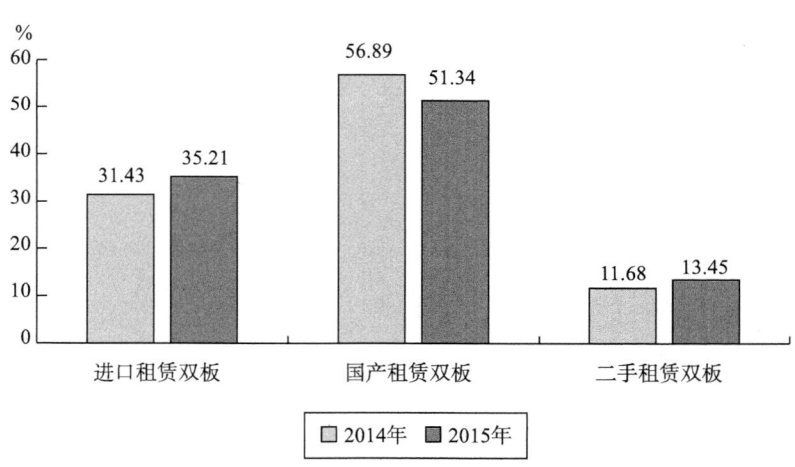

图1-13　2014年、2015年国内滑雪场新增租赁双板结构

关于租赁单板的数量，各滑雪场差异较大。由于缺乏有效的统计数据，仅依据对市场的判断，估算每年新增的租赁单板数量在4000副左右。每年新增租赁雪服的数量，仅依据对市场的判断，估算为3万套左右。

第四节 主要滑雪场人力资源状况

为便于了解国内滑雪场的人力资源状况，本报告人力资源调研小组选取了国内以下滑雪场作为样本来进行调查研究（以下简称"样本滑雪场"）。

表1-9 样本滑雪场清单

省份	序号	滑雪场
黑龙江	1	亚布力滑雪场
	2	亚布力阳光度假村
	3	帽儿山滑雪场
吉林	4	北大壶滑雪场
	5	万达长白山国际滑雪场
	6	万科松花湖滑雪场
辽宁	7	东北亚滑雪场
	8	怪坡滑雪场
河北	9	万龙滑雪场
	10	云顶滑雪场
	11	长城岭滑雪场
	12	多乐美地滑雪场
	13	太舞滑雪场
北京	14	南山滑雪场
	15	军都山滑雪场
河南	16	伏牛山滑雪场
山西	17	梅苑南山滑雪场
	18	采薇庄园滑雪场
四川	19	西岭雪山滑雪场
	20	太子岭滑雪场
湖北	21	神农架滑雪场
浙江	22	大明山滑雪场
重庆	23	金佛山滑雪场
陕西	24	照金滑雪场

续表

省份	序号	滑雪场
甘肃	25	松鸣岩滑雪场
	26	兴隆山滑雪场
新疆	27	丝绸之路滑雪场
	28	天山滑雪场

根据28家样本滑雪场反馈的数据，形成表1-10。滑雪场高层管理人员平均每家滑雪场3.75人，中层管理人员平均每家滑雪场7.68人。平均每家滑雪场的教练人数为27.36人。28家滑雪场从业20年以上的人员合计为110人，平均每家滑雪场不到4人。

表1-10　2015年样本雪场核心人力资源统计　　　　　　　　　　单位：人

人员类别		从业20年以上	从业10~20年	从业5~10年	小计	平均每家雪场人数
管理人员	高层	14	58	33	105	3.75
	中层	20	90	105	215	7.68
技术骨干	场地	16	44	59	119	4.25
	索道	16	44	59	119	4.25
	造雪	16	78	87	181	6.46
	雪地机械	5	24	52	81	2.89
	场馆	2	11	37	50	1.79
	教练	20	145	601	766	27.36
	市场	1	18	56	75	2.68
	网络	0	6	37	43	1.54
合计		110	518	1126	1754	62.64

统计显示，国内滑雪场高层管理人员占比为6.0%，中层管理人员占比为12.3%，教练技术骨干占比为43.7%（见图1-14）。

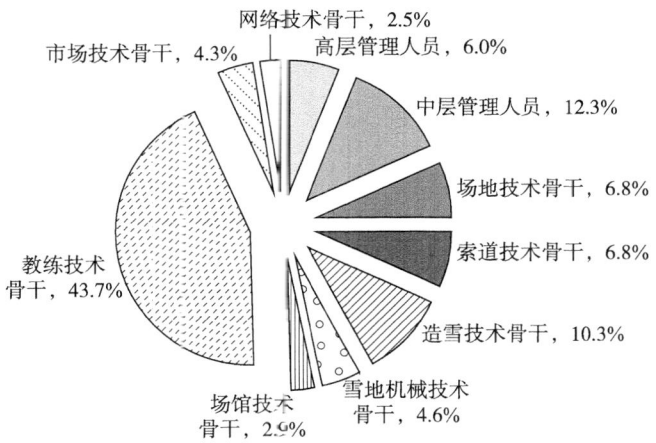

图1-14 2015年国内滑雪场核心人力资源从业类型分布

第五节 四季滑雪场所

一、室内滑雪馆

截至2015年，国内合计有9家室内滑雪馆投入运营。其中长沙三只熊和石家庄四季常青为2015年新增的室内滑雪馆项目（见表1-11）。此外，各类公开信息显示，国内在建及拟建的室内滑雪场项目如下

· 万达系：哈尔滨、广州、无锡、成都等4家（建筑面积分别为8万平方米、7.5万平方米、1.75万平方米及7.5万平方米）；

· 乔波系：南京、广东等（计划10家左右）；

· AST奥悦系：齐齐哈尔、株洲云龙等（计划10多个项目）；

· 中弘：御马坊新奇世界；

· 温州：文成西坑镇"天鹅堡"；

· 重庆：武隆仙女山（1.7万平方米）、天籁谷（5700平方米）；

· 湖南：长沙大王山、岳阳洞氮；

· 上海、湖北武汉、河北邯郸等。

表 1-11　国内运营中的室内滑雪馆基本信息

名称	地点	开业年份	总面积/万平方米	戏雪面积/万平方米	雪道数/条	最长道/米	拖牵/条	魔毯/条
乔波北京	北京顺义	2005	2	—	2	275	2	2
乔波绍兴	浙江绍兴	2009	2	—	2	275	1	2
阿尔卑斯	深圳世界之窗	2003	0.43	0.1	1	100	0	1
伏牛山	河南洛阳	2009	0.8	—	1	200	0	1
瑞祥	湖南浏阳	2011	1.2	—	2	180	0	2
达永山	内蒙古满洲里	2005	1.2	—	1	200	0	1
抚顺冠翔	辽宁抚顺	2014	0.8	0.3	1	50	0	1
三只熊	长沙	2015	1.26	—	1	170	0	2
四季常青	石家庄	2015	1.1	0.1	1	150	0	1

注：上海银七星室内滑雪场面积2.4万平方米，最长雪道380米，2010年歇业。

二、旱雪及室内滑雪训练场地

根据成都旱雪尖峰董事长提供的资料，全球旱雪分布情况如图1-15所示，中国旱雪场地数量已排名全球第二。

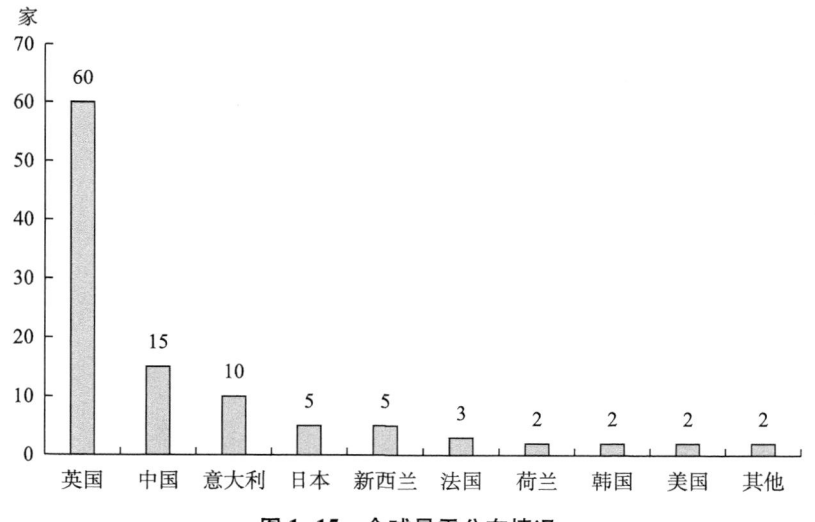

图 1-15　全球旱雪分布情况

图 1-16 显示了国内已建成和拟建的旱雪场地分布。

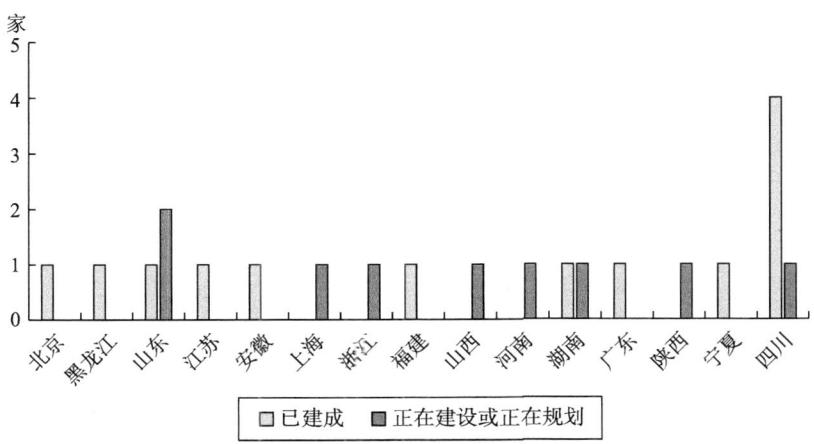

图 1-16　2015 年国内旱雪场地分布情况

除旱雪外，目前北京、上海两地已建成室内模拟训练基地，北京有雪乐山和思凯泰思两家，上海为零度滑雪。

第二章 2015年滑雪者情况

第一节 滑雪者人次及分布

根据统计数据分析测算，2014—2015年雪季，国内滑雪人次为1250万（室内滑雪馆人次数据按2014年全年数据计入），相比2013—2014年雪季增长21.36%，相比2009—2010年雪季增长98.41%（见图2-1）。

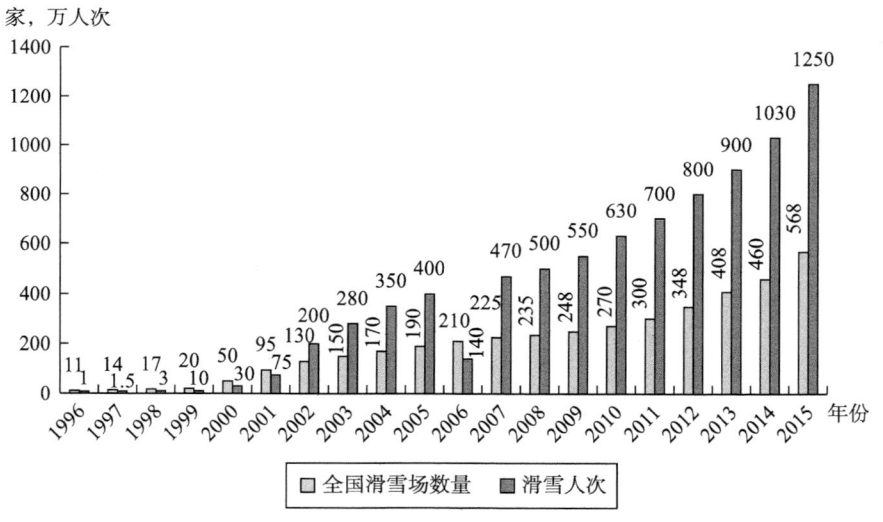

图2-1 2015年国内滑雪场数量及滑雪人次对比

按各区域典型滑雪场提供的滑雪人次数据，初步整理出滑雪人次分布情况如表2-1所示。2014—2015年雪季，北京滑雪场总滑雪人次为169万，为全国之最；其次是黑龙江，为149万；再次是吉林，为96万；山东、河北以85万并列第四。

表2-1 2014—2015年雪季滑雪人次按目的地分布

序号	省份	滑雪场总数量/家	滑雪人次/万人次
1	北京	23	169
2	黑龙江	120	149
3	吉林	37	96
4	山东	51	85
5	河北	40	85
6	新疆	52	77
7	山西	32	72
8	浙江	17	70
9	辽宁	31	65
10	内蒙古	26	59
11	河南	33	58
12	四川	10	42
13	陕西	21	41
14	天津	12	40
15	江苏	13	29
16	甘肃	11	27
17	湖南	7	25
18	重庆	10	21
19	湖北	4	15
20	宁夏	7	8
21	贵州	4	5
22	青海	3	4
23	云南	2	3
24	福建	1	2
25	广东	1	2
合计		568	1250

按七大区域统计，华北滑雪人次占比最大，为34.01%；其次为东北，占比24.83%（见图2-2）。

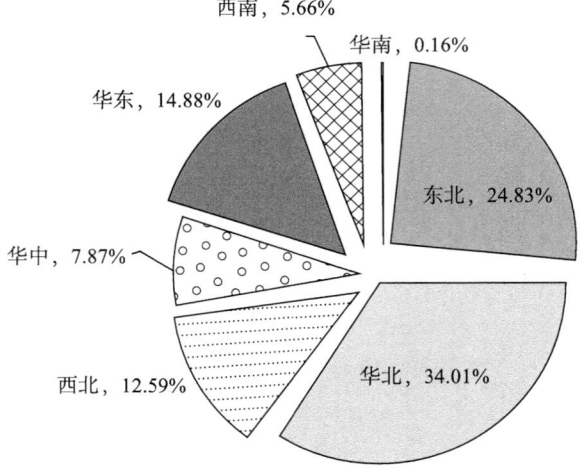

图 2-2　2014—2015 年雪季滑雪人次按区统计占比

第二节　滑雪者客源地及特征

从客源地角度分析滑雪者是相当重要的，但目前暂没有切实可行的收集信息的办法。本报告试图以全国各地活跃程度相对较高的 QQ 滑雪群为样本，对滑雪者客源地及特征作初步分析，但很遗憾，研究结果发现样本与客源地并未能构成较强的关联性。从表 2-2 的统计中可以看到，QQ 滑雪群中，男女比例为 63.88∶36.12，"80 后"占比 45.36%，标注"单身"的人群占比 23.91%。

表 2-2　2015 年活跃度高的 QQ 滑雪群成员分析

区域	样本 QQ 滑雪群活跃人数/人	男性成员数/人	男性成员占比/%	"80 后"成员数/人	"80 后"成员占比/%	单身成员数/人	单身成员占比/%
华北	23540	14658	62.27	11092	47.12	5719	24.29
东北	22703	15711	69.20	9636	42.44	5676	25.00
华东	6966	3975	57.06	3294	47.29	1754	25.18
华中	5563	3270	58.78	2478	44.54	636	11.43
西北	4643	2974	64.05	2133	45.94	1340	28.86

续表

区域	样本QQ滑雪群活跃人数/人	男性成员数/人	男性成员占比/%	"80后"成员数/人	"80后"成员占比/%	单身成员数/人	单身成员占比/%
西南	1890	1185	62.70	989	52.33	482	25.50
华南	410	208	50.73	189	46.10	104	25.37
合计	65715	41981	63.88	29811	45.36	15711	23.91

图2-3中QQ滑雪群活跃用户七大区域占比，与整体滑雪人次按区域占比基本可以吻合，从一个侧面表明网络活跃滑雪用户与滑雪目的地之间的关联性比与客源地之间的关联性更强。从活跃QQ滑雪群的数量以及群成员的规模来看，以目的地滑雪场为主题的QQ滑雪群活跃程度更高。

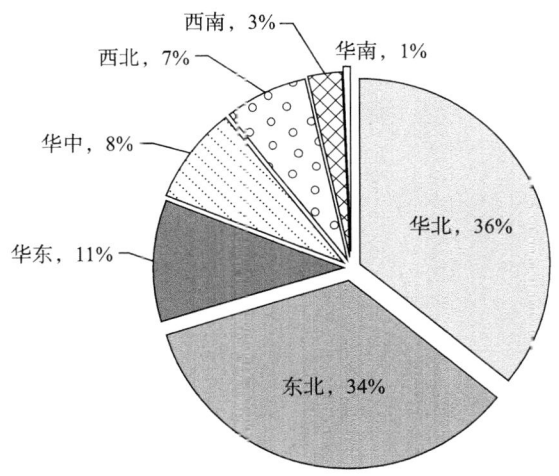

图2-3 2015年样本QQ滑雪群活跃用户各区域占比

第三节 滑雪者装备市场

从滑雪双板的零售市场调查来看，本报告共收到9个国际双板品牌中国总代理的反馈信息。2014年9大品牌合计零售双板10345副，2015年预计销售13280副，预计增长率为28.36%。考虑到统计不完整，同时零售市场有大量海淘行为等因素，估算全年零售双板市场销量为 2 万副左右。

  一个明显的现象是,单板零售市场反馈的数据远远高于双板零售市场。从收到的 3 个商家的反馈信息来看,2014 年零售单板销量合计 6063 副,2015 年预计销售量为 8900 副,年增长率 46.79%。按同样方式估算后,全年单板零售市场销量应在 3 万副左右,高出双板零售量 50%。

第三章　滑雪赛事

第一节　中国近代竞技滑雪历程

1957年，中国第一次全国滑雪比赛在吉林省通化市举行，从此拉开了中国近代竞技滑雪的序幕。

1959年，吉林市举办了全国第一届冬季运动会。20世纪80年代初，中国从近代滑雪跨越到现代滑雪的行列。

1981年，中国加入国际滑雪联合会（FIS），成为正式会员，随后成立了中国滑雪协会（CSA）。

目前，中国在黑龙江、吉林、辽宁、内蒙古、新疆等省（区、市）开展了越野滑雪、跳台滑雪、高山滑雪、自由式滑雪、单板滑雪等竞技滑雪项目（见表3-1）。

表3-1　雪上各项目注册单位及运动员情况

开展项目		注册单位数量/家	注册运动员数/人
越野滑雪		16	306
跳台滑雪		2	30
高山滑雪		10	94
自由式滑雪	空中技巧	5	51
	U型场地	6	37
	雪上技巧	4	28
单板滑雪	平行项目	9	81
	U型场地	9	56
合计		61	683

第二节 中国参加历届冬奥会情况

中国多次参加亚洲冬季运动会和冬季奥林匹克运动会（见表3-2）。1980年中国首次组团参加了第13届普莱锡德湖冬奥会。1998年长野冬奥会上，中国队夺得了中国滑雪第一枚奖牌（自由式滑雪女子空中技巧银牌）。2006年都灵冬奥会上，中国队夺取了中国滑雪第一枚金牌（自由式滑雪男子空中技巧）。至2014年索契冬奥会，中国已连续参加10届冬奥会。

表3-2 历届冬奥会滑雪比赛中国队参加情况

分项	小项	1980年第13届（美国普莱锡德湖）	1984年第14届（南联盟萨拉热窝）	1988年第15届（加拿大卡尔加里）	1992年第16届（法国阿尔贝维尔）	1994年第17届（挪威利勒哈默尔）	1998年第18届（日本长野）	2002年第19届（美国盐湖城）	2006年第20届（意大利托里诺）	2010年第21届（加拿大温哥华）	2014年第22届（俄罗斯索契）
越野滑雪	男子短距离						√	√	√	√	√
	男子10千米				√		√				
	男子个人赛	√	√	√				√	√	√	√
	男子双追逐			√	√						
	男子集体出发				√				√		√
	男子接力赛		√				√				
	男子竞速赛				√						
	男子团体短距离								√	√	√
	女子短距离										
	女子5千米	√	√	√	√		√				
	女子个人赛	√	√	√			√	√	√	√	√
	女子双追逐				√						
	女子20千米				√						
	女子集体出发				√				√		√
	女子接力赛		√				√			√	
	女子竞速赛				√			√	√	√	√
	女子团体短距离						√	√	√	√	

续表

分项	小项	1980年第13届（美国普莱锡德湖）	1984年第14届（南联盟萨拉热窝）	1988年第15届加拿大卡尔加里）	1992年第16届（法国阿尔贝维尔）	1994年第17届（挪威利勒哈默尔）	1998年第18届（日本长野）	2002年第19届（美国盐湖城）	2006年第20届（意大利都灵托里诺）	2010年第21届（加拿大温哥华）	2014年第22届（俄罗斯索契）
高山滑雪	男子大回转	√	√						√	√	√
	女子大回转	√	√		√				√	√	√
	男子回转	√	√						√	√	√
	女子回转	√	√		√				√	√	√
	女子超级大回转				√						
自由式滑雪	男子空中技巧								√	√	√
	女子空中技巧					√		√	√	√	√
	女子雪上技巧										√
单板滑雪	男子U型场地技巧								√		
	女子U型场地技巧							√	√	√	√
跳台滑雪	男子个人标准台								√		
	男子个人大跳台								√		
	男子团体								√		

第三节 国内举办过的重要赛事

全国冬季运动会作为级别最高的全国综合性冬季运动会，于1959年首次举办，每4年举办一届。

我国曾承办过的重要国际赛事有：

（1）综合性运动会：1996年2月哈尔滨，第三届亚洲冬季运动会；2007年2月长春，第七届亚洲冬季运动会；2009年2月哈尔滨，第二十四届世界大学生冬季运动会。

（2）单项比赛：2006年3月长春，越野滑雪世界杯短距离总决赛；2007年2月长春，越野滑雪世界杯；2003年2月至2015年12月，连续多年举办自由式滑雪空中技巧及雪上技巧世界杯；2011年2月，单板滑雪U型场地技巧世界杯；2004年3月至2015年12月，连续多年举办FIS高山滑雪积分赛及远东杯。

第四节　国内已建设的竞技滑雪场

1996年以前，中国滑雪场基本上由政府投资兴建，如1957年吉林省通化市兴建了中华人民共和国第一座滑雪场，1986年及1995年先后建成了亚布力、北大壶两个规模较大的滑雪场。

政府对滑雪场的直接投入，以及交通、水利、电力、通信、环保等公共基础设施的改善，极大促进了民营企业投资滑雪场的热情。经过近20年的发展，目前集竞赛、休闲、会议接待等功能于一身，承办过国际综合性或单项比赛的较大型滑雪场有亚布力滑雪场、北大壶滑雪场、万龙滑雪场、云顶滑雪场、长白山万达滑雪场、帽儿山滑雪场、多乐美地滑雪场、乌吉密滑雪场、长春净月潭滑雪场、新疆丝绸之路滑雪场、新疆阿勒泰将军山滑雪场等。

第二篇

2016 年度中国滑雪产业核心数据报告

第四章 2016年滑雪场情况

第一节 滑雪场数量及分布

根据2016年版《中国滑雪场大全》提供的信息，剔除戏雪娱雪乐园的部分，同时根据卡宾研究团队的统计资料，结合实际调研情况复核修正，2016年全国滑雪场数量达到646家，相比2015年新增78家，增幅为13.73%。

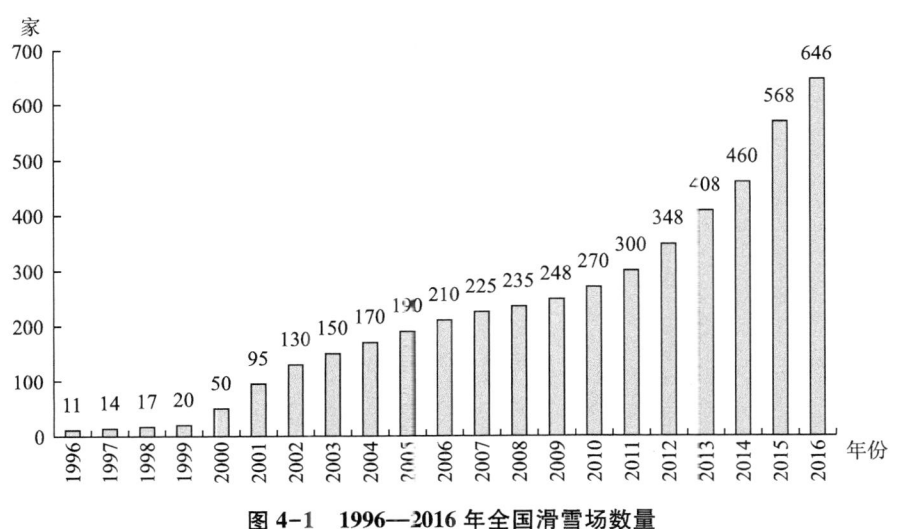

图4-1 1996—2016年全国滑雪场数量

646家滑雪场分布于全国27个省（区、市），其中，黑龙江有滑雪场122家，为全国之冠（见图4-2、表4-1）。

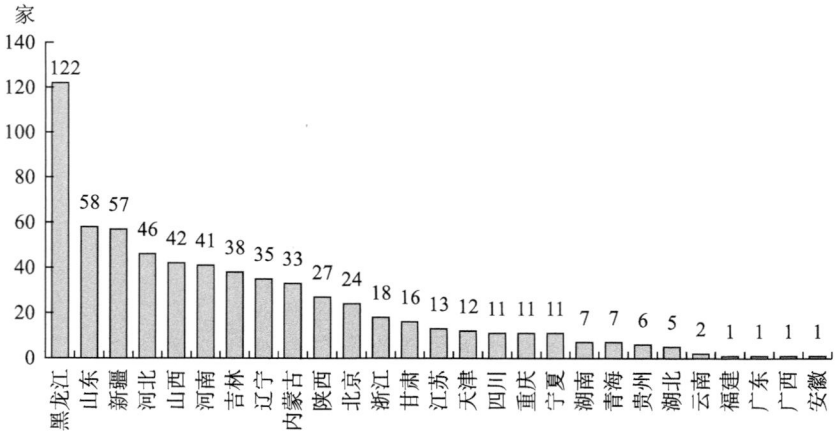

图 4-2 2016 年全国各省（区、市）滑雪场数量

表 4-1 2016 年全国各省（区、市）滑雪场数量

排序	省份	滑雪场数量/家	与 GOSKI 建立天气预报合作的雪场数/家
1	黑龙江	122	37
2	山东	58	26
3	新疆	57	33
4	河北	46	25
5	山西	42	22
6	河南	41	14
7	吉林	38	26
8	辽宁	35	26
9	内蒙古	33	15
10	陕西	27	13
11	北京	24	24
12	浙江	18	7
13	甘肃	16	9
14	江苏	13	5
15	天津	12	7
16	四川	11	8
17	重庆	11	5
18	宁夏	11	5
19	湖南	7	3

续表

排序	省份	滑雪场数量/家	与GOSKI建立天气预报合作的雪场数/家
20	青海	7	0
21	贵州	6	1
22	湖北	5	3
23	云南	2	2
24	福建	1	1
25	广东	1	1
26	广西	1	0
27	安徽	1	0
合计		646	318

全国34个省级行政区中，目前仅香港、澳门、台湾、上海、江西、西藏及海南尚未建成滑雪场馆设施。据了解，上海、江西、西藏都有正在进行的滑雪场馆类投资项目。

全国滑雪场按区域分布情况如图4-3、图4-4所示。

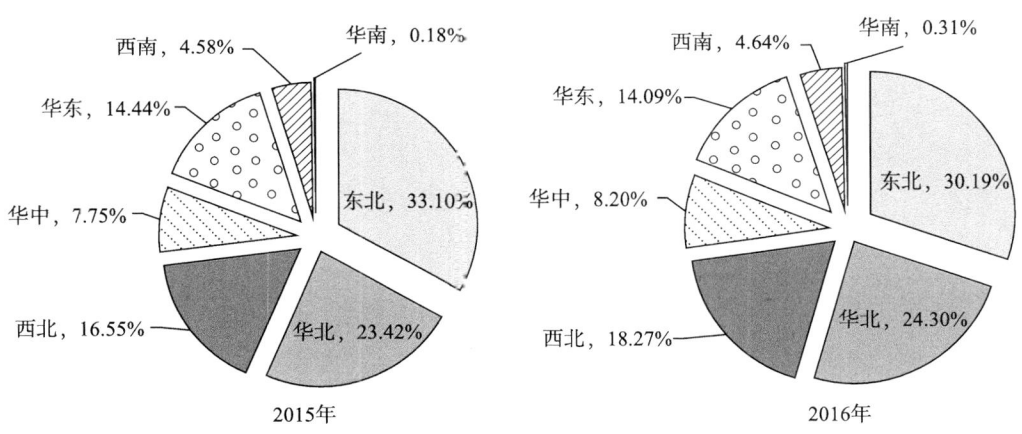

图4-3 2015年、2016年全国滑雪场分布（按区域）

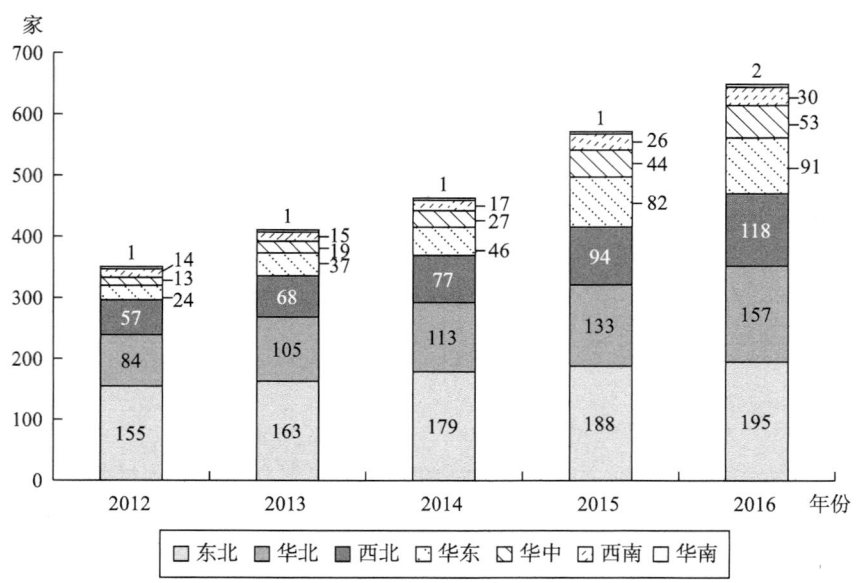

图 4-4 2012—2016 年全国滑雪场分布（按区域）

第二节 滑雪场分类统计信息

一、按核心目标客群分类

按滑雪场的核心目标客群的差异，国内滑雪场分为旅游体验型、城郊学习型以及目的地度假型三类，占比分别为 75%、22% 及 3%（详细特征见表 4-2）。

表 4-2 2016 年国内滑雪场按核心目标客群分类

滑雪场类型	数量占比	客群定位	主要体现滑雪属性	滑雪场特征	客群特征	典型案例
旅游体验型	75%	旅游观光客	旅游属性	设施简单，只有初级道。位置一般在旅游景区或城郊	90%以上为一次性体验客户，客人平均停留时间 2 小时	雪世界、鸟巢

续表

滑雪场类型	数量占比	客群定位	主要体现滑雪属性	滑雪场特征	客群特征	典型案例
城郊学习型	22%	本地居民	运动属性、旅游属性	山体落差不大,位于城市郊区,开发有初级、中级、高级雪道	本地自驾客人占比很大,平均停留时间为3~4小时	南山、军都山、万科石京龙
目的地度假型	3%	度假人群	度假属性、运动属性、旅游属性	山体有一定规模,除有齐全的雪道产品外,还有住宿等设施的配套	过夜消费占比较大,客人平均停留时间在1天以上	万科松花湖、万达长白山、北大壶、亚布力、万龙、云顶、太舞

二、按垂直落差统计

滑雪场垂直落差是衡量滑雪场所在山地的资源规模的一个重要指标。按滑雪场实际开发雪道的垂直落差,将国内滑雪场按以下三类统计:垂直落差超过300米的滑雪场19家、垂直落差在100~300米的滑雪场120家以及垂直落差小于100米的滑雪场507家(见图4-5)。

垂直落差超过300米的雪场的详细信息见表4-3,与2015年相比没有变化。但需要注意的是,2016年新开业的崇礼富龙滑雪场规划为落差480米,但因一期开发落差不足300米,暂未统计在内;2017年1月15日开业的新疆阿尔泰山野雪公园落差超过1000米,首开直升机滑雪,未录入2016年报告。

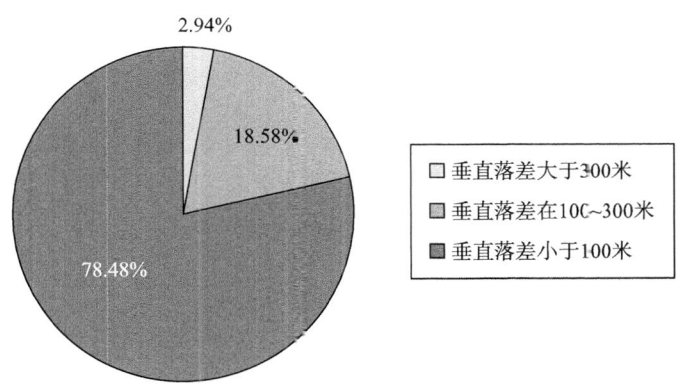

图4-5 2016年国内滑雪场按垂直落差统计占比

表 4-3　2016 年国内垂直落差超过 300 米的滑雪场

排序	滑雪场名称	已开发垂直落差/米	山顶海拔/米	山脚海拔/米	所在省份
1	长白山天池雪	950	2600	1650	吉林
2	亚布力体委	885	1360	475	黑龙江
3	北大壶	870	1404	534	吉林
4	云南香格里拉	662	3980	3318	云南
5	万科松花湖	600	935	335	吉林
6	万龙	580.3	2110.3	1530	河北
7	新疆丝绸之路	580	2440	1860	新疆
8	亚布力阳光	540	995	455	黑龙江
9	太舞	510	2062	1552	河北
10	美林谷	480	1660	1180	内蒙古
11	云顶	420	2100	1680	河北
12	阿勒泰将军山	405	1320	915	新疆
13	伏牛山	400	1931	1565	河南
14	丹东天桥沟	392	878	486	辽宁
15	万达长白山	380	1200	820	吉林
16	多乐美地	323	1963	1640	河北
17	万科石京龙	310	836	526	北京
18	帽儿山	308	626	318	黑龙江
19	长城岭	300	2060	1760	河北

如表 4-3 所示，垂直落差超过 300 米的 19 家滑雪场中，有 5 家位于河北（全部落户崇礼），有 4 家位于吉林，有 3 家位于黑龙江，此外新疆有 2 家，内蒙古、辽宁、河南、云南、北京各 1 家。需要说明的是，长白山天池雪滑雪场开发出的雪道垂直落差居于全国之首，但提升设施仅依赖于压雪车和雪地摩托；北京延庆的万科石京龙滑雪场垂直落差达到 310 米，是全北京落差最大的滑雪场，在其他统计资料中经常被遗漏。

三、按雪道面积统计

雪道面积是衡量滑雪场大小的另一个重要维度。2016 年，北大壶及万龙扩建力度较大，和万科松花湖一起成为国内雪道面积超过 100 公顷的滑雪场（见表 4-4）。

表 4-4 2016 年按雪道面积统计的滑雪场数据

雪道面积/公顷	滑雪场数量/家	滑雪场名称
>100	3	万科松花湖、北大壶、万龙
50~100	5	亚布力阳光、万达长白山、云顶……
30~50	7	南山、牙克石……
10~30	26	万科石京龙……
5~10	87	
<5	518	
合计	646	

注：①部分数据参照北京硕华基公司提供的工程资料；②亚布力如果按三山联网的范围计算，雪道面积在100公顷以上。

第三节 滑雪场设施

一、滑雪场上行设施

（一）滑雪场索道

2016 年全国滑雪场架空索道数量及分布如表 4-5 所示。根据脱挂式架空索道分布统计，吉林省合计 17 条，排名第一；河北省合计 13 条，排名第二；黑龙江省合计 6 条，排名第三（见表 4-6）（此项统计中，只包括用于滑雪的索道，不包括运输用途的索道）。

表 4-5 2016 年全国滑雪场架空索道数量及分布

排序	省份	架空索道数量/条	有架空索道分布的滑雪场数量/家
1	黑龙江	44	25
2	河北	30	10
3	辽宁	29	22
4	吉林	26	8
5	北京	24	12
6	新疆	10	7
7	内蒙古	6	5
8	山西	5	4

续表

排序	省份	架空索道数量/条	有架空索道分布的滑雪场数量/家
9	甘肃	5	3
10	四川	4	2
11	河南	3	2
12	湖北	3	2
13	山东	3	3
14	云南	3	1
15	重庆	2	2
16	贵州	2	2
17	陕西	1	1
18	天津	1	1
遗漏估计		25	25
合计		226	137

表4-6 2016年全国滑雪场脱挂式架空索道分布

雪场	2016年数量/条	所在省份
万科松花湖	6	吉林
万达长白山	5	吉林
北大壶	4	吉林
万龙	4	河北
云顶	3	河北
太舞	3	河北
亚布力体委	3	黑龙江
亚布力阳光	2	黑龙江
富龙	2	河北
鲁能长白山	2	吉林
多乐美地	1	河北
帽儿山	1	黑龙江
合计	36	

（二）滑雪场魔毯

魔毯数据参照了道沃机电网站数据。截至2016年，全国滑雪场共计有850条魔毯处于运营中，包括2016年新增的232条魔毯。全部魔毯总长度约128千米（见图4-6）。

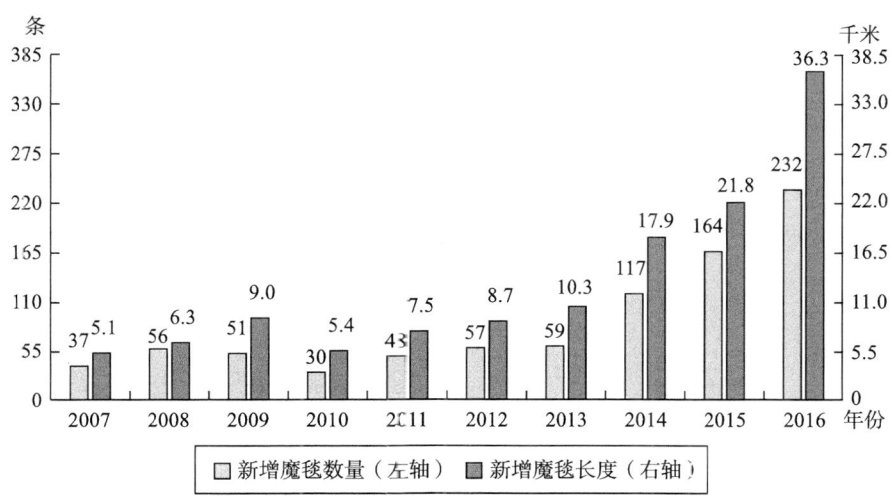

图 4-6 2007—2016 年滑雪场新增魔毯数量及长度

二、滑雪场场地设施

国内滑雪场全部压雪车数量约为 410 台。2016 年，国内新增压雪车数量为 80 台，其中进口车 65 台（见图 4-7）。本数据主要来源于压雪车供应商以及卡宾集团研究中心数据。

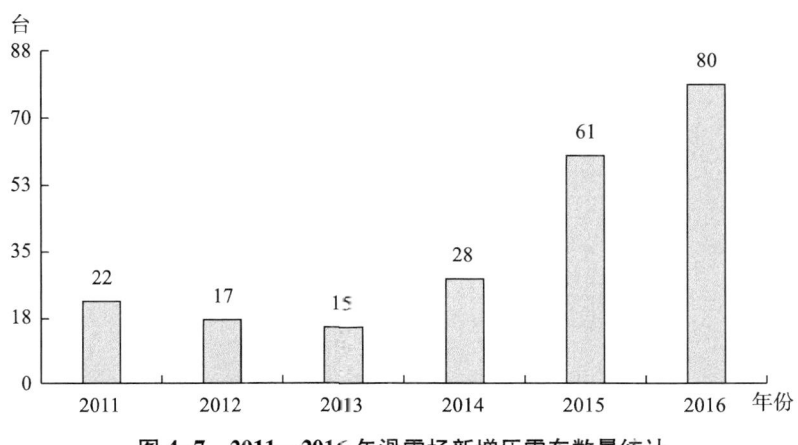

图 4-7 2011—2016 年滑雪场新增压雪车数量统计

2016 年，全国滑雪场新增造雪机 1180 台，全部造雪机数量合计约 5180 台。其中，国产造雪机占比为 15%（见图 4-8）。

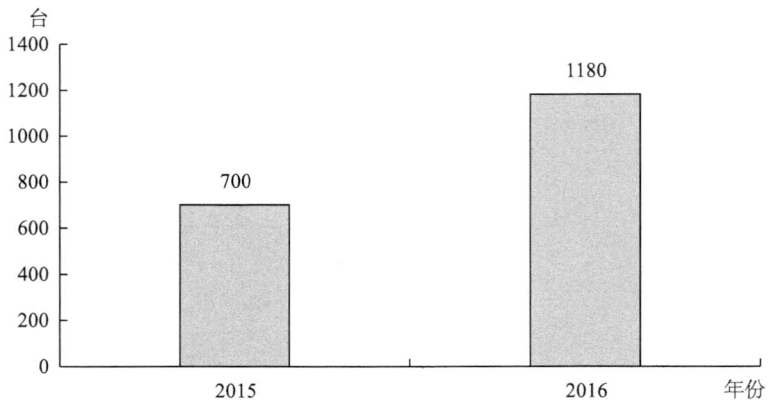

图 4-8 2015 年、2016 年滑雪场新增造雪机数量统计

三、滑雪场租赁双板

根据主要雪板供应商提供的信息,截至 2016 年,雪场租赁双板数量合计约 48.5 万副,相比 2015 年增长 38.57%。其中,进口租赁双板增幅高于国产租赁双板增幅(见图 4-9)。

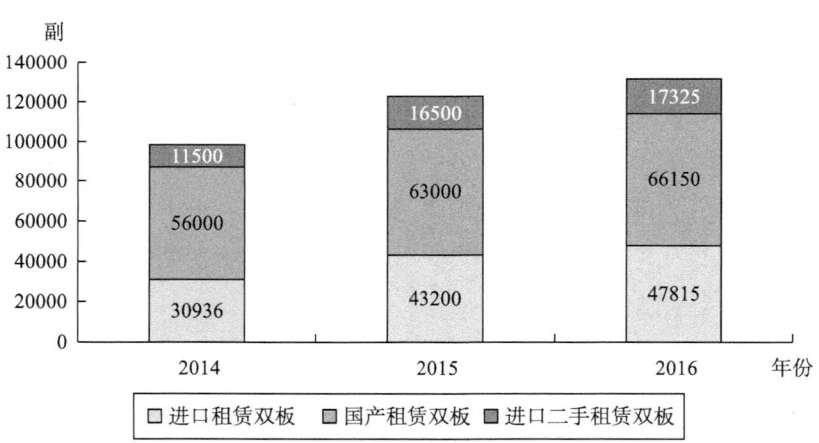

图 4-9 2014—2016 年滑雪场新增租赁双板数量统计

第四节 滑雪教练统计数据

根据 100 家滑雪场调研资料，滑雪教练员总数共计 4810 人，平均每家滑雪场教练员 48 人。从性别统计来看，63% 为男性教练员，37% 为女性教练员；从教学经验来看，5 年以上教学经验的教练员人数所占比重为 56%，教学经验低于 5 年的教练员人数约占 44%；从受教育水平结构统计数据来看，滑雪教练中 50% 为高中或中专学历，15% 为大专及大专以上学历，35% 为高中以下学历（见表 4-7、图 4-10、图 4-11）。

表 4-7 2016 年滑雪教练统计数据　　　　　　　　　　单位：人

指标	数量
滑雪教练员人数	4810
平均每家滑雪场教练员人数	48
5 年以上教学经验的教练员人数	2681
教学经验低于 5 年的教练员人数	2129
男性教练员人数	3042
女性教练员人数	1768

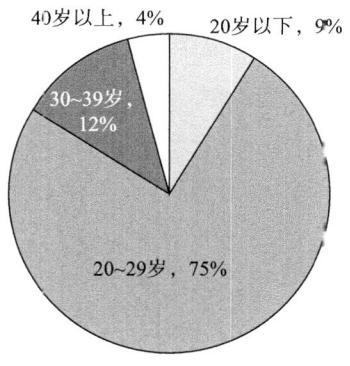

图 4-10 2016 年滑雪教练年龄结构统计数据

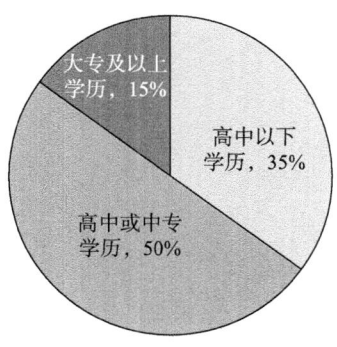

图 4-11 2016 年滑雪教练受教育水平结构统计数据

第五节 四季滑雪场所

一、室内滑雪馆

随着近两年国内室内滑雪馆数量不断增长（见图4-12），目前在室内滑雪馆数量全球排名中，中国已经占据绝对第一的位置。2017年6月，万达哈尔滨室内滑雪馆将正式开业，其规模远远大于迪拜室内滑雪馆，届时中国室内滑雪馆无论从数量上还是规模上都将成为世界第一。毫无疑问，室内滑雪馆的发展将改变整体市场格局，并将为整个滑雪市场输送源源不断的客流。

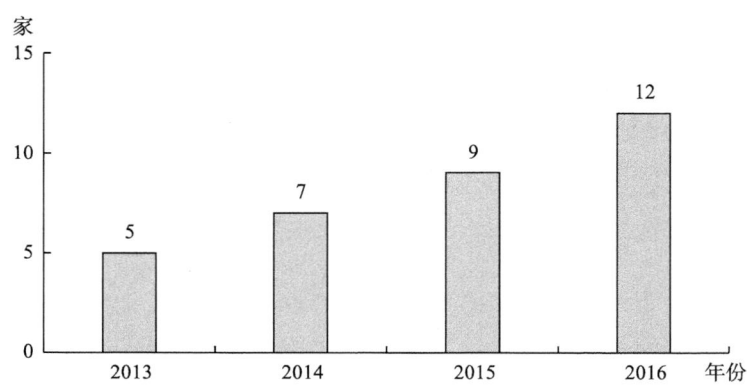

图4-12 2013—2016年已投入运营的室内滑雪馆数量

二、旱雪

旱雪场地作为滑雪的替代品，近几年在国内得到了长足的发展。尖峰旱雪是国内旱雪的主要供应商，根据尖峰旱雪提供的资料，截至2016年年底，国内已投入使用的尖峰旱雪场地达到18家（见图4-13），另外有5家处于在建状态。

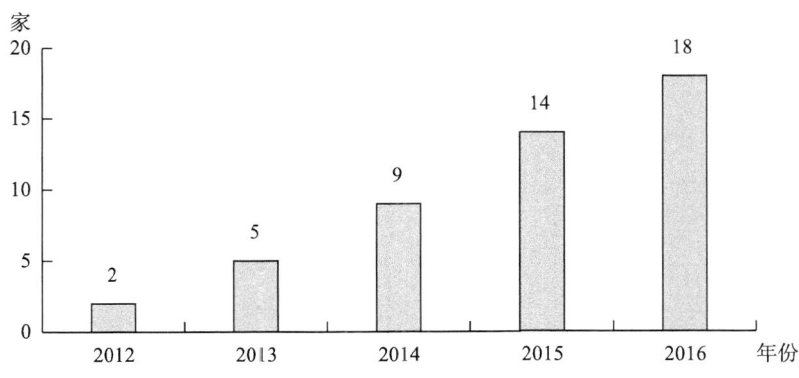

图 4-13 2012—2016 年已投入运营的尖峰旱雪场地数量

三、室内滑雪模拟训练场地

根据室内滑雪模拟器主要供应商提供的信息,国内目前共有 25 台滑雪模拟设备。以雪乐山俱乐部为例,LeSki Club 已有 3 家室内滑雪训练中心在北京开业,每家训练中心接待滑雪人次约 1 万。按计划,2017 年 LeSki Club 将在北京新开另外 3 家训练中心,北京的总目标为 10 家。

第五章 2016年滑雪者情况

第一节 滑雪者人次及分布

在关于滑雪市场的各层次交流中,被问及最多的一个问题就是:中国到底有多少人滑雪?图5-1试图给出一部分相对合理的答案。根据测算,2016年,我国全部滑雪人次为1510万,全部参与滑雪的人数为1133万人,人均滑雪次数为1.33次。在全部滑雪人数中,一次性体验者所占比例由2015年的80%下降到78%。

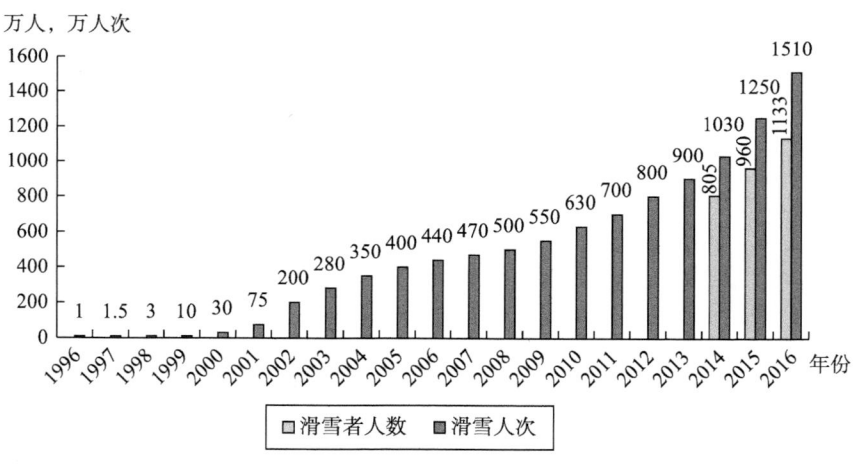

图5-1 2016年滑雪人次及滑雪者人数

滑雪人次按目的地省份的分布如表5-1所示。其中,河北、吉林、新疆、山西、河南及甘肃6个省份增长量均超过20万人次。滑雪人次按目的地区域的分布如图5-2所示。

表 5-1　2015 年、2016 年滑雪人次分布（按目的地省份）

省份	2015 年			2016 年		
	排序	滑雪场数量/家	滑雪人次/万人次	排序	滑雪场数量/家	滑雪人次/万人次
北京	1	23	169	1	24	171
黑龙江	2	120	149	2	122	158
吉林	3	37	96	4	38	118
山东	4	51	85	6	58	98
河北	5	40	85	3	46	122
新疆	6	52	77	5	57	99
山西	7	32	72	7	42	96
浙江	8	17	70	9	18	79
辽宁	9	31	65	11	35	72
内蒙古	10	26	59	10	33	76
河南	11	33	58	8	41	82
四川	12	10	42	13	11	50
陕西	13	21	41	12	27	54
天津	14	12	40	15	12	39
江苏	15	13	29	16	13	29
甘肃	16	11	27	14	16	48
湖南	17	7	25	17	7	27
重庆	18	10	21	18	11	24
湖北	19	4	15	19	5	18
宁夏	20	7	8	20	11	15
贵州	21	4	5	21	6	10
青海	22	3	4	22	7	9
云南	23	2	4	23	2	4
福建	24	1	2	24	1	3
广东	25	1	2	25	1	3
广西	26	0	0	26	1	3
安徽	27	0	0	27	1	3
合计		568	1250		646	1510

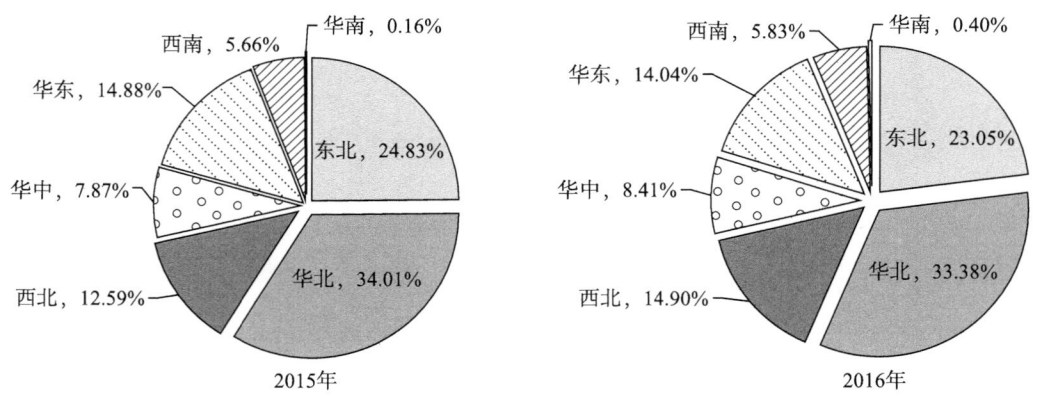

图 5-2　2015 年、2016 年滑雪人次分布（按目的地区域）

第二节　滑雪者特征：移动互联网数据

从需求侧的角度出发，如何清晰地描绘出中国滑雪者的画像至关重要。本报告联合国内相对活跃的四个专注于滑雪消费领域的移动端平台，它们从各自的角度提供了部分维度的分析报告，包括 GOSKI、滑呗、滑雪族以及乐点滑雪。客观上讲，滑雪移动端的用户基本上是已经获得一定信息量及资源的滑雪爱好者，一次性体验用户使用移动端的少之又少。因此本节描绘的滑雪者的特征更多地反映出滑雪爱好者的特征。

一、GOSKI 报告

由于 GOSKI 团队及资源与单板有更多的联系，因此 GOSKI 报告更多地反映出单板滑雪者的特征。

GOSKI 用户客源地分布以北京、辽宁、吉林等省份为主，其次是黑龙江、山东和新疆等地，其他省份仅占 23.64%。此外，GOSKI 用户以男性为主，且 57.49% 的用户为单板用户，74% 为中级雪友，63% 为 iOS 用户（见图 5-3、图 5-4）。

GOSKI 用户数据统计显示，GOSKI 用户最喜爱的滑雪场标签前十名中，万科松花湖占据首位，其次是万龙、北大壶等；Burton 成为 GOSKI 用户最喜爱的品牌标签，其次是 NI-TRO、DC 等（见图 5-5、图 5-6）。

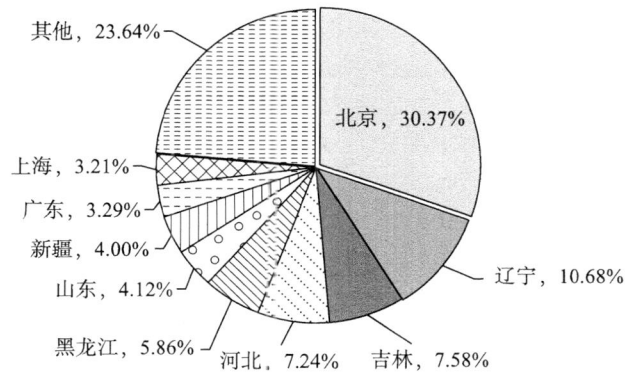

图5-3 2016年GOSKI用户客源地分布（按省份）

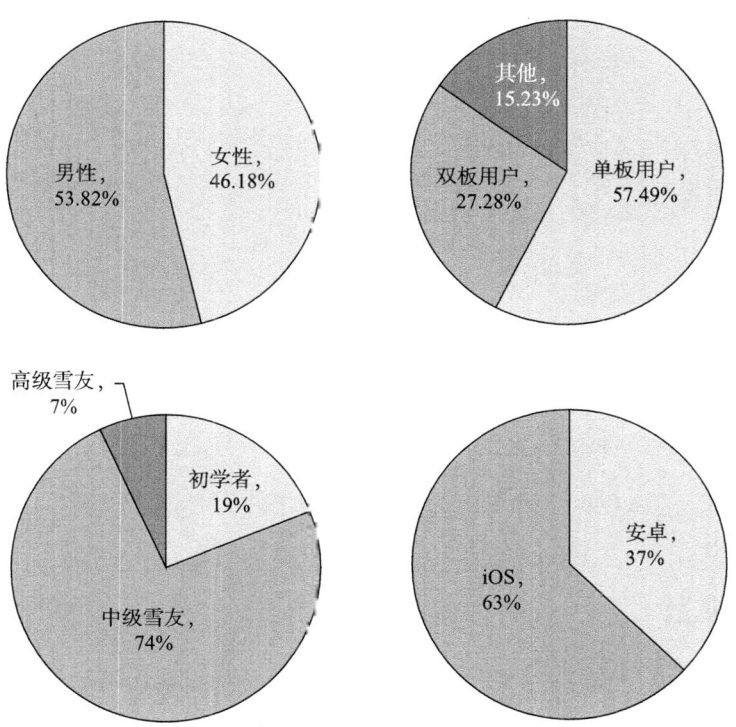

图5-4 2016年GOSKI用户特征

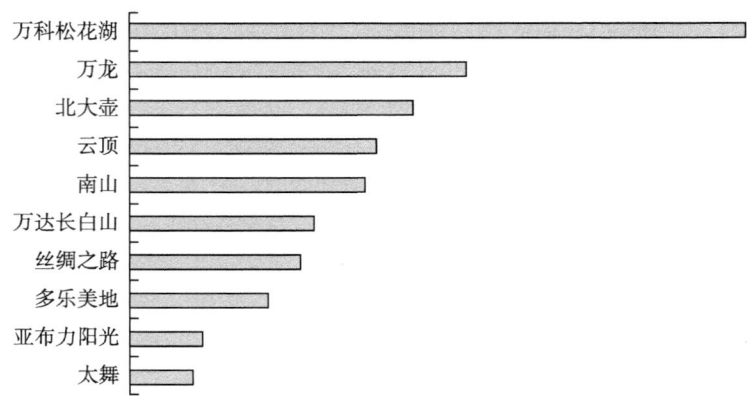

图 5-5　2016 年 GOSKI 用户最喜爱的滑雪场标签前十名

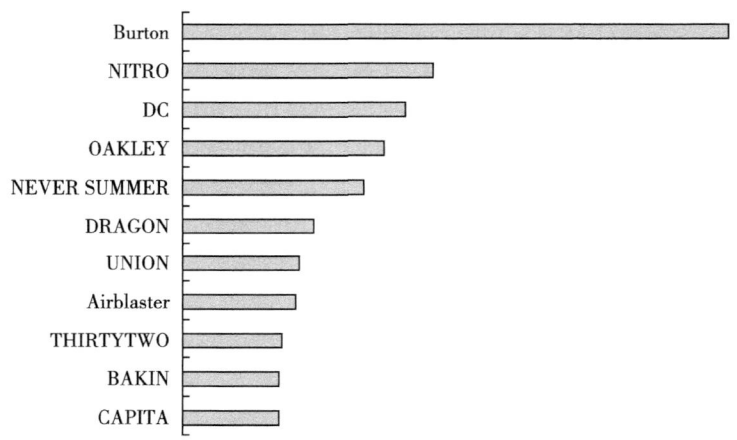

图 5-6　2016 年 GOSKI 用户最喜爱的品牌标签前十名

二、滑呗报告

使用滑呗运动软件记录的滑雪者,被我们认定为相对狂热的滑雪爱好者。因此,滑呗运动数据更多地反映出滑雪发烧友的特性。

在与滑呗的沟通过程中,我们发现在滑呗 App 上注册的滑雪俱乐部高达 481 家。由于滑呗要求每位用户只能选择一家俱乐部注册,因此对俱乐部客户的数据研究能有效地从一个侧面反映出各个俱乐部的不同滑雪者特征。

2016 年,滑呗运动数据覆盖的滑雪场总数共 348 家,其中国内滑雪场 180 家。用户总数达 179632 人,人均滑行记录 22.3 千米(见表 5-2)。注册滑雪俱乐部 481 家,俱乐部注册用户人数38021人,平均每个俱乐部用户79人(见表5-3)。

在2016年滑呗运动数据记录的滑雪场基础信息中,万科松花湖记录人数为4322人,记录总里程为228687千米,位列第一,其次是万龙和北大壶等滑雪场(见表5-4)。在滑呗运动数据记录的滑雪俱乐部基础信息中,1031滑雪俱乐部以记录人数649人和记录总里程数36058千米占据首位(见表5-5)。

表5-2 2016年滑呗基础信息

指标	数量
滑呗运动数据覆盖的滑雪场总数/家	348
滑呗运动数据覆盖的国内滑雪场数量/家	180
滑呗运动数据覆盖的国外滑雪场数量/家	168
滑呗运动数据用户总数/人	179632
滑呗运动轨迹记录人数/人	53271
滑呗运动轨迹累计数/千米	1188729
滑呗运动轨迹人均滑行记录数/千米	22.3

表5-3 2016年滑呗注册滑雪俱乐部基础信息

指标	数量
注册滑雪俱乐部总数/家	481
俱乐部注册用户数/人	38021
平均每个俱乐部用户数/人	79
滑雪俱乐部滑行总里程数/千米	490826
滑雪俱乐部人均滑行里程数/千米	13

表5-4 2016年滑呗运动数据记录的滑雪场基础信息

排名	滑雪场名称	记录人数/人	记录总里程数/千米	人均里程数/千米	人均滑行落差/米
1	万科松花湖	4322	228687	53	11917
2	万龙	3463	209779	61	13688
3	北大壶	1908	85229	45	10759
4	太舞	1847	84891	46	10042
5	亚布力	1428	129996	91	19686
6	富龙	1300	23758	18	3310

续表

排名	滑雪场名称	记录人数/人	记录总里程数/千米	人均里程数/千米	人均滑行落差/米
7	云顶	1278	94309	74	10217
8	南山	1024	18128	18	2805
9	万达长白山	977	28895	30	6040
10	多乐美地	953	33974	36	7249
11	怀北	951	15948	17	3171
12	庙香山	769	14000	18	3544
13	万龙八易	675	13852	21	3181
14	帽儿山	667	20921	31	7015
15	长城岭	497	14308	29	5463
16	怪坡	422	4157	10	2102
17	渔阳	342	5993	18	3451
18	军都山	337	3209	10	1552
19	丝绸之路	331	15374	46	9628
20	美林谷	319	10924	34	6124

表 5-5 2016 年滑呗运动数据记录的滑雪俱乐部基础信息

排名	俱乐部名称	记录人数/人	记录总里程数/千米	人均里程数/千米	人均滑行落差/米
1	1031滑雪俱乐部	649	36058	56	25474
2	炫酷之旅俱乐部	352	6369	18	11951
3	广东滑雪俱乐部	320	26904	84	34050
4	西安冰峰俱乐部	271	5794	21	8719
5	长春极限俱乐部	266	5055	19	10306
6	雪峰滑雪俱乐部	264	50186	190	58076
7	远山滑雪俱乐部	257	23098	90	33429
8	风暴俱乐部	247	6458	26	10211
9	雪线单板俱乐部	229	5445	24	12148
10	疯滑雪跃俱乐部	217	8775	40	17724
11	雪蛙族俱乐部	197	3297	17	9837
12	天津零度户外俱乐部	186	8943	48	21589
13	巅峰九七俱乐部	184	5843	32	14845
14	铲雪大队俱乐部	182	4401	24	11489
15	678滑雪俱乐部	178	5340	30	16465

续表

排名	俱乐部名称	记录人数/人	记录总里程数/千米	人均里程数/千米	人均滑行落差/米
16	Sstyle雪风俱乐部	144	8128	56	30038
17	中国魔诺滑雪俱乐部	106	10876	103	34877
18	吉林雪者联盟俱乐部	146	5625	39	26703
19	盘锦彩虹俱乐部	143	5075	35	18300
20	Veneer单板俱乐部	105	7282	69	28956

三、滑雪族报告

北京、辽宁及河北三省（市）是滑雪族用户的主要客源地，占全国的61.10%，其中，北京为33.67%，辽宁为16.76%，河北为10.67%。其余依次为黑龙江、吉林、上海、山东、天津和陕西等地，所占比例分别为4.53%、4.31%、3.97%、2.94%、2.55%及2.24%。此外，还有18.36%分布在其他地区，与北京、辽宁、河北相比，具有较大差距（见图5-7）。

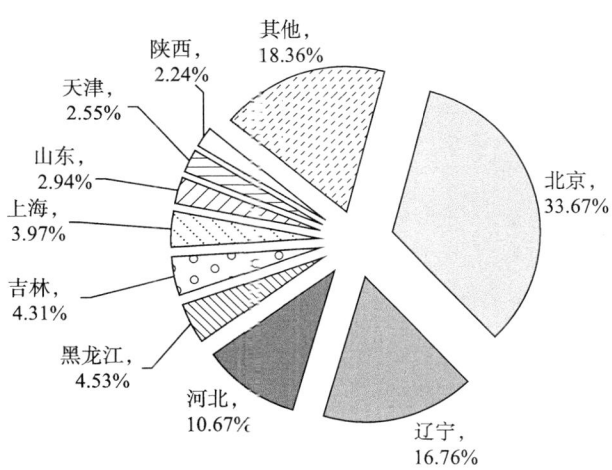

图5-7 2016年滑雪族用户客源地分布（按省份）

基于50家样本滑雪场的滑雪族交易数据如表5-6所示，滑雪票、滑雪教学、冬令营和酒店2016年的线上交易额与2015年相比有了明显提升。2015—2016年，滑雪票线上交易额增加了1300万元，滑雪教学线上交易数据增加了338万元，冬令营线上交易数据增加了177万元，酒店线上交易数据增加了418万元。

表5-6 2016年滑雪族线上交易数据（基于50家样本滑雪场） 单位：万元

产品	2015年线上交易数据	2016年线上交易数据
滑雪票	300	1600
滑雪教学	31	369
冬令营	120	297
酒店	46	464

表5-7为50家样本滑雪场的滑雪族滑雪票线上交易数据，2015—2016年北京/天津、河北以及东北地区的滑雪族滑雪票线上交易数据，包括线上交易总额、人均消费金额及交易次数都有了明显变化。线上交易总额与交易次数快速提升，人均消费在北京/天津、河北有所下降，东北则出现了小幅提升。北京/天津、河北、东北地区的线上交易额分别增加了1881754元、9966533元和2221265.5元，人均消费金额分别增加了-331元、-268元、57.5元，交易次数分别增加了16420次、14696次、8076次。2016年，西北/山东线上交易总额、人均消费金额及交易次数均较小，与其他三个地区相比存在着较大差距。

表5-7 2016年滑雪族滑雪票线上交易数据（基于50家样本滑雪场）

区域	2015年			2016年		
	线上交易总额/元	人均消费金额/元	交易次数/次	线上交易总额/元	人均消费金额/元	交易次数/次
北京/天津	98800	450	220	1980554	119	16640
河北	2269088	988	2297	12235621	720	16993
东北	317048	206.5	1539	2538313.5	264	9615
西北/山东	—	185282.3	49.3	3510	—	—

四、乐点滑雪报告

据乐点滑雪报告，中国滑雪爱好者选择的境外目的地48%集中于日本，其余依次为欧洲、北美、新西兰和韩国，占比分别为23%、19%、4%、5%，其他地方仅占1%（见图5-8）。

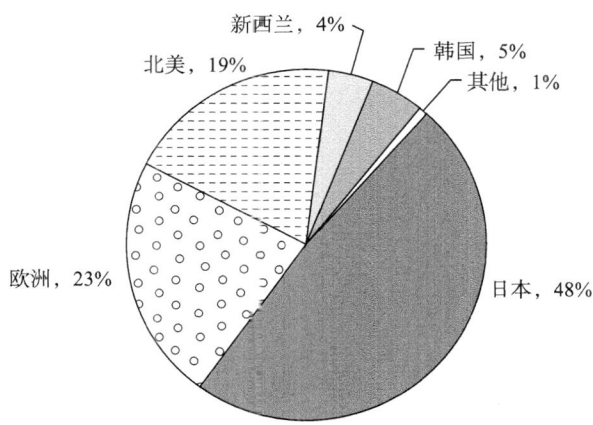

图5-8 2016年中国滑雪爱好者的境外目的地选择

第三节 滑雪者装备市场

滑雪者装备市场是反映滑雪者特征的一个非常重要的方面，但很遗憾，由于涉及品类相对复杂、获取信息的难度相对较大，截至本报告完成，并未能获取到足够的有效信息，因此本节仅提供相对有限的部分双板以及单板的零售数据，供参考。

对9大和3大国际品牌提供的数据进行整理发现，2014—2016年双板零售量远高于单板零售量，但增长率低于单板零售量。2014—2016年，双板、单板零售量分别增加了4155副、4764副，增长率分别为40.16%、78.93%。

2014—2015年，双板零售量增加了2935副，增长率为28.37%；单板零售量增加了2864副，增长率为47.45%。2015—2016年，双板零售量增加了1220副，增长率为9.19%；单板零售量增加了1900副，增长率为21.35%（见图5-9、图5-10）。

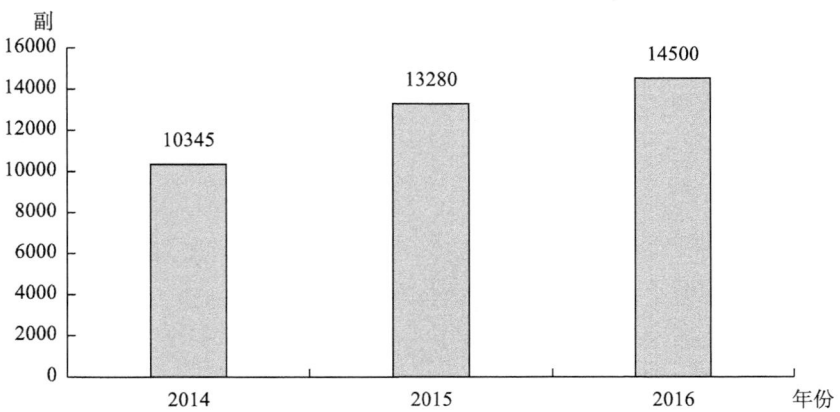

图 5-9　2014—2016 年中国双板零售量

注：基于 9 大国际品牌提供的数据整理。

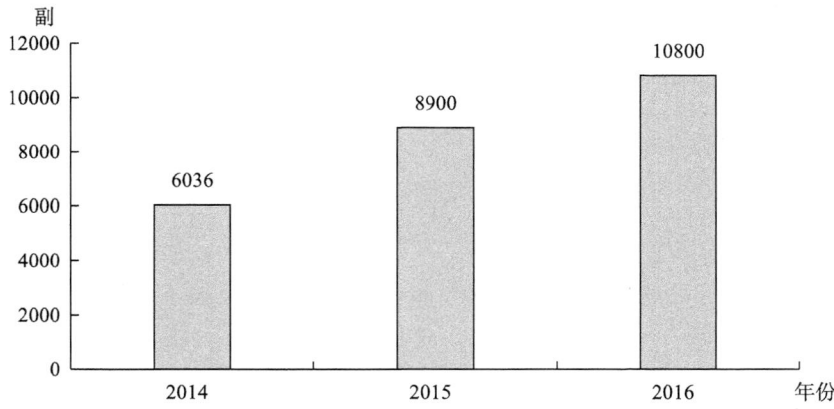

图 5-10　2014—2016 年中国单板零售量

注：基于 3 大国际品牌提供的数据整理。

第三篇

2017年度中国滑雪产业核心数据报告

第六章 2017年滑雪场情况

第一节 滑雪场数量及分布

一、现有滑雪场数量及分布

2017年国内滑雪场新增57家（含室内馆），总数达703家（见图6-1），增幅8.82%。新增的57家滑雪场中，有20家滑雪场建设有架空索道。截至2017年年底，在全国703家滑雪场中，有架空索道的滑雪场有145家，其分布见图6-2。

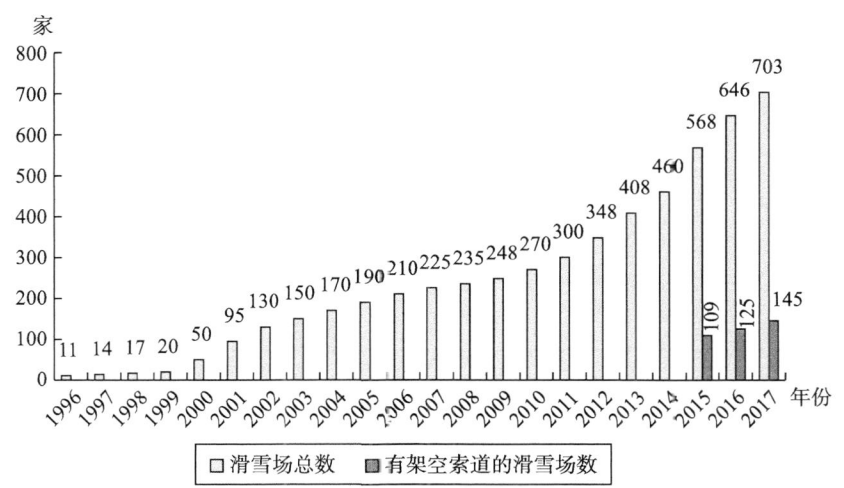

图6-1 1996—2017年中国滑雪场数量统计

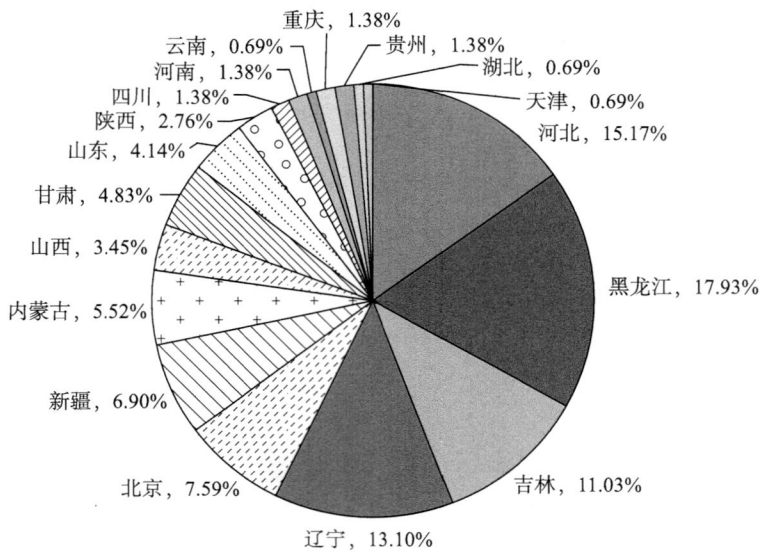

图 6-2 2017 年中国有架空索道的滑雪场分布（按省份）

703 家滑雪场分布于全国 27 个省（区、市）。黑龙江省滑雪场数量为 124 家，为全国之冠（见表 6-1）。

表 6-1 2017 年中国滑雪场数量分布（按省份）　　　　　　　　　　单位：家

排序	省份	2017年滑雪场数量	2016年滑雪场数量	2017年新增滑雪场数量
1	黑龙江	124	122	2
2	山东	61	58	3
3	新疆	59	57	2
4	河北	58	46	12
5	山西	45	42	3
6	河南	42	41	1
7	吉林	41	38	3
8	辽宁	37	35	2
9	内蒙古	37	33	4
10	陕西	31	27	4
11	北京	24	24	0
12	甘肃	20	16	4
13	浙江	18	18	0
14	江苏	15	13	2

续表

排序	省份	2017年滑雪场数量	2016年滑雪场数量	2017年新增滑雪场数量
15	重庆	14	11	3
16	天津	13	12	1
17	宁夏	12	11	1
18	四川	11	11	0
19	贵州	10	6	4
20	湖南	8	7	1
21	青海	7	7	0
22	湖北	7	5	2
23	安徽	3	1	2
24	云南	2	2	0
25	广西	2	1	1
26	福建	1	1	0
27	广东	1	1	0
合计		703	646	57

与2016年相同，在全国34个省级行政区中，仅香港、澳门、台湾、上海、江西、西藏及海南尚未建成滑雪场馆设施。河北省新增滑雪场12家，增幅第一，遥遥领先。

如前所述，本报告中的滑雪场数量及滑雪人次都已包含室内滑雪馆，但不包含旱雪及模拟滑雪器等仿真场馆设施及产生的滑雪人次。在新增57家雪场中，有9家新开的室内滑雪馆。截至2017年年底，国内开业的室内滑雪馆已达21家（见图6-3、表6-2）。

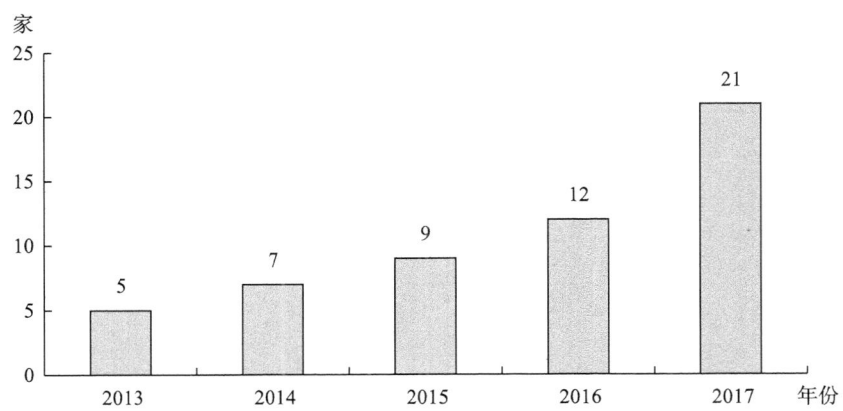

图6-3　2013—2017年国内已投入运营的室内滑雪馆数量

除此之外，依据各方面的公开信息，目前已经完成规划设计、处于在建状态的室内滑雪馆有19家左右，其中有11家预计的开业时间为2018年，其余预计在2019年开业。

在已开业的室内场馆中，哈尔滨万达娱雪乐园最有代表性。哈尔滨万达娱雪乐园于2017年6月30日正式营业，是目前全球最大的室内滑雪场。根据业内调查结果，经过半年时间的运营，哈尔滨万达娱雪乐园在2017年已实现20万滑雪人次的业绩。

表6-2 2017年已建成并投入运营的室内滑雪馆

序号	省份	名称	所属城市	开业时间
1	广东	阿尔卑斯冰雪世界	深圳	2000年7月
2	内蒙古	达永山滑雪馆	满洲里	2005年12月
3	北京	乔波滑雪馆（北京）	顺义	2005年8月
4	浙江	乔波冰雪世界（绍兴）	绍兴	2009年9月
5	河南	伏牛山四季冰雪乐园	洛阳	2010年5月
6	湖南	瑞祥冰雪世界	浏阳	2011年10月
7	广西	冰河世纪滑雪场	来宾	2014年10月
8	湖南	三只熊冰雪王国	长沙	2015年7月
9	河北	西部长青室内冰雪馆	石家庄	2015年9月
10	浙江	文成天鹅堡滑雪场	温州	2015年10月
11	陕西	秦岭四季滑雪场	安康	2016年4月
12	河北	四季滑雪馆	邯郸	2016年5月
13	重庆	仙女山冰雪城	重庆	2016年7月
14	浙江	青田乐园室内滑雪场	丽水	2016年7月
15	湖南	桃花雪缘四季滑雪场	常德	2017年2月
16	河北	青青四季滑雪滑草乐园	邯郸	2017年5月
17	黑龙江	哈尔滨万达娱雪乐园	哈尔滨	2017年6月
18	贵州	荔波冰雪水世界主题乐园室内滑雪场	荔波	2017年8月
19	贵州	遵义思达欢乐谷室内滑雪馆	遵义	2017年9月
20	贵州	奇缘谷冰雪小镇室内滑雪场	安顺	2017年10月
21	安徽	马鞍山启迪乔波冰雪世界	马鞍山	2017年11月

二、滑雪场规划设计项目及分布

表6-3汇总了2016—2017年国内主要规划设计单位签订的滑雪场规划设计项目，同

样反映出河北省冰雪产业的活跃程度。河北共有项目18个,占全部样本项目的28%。

表6-3　2016—2017年国内主要规划设计单位滑雪场项目分布

编号	省份	项目数/个
1	河北	18
2	山西	5
3	甘肃	5
4	内蒙古	5
5	四川	3
6	新疆	3
7	吉林	3
8	湖北	3
9	湖南	2
10	宁夏	2
11	陕西	2
12	北京	2
13	重庆	2
14	贵州	2
15	其他	7
	合计	64

第二节　滑雪场分类统计信息

一、按核心目标客群分类

按核心目标客群可以将国内滑雪场分为旅游体验型、城郊学习型及目的地度假型三类。此三类滑雪场在全部滑雪场中的占比分别为75%、22%和3%(见表6-4)。

表 6-4 2017 年中国滑雪场按核心目标客群分类

滑雪场类型	数量占比	客群定位	主要体现滑雪属性	滑雪场特征	客群特征	典型案例
旅游体验型	75%	旅游观光客	旅游属性	设施简单，只有初级道。位置一般在旅游景区或城郊	90%以上为一次性体验客户，客人平均停留时间 2 小时	雪世界、鸟巢
城郊学习型	22%	本地居民	运动属性、旅游属性	山体落差不大，位于城市郊区，开发有初级、中级、高级雪道	本地自驾客人占比很大，平均停留时间为 3~4 小时	南山、军都山、万科石京龙
目的地度假型	3%	度假人群	度假属性、运动属性、旅游属性	山体有一定规模，除有齐全的雪道产品外，还有住宿等设施的配套	过夜消费占比较大，客人平均停留时间在 1 天以上	万科松花湖、万达长白山、北大壶、亚布力、万龙、富龙、云顶、太舞

在有架空索道的 145 家滑雪场中，旅游体验型滑雪场 21 家，占比 14.5%；城郊学习型滑雪场 107 家，占比 73.8%；目的地度假型滑雪场 17 家，占比 11.7%（见图 6-4）。

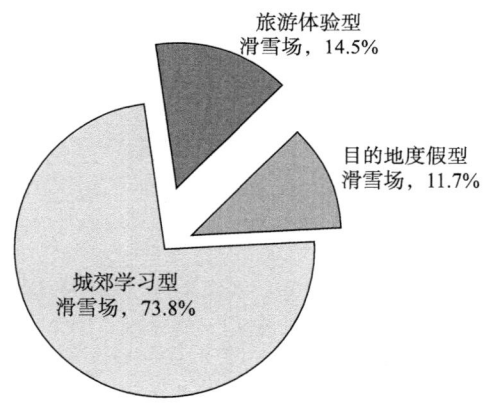

图 6-4 2017 年有架空索道的滑雪场按核心目标客群分类

二、按垂直落差统计

滑雪场垂直落差是衡量滑雪场所在山地的资源规模的一个重要指标。按滑雪场实际开发雪道的垂直落差，将国内滑雪场按以下三类统计：垂直落差超过 300 米的滑雪场 24 家、垂直落差在 100~300 米的滑雪场 138 家以及垂直落差小于 100 米的滑雪场 541 家（见图 6-5）。

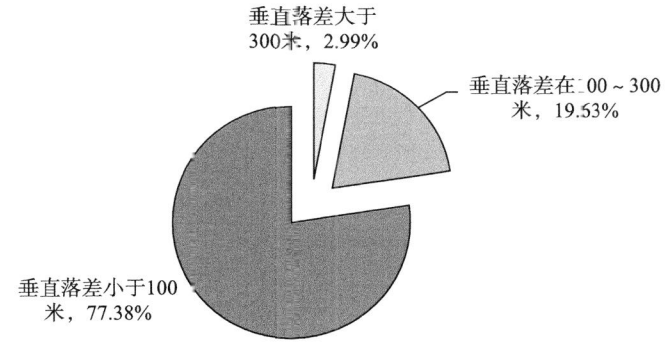

图 6-5　2017 年国内滑雪场按垂直落差统计占比

如表 6-5 所示，垂直落差超过 300 米的 24 家滑雪场中，有 7 家位于河北（全部落户崇礼区），有 4 家位于吉林，黑龙江、新疆各 3 家，内蒙古 2 家，辽宁、河南、云南、甘肃、北京各 1 家。

表 6-5　2017 年国内垂直落差超过 300 米的滑雪场

排序	滑雪场名称	已开发垂直落差/米	所在省份
1	阿尔泰山野雪公园	>1000	新疆
2	长白山天池雪	>900	吉林
3	亚布力体委	885	黑龙江
4	北大壶	870	吉林
5	云南香格里拉	662	云南
6	万科松花湖	600	吉林
7	万龙	580	河北
8	新疆丝绸之路	580	新疆
9	亚布力阳光	540	黑龙江
10	太舞	510	河北
11	富龙	480	河北
12	美林谷	480	内蒙古
13	岱海	468	内蒙古
14	云顶	420	河北
15	阿勒泰将军山	405	新疆
16	伏牛山	400	河南
17	丹东天桥沟	392	辽宁
18	万达长白山	380	吉林

续表

排序	滑雪场名称	已开发垂直落差/米	所在省份
19	多乐美地	323	河北
20	翠云山银河	315	河北
21	万科石京龙	310	北京
22	帽儿山	308	黑龙江
23	抱龙山凤凰岭	304	甘肃
24	长城岭	300	河北

垂直落差排在前两位的已开发滑雪场均属于纯天然滑雪场，没有索道设施，依靠雪地摩托、压雪车（雪猫）、直升机等移动设施解决滑雪者上行需求。其他22家滑雪场都有架空索道。

三、按雪道面积统计

雪道面积是衡量滑雪场大小的另一个重要维度。2017年，除新建滑雪场外，吉林北大壶、长春庙香山，以及崇礼的万龙、富龙、云顶等已开业滑雪场也纷纷加大了扩建力度。

截至2017年年底，雪道面积超过30公顷的滑雪场共计28家，在全部滑雪场中占比3.98%。雪道面积超过30公顷的滑雪场名录详见表6-6。

表6-6 2017年按雪道面积统计的滑雪场数据

雪道面积/公顷	滑雪场数量/家	滑雪场名称
>100	6	阿勒泰阿尔泰山野雪公园、长白山天池雪、万科松花湖、万龙、北大壶、云顶
50~100	7	万达长白山、太舞、富龙、亚布力阳光、亚布力体委、太白鳌山、丝绸之路
30~50	15	将军山、多乐美地、玉龙湾、南山、狼牙山、白登山、翠云山银河、太子岭、伏牛山、西岭雪山、乌金山李宁、七山、抱龙山凤凰岭、岱海、渔阳
10~30	34	
5~10	105	
<5	536	
合计	703	

根据估算，国内雪道总面积大约在3500公顷，其中，表6-6中所列28家滑雪场的雪道面积之和占比超过40%。国内雪道总长度超过1000千米，所列28家滑雪场的雪道总长超过500千米。

第三节 滑雪场硬件设施

一、滑雪场上行设施

(一) 滑雪场架空索道

截至 2017 年年底,国内滑雪场中建成并投入使用的架空索道总数为 236 条,分布于 145 家滑雪场中(见图 6-6)。河北、黑龙江、吉林分别以 46 条、39 条、37 条位居前三,三省合计总共建成 122 条架空索道,占全部架空索道的 51.69%(见表 6-7)。

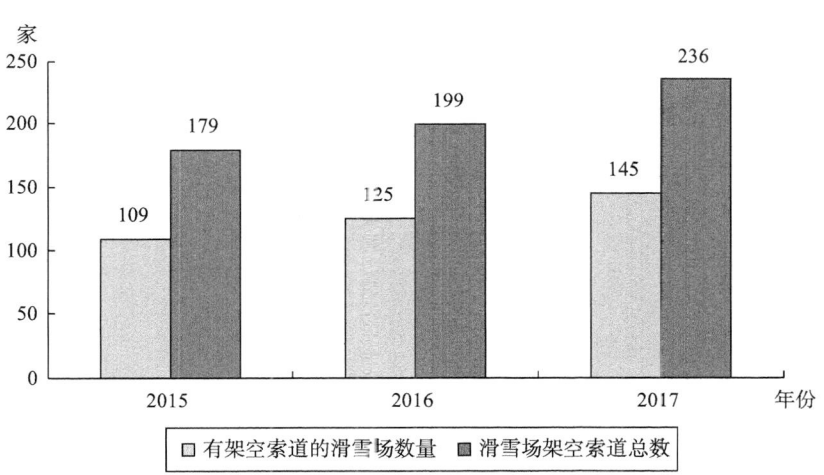

图 6-6　2015—2017 年中国有架空索道的滑雪场及滑雪场架空索道数量

表 6-7　2017 年中国滑雪场架空索道数量及分布

序号	省份	架空索道数量/条	架空索道分布的滑雪场数量/家
1	河北	46	22
2	黑龙江	39	26
3	吉林	37	16
4	辽宁	28	19
5	北京	19	11

续表

序号	省份	架空索道数量/条	架空索道分布的滑雪场数量/家
6	新疆	16	10
7	内蒙古	9	8
8	山西	8	5
9	甘肃	8	7
10	山东	6	6
11	陕西	5	4
12	四川	3	2
13	河南	3	2
14	云南	3	1
15	重庆	2	2
16	贵州	2	2
17	湖北	1	1
18	天津	1	1
合计		236	145

在架空索道中，脱挂式架空索道的数量是滑雪场规模和效率的集中体现。2015—2017年，国内脱挂式架空索道发展迅猛，由26条增长到48条，有脱挂式架空索道的滑雪场也由10家增长到了18家（见图6-7）。

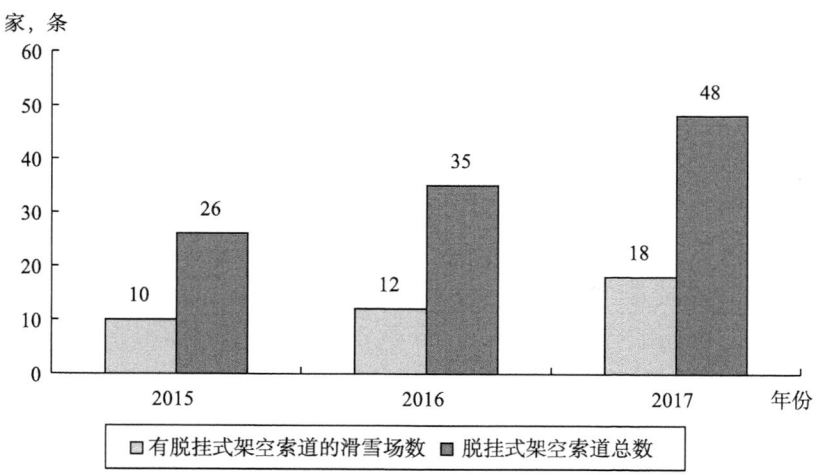

图6-7 2015—2017年中国滑雪场脱挂式架空索道数量统计

图 6-8 统计了 2015—2017 年脱挂式架空索道中进口和国产的数量。很明显，国产脱挂式架空索道的发展相当迅猛，从 2015 年的 2 条增长到 2017 年的 15 条。

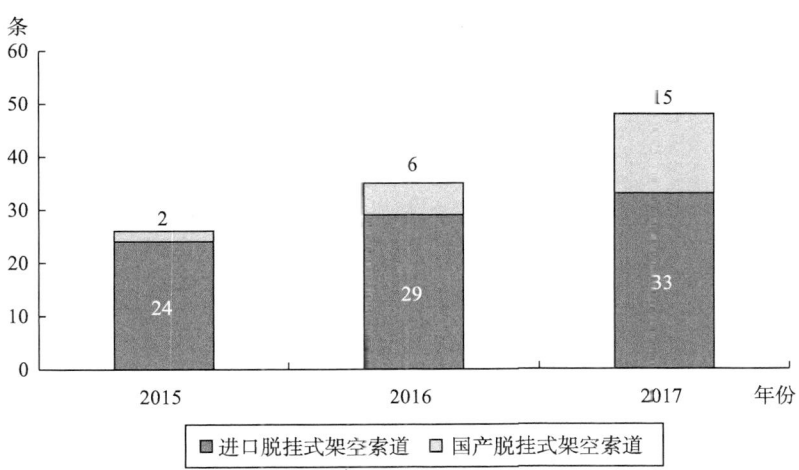

图 6-8　2015—2017 年中国滑雪场进口、国产脱挂式架空索道数量

用于滑雪的 48 条脱挂式架空索道中，河北省 18 条，分布于 5 家雪场，全部集中在张家口市崇礼区；吉林省 18 条，分布于 5 家雪场；黑龙江省 6 条，分布于 3 家雪场；陕西、内蒙古、新疆各建成 2 条（见图 6-9、表 6-8）（此项统计中，只包括用于滑雪的索道，不包括运输用途的索道）。

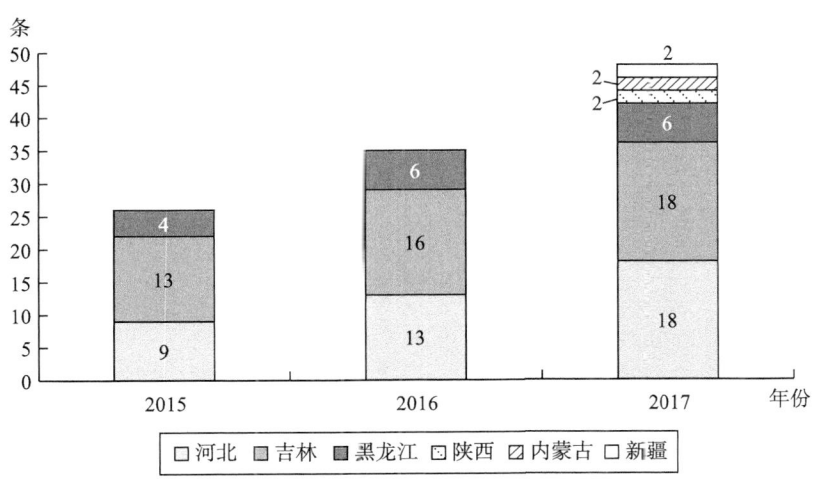

图 6-9　2015—2017 年中国滑雪场脱挂式架空索道按分布省份统计

表 6-8　2017年中国滑雪场按脱挂式架空索道数量排名　　　　　　单位：条

序号	滑雪场	2017年	省份
1	万科松花湖	6	吉林
2	万达长白山	5	吉林
3	万龙	5	河北
4	北大壶	4	吉林
5	云顶	4	河北
6	太舞	3	河北
7	富龙	3	河北
8	亚布力体委	3	黑龙江
9	鲁能长白山	2	吉林
10	翠云山银河	2	河北
11	亚布力阳光	2	黑龙江
12	太白鳌山	2	陕西
13	凉城岱海	2	内蒙古
14	庙香山	1	吉林
15	多乐美地	1	河北
16	帽儿山	1	黑龙江
17	丝绸之路	1	新疆
18	将军山	1	新疆
	合计	48	

（二）滑雪场魔毯

魔毯数据来源于道沃机电、娅豪等国内主要供应商。截至2017年，国内滑雪场共计有1076条魔毯处于运营中（见图6-10），包括2017年新增的226条魔毯（见图6-11）。全部魔毯总长度约157千米。

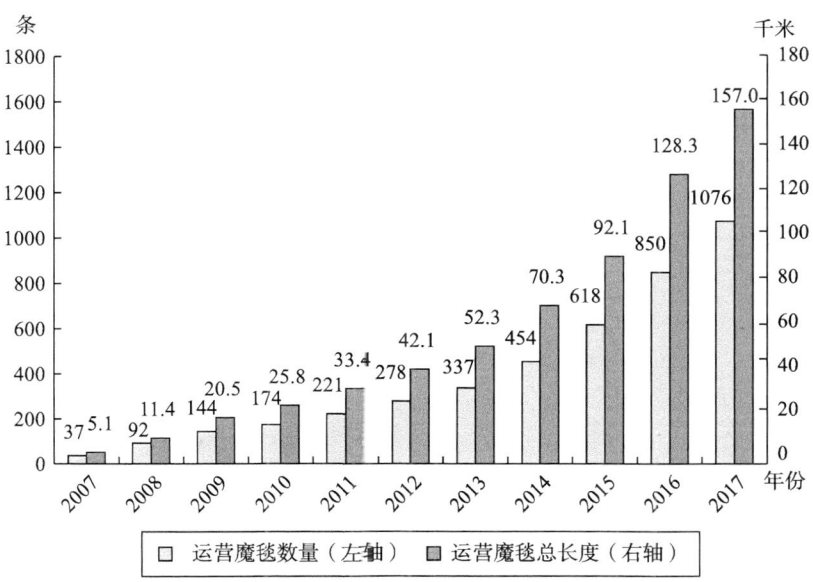

图 6-10 2007—2017 年滑雪场运营魔毯总数量及总长度

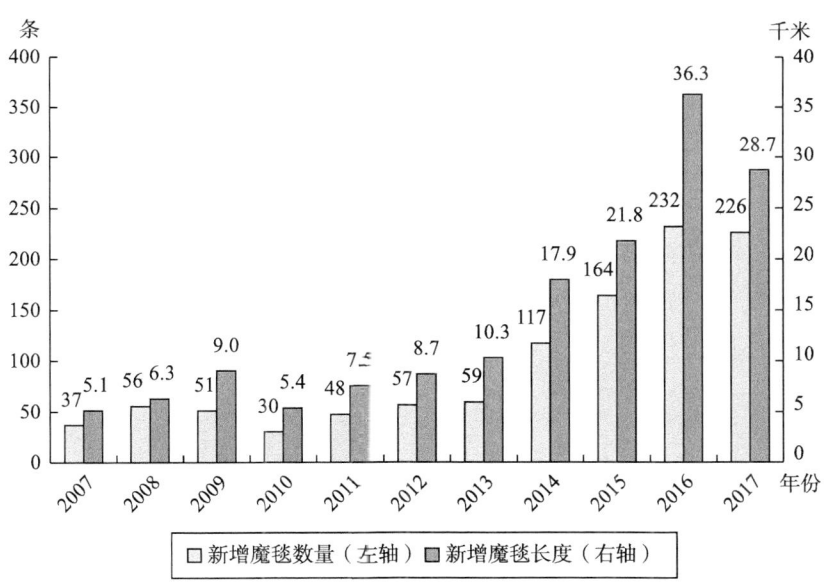

图 6-11 2007—2017 年滑雪场新增魔毯数量及长度

三、滑雪场场地设施

（一）压雪车

根据主要压雪车供应商统计数据，国内滑雪场全部压雪车数量约为485台。2017年，国内新增压雪车75台，略低于2016年的80台。其中，进口新车48台，同比下降幅度较大（见图6-12）。

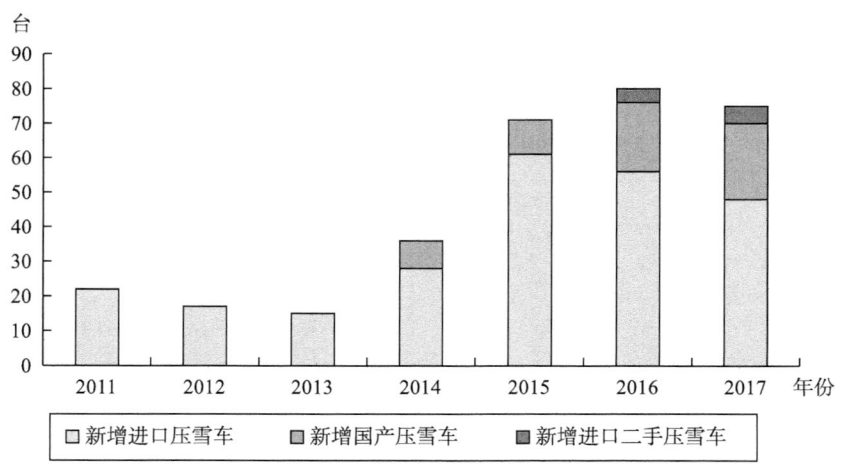

图6-12　2011—2017年中国滑雪场新增压雪车数量

本报告首次引入了对中国海关进口压雪车相关数据的研究（见表6-9）。数据表明，国内进口压雪车的主要产地依次为意大利、德国、加拿大、美国等。

表6-9　2011—2017年中国压雪车进口数据　　　　　　　　　　　　单位：台

贸易伙伴	数量						
	2011年	2012年	2013年	2014年	2015年	2016年	2017年1—11月
全球	22	24	23	31	68	68	58
意大利	12	18	10	18	28	28	25
德国	2	3	6	7	16	20	24
加拿大	1	1	2	4	12	11	6
美国	2	1	2	1	4	7	2
其他	5	1	3	1	8	2	1

资料来源：中国海关，北京龙之讯信息咨询有限公司。

（二）造雪机

2017年，全国滑雪场新增造雪机1420台（见图6-13），全部造雪机合计约6600台。其中，国产造雪机占比约为15%。

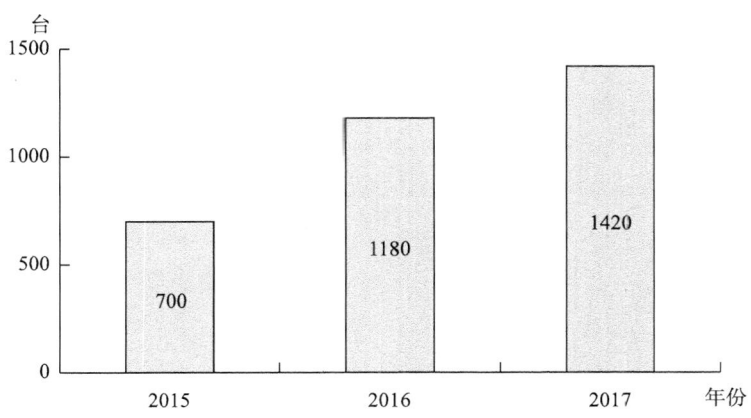

图6-13　2015—2017年滑雪场新增造雪机数量统计

三、滑雪场租赁设施

根据中国海关进口数据分析，双板脱落器的进口数量高速增长，而同时各类滑雪板的进口数量下跌幅度明显，从一个侧面反映出国产滑雪板的增幅显著（见图6-14）。

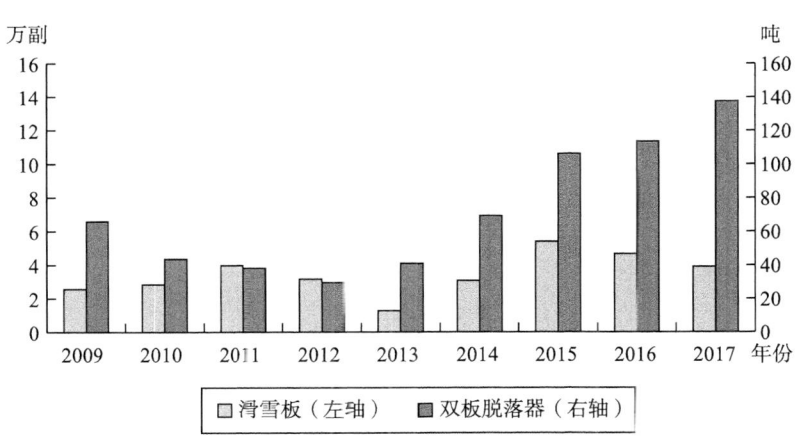

图6-14　2009—2017年中国滑雪板及双板脱落器进口数据

资料来源：中国海关，北京龙之讯信息咨询有限公司。

根据主要国际品牌滑雪板供应商提供的信息，滑雪场租赁双板中，进口国际品牌数量稳中有升。2017年新投入市场的进口租赁板数量突破5万副（见图6-15），其中包括某知名大品牌公司实施的与滑雪场合作租赁项目。整体市场租赁双板总数在60万副以上，平均每家滑雪场的租赁双板数接近900副。

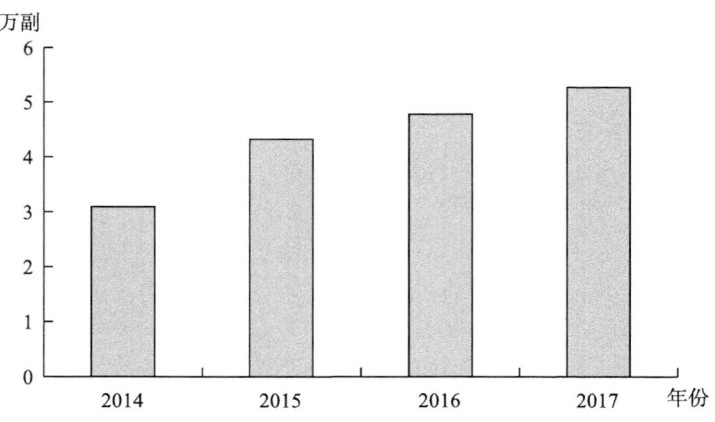

图6-15　2014—2017年中国滑雪场新增进口租赁双板数量

第四节　滑雪场软件设施

一、信息化管理：iSNOW冰雪企业云服务案例

图6-16为2017年iSNOW冰雪企业云服务滑雪场分布状况，其中，41%的iSNOW冰雪企业云服务滑雪场位于华北地区，23%位于东北地区，15%位于西北地区，13%位于华东地区，8%位于西南地区。

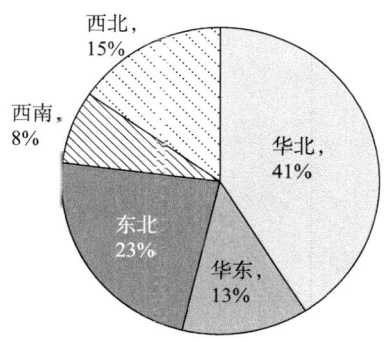

图 6-16　2017 年 iSNOW 冰雪企业云服务滑雪场分布

2017 年 iSNOW 冰雪企业云服务产品主要有滑雪票、教练、训练营、酒店及其他。其中，67% 为滑雪票，教练、训练营、酒店分别为 14%、5%、5%。此外，还包含 9% 的其他产品（见图 6-17）。

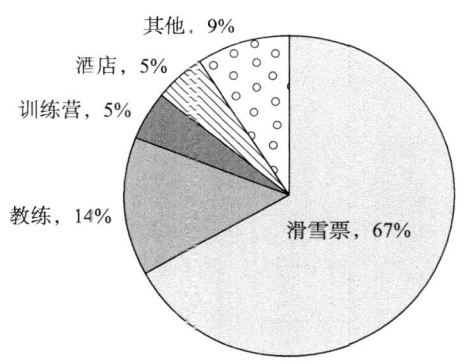

图 6-17　2017 年 iSNOW 冰雪企业云服务产品占比

图 6-18 为 2016 年和 2017 年 iSNOW 冰雪企业云服务情况，移动支付和"现金+卡"支付两类支付方式有了明显变化。2016 年移动支付和"现金+卡"支付比重基本持平。2016 年之后，移动支付手段快速上升至总支付比例的 73%，占据主导地位，"现金+卡"支付占比大大降低，从 49% 下降至 27%。

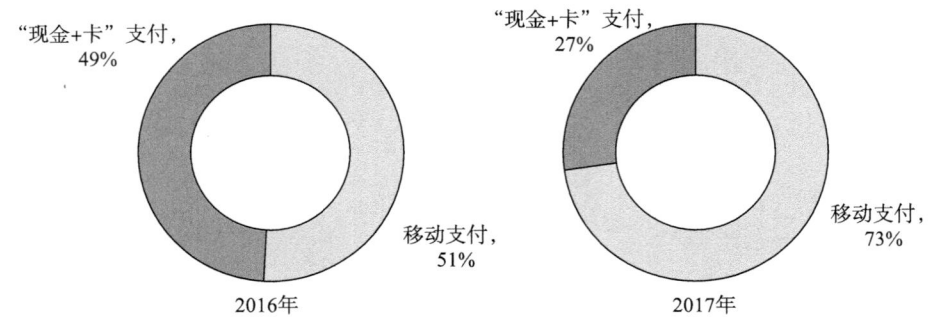

图 6-18　2016 年、2017 年 iSNOW 冰雪企业云服务情况

2017 年 iSNOW 冰雪企业云服务线上交易与 2016 年相比，除 4 月和 9 月之外，各月份的变化率均较大。2016 年 iSNOW 冰雪企业云服务线上交易最大值出现在 11 月，最小值出现在 5 月。2017 年 iSNOW 冰雪企业云服务线上交易最大值出现在 12 月，远高于 3000 万元，最小值出现在 4 月，不足 30 万元。

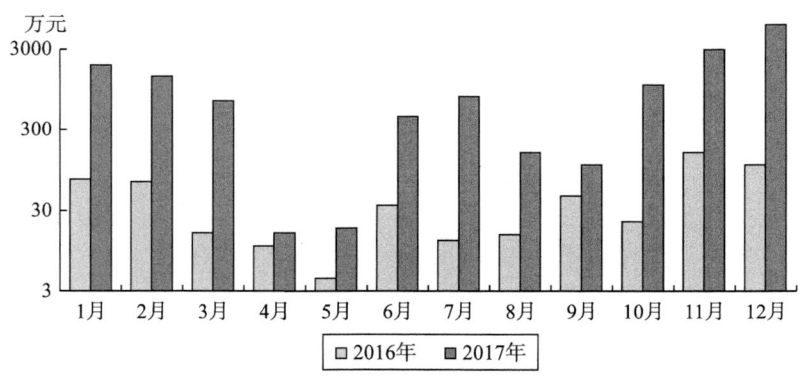

图 6-19　2016 年、2017 年 iSNOW 冰雪企业云服务线上交易

2016—2017 年 iSNOW 冰雪企业云服务客流量对比如图 6-20 所示。客流量与线上交易有着较强的相关性，客流量越大，企业云服务的线上交易越高。10 月至次年 3 月是 iSNOW 冰雪企业云服务客流量的高峰期，4—5 月、8—9 月客流量较小。2016 年 iSNOW 冰雪企业云服务客流量最大值出现在 12 月，约 5 万人，最小值出现在 9 月，略高于 50 人。2017 年 iSNOW 冰雪企业云服务客流量最大值同样出现在 12 月，超越了 500 万人，最小值出现在 4 月，低于 500 人。

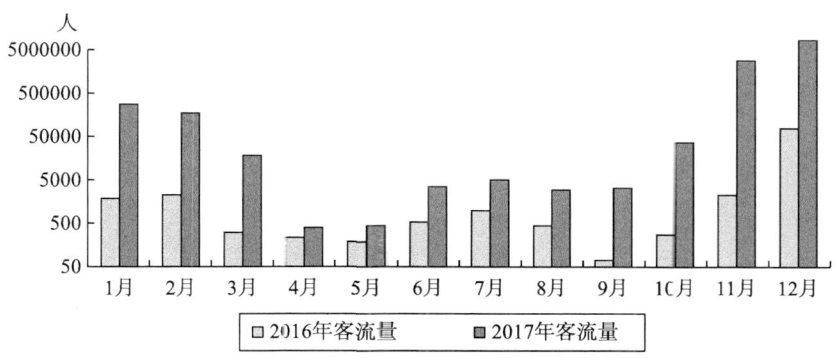

图 6-20 2016 年、2017 年 iSNOW 冰雪企业云服务客流量对比

二、大数据分析及服务：崇礼移动大数据报告案例[①]

来访崇礼的人数在不同的月份差异较大。2017 年 6—9 月为主要的变化期，6 月开始，来访崇礼的人数快速上升，至 8 月达到最大值 119.18 万人，8—9 月后人数快速下降，此后保持在稳定水平（见图 6-21）。

在来访崇礼的人流量中，以省内漫入为主要的流量来源，省外漫入崇礼的人流量占比较低。2017 年 1—11 月，省内漫入崇礼的人流量占比均值为 66.36%，人流量占比最高值在 4 月，占比为 75.20%，最低值在 8 月，占比为 57.32%。省外漫入崇礼的人流量占比均值为 33.64%，最高值在 8 月，占比为 42.68%，最低值在 4 月，占比为 24.80%（见图 6-22、图 6-23）。

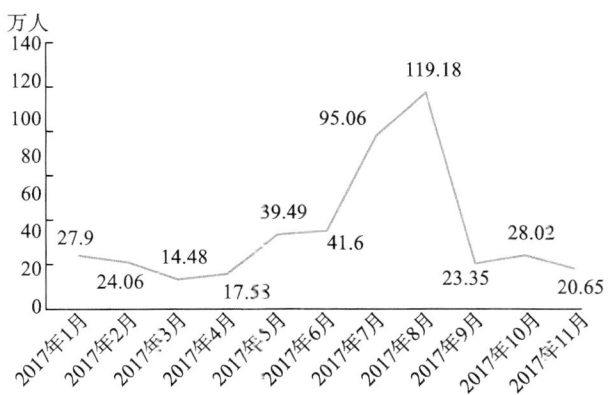

图 6-21 2017 年 1—11 月来访崇礼的人数

---

① 崇礼区政府授权使用。

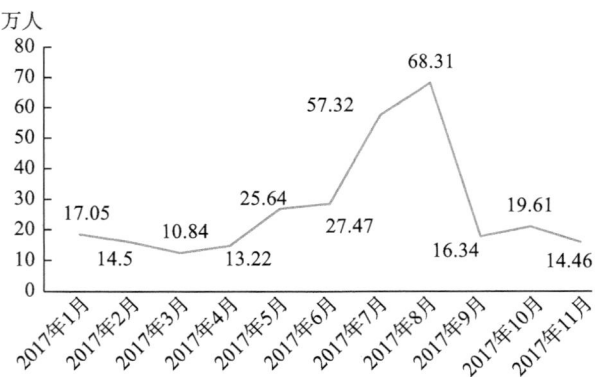

图 6-22 2017 年 1—11 月省内漫入崇礼人流量

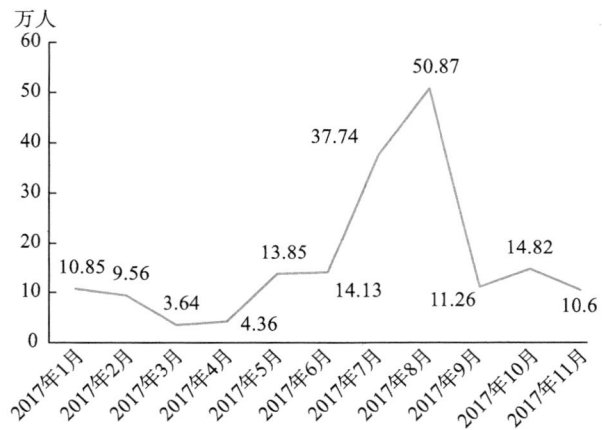

图 6-23 2017 年 1—11 月省外漫入崇礼人流量

2017 年 4 月，漫入崇礼人群逗留时长以短时为主，逗留时长超过三天的人群较少，且多集中于崇礼周边地区，如图 6-24 所示。漫入崇礼逗留时长 1~2 天的用户占所有用户的 67.65%，3~9 天的为 20.16%，10 天的为 12.19%。在逗留时间超过 3 天的不到 30% 的用户中，河北省内、北京、天津及内蒙古为主要的人流来源，河北省内与北京两地的用户占 70% 左右，天津与内蒙古两地约占 15%（见图 6-25）。

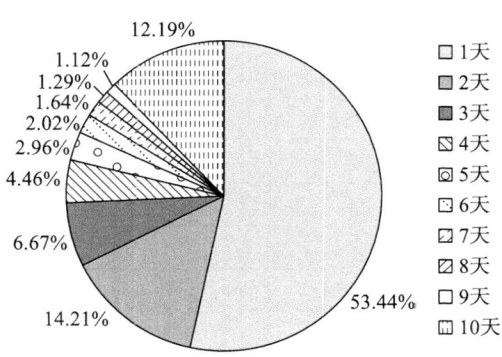 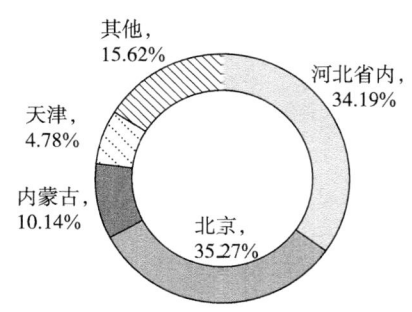

图 6-24　2017 年 4 月漫入崇礼逗留时长　　图 6-25　2017 年 4 月逗留时长 3 天以上的用户地区分布

在漫入崇礼的人群中，56.8%为男性，43.2%为女性；从年龄结构来看，漫入崇礼的人群以 20~40 岁、40~60 岁的青壮年为主，占比分别为 43.9%、41.8%；0~20 岁及 60 岁以上的青少年和老年人占比较低，合计仅占 14.3%（见图 6-26）。

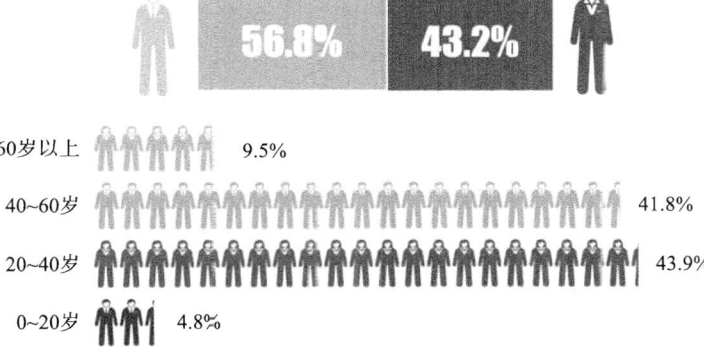

图 6-26　2017 年 4 月漫入崇礼人群的性别与年龄结构

表 6-10 为漫入崇礼人群的地区分布，以北京、内蒙古、天津和山西较多。这些地区因为距离较近，在短时间内可以往返，因此漫入量远高于其他地区。辽宁、山东等地漫入量与北京、内蒙古相比有较大差距。

表 6-10　2017 年 4 月漫入崇礼人群的地区分布　　　　　　　　　　　单位：人

省份	漫入量
北京	148862
内蒙古	32070

续表

省份	漫入量
天津	9890
山西	9455
辽宁	6816
山东	6812
河南	5999
上海	5249
广东	4980
江苏	4052

根据大数据报告分析，进入崇礼的交通以自驾及其他为主，辅之以铁路和客运等交通方式。北京与天津由于距离较近，且经济条件与生活水平较高，自驾成为越来越多的工作者所钟爱的出行方式。崇礼周边的县区由于距离较近，客运成为居民和旅行团出行可能的选择。此外，对于距离较远的游客来说，铁路具有承载力大、准时性高、价格便宜等优点，成为优先选择（见图6-27）。

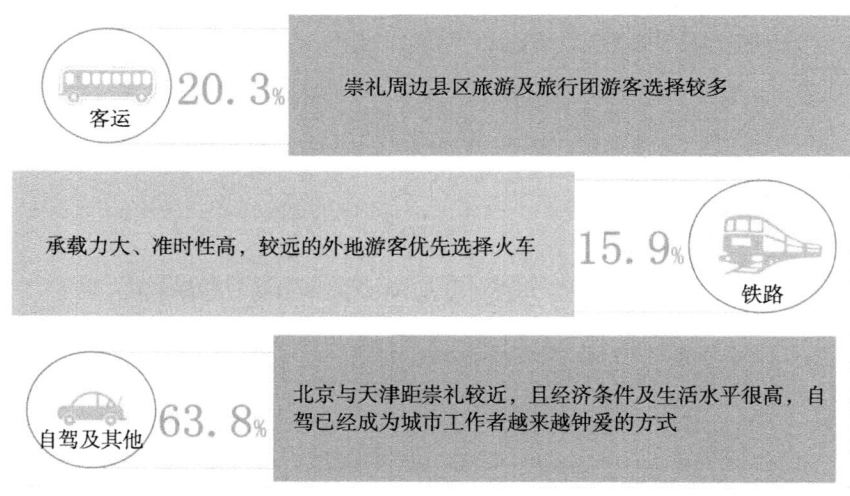

图6-27 崇礼移动大数据报告案例分析

三、滑雪教练培训认证[①]

截至 2017 年年底，全国从事滑雪教学工作的滑雪指导员约为 2 万人，其中考取国家体育总局和人事部颁发的滑雪社会体育指导员证书的指导员合计 9177 人，占比 46%。

此外，国内滑雪指导员和爱好者考取各类境外滑雪指导员协会执照成为趋势，如美国 PSIA、加拿大 CSIA、新西兰 NZSIA、英国相关协会、奥地利相关协会及日本相关协会等。2017 年累计 900 余人获得境外机构颁发的滑雪指导员执照，2016 年及 2015 年分别为 700 人和 300 人。

第五节　四季仿真滑雪场所

一、旱雪

旱雪场地作为滑雪的替代品，近几年在国内得到了长足的发展（见图 6-28）。尖峰旱雪是国内旱雪的主要供应商。根据尖峰旱雪提供的资料，截至 2017 年年底，国内已投入使用的尖峰旱雪场地达到 21 家（见图 6-29）。

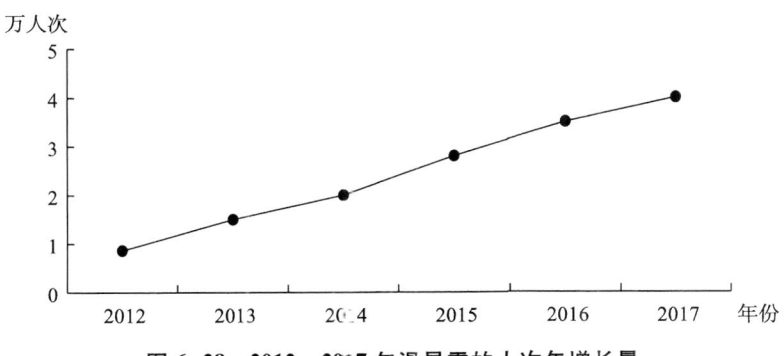

图 6-28　2012—2017 年滑旱雪的人次年增长量

资料来源：成都四季滑雪场。

---

① 资料整理：魔法滑雪学院张岩。

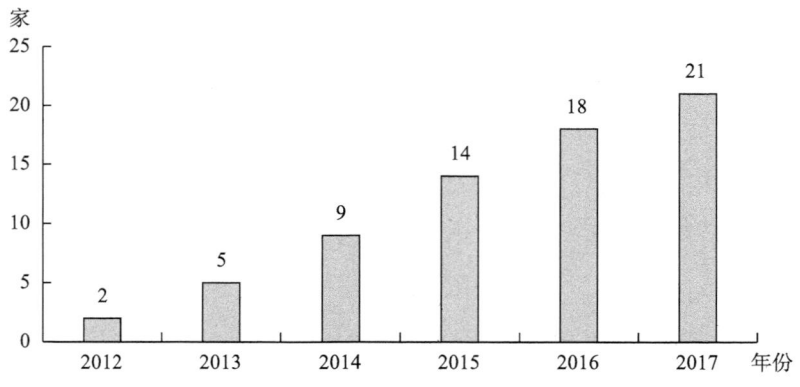

图 6-29　2012—2017 年已投入运营的尖峰旱雪场地数量

除尖峰旱雪外,其他品牌的旱雪类产品也都发展很快。比如,极速旱雪已建成并投入运营 10 家场馆,同时还有 5 家在建。

二、室内滑雪模拟训练场地

以雪乐山俱乐部为例,LeSki Club 已有 12 家室内滑雪训练中心在北京开业,合计投入模拟滑雪设备 28 台,预计全年运营将产生 14 万滑雪人次。雪乐山目前聘用滑雪教练 59 人。

第七章 2017年滑雪者情况

第一节 滑雪者人次及分布

2017年全年，中国到底有多少人滑过雪？根据本报告研究测算，在全部1750万滑雪人次中，滑雪者人数约为1210万人，相比2016年的1133万人，上涨6.8%（见图7-1）。其中，一次性体验者人数占比由2016年的77.8%下降为75.2%。2017年，人均滑雪次数由2016年的1.33次上升为1.45次。

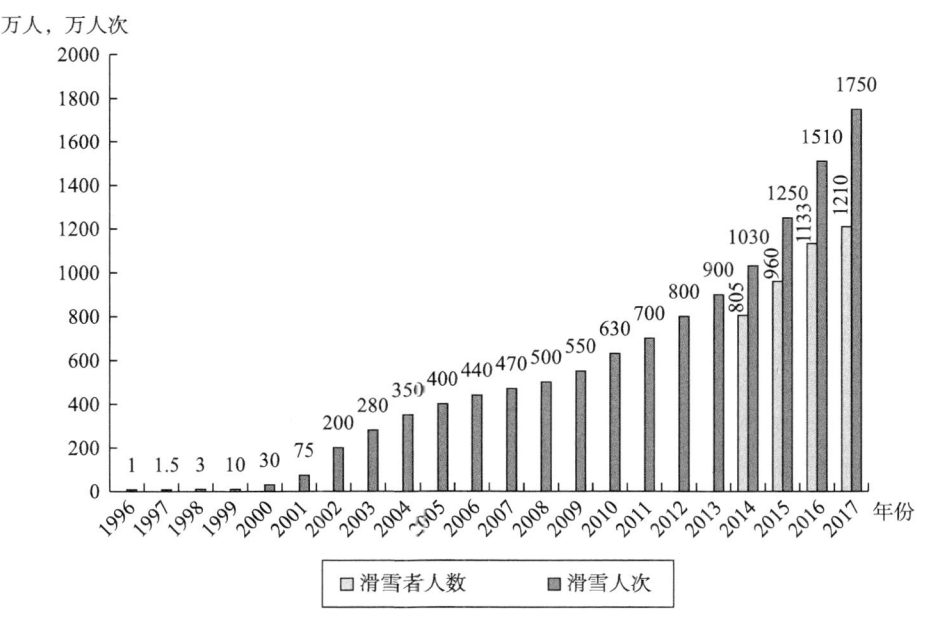

图7-1 1996—2017年滑雪人次及滑雪者人数

2017年，滑雪人次增量在10万以上的省份依次为河北、黑龙江、吉林、贵州、山西、陕西、浙江、江苏。其中，河北增长54万人次，与新增12家雪场有关；黑龙江增长38万人次，与哈尔滨万达娱雪乐园有关；新疆减少13万人次，与社会稳定状况有关。

表7-1 2016年、2017年滑雪人次分布（按目的地滑雪场省份）

省份	2017年			2016年		
	排序	滑雪场数量/家	滑雪人次/万人次	排序	滑雪场数量/家	滑雪人次/万人次
黑龙江	1	124	196	2	122	158
河北	2	58	176	3	46	122
北京	3	24	167	1	24	171
吉林	4	41	147	4	38	118
山西	5	45	110	7	42	96
山东	6	61	104	6	58	98
浙江	7	18	91	9	18	79
河南	8	42	90	8	41	82
新疆	9	59	86	5	57	99
内蒙古	10	37	84	10	33	76
辽宁	11	37	69	11	35	72
陕西	12	31	68	12	27	54
四川	13	11	58	13	11	50
甘肃	14	20	56	14	16	48
天津	15	13	40	15	12	39
江苏	16	15	39	16	13	29
湖南	17	8	33	17	7	27
重庆	18	14	33	18	11	24
贵州	19	10	30	21	6	10
湖北	20	7	21	19	5	18
宁夏	21	12	18	20	11	15
青海	22	7	10	22	7	9
安徽	23	3	10	27	1	3
广西	24	2	6	26	1	3
云南	25	2	4	23	2	4
福建	26	1	3	24	1	3
广东	27	1	3	25	1	3
合计		703	1750		646	1510

第二节　滑雪者特征：移动互联网数据

从多个维度为中国滑雪者画像，是我们作为从业者的终极使命。本报告继续联合国内相对活跃的同伴，它们从各自的角度提供了多方位、多维度的分析报告。

一、雪族科技——滑雪族

滑雪族，雪族科技旗下品牌，国内最早的垂直冰雪企业信息化服务平台。自 2014 年成立伊始，滑雪族就成了滑雪及广泛极限运动爱好者的前行伴侣。在这里，可以把滑雪场经历趣事以图文或视频的方式记录下来，和广大雪友分享，可以与好友或家人一起组队，参与最具娱乐性的大众滑雪体验。滑雪族通常采取用户分布地、用户自画像、用户装备以及雪季和非雪季阅读量等指标进行系统化的分析和应用。

（一）滑雪族用户分布地分析

图 7-2 为滑雪族用户分布地。滑雪族以北京、河北和黑龙江用户为主，其次为河南、辽宁和吉林等地。滑雪族用户分布高度集中，北京、河北和黑龙江用户占滑雪族用户总数的一半以上，其他地区分布仅占 44%。

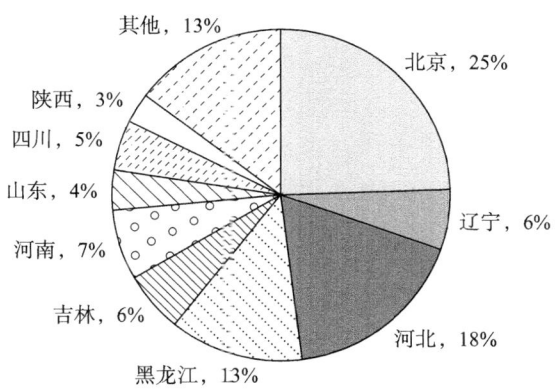

图 7-2　2017 年滑雪族用户分布地

(二)滑雪族用户自画像分析

根据对滑雪族用户的性别与终端分析发现,滑雪族用户53%为男性,47%为女性,男女比例基本持平。从终端来看,iPhone用户占滑雪族用户的75%,远高于其他用户终端的占比,安卓用户终端占19%,Windows Phone 7用户终端占5%,其他未知用户终端仅占1%,整体呈现出以iPhone用户终端为主导的趋势(见图7-3)。

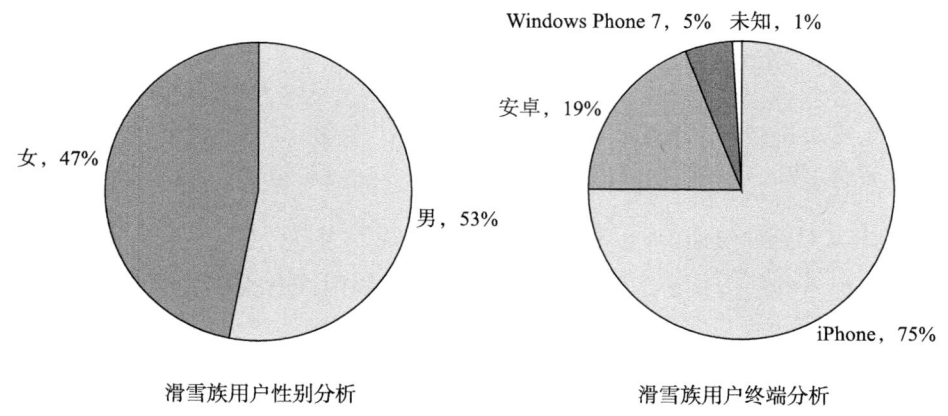

图7-3 2017年滑雪族用户性别、终端分析

(三)滑雪族用户装备分析

滑雪族用户装备中单双板占比具有较大差异。67%的滑雪族用户使用的是双板,使用单板的仅有33%。同时,74%的滑雪族用户使用的装备来自租赁,仅有26%为自带(见图7-4)。

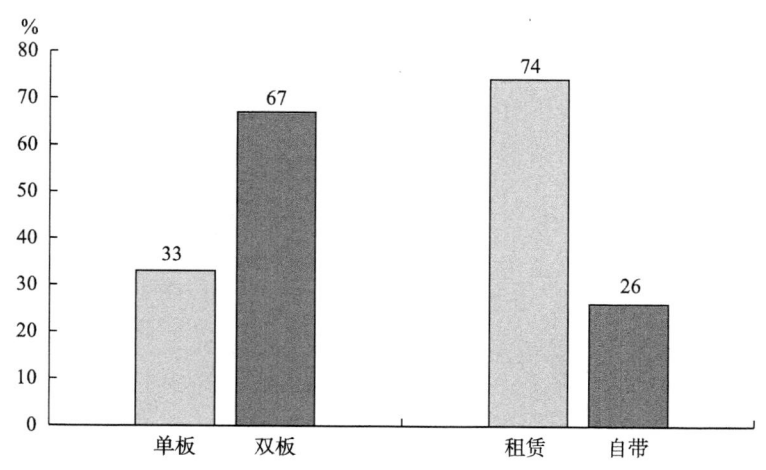

图7-4 2017年滑雪族用户装备占比

（四）滑雪族雪季和非雪季阅读量分析

在滑雪族雪季（1—4月、10—12月）和非雪季（4—10月）阅读量分析中，滑雪族雪季阅读量共7652661次，阅读量占比65.09%，非雪季阅读量共1937707次，阅读量占比34.91%，具有较明显的季节性特征（见表7-2）。

表7-2　2017年滑雪族雪季和非雪季阅读量分析

季节	阅读量/次	阅读量占比/%
雪季	7652661	65.09
非雪季	1937707	34.91

二、GOSKI报告

由于GOSKI团队及资源与单板有更多的联系，因此GOSKI报告更多地反映出单板滑雪者的特征。

图7-5为GOSKI用户客源地占比。GOSKI用户以来自北京、辽宁、吉林和河北等省份为主，所占比例为66.79%，其他省份或地区所占比例较小。用户男女比例均衡，以单板用户为主，辅之以24.9%的双板和16.2%的其他用户（见图7-6）。

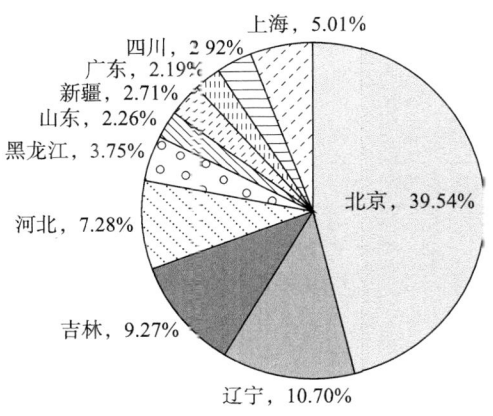

图7-5　2017年GOSKI用户客源地占比

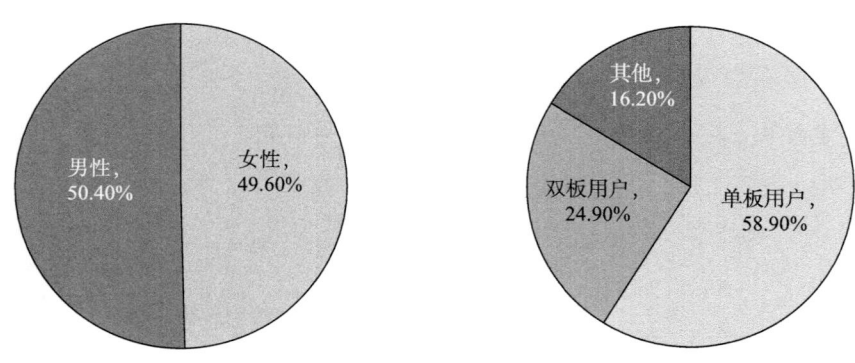

图7-6　2017年GOSKI用户特征

三、滑呗报告

根据滑呗基础信息报告，2017年滑呗覆盖的国内外滑雪场总数共354家，62%为国内滑雪场，38%为国外滑雪场。滑呗覆盖的用户总数约373137人，运动轨迹记录人数共96444人，运动轨迹累计3448300千米，运动轨迹人均滑行记录35千米（见表7-3）。

表7-3　2017年滑呗基础信息

指标	数量
覆盖的滑雪场总数/家	354
覆盖的国内滑雪场数量/家	219
覆盖的国外滑雪场数量/家	191
用户总数/人	373137
2017年运动轨迹记录人数/人	96444
2017年运动轨迹累计数/千米	3448300
运动轨迹人均滑行记录/千米	35

2017年，滑呗运动数据记录总里程数排名前20的滑雪场如表7-4所示，记录了滑雪场人数和总里程数等指标。记录总里程数最多的为万龙度假天堂，记录人数为8347人，人均里程76.01千米；其次为松花湖度假区，总里程数580569.18千米，记录人数为9353人，人均里程62.07千米；总里程数最小的是梦都美滑雪场，记录总里程数为19225.87千米，记录人数为347人。

表 7-4 2017 年滑呗运动数据记录

排名	滑雪场名称	记录人数/人	记录总里程数/千米	人均里程/千米	人均滑行落差/米
1	万龙度假天堂	8347	634493.84	76.01	15.69
2	松花湖度假区	9353	580569.18	62.07	13.4
3	密苑云顶乐园	5155	313796.49	60.87	10.53
4	北大壶度假区	4919	272470.24	55.39	12.65
5	亚布力阳光	2877	269435.85	93.65	19.66
6	太舞滑雪小镇	3825	176659.33	46.19	9.69
7	万达长白山	3182	113471.25	35.66	7.11
8	多乐美地	2020	79504.12	39.36	7.58
9	帽儿山滑雪场	3101	79435.99	25.62	8.36
10	富龙四季小镇	1852	72315.56	39.05	4.2
11	丝绸之路滑雪场	968	53750.64	55.53	10.48
12	南山滑雪场	2316	49158.73	21.23	3.14
13	庙香山滑雪场	1670	39666.99	23.75	4.06
14	亚布力滑雪场	1042	35936.31	34.49	7.16
15	美林谷滑雪场	682	34781.77	51	8.63
16	长城岭滑雪场	1171	34172.43	29.18	6.48
17	怀北国际滑雪场	1764	33748.7	19.13	3.32
18	万龙八易滑雪场	1269	30848.72	24.31	3.52
19	天桥沟滑雪场	633	19967.54	31.54	0.05
20	梦都美滑雪场	347	19225.87	55.41	11.91

2017 年滑呗注册滑雪俱乐部总数共 872 家，注册用户达 48876 人，平均每个俱乐部用户数 56 人，滑行总里程数共 1624824 千米，人均滑行里程数 29 千米（见表 7-5）。

表 7-5 2017 年滑呗注册滑雪俱乐部基础信息

指标	数量
注册总数/家	872
注册用户数/人	48876
平均每个俱乐部用户数/人	56
2017 年滑行总里程数/千米	1624824
2017 年人均滑行里程数/千米	29

表 7-6 为 2017 年滑呗滑雪俱乐部运动轨迹。1031 滑雪俱乐部一马当先，记录人数 637 人，记录总里程数 100606.27 千米。虽然总里程数最高，但由于记录人数较多，人均里程仅 157.94 千米，人均滑行落差较小。翼龙滑雪俱乐部因为记录的人数较少，总里程较大，因此人均里程最大，人均滑行落差也是最大的。

表 7-6 2017 年滑呗滑雪俱乐部运动轨迹

排名	俱乐部名称	记录人数/人	记录总里程数/千米	人均里程/千米	人均滑行落差/米
1	1031 滑雪俱乐部	637	100606.27	157.94	30.7
2	雪峰滑雪俱乐部	263	96990.85	368.79	78.96
3	广东滑雪俱乐部	307	56911.24	185.38	37.94
4	吉林雪者联盟	200	56515.9	282.58	36.04
5	远山滑雪俱乐部	334	54223.75	162.35	50.08
6	中国魔诺滑雪俱乐部	162	49912.31	308.1	60.03
7	星禹户外滑雪俱乐部	464	44719.04	96.38	18.09
8	翼龙滑雪俱乐部	88	35179.31	399.76	81.14
9	天津零度户外	203	30614.47	150.81	28.21
10	零度滑雪	165	26866.83	162.83	35.43
11	疯滑雪跃俱乐部	174	24230.58	139.26	28.6
12	Sstyle 雪风户外	176	23879.68	135.68	44
13	大庆 DCS 滑雪俱乐部	115	23608.01	205.29	27.72
14	炫酷之旅滑雪俱乐部	205	22000.34	107.32	19.76
15	长春极限俱乐部	291	19475.45	66.93	13.95
16	盘锦彩虹俱乐部	115	19401.62	168.71	24.57
17	极影者	163	18572.41	113.94	31.11
18	西安冰峰滑雪俱乐部	219	17732.92	80.97	15.56
19	Veneer 单板俱乐部	138	14595.64	105.77	36.5
20	678 滑雪俱乐部	86	14242.32	165.61	20.44

四、乐点滑雪报告

根据乐点报告，中国滑雪者选择去日本滑雪的人数增长明显，由 2016 年的 48% 上升到 2017 年的 55%（见图 7-7）。其次是欧洲。在欧洲国家中，瑞士明显靠前，法国、奥地利、意大利紧随其后。

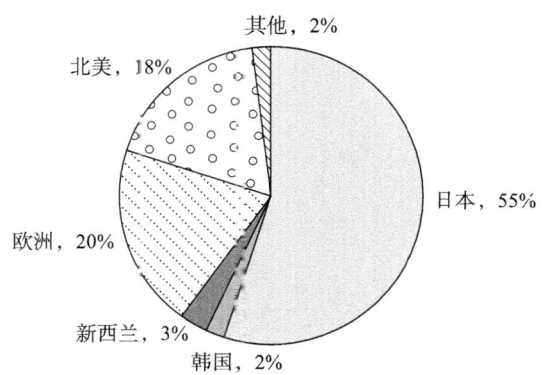

图 7-7　2017 年中国滑雪爱好者境外目的地选择占比

第三节　滑雪者装备市场

尽管绝大多数品牌商都提供了相关数据，但关于滑雪者装备市场的描述仍然是本报告中最薄弱的部分。对于绝大部分专业渠道（街边店等），滑雪装备零售市场一直处于平台期，并没有太大变化。需要重点关注的是：①青少年滑雪市场已经全面启动，青少年滑雪装备值得重点关注；②迪卡侬的滑雪品牌 Wed'ze 增长势头强劲，年增长达到 30%。

截至 2017 年年底，魔法滑雪学院分校及营地从 3 家增长到 10 家，增长 230%；持证专职教练 220 人，兼职教练 80 人，年增长 160%；2015 年教学 3100 人次，2016 年为 10900 人次，2017 年为 23000 人次，年增长 110%；教学收入 900 万元，年增长 210%；教学复购率 67%；教学转化率 32%（达到 3~4 级标准）。

第四篇

2018年度中国滑雪产业核心数据报告

第八章 2018年滑雪场情况

第一节 滑雪场数量及分布

滑雪场除传统意义上的户外滑雪场及室内滑雪馆外,也包括近几年国内蓬勃发展的旱雪场地以及滑雪模拟器场馆。

一、滑雪场(含室内滑雪馆)

2018年国内滑雪场新增39家(含室内滑雪馆),总数达742家,同比上升5.55%。新增的39家滑雪场中,有2家滑雪场建设有架空索道。截至2018年年底,全国有架空索道的雪场数量达到149家(除2家新建雪场外,另有2家已开业雪场新建架空索道)(见图8-1)。

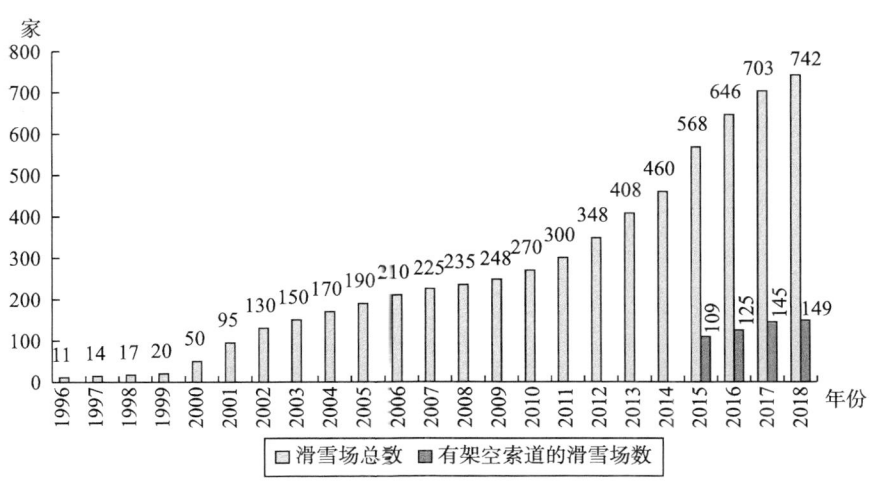

图8-1 1996—2018年中国滑雪场数量统计

742家滑雪场分布于全国28个省（区、市）。其中，滑雪场数量排名前5的省份依次为黑龙江、山东、新疆、河北和山西。2018年，内蒙古自治区新增滑雪场数量最多，其次是山东及湖北（见表8-1）。

表8-1 2017年、2018年中国滑雪场数量分布（按省份）　　　　　单位：家

排序	省份	2018年	2017年	2018年新增
1	黑龙江	124	124	0
2	山东	65	61	4
3	新疆	60	59	1
4	河北	59	58	1
5	山西	48	45	3
6	河南	43	42	1
7	吉林	43	41	2
8	内蒙古	42	37	5
9	辽宁	38	37	1
10	陕西	34	31	3
11	北京	24	24	0
12	甘肃	21	20	1
13	浙江	19	18	1
14	江苏	17	15	2
15	重庆	16	14	2
16	天津	13	13	0
17	宁夏	13	12	1
18	四川	11	11	0
19	湖北	11	7	4
20	贵州	10	10	0
21	湖南	9	8	1
22	青海	8	7	1
23	云南	4	2	2
24	安徽	3	3	0
25	广西	2	2	0
26	江西	2	0	2
27	广东	2	1	1
28	福建	1	1	0
	合计	742	703	39

在2018年新增的39家滑雪场中，有5家新开的室内滑雪馆。截至2018年年底，国内开业的室内滑雪馆已达26家（见图8-2）。

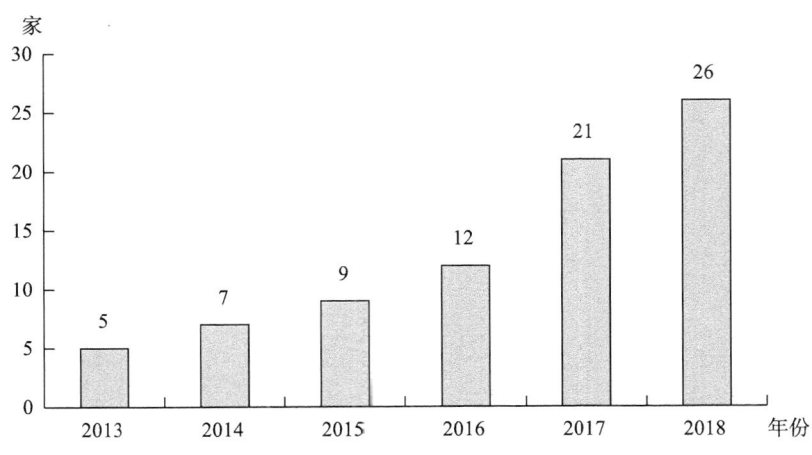

图8-2　2013—2018年国内已投入运营的室内滑雪馆数量

表8-2汇总了2018年国内部分主要规划设计单位签订的滑雪场规划设计项目，可以看出，河北、吉林、新疆的相对活跃程度较高。

表8-2　2018—2019年国内主要规划设计单位滑雪场项目分布　　　　单位：个

序号	省份	项目数
1	河北	7
2	吉林	4
3	新疆	3
4	山西	2
5	四川	2
6	辽宁	2
7	青海	1
8	安徽	1
9	山东	1
10	湖北	1
11	黑龙江	1
12	福建	1
合计		26

二、旱雪场地

2018年，旱雪场地发展势头强劲，成为滑雪场馆领域新增长极。中国旱雪场地目前使用的旱雪毯以金针菇式旱雪毯为主。根据尖锋旱雪提供的资料，截至2018年年底，国内旱雪场总数已超过30家（见图8-3）。

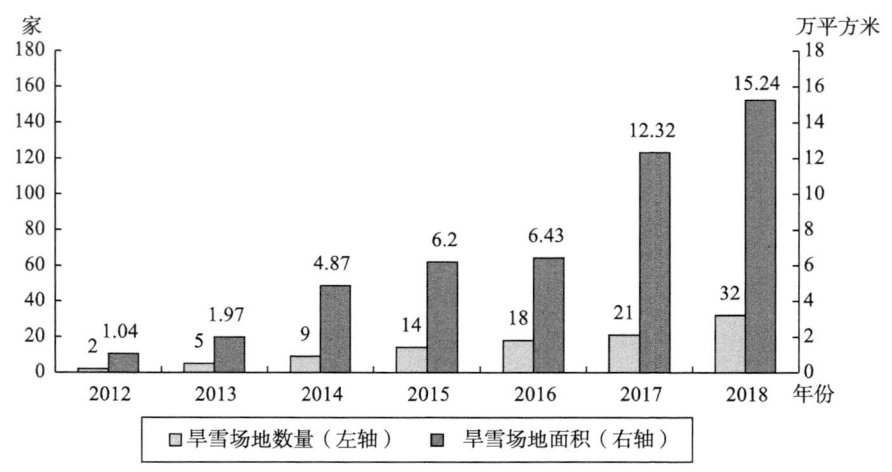

图8-3 2012—2018年旱雪场地数量及面积

从旱雪场地的面积分布来看，目前，山东、四川、北京、湖北、广东依次位居全国前五。

三、滑雪模拟器

2018年，滑雪模拟器市场同样呈现迅速增长态势。雪梦都提供的报告显示，截至2018年年底，全国滑雪模拟器场馆已达62家，投入使用的各类滑雪模拟器达到145台。其中，北京、上海、广东分别以43.45%、20%、7.59%的市场份额位居前列。

第二节 滑雪场分类统计信息

一、按核心目标客群分类

按核心目标客群分类，国内滑雪场分为旅游体验型、城郊学习型及目的地度假型三类。此三类滑雪场在全部滑雪场中占比分别为75%、22%及3%（见表8-3）。

表8-3　2018年中国滑雪场按核心目标客群分类

滑雪场类型	数量占比	客群定位	主要体现滑雪属性	滑雪场特征	客群特征	典型案例
旅游体验型	75%	旅游观光客	旅游属性	设施简单，只有初级道。位置一般在旅游景区或城郊	90%以上为一次性体验客户，客人平均停留时间2小时	西岭雪山、大明山、神农架
城郊学习型	22%	本地居民	运动属性、旅游属性	山体落差不大，位于城市郊区，开发有初级、中级、高级雪道	本地自驾客人占比很大，平均停留时间为3~4小时	南山、军都山、万科石京龙、探路者嵩顶
目的地度假型	3%	度假人群	度假属性、运动属性、旅游属性	山体有一定规模，除有齐全的雪道产品外，还有住宿等设施的配套	过夜消费占比较大，客人平均停留时间在1天以上	万科松花湖、万达长白山、北大壶、亚布力、万龙、太舞、富龙、云顶

在有架空索道的149家滑雪场中，旅游体验型滑雪场22家，占比14.77%；城郊学习型滑雪场108家，占比72.48%；目的地度假型滑雪场19家，占比12.75%（见图8-4）。

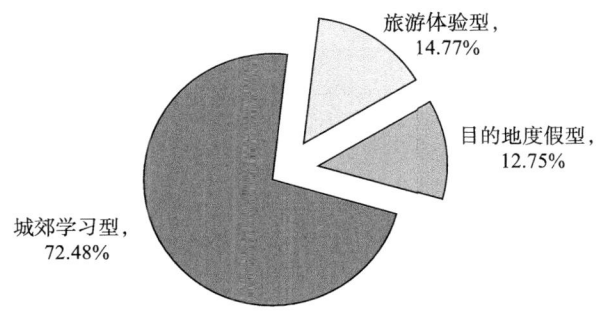

图8-4　2018年有架空索道的滑雪场按核心目标客群分类比例

二、按垂直落差统计

滑雪场垂直落差是衡量滑雪场所在山地的资源规模的一个重要指标。按滑雪场实际开发雪道的垂直落差，国内滑雪场按以下三类统计：垂直落差超过300米的滑雪场26家，占比3.5%；垂直落差在100～300米的滑雪场140家，占比18.87%；垂直落差小于100米的滑雪场576家，占比77.63%（见图8-5）。表8-4列出了国内目前有架空索道的垂直落差前十位的滑雪场。

垂直落差超过300米的26家滑雪场中，有7家位于河北（全部落户张家口市崇礼区），吉林、新疆各4家，黑龙江、内蒙古各3家，辽宁、河南、云南、甘肃、北京各1家。

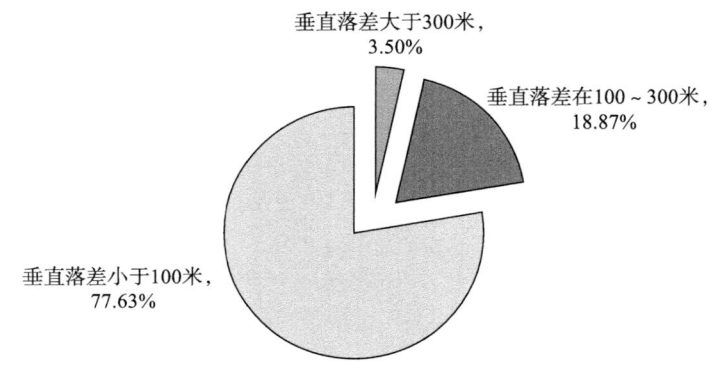

图8-5　2018年中国滑雪场按垂直落差统计占比

表8-4　2018年中国垂直落差前十大滑雪场　　　　　单位：米

排序	滑雪场名称	已开发垂直落差	所在省份
1	亚布力体委	885	黑龙江
2	北大壶	870	吉林
3	新疆丝绸之路	700	新疆
4	云南香格里拉	662	云南
5	万科松花湖	600	吉林
6	万龙	580	河北
7	亚布力阳光	540	黑龙江
8	太舞	510	河北

续表

排序	滑雪场名称	已开发垂直落差	所在省份
9	富龙	480	河北
10	美林谷	480	内蒙古

注：不含野雪场地。

此外，目前国内已开发3处野雪场地——新疆阿尔泰山野雪公园、吉林长白山天池雪以及2018年新开发的新疆可可托海，主要用雪地摩托、压雪车（雪猫）、直升机等移动设施解决滑雪者上行需求。其中，新疆可可托海滑雪场计划于2019年雪季开通索道设施。

三、按雪道面积统计

雪道面积是衡量滑雪场大小的另一个重要维度。2018年，在造雪面积方面，以新疆丝绸之路的改扩建力度最为突出，一举跃居国内造雪面积首位。截至2018年年底，雪道面积超过30公顷的滑雪场共计29家，占比3.91%；有架空索道的滑雪场中，雪道面积超过30公顷的为26家，占比为17.46%（见表8-5）。

表8-5 2018年按雪道面积统计的滑雪场数据

雪道面积/公顷	滑雪场数量/家	占比/%	有架空索道的滑雪场/家	占比/%
>100	8	1.08	5	3.36
50~100	6	0.81	6	4.03
30~50	15	2.02	15	10.07
10~30	35	4.72	35	23.49
5~10	106	14.29	88	59.06
<5	572	77.09	0	0
合计	742	100.00	149	100.00

不含野雪场地，目前国内按雪道面积排名的前十大滑雪场如表8-6所示。

表 8-6　2018 年中国雪道面积前十大滑雪场　　　　　　　　　　单位：公顷

排序	滑雪场名称	已开发雪道面积	所在省份
1	万科松花湖	175	吉林
2	万龙	140	河北
3	北大壶	126	吉林
4	万达长白山	100	吉林
4	云顶	100	河北
6	太舞	80	河北
7	富龙	75	河北
8	丝绸之路	70	新疆
9	亚布力阳光	50	黑龙江
9	鳌山	50	陕西

注：不含野雪场地。

根据估算，国内雪道总面积大约为 3500 公顷，其中，雪道面积超过 30 公顷的 29 家滑雪场的雪道面积之和占比超过 40%。

四、按营业天数统计

根据美团门票提供的数据，国内营业天数在 80 天以内的滑雪场占比大约为 36%（见图 8-6）。

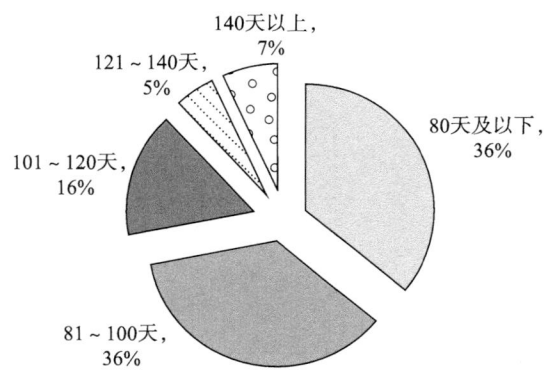

图 8-6　2018 年滑雪场按营业天数统计占比

五、其他

（一）夜场

目前国内开放夜场的滑雪场有南山、军都山、万龙八易、北京莲花山、万达长白山、万科松花湖、丝绸之路、西岭雪山、怀北、怪坡、东北亚、富龙、庙香山、将军山、万科石京龙等。

（二）微信公众号及天猫店

据统计，国内已开通微信公众号的滑雪场有 400 多家，开通天猫店的滑雪场不到 20 家。

（三）自助取票机及闸机

自助取票机及闸机在滑雪场的运用越来越广泛，比较有代表性的有万龙、富龙、太舞、翠云山银河、万科松花湖、北大壶、多乐美地、沈阳怪坡、乌金山李宁、南山、太白鳌山等。

第三节 滑雪场硬件设施

一、滑雪场上行设施

（一）滑雪场架空索道

2015—2018 年，滑雪场架空索道总数与有架空索道的滑雪场数量均有所增加，且滑雪场架空索道总数增长率高于有架空索道的滑雪场数量增长率。有架空索道的滑雪场数量从 109 家上升至 149 家，共增加了 40 家，年均增长率为 36.70%；滑雪场架空索道总数从 179 条上升至 250 条，共增加了 71 条，年均增长率为 39.66%（见图 8-7）。

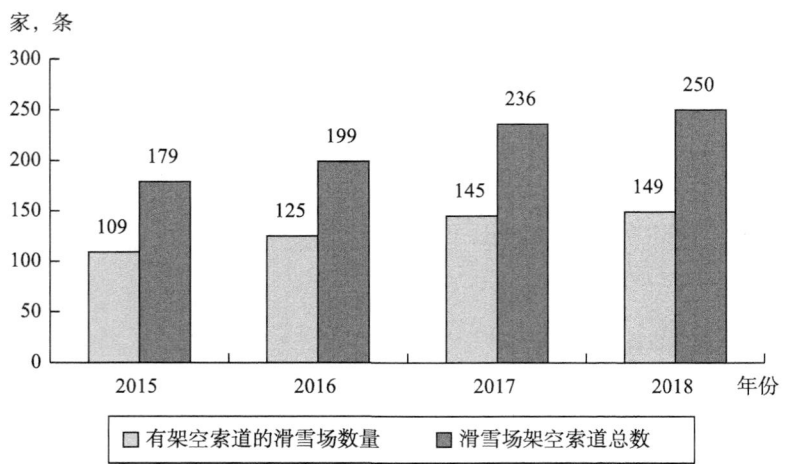

图 8-7 2015—2018 年有架空索道的雪场及雪场架空索道数量

滑雪场按索道条数统计占比结果如表 8-7 所示，国内建成并投入使用的索道数量共 250 条，分布于 149 家滑雪场中。其中，拥有 4 条及以上索道的滑雪场有 10 家，占滑雪场总数的 6.71%；拥有 3 条索道的滑雪场有 12 家，占滑雪场总数的 8.05%；拥有 2 条索道的滑雪场有 30 家，占滑雪场总数的 20.13%；拥有 1 条索道的滑雪场有 97 家，占滑雪场总数的 65.10%。

表 8-7 2018 年滑雪场按索道条数统计占比

索道数量分级	滑雪场数量/家	占比/%
4 条及以上	10	6.71
3 条	12	8.05
2 条	30	20.13
1 条	97	65.10
合计	149	100.00

截至 2018 年年底，国内滑雪场中建成并投入使用的架空索道总数为 250 条，分布于 149 家雪场中。河北、黑龙江、吉林分别以 49 条、39 条、37 条位居前三（见表 8-8）。三省合计建成 125 条架空索道，占全国架空索道的 50%。

表 8-8 2018 年中国滑雪场架空索道数量及分布

排序	省份	架空索道数量/条	有架空索道的滑雪场数量/家
1	河北	49	22
2	黑龙江	39	26
3	吉林	37	16
4	辽宁	28	19
5	北京	20	12
6	新疆	19	10
7	内蒙古	15	10
8	山西	8	5
9	甘肃	8	7
10	山东	6	6
11	陕西	5	4
12	四川	3	2
13	河南	3	2
14	云南	3	1
15	重庆	3	3
16	贵州	2	2
17	湖北	1	1
18	天津	1	1
	合计	250	149

脱挂式架空索道的数量更是滑雪场规模和效率的集中体现。2015—2018 年，国内脱挂式架空索道发展迅猛，由 2015 年的 26 条增长到 2018 年的 54 条，有脱挂式架空索道的滑雪场也由 10 家增长到了 19 家（见图 8-8、表 8-9）。

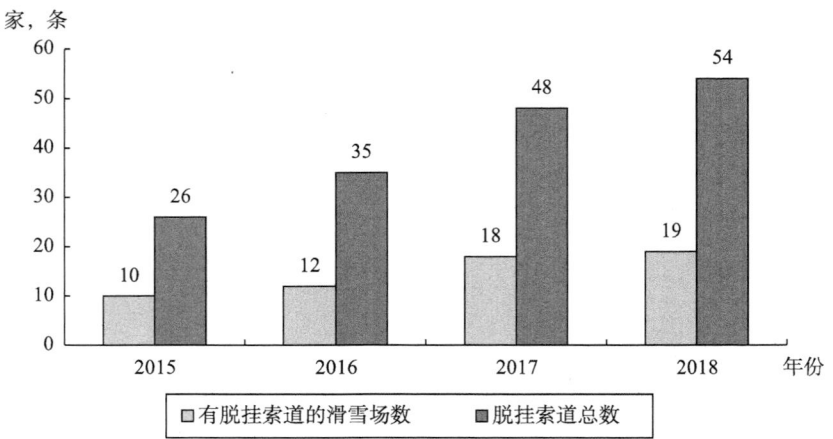

图 8-8 2015—2018 年中国滑雪场脱挂式架空索道数量

表 8-9 2018 年中国滑雪场按脱挂式架空索道数量排名　　　　单位：条

序号	排名	滑雪场	脱挂式架空索道数	所在省份
1	1	万科松花湖	6	吉林
2	1	万龙	6	河北
3	3	万达长白山	5	吉林
4	3	太舞	5	河北
5	5	北大壶	4	吉林
6	5	云顶	4	河北
7	7	丝绸之路	3	新疆
8	7	富龙	3	河北
9	7	亚布力体委	3	黑龙江
10	10	太白鳌山	2	陕西
11	10	鲁能长白山	2	吉林
12	10	翠云山银河	2	河北
13	10	亚布力阳光	2	黑龙江
14	10	凉城岱海	2	内蒙古
15	15	庙香山	1	吉林
16	15	多乐美地	1	河北
17	15	帽儿山	1	黑龙江
18	15	长春莲花山	1	吉林
19	15	将军山	1	新疆
		合计	54	

图 8-9 统计了 2015—2018 年脱挂式架空索道中进口和国产的数量关系。很明显，国产脱挂式架空索道的发展相当迅猛，从 2015 年的 2 条增长到 2018 年的 18 条。

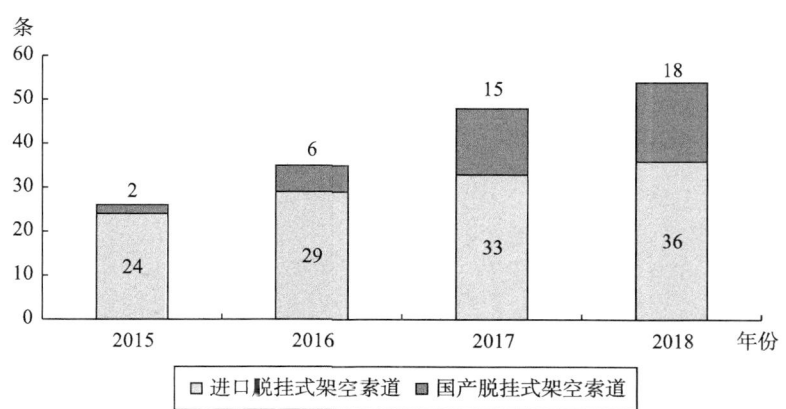

图 8-9　2015—2018 年中国滑雪场进口、国产脱挂式架空索道数量

2018 年，54 条用于滑雪的脱挂式架空索道中，河北建成 21 条，分布于 7 家雪场，全部集中在张家口市崇礼区；吉林建成 19 条，分布于 6 家雪场；黑龙江建成 6 条，分布于 3 家雪场；新疆建成 4 条，分布于 2 家雪场；陕西、内蒙古各建成 2 条（见图 8-10）（此项统计中只包括用于滑雪的索道，不包括运输用途的索道）。

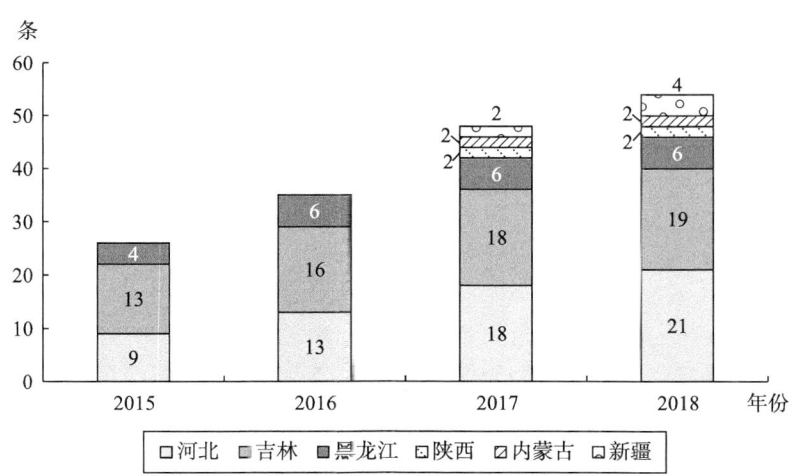

图 8-10　2015—2018 年中国滑雪场脱挂式架空索道按分布省份统计

（二）滑雪场魔毯

魔毯数据来源于道沃机电、娅豪等国内主要供应商。截至 2018 年，国内滑雪场共计有 1196 条魔毯处于运营中，包括 2018 年新增的 120 条魔毯。全部魔毯总长度约 176 千米（见图 8-11、图 8-12）。

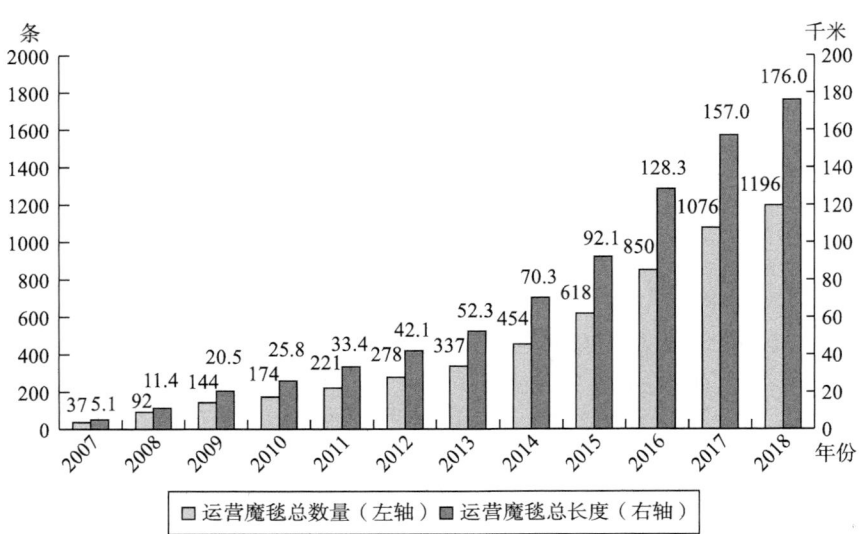

图 8-11　2007—2018 年滑雪场运营魔毯总数量及总长度

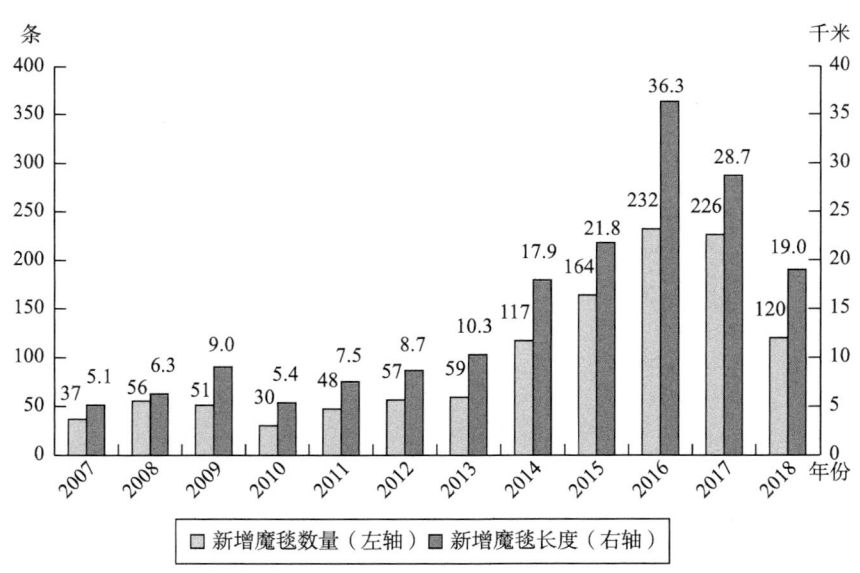

图 8-12　2007—2018 年滑雪场新增魔毯数量及长度

二、滑雪场场地设施

(一) 压雪车

根据主要压雪车供应商统计数据,国内滑雪场全部压雪车数量约为541台。2018年,国内新增压雪车数量为56台,低于2017年的75台。其中,进口新车36台,同比下降幅度较大(见图8-13)。

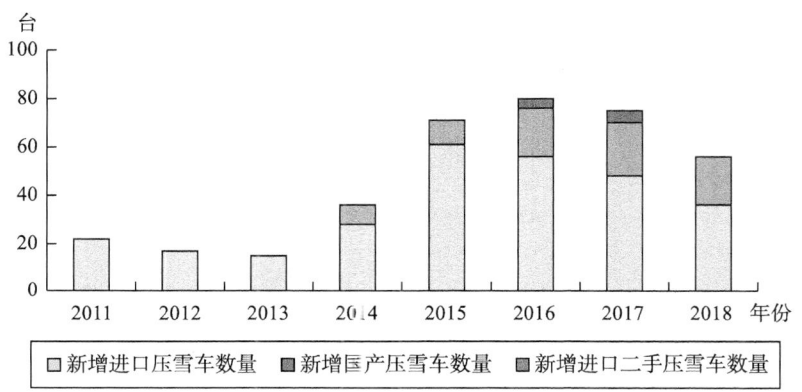

图8-13 2011—2018年中国滑雪场新增压雪车数量统计

通过对中国海关进口压雪车相关数据的研究(见表8-10),2018年国内进口压雪车的主要产地为意大利、德国。

2018年,压雪车市场出现了一个新的现象,租赁压雪车业务显著提升。据业内人士估计,用于租赁的压雪车保有量已经超过30台。

表8-10 2013—2018年中国进口压雪车数据

进口国	2013年/台	2014年/台	2015年/台	2016年/台	2017年/台	2017年1—11月/台	2018年1—11月/台	2018年同比增长率/%
合计	23	31	68	68	60	58	52	-10.34
意大利	10	18	28	28	24	24	31	29.17
德国	6	7	16	20	27	25	20	-20
中国	0	0	0	0	0	0	1	—
芬兰	1	1	0	0	0	0	0	
奥地利	0	0	1	0	0	0	0	
加拿大	2	4	12	11	6	6	0	-100

续表

进口国	2013 年/台	2014 年/台	2015 年/台	2016 年/台	2017 年/台	2017 年 1—11 月/台	2018 年 1—11 月/台	2018 年同比增长率/%
日本	2	0	7	1	1	1	0	-100
俄罗斯	0	0	0	1	0	0	0	—
美国	2	1	4	7	2	2	0	-100

资料来源：中国海关，北京龙之讯信息咨询有限公司。

（二）造雪机

2018 年，全国滑雪场新增造雪机 810 台，远远低于 2017 年的 1420 台（见图 8-14）。截至 2018 年年底，全部造雪机数量合计约 7410 台。

和压雪车有类似之处，2018 年，造雪机租赁业务也受到市场欢迎，用于租赁的造雪机数量估计为 60 台。

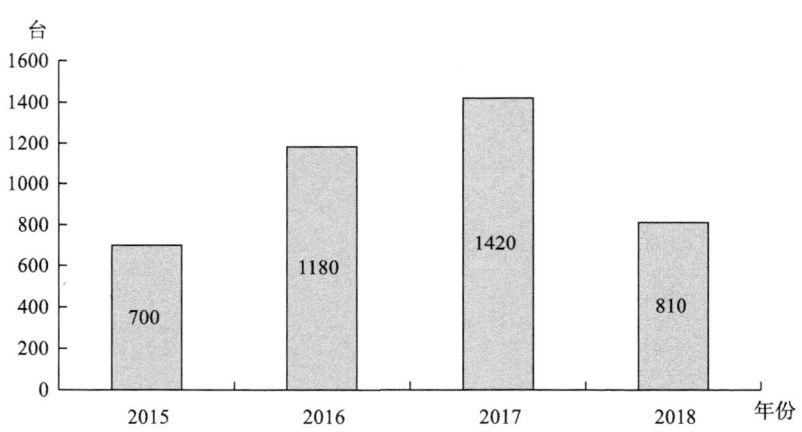

图 8-14 2015—2018 年滑雪场新增造雪机数量

三、滑雪场租赁设施

根据中国海关进口数据，双板脱落器的进口数量经过前几年的高速增长后，2018 年有明显回落。同时各类滑雪板的进口数量继续下跌（见图 8-15）。

根据主要国际品牌滑雪板供应商提供的信息，滑雪场租赁双板中，进口国际品牌产品相比 2017 年有明显回落（见图 8-16）。整体市场租赁双板总数在 60 万副以上，平均每家雪场的租赁双板数接近 900 副。

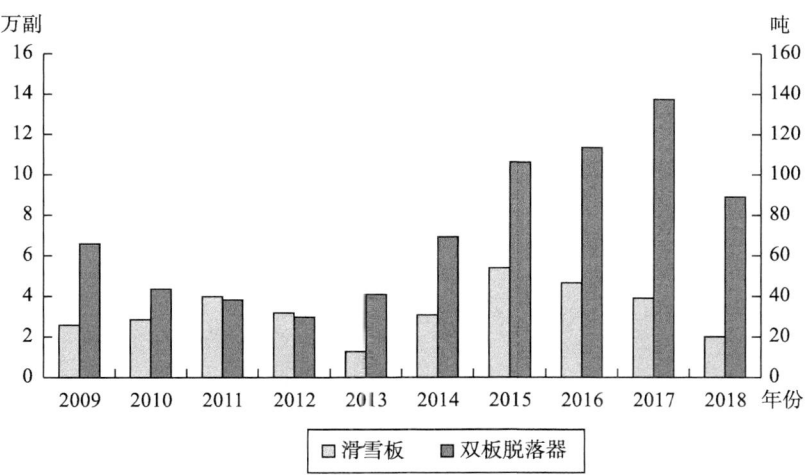

图 8-15　2009—2018 年中国进口滑雪板和双板脱落器数据

资料来源：中国海关，北京龙之讯信息咨询有限公司。

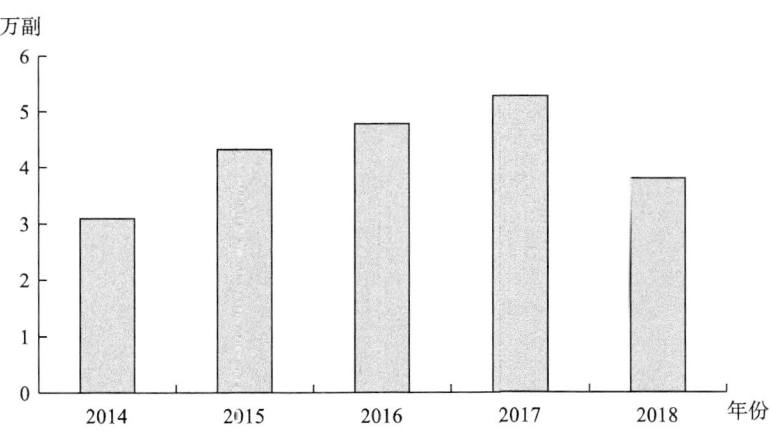

图 8-16　2014—2018 年滑雪场新增进口租赁双板数量

第九章 2018年滑雪者情况

第一节 滑雪者人次及分布

本期报告引入总滑雪人次的概念,将旱雪场地以及滑雪模拟器场馆产生的滑雪人次一并计算在内。截至2018年年底,国内总滑雪人次统计为2113万,其中滑雪场产生的滑雪人次为1970万,旱雪场地产生的滑雪人次为85万,滑雪模拟器产生的滑雪人次为58万。

按本报告测算,2018年全年滑雪者人数约为1320万人,相比2017年的1210万人,上浮9.09%。其中,一次性体验者人数占比为75.38%,与2017年的75.2%基本持平。2018年,滑雪场人均滑雪次数由2017年的1.45次上升为1.49次(见图9-1)。

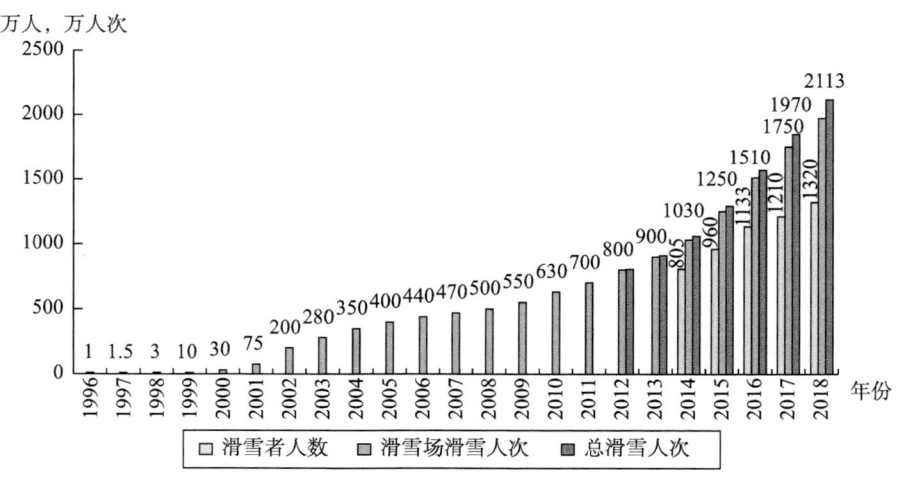

图9-1 1996—2018年总滑雪人次、滑雪场滑雪人次及滑雪者人数

滑雪场滑雪人次增量榜中，山东、江苏受气候变化的影响，部分滑雪场营业天数明显下降。黑龙江增长12.76%，与哈尔滨融创娱雪乐园有关（见表9-1）。在滑雪场的1970万滑雪人次中，室内滑雪馆所产生的滑雪人次约为166万。

表9-1 2017年、2018年滑雪场滑雪人次分布（按目的地滑雪场省份）

排序	省份	2018年滑雪场数量/家	2018年滑雪人次/万人次	同比增长/%	2017年滑雪场数量/家	2017年滑雪人次/万人次
1	黑龙江	124	221	12.76	124	196
2	河北	59	210	19.32	58	176
3	吉林	43	184	25.17	41	147
4	北京	24	176	5.39	24	167
5	山西	48	115.5	5.00	45	110
6	浙江	19	100	9.89	18	91
7	内蒙古	42	97.8	16.43	37	84
8	新疆	60	96	11.63	59	86
9	山东	65	94	-9.62	61	104
10	河南	43	93.4	3.78	42	90
11	陕西	34	82	20.59	31	68
12	辽宁	38	73	5.80	37	69
13	四川	11	72	24.14	11	58
14	甘肃	21	65	16.07	20	56
15	天津	13	44	10.00	13	40
16	重庆	16	40	21.21	14	33
17	湖南	9	39.3	19.09	8	33
18	江苏	17	36.8	-5.64	15	39
19	贵州	10	33	10.00	10	30
20	湖北	11	24	14.29	7	21
21	宁夏	13	20	11.11	12	18
22	青海	8	12.5	25.00	7	10
23	安徽	3	10	0.00	3	10
24	云南	4	8	100.00	2	4
25	广东	2	8	166.67	1	3
26	广西	2	6	0.00	2	6
27	江西	2	5	—	0	0

续表

排序	省份	2018年滑雪场数量/家	2018年滑雪人次/万人次	同比增长/%	2017年滑雪场数量/家	2017年滑雪人次/万人次
28	福建	1	4	33.33	1	3
	合计	742	1970	12.57	703	1750

旱雪场地的滑雪人次主要取决于场地位置以及旱雪雪道面积，根据尖锋旱雪提供的统计报告，可以对2018年旱雪滑雪人次的分布有所了解（见表9-2）。

表9-2　2018年旱雪场地滑雪人次分布　　　　　　　单位：万人次

省份	滑雪人次
新疆	1
四川	8.5
上海	0.5
陕西	1
山东	10.5
辽宁	0.5
江苏	12
湖南	4
湖北	6.5
黑龙江	3.7
河北	1.5
贵州	2.5
广东	13.5
甘肃	3.5
福建	1.5
北京	12.5
安徽	2
合计	85.2

根据雪梦都蔡天慧先生提供的专业报告，2018年滑雪模拟器产生的58万滑雪人次大致分布如图9-2所示。

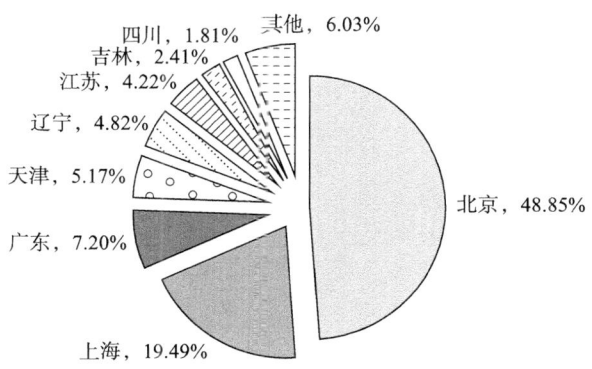

图 9-2　2018 年滑雪模拟器滑雪人次分布

第二节　滑雪者特征

本报告中,由美团门票的大数据呈现的美团滑雪消费者的特征,基本可以反映出市场的整体轮廓。另外,滑雪圈内各家线上小伙伴也提供了滑雪爱好者特征报告,还有众信旅游分享的出境滑雪者的相关信息。

一、美团 2018 年滑雪消费者特征报告

美团 2018 年滑雪消费者特征报告全方位地从用户性别及年龄段占比、客源地与目的地、用户购买次数与复购时间间隔、入园人次排名等 9 个指标评估滑雪消费者特征。

(一) 用户性别及年龄段占比

美团 2018 年滑雪消费者滑雪消费者特征报告指出,2018 年滑雪消费者男女占比分别为 49%、51%,女性占比较高(见图 9-3)。从年龄段占比来看,20～34 岁的滑雪消费者占有较大比例,占比达 73%,其他年龄段仅占 27%(见图 9-4)。

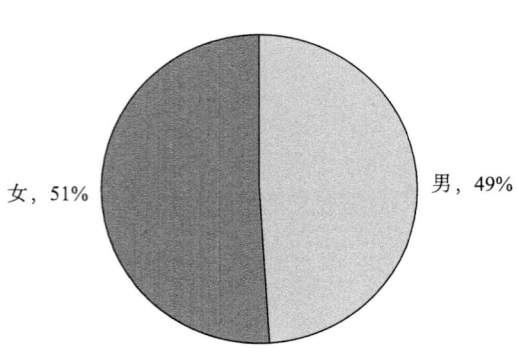

图 9-3　2018 年滑雪消费者性别占比

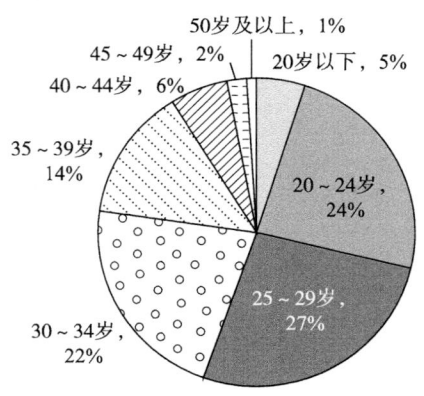

图 9-4　2018 年滑雪消费者年龄段占比

(二) 客源地与目的地

表 9-3 为旱雪场地滑雪人次前二十大客源地和目的地。排名第一的客源地是北京，目的地也是北京。其次客源地是西安，目的地是沈阳。排名最后的客源地为杭州，目的地为张家口。

表 9-3　2018 年旱雪场地滑雪人次前二十大客源地和目的地

排名	客源地	目的地
1	北京	北京
2	西安	沈阳
3	沈阳	西安
4	天津	天津
5	乌鲁木齐	乌鲁木齐
6	大连	哈尔滨
7	济南	太原
8	青岛	大连
9	深圳	济南
10	上海	青岛
11	太原	吉林
12	郑州	石家庄
13	兰州	深圳
14	石家庄	郑州
15	哈尔滨	兰州
16	成都	六盘水

续表

排名	客源地	目的地
17	长春	长春
18	吉林	银川
19	武汉	保定
20	杭州	张家口

（三）用户购买次数与复购时间间隔

用户购买次数如图9-5所示。其中，91%的用户购买1次，用户购买2次的比例为7%，仅有2%的用户购买3次及以上。

用户复购时间间隔占比如图9-6所示。45%的用户复购时间间隔为1天，29%的用户复购时间间隔为2~10天，10%的用户复购时间间隔为11~30天，15%的用户复购时间间隔为31天及以上。

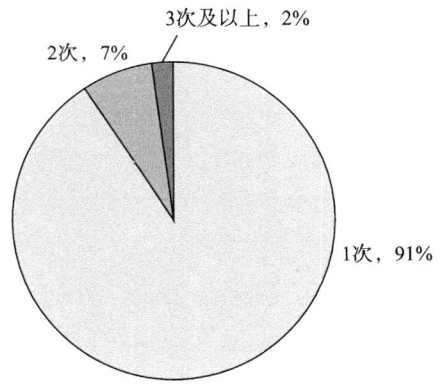

图9-5　2018年用户购买次数占比

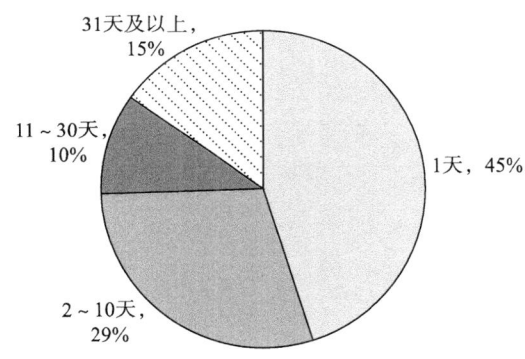

图9-6　2018年用户复购时间间隔占比

（四）入园人次排名

根据2017年、2018年旱雪场地滑雪人次统计发现，2018年旱雪场地滑雪人次与2017年的排名相比虽然有所变动，但变动较小（贵州和广东除外）。相反地，2018年同比增长率变化较大。贵州、广东、安徽、重庆和江西等地2018年同比增长率高达200%以上，最大值贵州2018年同比增长率达560%。吉林、江苏2018年同比下降较快，增长率均为-14%（见表9-4）。

表 9-4　2017 年、2018 年旱雪场地滑雪人次

省份	2017 年人次排名	2018 年人次排名	2018 年同比增长率/%
北京	1	1	5
辽宁	2	2	-6
山东	4	3	12
陕西	3	4	-5
河北	5	5	-6
山西	7	6	-5
天津	6	7	-6
新疆	9	8	25
吉林	8	9	-14
黑龙江	12	10	14
河南	10	11	3
甘肃	11	12	-6
浙江	13	13	16
内蒙古	14	14	3
贵州	22	15	560
四川	18	16	64
广东	21	17	243
宁夏	15	18	6
湖北	16	19	6
江苏	17	20	-14
青海	20	21	25
湖南	19	22	-2
安徽	23	23	266
重庆	24	24	239
江西	25	25	221

（五）"滑雪+X"

"滑雪+X"品类占比中，景点、温泉、泛主题乐园占比较高，分别为 27.7%、25.1% 及 20.1%。而动植物园、展览馆、其他品类占比较小，分别为 7.9%、7.3% 及 11.8%（见图 9-7）。

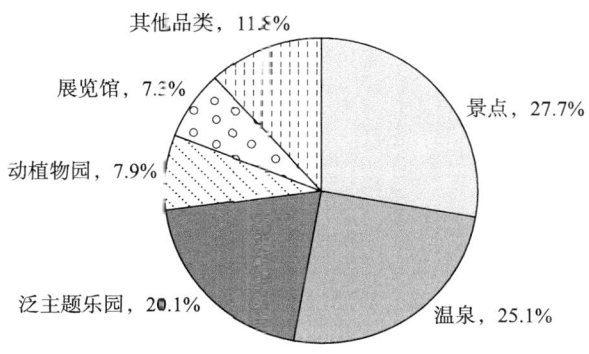

图 9-7 2018 年 "滑雪+X" 品类占比

（六）用户评论

用户评论中亲子相关评论占评论总数的 8.2%，亲子相关评论的平均得分为 3.6 分，低于总评论的平均得分 3.7 分（见表 9-5）。

表 9-5 2018 年用户评论分析

类型	评论数占比/%	平均得分/分（满分 5 分）
亲子相关评论	8.2	3.6
总评论	100	3.7

（七）雪季客流变化趋势

对 2018 年雪季客流变化趋势的分析表明，2018 年 1 月 1 日至 2018 年 2 月 26 日、2018 年 12 月 3 日至 2018 年 12 月 31 日是雪季客流较大的时间段，2 月 26 日与 12 月 3 日是两个重要的节点日期。2018 年 2 月 19 日客流量达到最大值，客流量为全年客流量的 18%，其次为 2 月 12 日，客流量为全年客流量的 12%。全年客流量最小时，接近于 0。

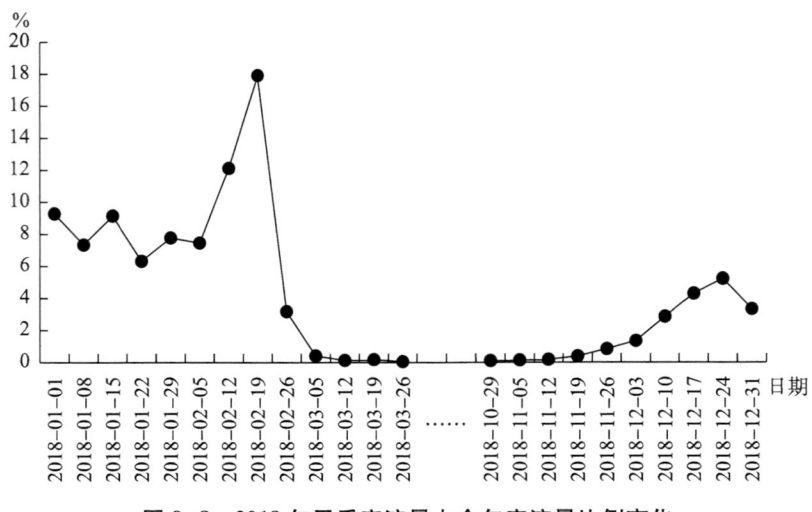

图 9-8 2018 年雪季客流量占全年客流量比例变化

(八) 入园人次排名

表 9-6 为滑雪场入园人次排名情况。滑雪场数量与入园人次数量呈现出不匹配现象。滑雪场数量排名第一的山东，入园人次排名仅为第三；滑雪场数量排名第二的黑龙江，入园人次排名为第 11；相反，滑雪场数量排名较后的广东、贵州等地，入园人次排名较前。

表 9-6 2018 年滑雪场入园人次排名

省份	滑雪场数量排名	入园人次排名
山东	1	3
黑龙江	2	11
河北	3	5
辽宁	4	2
北京	5	1
吉林	6	8
河南	7	10
内蒙古	8	14
山西	9	6
新疆	10	9
陕西	11	4
天津	12	7
甘肃	13	12
江苏	14	20

续表

省份	滑雪场数量排名	入园人次排名
浙江	15	13
宁夏	16	18
湖北	17	19
四川	18	16
青海	19	21
重庆	20	24
湖南	21	22
贵州	22	15
安徽	23	23
广东	24	17
广西	25	27
云南	26	26
上海	27	28
江西	28	25
福建	29	29
西藏	30	30

（九）人均消费金额排名

滑雪场人均消费金额排名如表9-7所示，广西、浙江、贵州分别占据前3位，山东、天津和广东排名较为靠后。

表9-7 2018年滑雪场人均消费金额排名

省份	人均消费金额排名
广西	1
浙江	2
贵州	3
湖北	4
四川	5
安徽	6
云南	7
重庆	8
新疆	9
江苏	10
甘肃	11

续表

省份	人均消费金额排名
河北	12
黑龙江	13
北京	14
宁夏	15
陕西	16
吉林	17
青海	18
辽宁	19
山东	20
天津	21
广东	22

二、滑雪爱好者特征报告

（一）用户自画像及分析

根据滑雪爱好者特征报告，用户男女性别比例分别为64.33%、35.67%，男性占比远高于女性，男女比例不平衡（见图9-9）。

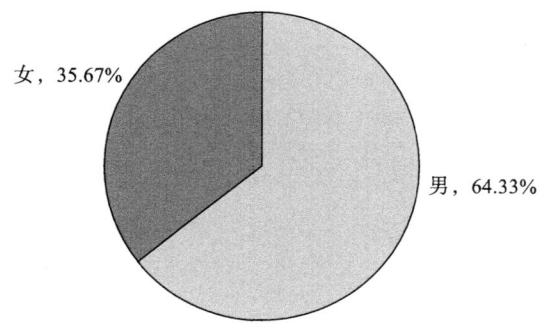

图9-9 2018年用户性别占比

（二）用户年龄结构分析

根据滑雪爱好者特征报告，用户年龄段集中于20~30岁、30~40岁，两个年龄段的滑雪爱好者占比共计79.3%，而0~20岁、40~50岁及50岁以上的用户占比约20.7%，所占比例较小（见图9-10）。

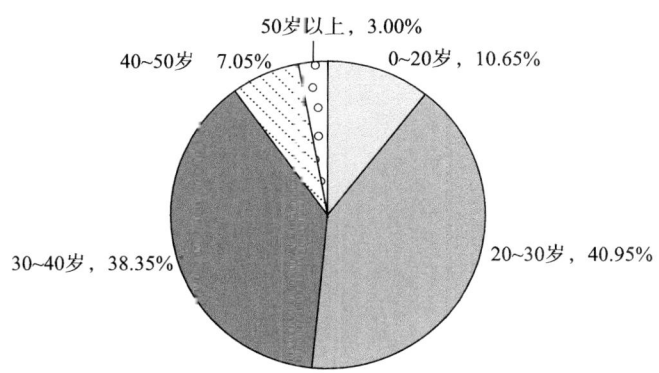

图 9-10　2018 年用户年龄段占比

（三）用户分布地分析

通过对用户分布地进行分析，北京、河北和吉林三地占有较大比重，分别为 31.11%、16.01%、11.17%。其次为黑龙江、辽宁、上海等地（见图 9-11）。

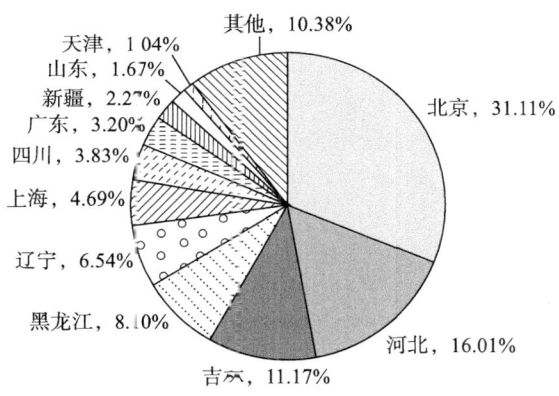

图 9-11　2018 年用户地域分布

（四）滑雪水平分析

通过对用户滑雪水平进行分析发现，国内具有高级滑雪水平的滑雪爱好者较少，占比不到 1/4。大多数滑雪爱好者处于初级水平，占 44.67%，具有中级滑雪水平的滑雪爱好者占 33.33%，具有高级滑雪水平的滑雪爱好者仅占 22.00%（见图 9-12）。

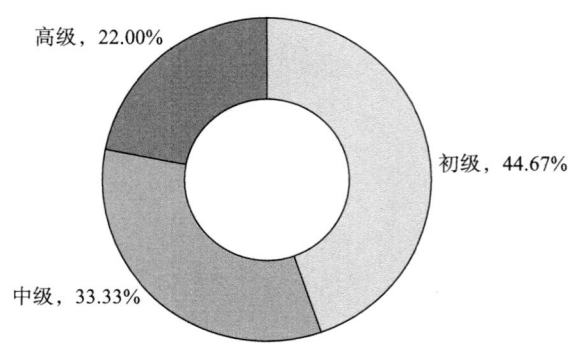

图9-12 2018年用户滑雪水平占比

（五）用户关注的内容类型

滑雪族用户、GOSKI用户、滑呗用户关注的内容类型具有较大差别。

滑雪族用户中关注奇趣内容类型的用户较多，约占一半以上。装备、热点和技术等内容的关注度较低，呈现分化的趋势（见图9-13）。

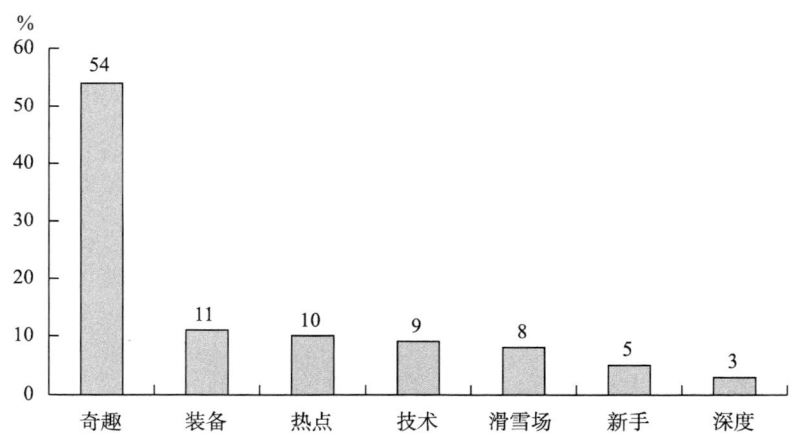

图9-13 2018年滑雪族用户关注内容类型

与滑雪族用户不同的是，GOSKI用户关注内容类型较多，且分布均匀。关注的20%为雪友动态，19%为教学，16%为装备，其次为大神视频、赛事新闻、旅行等（见图9-14）。

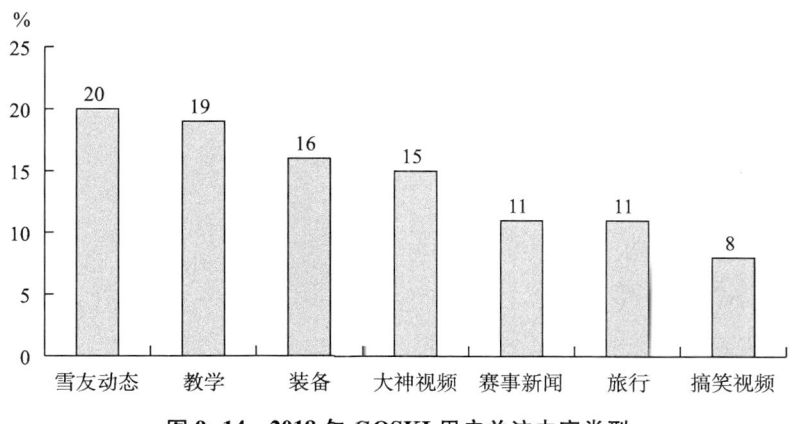

图 9-14 2018 年 GOSKI 用户关注内容类型

滑呗用户关注的内容类型 37.40% 集中于攻略，其次是技术、人物和活动等，关注装备与教学的用户较少（见图 9-15）。

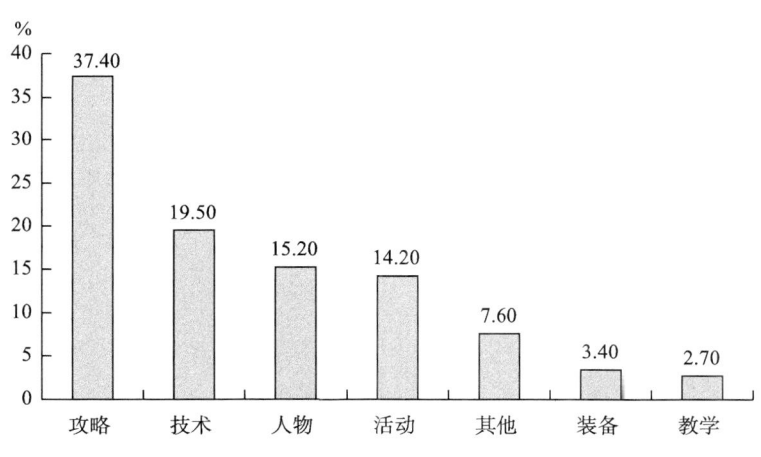

图 9-15 2018 年滑呗用户关注内容类型

（六）记录轨迹最多的滑雪场前十名

滑雪族记录轨迹前十名滑雪场分别为松花湖度假区、万龙度假天堂、密苑云顶乐园、北大壶度假区、太舞滑雪小镇、富龙四季小镇、万达长白山国际度假区、南山滑雪场、怀北国际滑雪场、亚布力阳光国际滑雪场。

GOSKI 记录轨迹前十名滑雪场分别为万龙度假天堂、密苑云顶乐园、富龙四季小镇、北大壶度假区、松花湖度假区、怀北国际滑雪场、南山滑雪场、万龙八易滑雪场、万达长白山国际度假区、太舞滑雪小镇。

滑呗记录轨迹前十名滑雪场分别为万龙度假天堂、松花湖度假区、密苑云顶乐园、北大壶度假区、亚布力阳光国际滑雪场、太舞滑雪小镇、富龙四季小镇、万达长白山国际度假区、翠云山银河滑雪场、怀北国际滑雪场。

（七）滑雪场好评率排行前十名

滑雪族好评率前十名滑雪场分别是松花湖度假区、万龙度假天堂、密苑云顶乐园、北大壶度假区、太舞滑雪小镇、富龙四季小镇、万达长白山国际度假区、亚布力阳光国际滑雪场、翠云山银河滑雪场、丝绸之路滑雪场。

GOSKI好评率前十名滑雪场分别为万龙滑雪场、万达长白山国际度假区滑雪场、太舞滑雪小镇、松花湖滑雪场、富龙滑雪场、南山滑雪场（北京）、密苑云顶乐园、长白山天池雪滑雪场、北大壶滑雪场、渔阳国际滑雪场。

滑呗好评率前十名滑雪场分别为松花湖度假区、万龙度假天堂、翠云山银河滑雪场、北大壶度假区、富龙四季小镇、万达长白山国际度假区、丝绸之路滑雪场、亚布力阳光国际滑雪场、太舞滑雪小镇、密苑云顶乐园。

三、出境滑雪者特征

众信旅游提供的出境滑雪者特征报告显示，产品天数为6~8天、人均客单价在8000~12000元的产品最受欢迎。客群年龄在25~40岁，男女比例为6∶4。集客地主要集中在北京、天津、上海。滑雪目的地以日本为主，超过65%，主要集中在三大目的地：北海道地区，包括二世古、富良野、留寿都、喜乐乐、旭岳等；长野地区，如白马、志贺、斑尾等；东北方向，如安比高原、藏王、零石等。其他目的地包括欧洲，以法国三峡谷为主，其次是瑞士、奥地利；北美、新西兰也在初期发展中。

第三节 滑雪者装备市场

2018年，本报告收集到了来自迪卡侬（DECATHLON）、博登（Burton）、GOSKI等品牌的更完整的单板品牌零售相关数据。2018年单板年总销量为3.8万副左右，同比增长超过25%，单板鞋销量为5万双。

同单板市场相比，双板市场相对疲软，年销售总量在1.5万副左右，同比增长5%左右。双板部分数据感谢迪卡侬、海德（HEAD）、金鸡（ROSSIGNOL）、伊兰（ELAN）等品牌的大力支持。

另外，2018年滑雪装备线上销售占比在1/3左右，并且有继续增长的趋势。

第五篇

2019年度中国滑雪产业核心数据报告

第十章 2019年滑雪场与滑雪人次情况

滑雪场与滑雪者是整个滑雪产业的两个核心，滑雪产业的全部业务和活动都围绕着这两个核心展开。因此，滑雪场馆数量与滑雪人次构成了滑雪产业最核心的两项指标。根据目前国内的实际情况，本报告将滑雪场馆分为滑雪场（包括户外滑雪场及室内滑雪馆）、旱雪场地以及模拟滑雪器健身馆。

第一节 滑雪场数量、滑雪人次以及滑雪者人数

2019年，国内滑雪场新增28家，包括5家室内滑雪场，总数达到770家，增幅3.77%。新增28家滑雪场中，有5家建设有架空索道，另有1家已开业滑雪场新建架空索道。截至2019年年底，全国770家滑雪场中，有架空索道的滑雪场达到155家，相比2018年的149家增长4.03%。国内滑雪场的滑雪人次由2018年的1970万上升到2019年的2090万，同比增幅为6.09%（见图10-1、图10-2）。

随着冬奥北京时间的临近，各项滑雪推广活动朝着纵深化方向发展，初学者转化率有明显提升。按本报告测算，2019年全年国内滑雪者约为1305万人，相比2018年的1320万人略有下降。其中，一次性体验滑雪者占比由2018年的75.38%下降为72.04%，滑雪爱好者比例有所上升。2019年，滑雪者在国内滑雪场的人均滑雪次数由2018年的1.49次上升为1.60次。

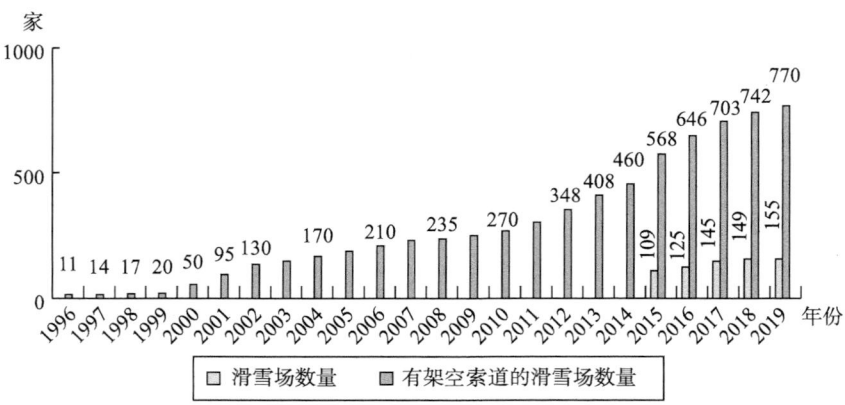

图 10-1　1996—2019 年中国滑雪场数量

注：统计数据包括户外滑雪场、室内滑雪馆，不含旱雪、模拟滑雪器等。

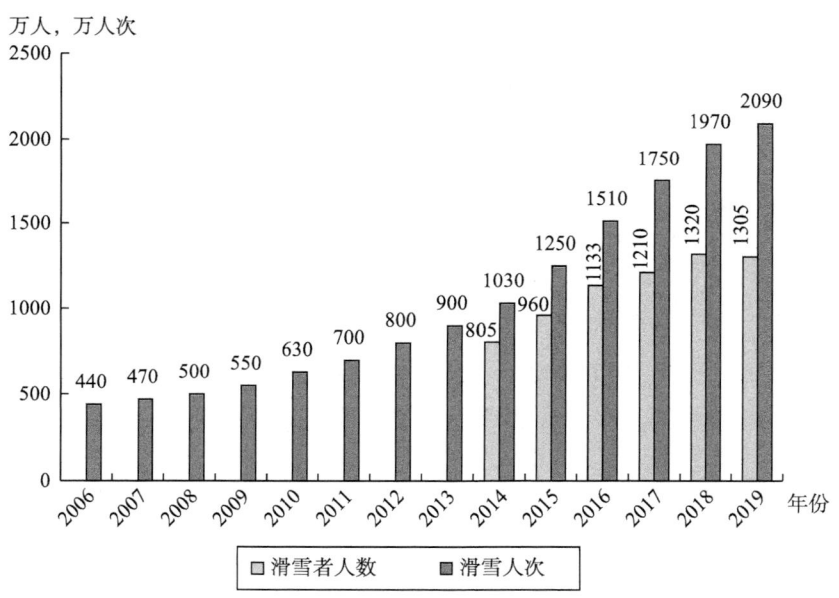

图 10-2　2006—2019 年中国滑雪场滑雪人次及滑雪者人数

注：统计数据包括户外滑雪场、室内滑雪馆，不含旱雪、模拟滑雪器等。

第二节 滑雪场及滑雪人次分布

770家滑雪场分布于全国28个省（区、市）。其中，滑雪场数量排名前5的省份为黑龙江、山东、新疆、河北和山西。2019年，湖北和新疆新增滑雪场数量最多（见表10-1）。

表10-1 2018年、2019年中国滑雪场数量分布（按省份） 单位：家

排序	省份	2018年	2019年	2019年新增
1	黑龙江	124	124	0
2	山东	65	67	2
3	新疆	60	65	5
4	河北	59	61	2
5	山西	48	49	1
6	吉林	43	45	2
7	河南	43	44	1
8	内蒙古	42	42	0
9	辽宁	38	38	0
10	陕西	34	35	1
11	北京	24	25	1
12	甘肃	21	22	1
13	浙江	19	20	1
14	江苏	17	18	1
15	重庆	16	16	0
16	湖北	11	16	5
17	宁夏	13	14	1
18	天津	13	13	0
19	四川	11	12	1
20	贵州	10	10	0
21	湖南	9	10	1
22	青海	8	8	0
23	云南	4	5	1
24	安徽	3	3	0
25	广东	2	3	1

续表

排序	省份	2018年	2019年	2019年新增
26	广西	2	2	0
27	江西	2	2	0
28	福建	1	1	0
	合计	742	770	28

2019年国内滑雪人次的分布如表10-2所示。河北、吉林、北京增长态势明显，滑雪人次超越黑龙江，成为前三。其中，河北、吉林两省全年滑雪人次突破200万大关。同时，国内滑雪市场在2019年明显出现分化的现象。2019年，共有13个省份的滑雪人次出现下跌。另外，融创集团接手万达的"融创雪世界"系列陆续开业，形成了持续的热点，广州、无锡、昆明均有不俗的表现。

表10-2 2018年、2019年滑雪场滑雪人次分布（按目的地滑雪场省份）

排序	省份	2018年滑雪场数量/家	2018年滑雪人次/万人次	2019年滑雪场数量/家	2019年滑雪人次/万人次	2019年滑雪人次增幅/%
1	河北	59	210	61	243	15.62
2	吉林	43	184	45	215	16.85
3	北京	24	176	25	189	7.27
4	黑龙江	124	221	124	186	-16.06
5	新疆	60	96	65	122	26.88
6	浙江	19	100	20	111	10.50
7	内蒙古	42	98	42	101	3.27
8	河南	43	93	44	96	2.78
9	山西	48	116	49	95	-18.01
10	山东	65	94	67	88	-6.38
11	陕西	34	82	35	74	-9.76
12	四川	11	72	12	68	-5.28
13	辽宁	38	73	38	67	-8.22
14	广东	2	8	3	65	712.50
15	甘肃	21	65	22	60	-8.46
16	江苏	17	37	18	54	45.92
17	天津	13	44	13	46	4.55
18	湖北	11	24	16	43	79.17

续表

排序	省份	2018年滑雪场数量/家	2018年滑雪人次/万人次	2019年滑雪场数量/家	2019年滑雪人次/万人次	2019年滑雪人次增幅/%
19	重庆	16	40	16	35	-12.50
20	湖南	9	39	10	34	-14.76
21	贵州	10	33	10	32	-3.03
22	宁夏	13	20	14	22	9.00
23	青海	8	13	8	15	20.00
24	安徽	3	10	3	12	20.00
25	云南	4	8	5	9	8.75
26	广西	2	6	2	5	-16.67
27	江西	2	5	2	4	-20.00
28	福建	1	4	1	2	-50.00
合计		742	1970	770	2090	6.09

第三节 滑雪场分类统计信息

一、室内滑雪馆

在2019年新增的28家滑雪场中，有5家新开的室内滑雪馆。截至2019年年底，国内开业的室内滑雪馆已达31家。

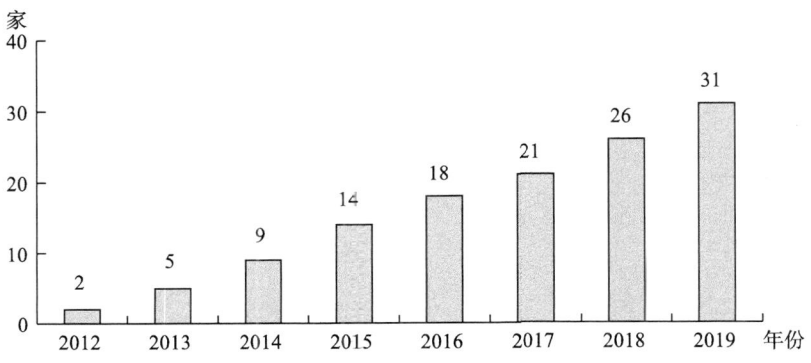

图10-3 2012—2019年国内已投入运营的室内滑雪馆数量

2019 年全年，国内 31 家室内滑雪馆滑雪人次合计 235 万。其中，最突出的当属广州融创雪世界。广州融创雪世界占地面积 7.5 万平方米，是全球第二大室内滑雪馆。从 2019 年 6 月 15 日开业到 2019 年 12 月 31 日，广州融创雪世界累计接待滑雪人次 55 万，有望成为全球接待量最大的室内滑雪馆。但同时，全球第一大室内滑雪馆——哈尔滨融创雪世界（原哈尔滨万达娱雪乐园）在 2019 年的表现则不容乐观，滑雪人次下跌幅度较大。

从表 10-3 可见，室内滑雪馆滑雪人次 2019 年增幅为 42%，对全部滑雪场滑雪人次的增长起到了决定性作用。

表 10-3　2018 年、2019 年室内滑雪馆滑雪人次统计

滑雪场类型	滑雪场数量/家	2019 年滑雪人次/万人次	2018 年滑雪人次/万人次	增幅/%
室内滑雪馆	31	235	166	42
户外滑雪场	739	1855	1804	3
全部滑雪场	770	2090	1970	6

二、目的地度假型滑雪场

按核心目标客群分类，国内滑雪场可分为旅游体验型、城郊学习型及目的地度假型三类。此三类滑雪场在全部滑雪场中占比分别为 77%、20% 及 3%（见表 10-4）。

表 10-4　2019 年中国滑雪场按核心目标客群分类

滑雪场类型	数量占比	客群定位	主要体现滑雪属性	滑雪场特征	客群特征	典型案例
旅游体验型	77%	旅游观光客	旅游属性	设施简单，只有初级道。位置一般在旅游景区或城郊	90%以上为一次性体验客户，客人平均停留时间 2 小时	西岭雪山、大明山、狼牙山
城郊学习型	20%	本地居民	运动属性、旅游属性	山体落差不大，位于城市郊区，开发有初级、中级、高级雪道	本地自驾客人占比很大，平均停留时间为 3~4 小时	南山、军都山、万科石京龙、探路者嵩顶
目的地度假型	3%	度假人群	度假属性、运动属性、旅游属性	山体有一定规模，除有齐全的雪道产品外，还有住宿等设施的配套	过夜消费占比较大，客人平均停留时间在 1 天以上	万科松花湖、万达长白山、北大湖、亚布力、万龙、太舞、富龙、云顶

在 2019 年 770 家滑雪场中，有 20 家左右符合目的地度假型滑雪场的特征。其中，有 8 家滑雪场可以被称为大型目的地滑雪度假村。

由表 10-5 可见，目的地度假型滑雪场的滑雪人次增长幅度要远远大于全部滑雪场滑雪人次的增长幅度，其中，大型目的地滑雪度假村滑雪人次的增长幅度又远远高于中型目的地滑雪度假村。

表 10-5　2018 年、2019 年目的地度假型滑雪场滑雪人次统计

滑雪场类型	滑雪场数量/家	2019 年滑雪人次/万人次	2018 年滑雪人次/万人次	增幅/%
大型目的地滑雪度假村	8	256	195	31
中型目的地滑雪度假村	12	88	72	22
全部滑雪场	770	2090	1970	6

三、垂直落差超过 300 米的滑雪场

滑雪场垂直落差是衡量滑雪场所在山地的资源规模的一个重要指标。按滑雪场实际开发雪道的垂直落差，我们将国内滑雪场按以下三类统计：垂直落差超过 300 米的滑雪场 26 家，占比 3.4%；垂直落差在 100～300 米的滑雪场 142 家，占比 18.44%；垂直落差小于 100 米的滑雪场 602 家，占比 78.18%（见图 10-4）。

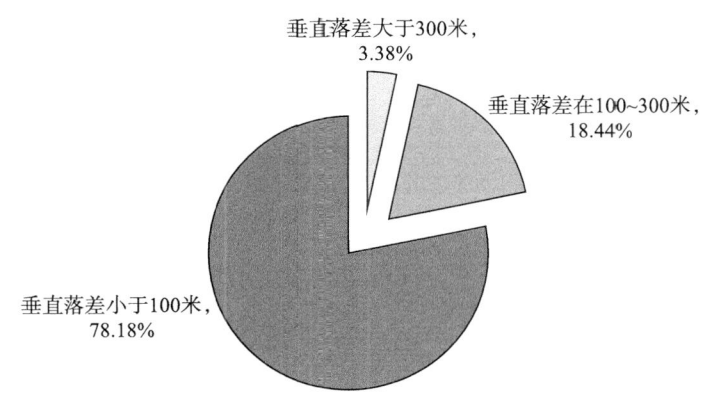

图 10-4　2019 年中国滑雪场按垂直落差统计占比

北京延庆小海坨新建成的国家高山滑雪中心是北京冬奥会高山滑雪主赛场，垂直落差超过 900 米，是目前国内有架空索道的滑雪场中垂直落差最大的场地。此外，黑龙江亚布

力和吉林北大壶两家滑雪场垂直落差均超过800米，是国内仅有的两家举办过亚洲冬季运动会的滑雪场。2019年，垂直落差超过300米的滑雪场滑雪人次统计为364万人次，相比2018年增长17%，远高于全部滑雪场总滑雪人次的增长幅度（见表10-6）。

表10-6　2019年垂直落差超过300米的滑雪场滑雪人次统计

滑雪场类型	滑雪场数量/家	2019年滑雪人次/万人次	2018年滑雪人次/万人次	增幅/%
垂直落差超过300米的滑雪场	26	364	312	17
全部滑雪场	770	2090	1970	6

四、雪道面积超过30公顷的滑雪场

雪道面积是衡量滑雪场大小的另一个重要维度。截至2019年年底，雪道面积超过30公顷的滑雪场共计30家，占比3.90%（见表10-7）。

表10-7　2019年按雪道面积统计的滑雪场数据

雪道面积/公顷	滑雪场数量/家	占比/%	2019年滑雪人次/万人次	2018年滑雪人次/万人次	增幅/%
>100	8	1.04	478	413	16
50~100	7	0.91			
30~50	15	1.95			
10~30	37	4.81	—	—	—
5~10	126	16.36			
<5	577	74.94			
合计	770	100.00	2090	1970	6

五、有架空索道的滑雪场

2019年，国内有架空索道的滑雪场统计为155家，相比2018年增加6家。本报告的研究重点将会越来越集中于有架空索道的滑雪场。其中，有4条及以上架空索道的8家滑雪场正好和前文统计的大型目的地滑雪度假村完全吻合。由表10-8可见，总体而言，架空索道数量越多的滑雪场滑雪人次增长幅度越大。155家有架空索道的滑雪场，滑雪人次合计为1015万，占总人次2090万的48.56%。有脱挂式缆车的滑雪场统计为22家，2019

年滑雪人次达到 354 万,同比增长 20%。

表 10-8　2019 年有架空索道的滑雪场统计信息

滑雪场类型	滑雪场数量/家	2019 年滑雪人次/万人次	2018 年滑雪人次/万人次	增幅/%
有架空索道 4 条及以上	8	256	195	31
有架空索道 3 条及以上	23	350	300	17
有架空索道 2 条及以上	57	615	535	15
有架空索道 1 条及以上	155	1015	904	12
有脱挂式缆车	22	354	295	20
全部滑雪场	770	2090	1970	6

六、滑雪人次超过 10 万的滑雪场

瑞士劳伦特先生在历年的《全球滑雪市场报告》中都会重点研究百万人次以上的滑雪场,以滑雪人次作为指标对滑雪场进行分类和筛选具有现实意义。2019 年,国内 770 家滑雪场中,滑雪人次占据前三名的仍是"三万",即万科松花湖、万达长白山以及万龙三家滑雪场。

2019 年全年滑雪人次超过 10 万以及 15 万的滑雪场的数量及人次增长信息如表 10-9 所示。770 家滑雪场中,滑雪人次超过 10 万人次的仅有 31 家,占滑雪场总量的 4.03%;但 31 家滑雪场合计产生了 609 万滑雪人次,占总滑雪人次的 29.14%。同时,从增幅的数据可以看到,滑雪人次越大的滑雪场同比增长幅度也越大。

表 10-9　2019 年滑雪人次超过 10 万的滑雪场信息

滑雪场类型	滑雪场数量/家	2019 年滑雪人次/万人次	2018 年滑雪人次/万人次	增幅/%
滑雪人次 15 万及以上	16	451	349	29
滑雪人次 10 万及以上	31	609	487	25
全部滑雪场	770	2090	1970	6

第四节　旱雪场地

根据尖锋旱雪提供的资料①，截至 2019 年年底，国内已建成的旱雪场总数已达到 45 家（见图 10-5）。但其中有 8 家处于超期停业状态，另有 1 家被拆除。

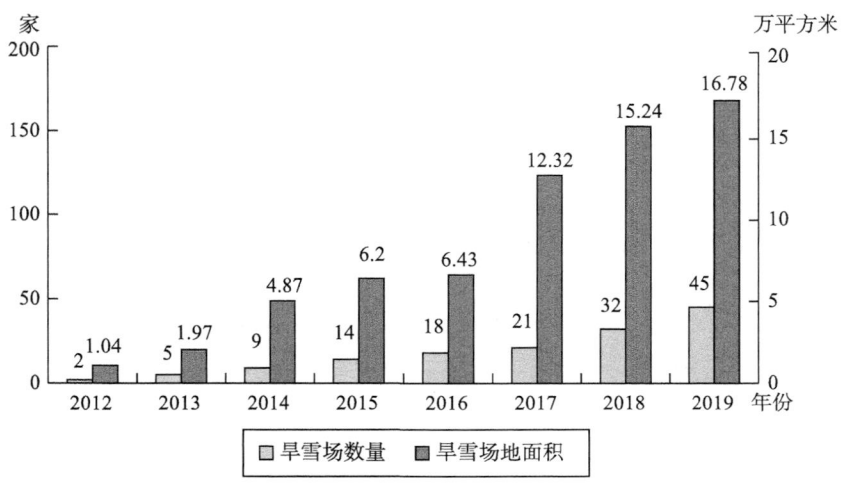

图 10-5　2012—2019 年已建成的旱雪场地及面积

旱雪场地分布如图 10-6 所示。目前，四川、北京、河北居于前三名，占比均超过 10%。

由于 2018 年统计的旱雪滑雪人次中包含了滑雪圈的人次，不能作为对比和参考的依据。2019 年剔除了滑雪圈的数据后，国内旱雪场产生的滑雪人次为 34.23 万人次（见图 10-7）。

---

①　世界金针菇旱雪（尖锋旱雪）的发明者和商标拥有者尖锋（旱雪先生）为本期报告提供了一份完整翔实的旱雪报告，本报告仅摘录其中部分重要信息。

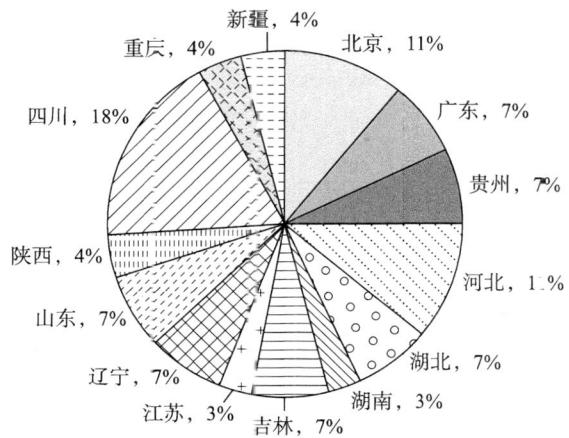

图 10-6 2019 年营运中的旱雪场分布

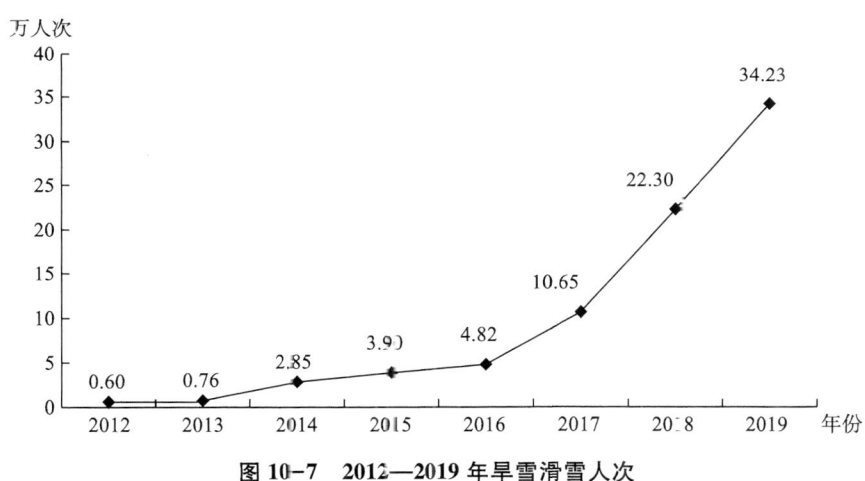

图 10-7 2012—2019 年旱雪滑雪人次

第五节 滑雪模拟器

2019 年，滑雪模拟器市场继续呈现加速增长态势。根据雪乐山提供的资料，截至 2019 年年底，雪乐山门店总数已达到 96 家。结合雪梦都提供的报告，截至 2019 年年底，全国滑雪模拟器场馆已达 140 家，投入使用的各类滑雪模拟器达到 400 台。据本报告测算，2019 年滑雪模拟器产生的滑雪人次在 78 万左右，相比 2018 年的 58 万，增长了 34.48%。

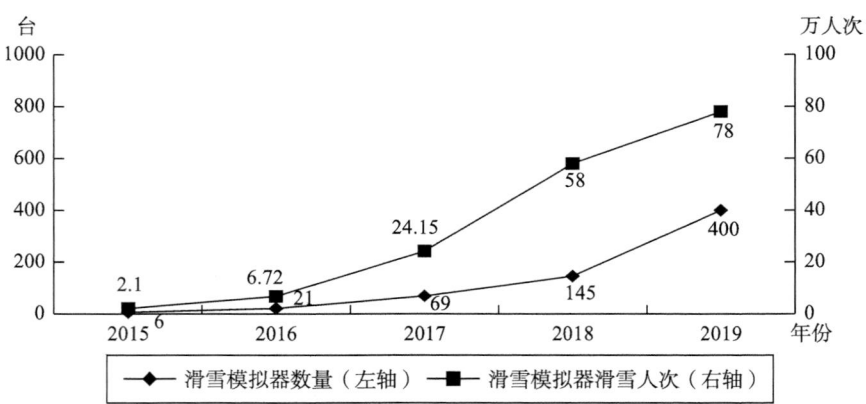

图 10-8　2015—2019 年滑雪模拟器数量及滑雪人次

第六节　总滑雪人次

综合旱雪以及滑雪模拟器的数据，2019 年总滑雪人次合计为 2202 万（见图 10-9）。

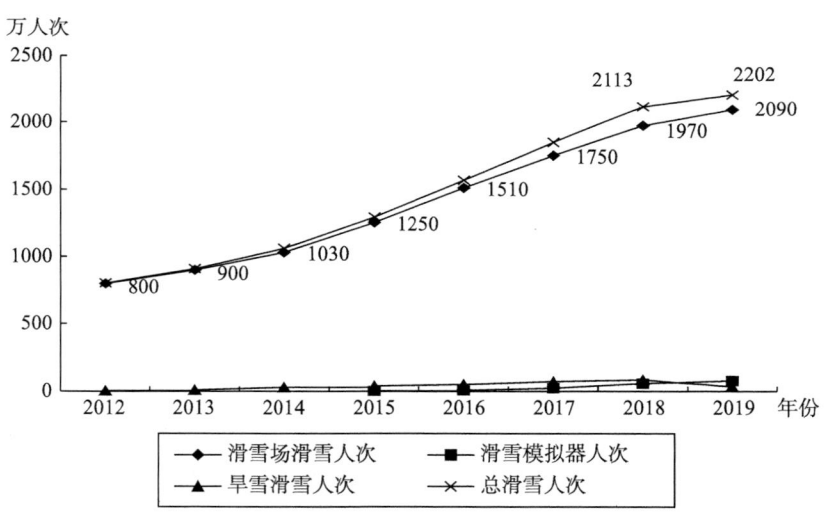

图 10-9　2012—2019 年总滑雪人次统计

第十一章　滑雪场硬件设施

第一节　滑雪场上行设施

一、滑雪场架空索道

截至 2019 年年底，国内滑雪场中建成并投入使用的架空索道总数为 261 条，分布于全国 22 个省（区、市）的 155 家滑雪场中（见图 11-1）。其中，河北、黑龙江、吉林分别以 49 条、40 条、39 条位列前三。三省合计总共建成 128 条滑雪架空索道，占全国滑雪架空索道总数的 49%（见表 11-1）。

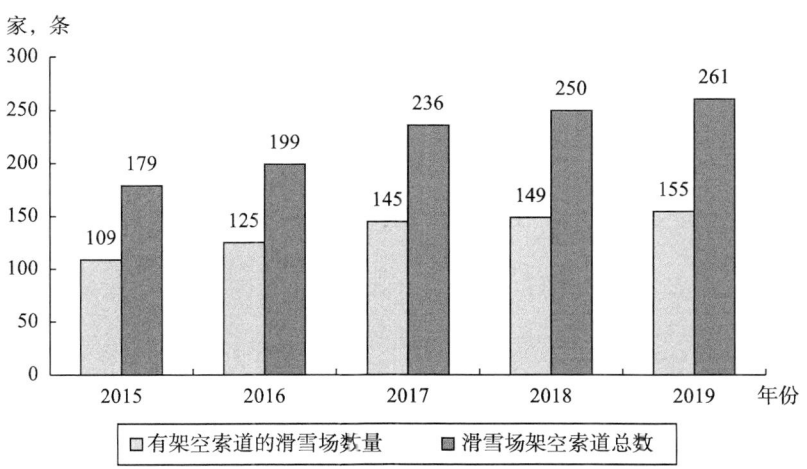

图 11-1　2015—2019 年有架空索道的滑雪场及滑雪场架空索道数量

表 11-1　2019 年中国滑雪场架空索道数量及分布

排序	省份	架空索道数量/条	有架空索道分布的滑雪场数量/家
1	河北	49	22
2	黑龙江	40	28
3	吉林	39	16
4	辽宁	28	19
5	北京	23	13
6	新疆	19	10
7	内蒙古	17	10
8	山西	8	5
9	甘肃	8	7
10	山东	6	6
11	陕西	5	4
12	四川	3	2
13	河南	3	2
14	云南	3	1
15	重庆	3	3
16	贵州	2	2
17	湖北	2	2
18	天津	1	1
19	广东	1	1
20	宁夏	1	1
	合计	261	155

2015—2019 年，国内脱挂式架空索道发展迅猛，由 2015 年的 26 条增长到 2019 年的 60 条，有脱挂式架空索道的滑雪场也由 10 家增长到了 22 家（见图 11-2）。

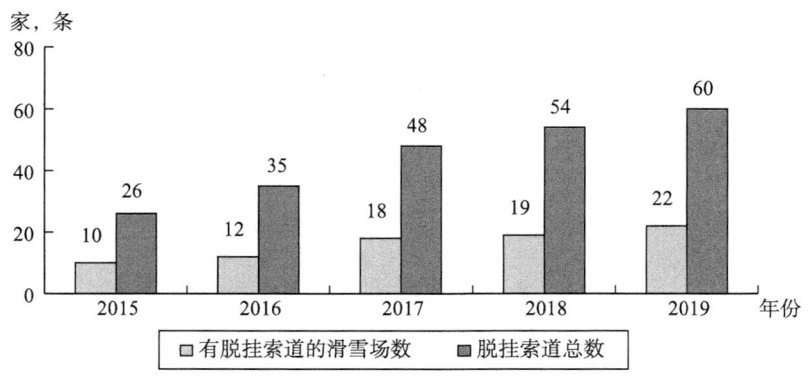

图 11-2　2015—2019 年中国滑雪场脱挂式架空索道数量

图 11-3 统计了 2015—2019 年脱挂式架空索道中进口和国产的数量关系。国产脱挂式架空索道的发展相当迅猛，从 2015 年的 2 条增长到 2019 年的 20 条。

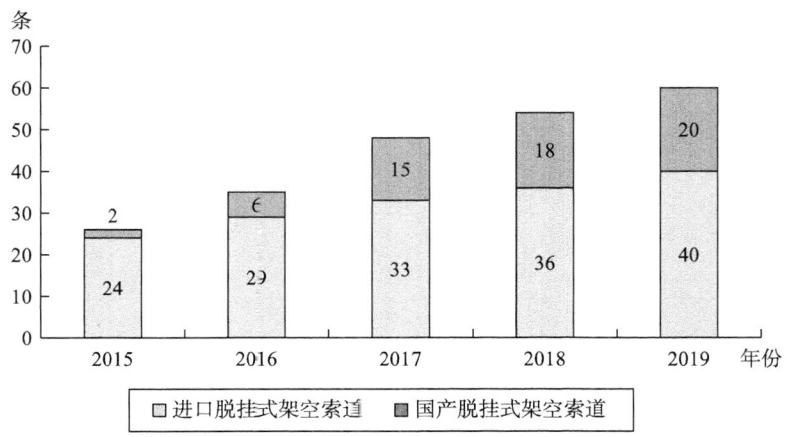

图 11-3　2015—2019 年中国滑雪场进口、国产脱挂式架空索道数量

60 条用于滑雪的脱挂式架空索道中，河北 21 条，分布于 6 家滑雪场，全部集中在张家口市崇礼区；吉林 19 条，分布于 6 家滑雪场；黑龙江 7 条，分布于 3 家滑雪场；新疆 4 条，分布于 2 家滑雪场；北京、内蒙古各建成 3 条，陕西建成 2 条，湖北建成 1 条（见图 11-4、表 11-2）（此项统计中，只包括用于滑雪的索道，不包括非滑雪用途的索道）。

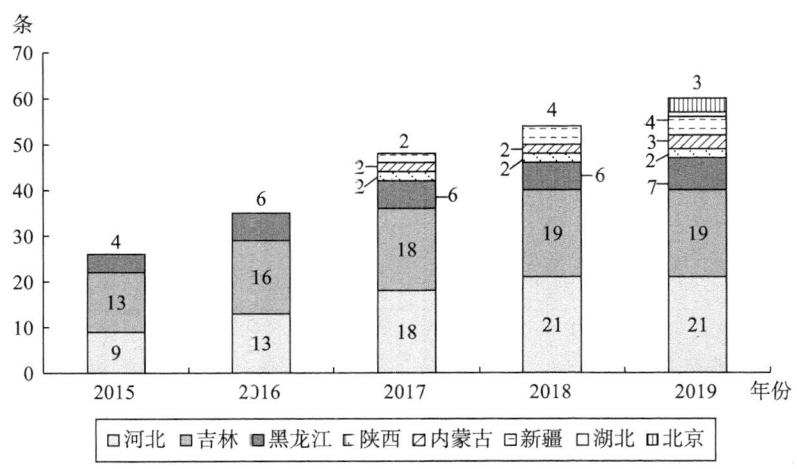

图 11-4　2015—2019 年中国滑雪场脱挂式架空索道按分布省份统计

2019 年，国内有脱挂式架空索道的滑雪场中，位于北京延庆小海坨的国家高山滑雪中

心最值得关注。该滑雪场目前已完成3条脱挂式架空索道的建设,并已投入赛事运营。作为北京冬奥会高山滑雪主赛场,其硬件设施必然会成为国内滑雪场的一个标杆。

表11-2 2019年中国滑雪场按脱挂式架空索道数量排名　　　　　　　　单位:条

序号	排名	滑雪场名称	数量	所在省份
1	1	万科松花湖	6	吉林
2	1	万龙	6	河北
3	3	万达长白山	5	吉林
4	3	太舞	5	河北
5	5	北大壶	4	吉林
6	5	云顶	4	河北
7	5	亚布力体委	4	黑龙江
8	8	国家高山滑雪中心	3	北京
9	8	丝绸之路	3	新疆
10	8	富龙	3	河北
11	11	太白鳌山	2	陕西
12	11	鲁能长白山	2	吉林
13	11	翠云山银河	2	河北
14	11	亚布力阳光	2	黑龙江
15	11	凉城岱海	2	内蒙古
16	16	庙香山	1	吉林
17	16	多乐美地	1	河北
18	16	帽儿山	1	黑龙江
19	16	长春莲花山	1	吉林
20	16	将军山	1	新疆
21	16	美林谷	1	内蒙古
22	16	绿葱坡	1	湖北
		合计	60	

二、滑雪场魔毯

对于全球最大的初级滑雪市场而言,魔毯在中国滑雪产业发展的过程中扮演着至关重要的角色。近两年,随着新增户外滑雪场数量的减少,魔毯市场也出现了较大幅度的回落。2019年,滑雪场魔毯新增21千米,略高于2018年(见图11-5)。

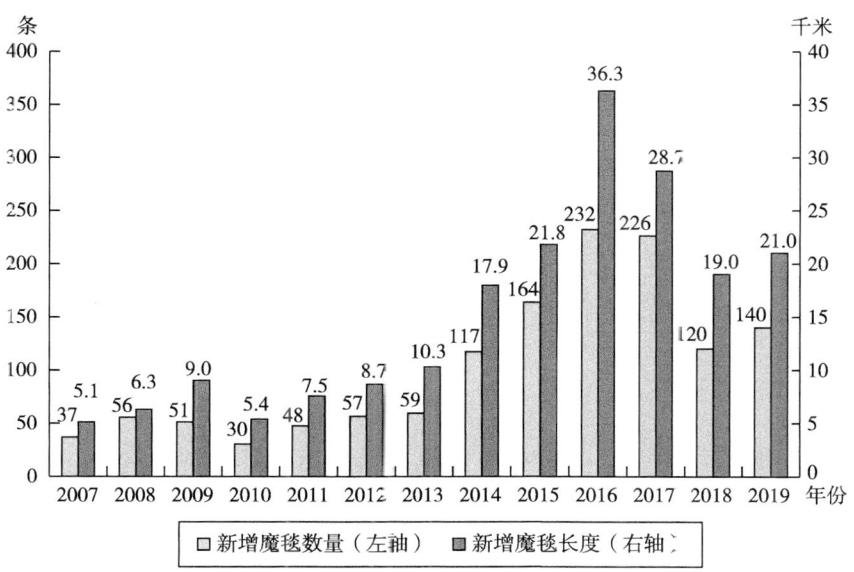

图 11-5　2007—2019 年滑雪场新增魔毯数量及长度

魔毯数据来源于国内主要魔毯供应商。截至 2019 年，国内滑雪场共计有 1336 条魔毯处于运营中，包括 2019 年新增的 140 条魔毯。全部魔毯总长度约 197 千米（见图 11-6）。

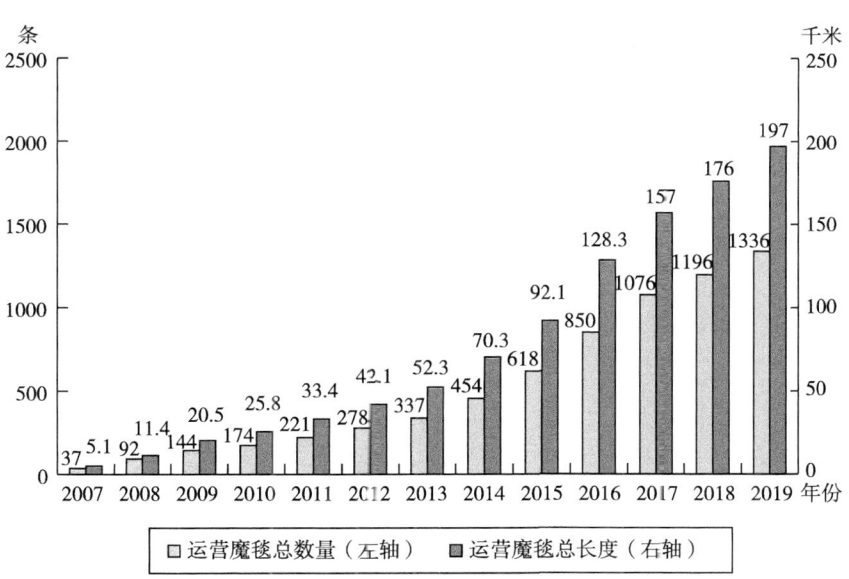

图 11-6　2007—2019 年滑雪场运营魔毯总数量及总长度

第二节　滑雪场场地设施

2019年,滑雪场场地设施中,压雪车和造雪机都有明显的增长,与北京冬奥会大额的采购订单直接相关。另外,近两年气候变化给造雪和雪道维护都造成了很大困扰,不少老滑雪场被迫改良压雪设备,增加造雪设备。

一、压雪车

根据主要压雪车供应商统计数据,国内滑雪场全部压雪车数量约为629台。如图11-7所示,2019年,国内新增压雪车数量为88台,远高于2018年的56台,其中包括国家高山滑雪中心采购的19台。进口新车合计61台,国产压雪车27台。

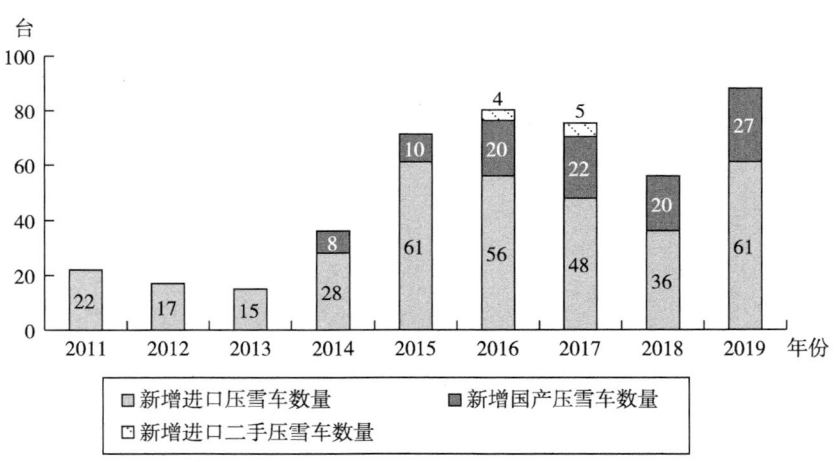

图11-7　2011—2019年中国滑雪场新增压雪车数量统计

二、造雪机

2019年,全国滑雪场新增造雪机1149台(包括冬奥会项目采购数量),相比2018年的810台增长41.85%(见图11-8)。截至2019年年底,全部造雪机数量约8559台[①]。

[①] 数据来源于主要造雪机设备供应商。

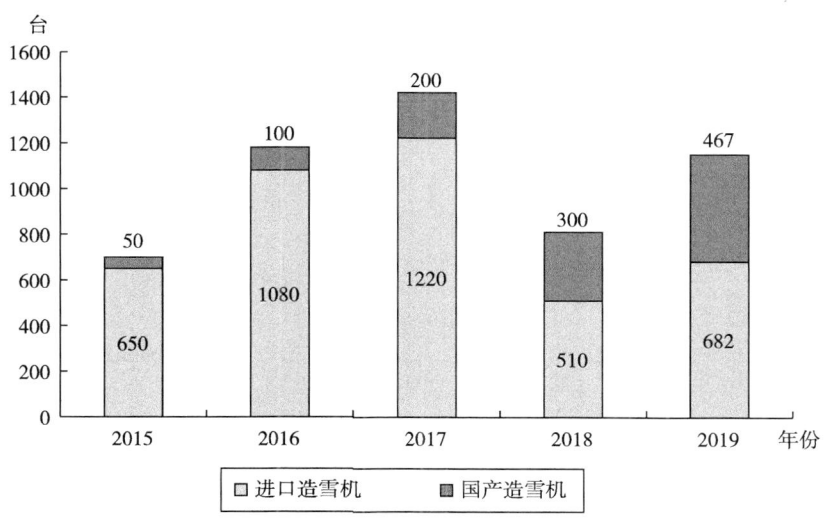

图 11-8 2015—2019 年滑雪场新增造雪机数量

第三节 滑雪场租赁设施

鉴于目前国内尚不具备独立生产双板脱落器的能力，因此，双板脱落器的海关进口数据基本能反映出国内双板市场的状态。而由于双板零售市场与双板租赁市场存在数量级上的差异，因此，进口脱落器的规模与租赁双板的数量关联性更强。

从海关数据分析可见，在经历了 2018 年的大幅度下跌之后，双板脱落器进口数量在 2019 年形成了强力反弹，同比增长 29.35%，由 2018 年的 92 吨上升到 119 吨。但相比 2017 年的 137.45 吨仍然有一定差距。

很遗憾，截至本报告成稿前，未能及时取得业界相关的数据来估算双板租赁市场 2019 年的表现，但从以往年度来看，双板脱落器海关进口数据的强力增长，一定程度上表明双板租赁市场向好。

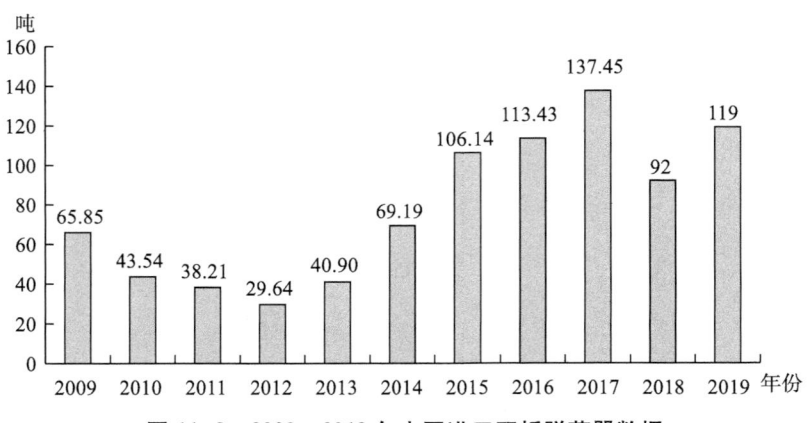

图 11-9　2009—2019 年中国进口双板脱落器数据

资料来源：中国海关，北京龙之讯信息咨询有限公司。

第十二章 滑雪者特征

本报告除获得了大量定向调查问卷的信息之外，携程旅游、马蜂窝滑雪、雪族科技以及滑呗等具备线上资源的平台机构都组织了专项小组，出具了完整的滑雪者特征报告。滑雪者这一群体也在这些数字的基础上逐渐变得立体起来。

第一节 滑雪者的性别

尽管每个数字都不可能反映出全貌，但通过横向数据对比可以发现部分线索，以便日后进一步去寻找更为准确的信息。

（1）与度假型滑雪场相比，当日往返型滑雪场的男女比例更为平衡；
（2）雪族科技与滑呗的报告中，男性占较大比例，说明滑雪爱好者以男性居多；
（3）马蜂窝滑雪的用户中，女性占比超过2/3；
（4）室内初级市场中，参与教学的人群可能以女性居多（见表12-1）。

表12-1 2019年滑雪者性别特征综合信息

指标	度假型滑雪场问卷	当日往返型滑雪场问卷	雪族科技报告	滑呗报告	马蜂窝滑雪报告	滑雪模拟器报告（雪乐山）	室内滑雪馆报告（融创雪世界）
男性占比/%	57.70	52.80	58	68	32	55	44.37
备注	根据各滑雪场人次综合计算		线上实际消费人群	线上用户	线上用户	到店客户	仅统计融创滑雪学校学员

第二节 滑雪者的年龄

(1) 度假型滑雪场滑雪者的平均年龄高于当日往返型滑雪场；

(2) 雪乐山以学习滑雪为主，40 岁以下滑雪者占比达到了 95%，而其中学龄前儿童滑雪者占比为 15%；

(3) 雪族科技以提供线上服务为主，40 岁以下滑雪者占比达到了 96%（见表 12-2）。

表 12-2 2019 年滑雪者年龄特征综合信息 （%）

滑雪者年龄分段	度假型滑雪场问卷	当日往返型滑雪场问卷	雪族科技报告	滑雪模拟器报告（雪乐山）	携程主题游滑雪数据
学龄前儿童（1~7 岁）	3.74	4.21	—	15	—
7~20 岁	10.74	17.06	6	19	22
20~30 岁	27.69	34.59	51	26	25
30~40 岁	33.66	28.19	39	35	30
40~50 岁	18.38	12.02	3	4	15
50 岁以上	5.79	3.93	1	1	8

第三节 滑雪者的其他特征

一、携程旅游报告（摘录）

滑雪游客中，单人出行最多，占比 29.3%；其次是亲子游客，占比 27.5%；情侣出行占比 22.8%；同事朋友占比 20.4%（见图 12-1）。除了比较资深的滑雪爱好者，亲子游客比例上升较快。携程滑雪订单中，带孩子滑雪的家庭中，孩子年龄最小的仅 2.5 岁，滑雪成为冬季亲子游的热门选择。

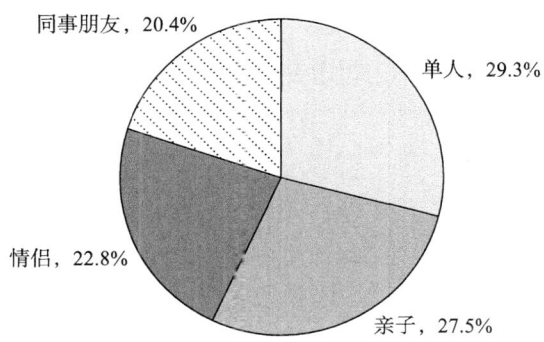

图 12-1 2019 年滑雪爱好者游伴分布

这些滑雪爱好者都来自哪里？根据携程主题游数据，地处南方、经济发展水平较高的上海人对滑雪的热情最高，成都和北京紧随其后，接下来依次是广州、武汉、杭州、苏州、南京、福州、深圳。

滑雪游要花多少钱？据携程主题游滑雪打包产品价格，国内滑雪人均消费2398元，国外滑雪人均消费9893元（见图12-2）。

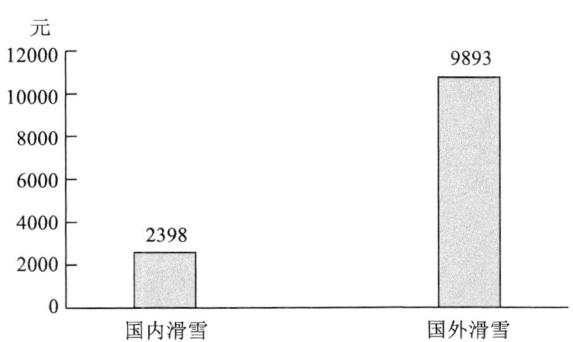

图 12-2　2019 年国内外滑雪人均消费

二、马蜂窝滑雪报告（摘录）

随着站内滑雪用户的逐步增加，马蜂窝2019年产生的滑雪类笔记数量同比增长349.89%，比2017年增长1120.64%。

三、雪族科技报告（摘录）

雪族科技线上记录的滑雪爱好者遍布全国各地，但仍以北京、河北及东北三省居多

（见图12-3）。从2017—2018年雪季、2018—2019年雪季的数据看，线上交易的比例明显增多，同时，移动支付占比在2018—2019年雪季已达82%（见图12-4）。

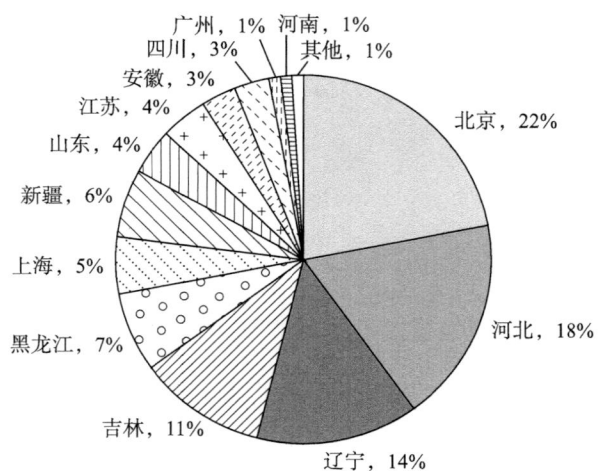

图12-3 2019年滑雪爱好者地域分布

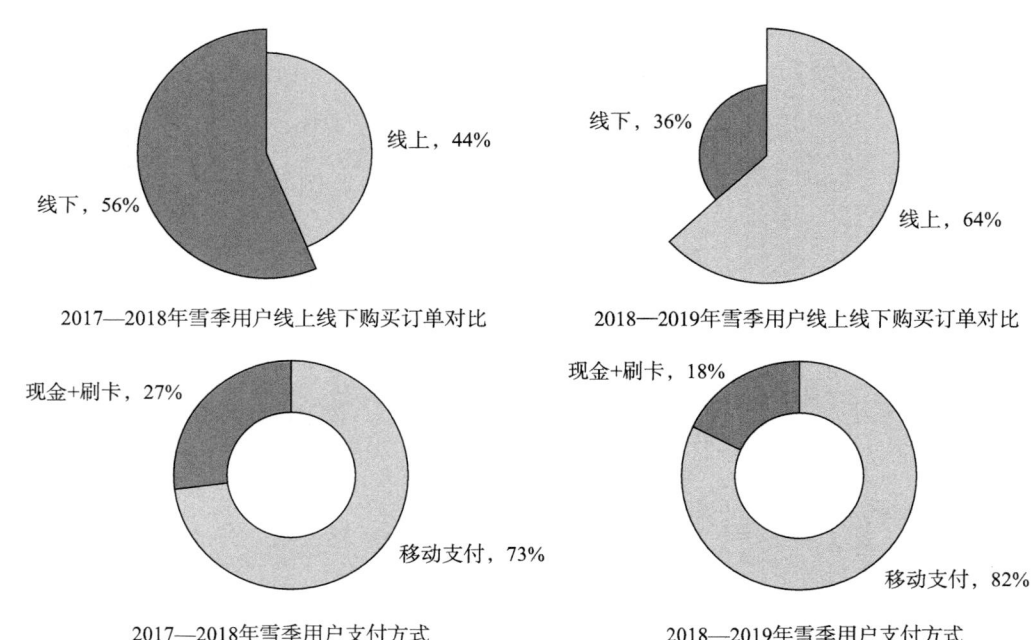

图12-4 2017—2018年雪季、2018—2019年雪季用户订单对比

四、滑呗报告（摘录）

截至 2019 年，在滑呗上被审核通过的注册俱乐部多达 1172 家（见图 12-5），覆盖全国 126 个城市（地级市及以上）、29 个省份（见图 12-6）；海外地区共有 13 个俱乐部。

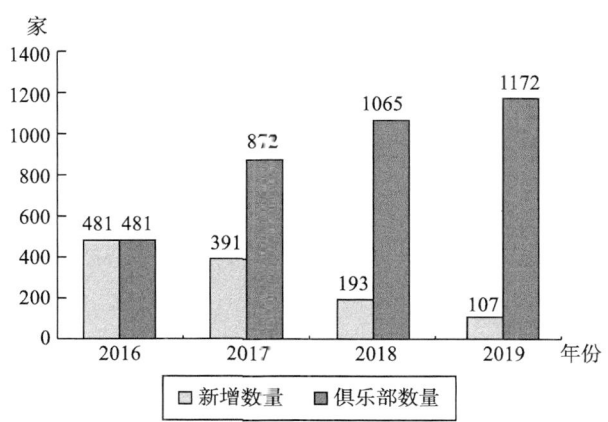

图 12-5　2019 年滑呗注册俱乐部数据统计

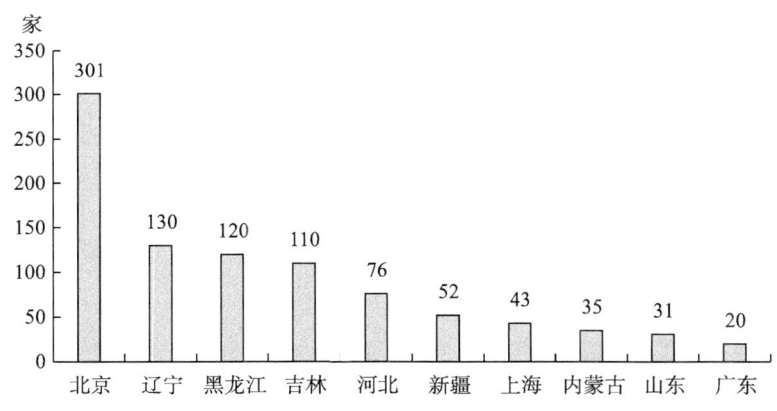

图 12-6　2019 年俱乐部数量前十名省份

第十三章 滑雪者装备市场

2019年的滑雪者装备市场陆续收到了更多积极的消息。总体而言，单板市场已进入高速增长期，预期整体年增长率在25%~30%。同时，双板市场也有复苏和启动的迹象。本章内容主要来源于法国迪卡侬Wed'ze滑雪品牌以及冷山GOSKI。

第一节 迪卡侬Wed'ze滑雪品牌中国报告

2019年，迪卡侬Wed'ze滑雪品牌已全面进入中国区的315家迪卡侬门店。店面数排名前三的城市为上海、北京、广州，Wed'ze滑雪品牌销售排名前三的城市连续五年均为北京、上海、成都。Wed'ze滑雪品牌在中国取得了连续五年保持增长的成绩。

从Wed'ze滑雪品牌不同品类的销售状况来看，单板的销量远远大于双板，儿童系列的滑雪装备增速高于成人系列。其中，2019年儿童单板和单板鞋的同比增长率均在40%左右。

Wed'ze滑雪服装的销量最为突出。2019年，成人和儿童滑雪服系列的销量超过150万件。

Wed'ze滑雪头盔和风镜销售量持续五年增长迅猛。成人系列和儿童系列2019年全年销量与2015年相比，均取得了100%以上的增长率。

第二节 冷山GOSKI报告

截至2019年，冷山开业店铺合计27家。2017—2018年雪季销售额为7500万元，2018—2019年雪季增长至9000万元，年增长率20%。客单价为2000元。

销售男款占比65%，女款占比35%。

从销售地域来看，北京及河北张家口崇礼占比40%，东北三省占比30%，长三角区域占比5%。

著名眼镜品牌Oakley在中国的销量每年增长1万副以上，近三个雪季销量分别为1万副、2万副、3万副。预计到2022—2023年雪季将达到6万副。

单板顶级品牌博顿在中国2018—2019年雪季零售额为1亿元，2019—2020年雪季为1.2亿元。预计未来数年每年将增长30%~50%。

冷山市场份额约为整个核心市场①的10%~15%，推测整体市场规模在6亿~9亿元。未来3年按每年30%的增长预测，2019—2020年雪季市场规模为10亿元，2020—2021年雪季为13亿元，2021—2022年雪季将达到15.6亿元。

根据美国SIA产业报告，美国滑雪市场单板零售业的市场规模为8亿~10亿美元，单板人群约为760万人，单板销售量为45万~50万片。中国目前的市场规模约为美国的10%。

---

① 核心市场指专业品牌市场，不含淘品牌等。

Report on Key Data of Ski Industry in China (2015-2019)

WU Bin, LI Yu, WEI Qinghua

General

I . Changes in Main Indicators of Ski Industry in China

In 2019, compared with 2015, the total number of ski resorts was 770, increased by 35.56% with 202 newly added ski resorts, but the growth rate was declined. By the end of 2019, among of these 770 resorts, 155 resorts were equipped with the aerial lifts, increased by 27.05% in 2019 compared with 122 in 2015. There were 31 indoor ski resorts in China, increased by 244.44% in 2019 compared with 9 in 2015. The number of domestic ski visits increased from 12.5 million in 2015 to 20.9 million in 2019, with a growth of 67.2%. As is shown in Figure 0-1 to Figure 0-4 for details.

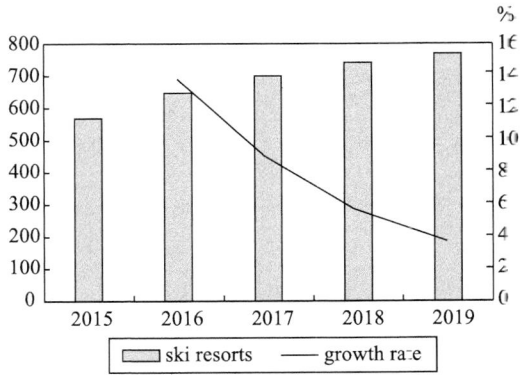

Figure 0-1　Number of Ski Resorts in China

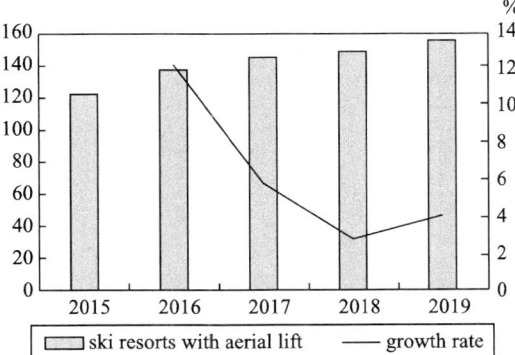

Figure 0-2　Number of Ski Resorts with Aerial Lift in China

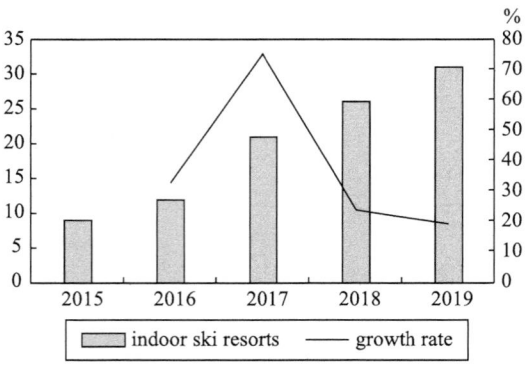

Figure 0-3 Number of Indoor Ski Resorts in China

Figure 0-4 Number of Ski Visits in China

Area of slopes is another important indicator to measure the size of one ski resort. By the end of 2019, there were 30 ski resorts with a total area of more than 30 hectares. Compared with 2015, this number was increased by 1.6% with 13 new ski resorts (shown in Table 0-1).

Table 0-1 Ski Resorts by Slope Area

Area of Slopes/hm²	2015	Percentage/%	2019	Percentage/%
>100	1	0.18	8	1.04
50~100	7	1.23	7	0.91
30~50	5	0.88	15	1.95
10~30	20	3.52	37	4.81
5~10	50	8.80	126	16.36
<5	485	85.39	577	74.94
Total	568	100.00	770	100.00

II. Changes in Main Indicators of Ski Industry in Provinces

1. Analysis of the Number of Ski Resorts

From 2015 to 2019, there were 202 newly added ski resorts in China. By the number of ski resorts, the top 5 provinces and autonomous regions owned the most ski resorts were Heilongjiang, Shandong, Xinjiang, Hebei and Shanxi. Unlike 2015, Shanxi surpassed Jilin and entered the top five in 2019. Sorted by the number of new ski fields, Hebei took the top rank with the number of 21 new ski resorts, followed by Shanxi, Shandong and Inner Mongolia, with 17, 16 and 16 resorts respectively. In addition, the number of ski resorts in Shanxi, Xinjiang and Hubei increased as well. See Figure 0-5 for details.

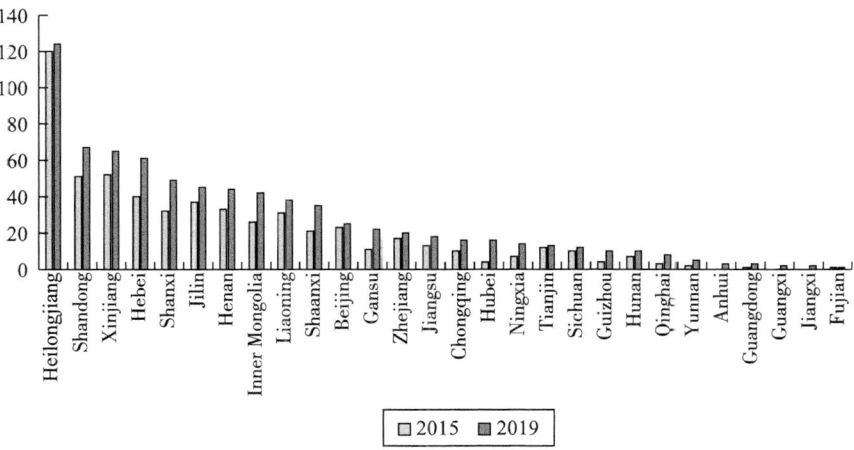

Figure 0-5　Number of Ski Resorts by Province

Ranked by the proportion of ski resorts in the national level, the top five provinces were Heilongjiang, Shandong, Xinjiang, Hebei and Shanxi, which accounted for 47.5% of the total. According to the growth of new ski resorts from 2015 to 2019, Hubei took the top rank with the number of 12 new resorts, followed by Guangdong, Qinghai and Yunnan, with 31.61%, 27.79% and 25.74% respectively. Some provinces such as Anhui, Guangxi and Jiangxi which did not have ski resorts before also began to develop skiing gradually. Conversely, Heilongjiang, Liaoning and Shandong with bigger bases had slower averaged annual growth rates. See Figure 0-6 for details.

Report on Key Data of *Ski* Industry in China (2015-2019)

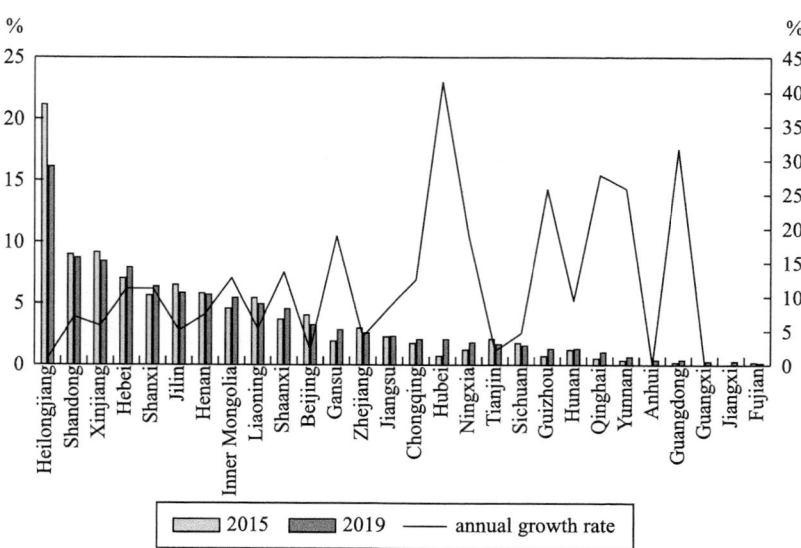

Figure 0-6 Number of Ski Resorts by Province and Changes in Average Annual Growth Rate

The distribution of ski resorts in China generally exhibited a decreasing tendency from north to south. In other words, ski resorts mainly concentrated in the Northeast and North regions in China like Heilongjiang, Hebei and Shandong, and in the south of the Yangtze River, such as Hubei, Yunnan and Anhui, ski resorts were less distributed and changed a little.

In order to facilitate a clearer understanding of the distribution of ski resorts in China, the whole country can be divided into seven regions: northeast, north, northwest, east, central, south and southwest. The distribution of ski resorts by regions was showed in Figure 0-7 and Figure 0-8. Among them, northeast region continuously took the top rank with the number of 57 newly added ski resorts in 2019, while its proportion dropped rapidly from 33.1% to 26.88%. North China was the second region with 50 new ski resorts, increased by 2.15% compared with 2015. And central and east regions increased by 28 and 27 respectively.

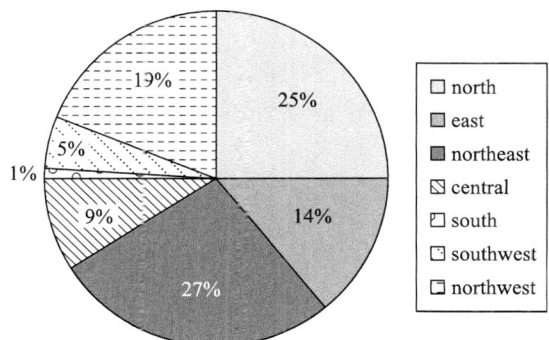

Figure 0-7　Distribution of Ski Resorts in all Regions(2015)

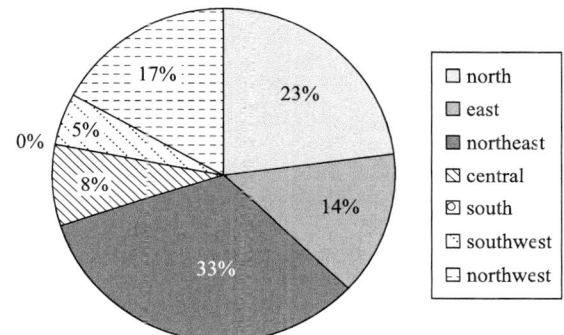

Figure 0-8　Distribution of Ski Resorts in all Regions(2019)

The distribution of total ski resorts by province was showed in Figure 0-9. In 2015, high-value areas of ski resorts were mainly concentrated in Heilongjiang, Xinjiang and Shandong, accounting for 9.2% to 21.3%. And most provinces in the south of the Yangtze River, such as Hubei, Anhui and Jiangxi were called low-value areas, owned less than 0.7% of ski resorts. The high-value areas in 2019 were basically the same as that in 2015 without any big changes. While the low-value areas like Hubei, Guizhou had significantly reduced and gradually transformed to the median areas.

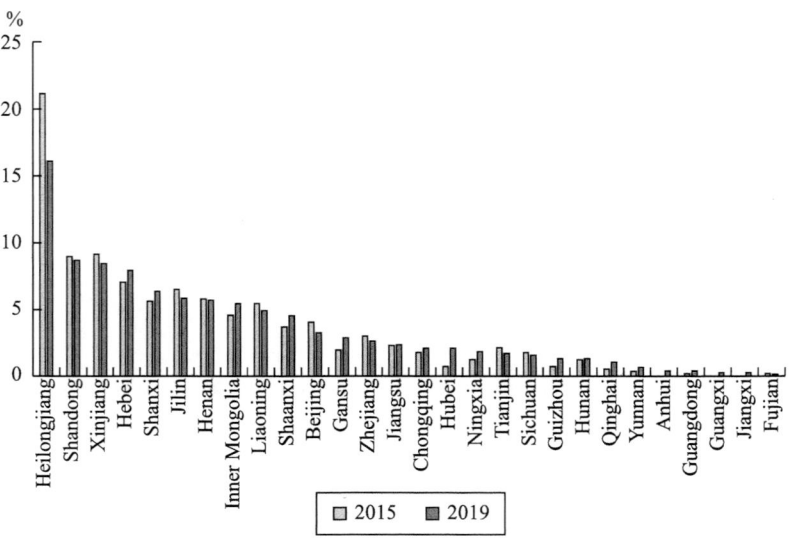

Figure 0-9　Proportion of Ski Resorts in China by Province

The average annual growth rate of ski resorts by province between 2015 and 2019 was shown in Figure 0-10. Due to the small base of ski resorts in 2015, Hubei, Guangdong, Guizhou, Yunnan and Qinghai were high-value areas with rapid average annual growth.

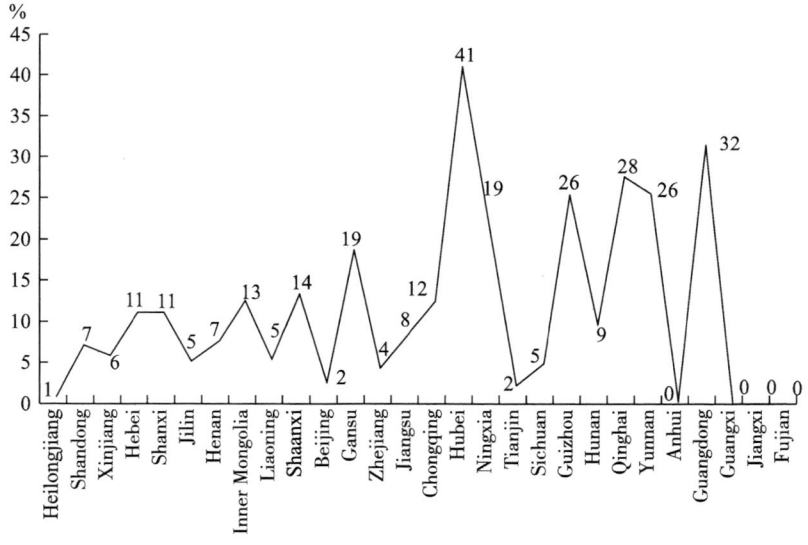

Figure 0-10　Growth Rate of Ski Resorts in China by Province(2015-2019)

2. Analysis of Ski Visits

The proportion of ski visits in China by province and changes in average annual growth rate were shown in Figure 0-11. The top 5 provinces and autonomous regions which owned the most ski visits were Hebei, Jilin, Beijing, Heilongjiang and Xinjiang. Among them, the proportion of ski visits in Hebei rose rapidly from the original fifth to the first, while the numbers of ski visits in Heilongjiang, Shandong and Beijing decreased slightly. The overall annual growth rate was 13.77% in China from 2015 to 2019. Guangdong ranked the first by increasing 630 thousand ski visits, with an average annual growth rate of 138.77%, followed by Guizhou, Qinghai and Yunnan with 59.05%, 39.16% and 31.61% respectively.

As a whole, the distribution of ski visits in China presented a gradually decreasing trend from north to south and from east to west. Ski visits were mainly concentrated in Northeast China, North China with more skiing resources and the eastern developed areas. In 2019, the number of ski visits in all provinces increased significantly with Hebei, Jilin and Guangdong having the most outstanding performance. Nevertheless, in South and Southwest China, such as Jiangxi, Guangxi and Fujian, ski visits were fewer and changed slightly.

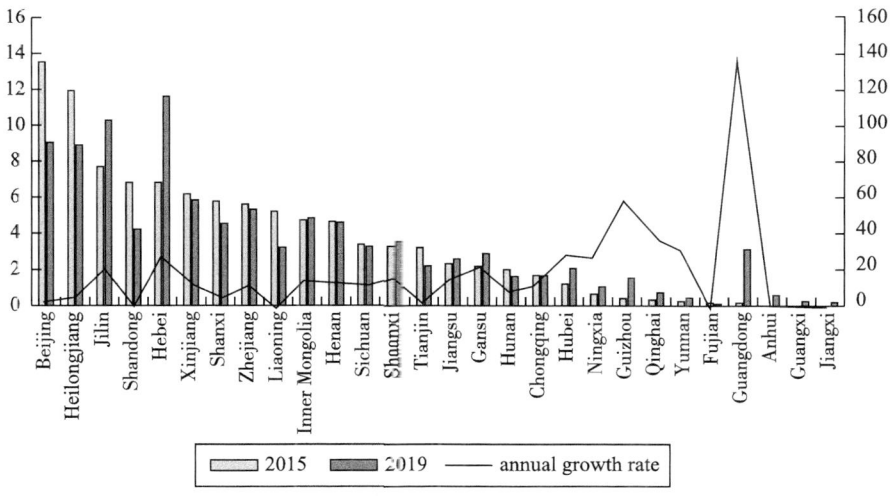

Figure 0-11 Proportion of Ski Visits in China by Province

In 2015, high-value areas of ski visits were only concentrated in Beijing, Heilongjiang and Jilin, accounting for 7.7% to 13.5%. And most provinces in the south of the Yangtze River, such as

Hubei, Guizhou and Yunnan were called low-value areas, owned less than 0.6% of ski visits. Compared with 2015, the scopes of high-value areas in 2019 were much larger. Hebei entered the high-value areas as well. Meanwhile, the low-value areas, which located in the south of the Yangtze River like Hubei, Guizhou, were gradually transformed to the median areas.

From 2015 to 2019, the spatial variation in average annual growth rate of ski visits in China was shown in Figure 0-12. On the contrary of ski visits which high-value areas distributed in the north of China, high-value areas of average annual growth rate mostly located in the south, such as Guangdong, Guizhou, accounting for 59.0% to 138.77%. In addition, Liaoning, Beijing and Shandong were low-value areas with smaller average annual growth rate of ski visits.

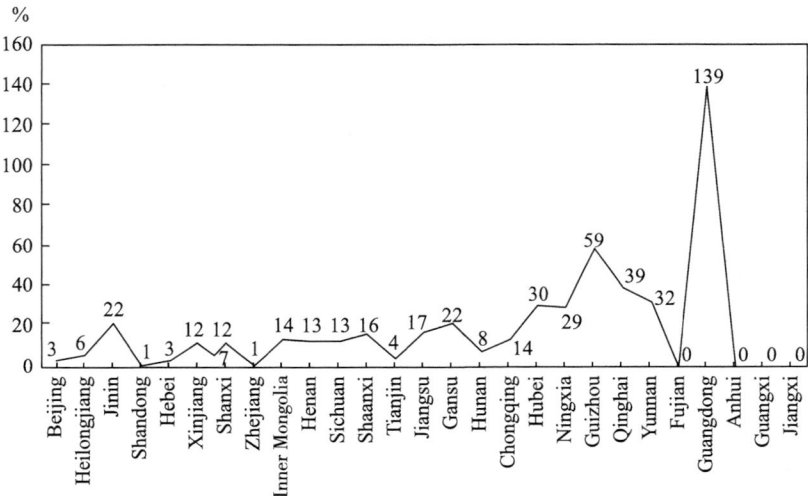

Figure 0-12　Average Annual Growth Rate of Ski Visits in China(2015-2019)

3. Analysis of Aerial Lifts

The total number of operating aerial lifts in domestic ski resorts in 2015 and 2019 were shown in Figure 0-13. And Figure 0-14 presented the number of ski resorts with aerial lifts in China in 2015 and 2019. Compared with 2015, there were 64 aerial lifts newly added in 2019, including 24 in Hebei, followed by Jilin, Inner Mongolia. In the past five years, the ski resorts with aerial lifts had developed rapidly from 122 in 2015 to 155 in 2019. Among the 33 ski resorts, there were 13 new resorts in Hebei, accounting for 39.4%, followed by Jilin, Heilongjiang and Inner Mongolia with 9,6 and 5 resorts respectively.

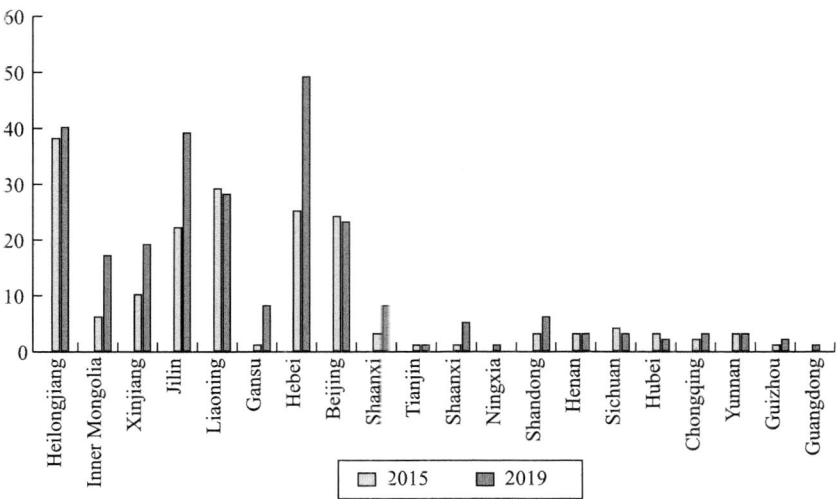

Figure 0-13　Number of Aerial Lifts in Ski Resorts in China

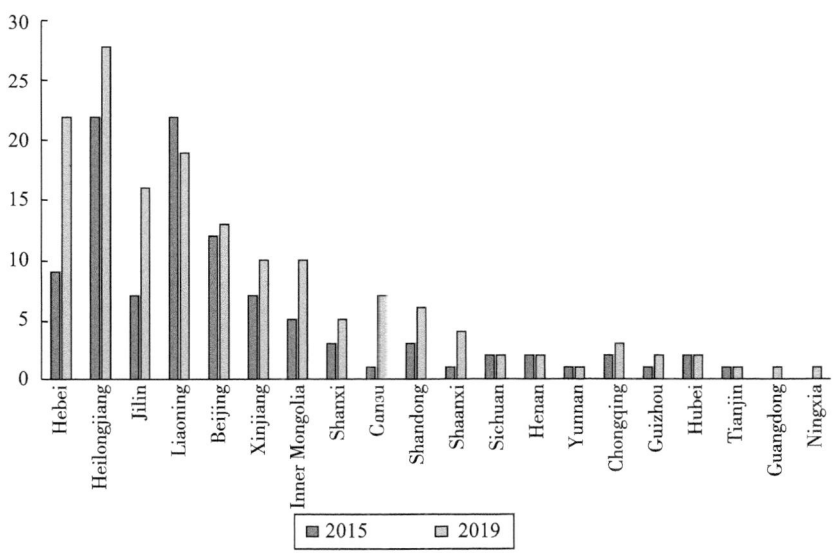

Figure 0-14　Number of Ski Resorts with Aerial Lift in China

All aerial lifts were mainly concentrated in Northeast China, North China and Xinjiang, followed by the central regions, and less distributed in the southwest and southeast coastal areas. There was a strong correlation between ski resorts with aerial lifts and distribution of aerial lifts because of the similar spatial distribution.

The distribution of aerial lifts in ski resorts by average annual growth rate was mostly low-value areas based from 2015 to 2019, being sparse in high-value areas. See Figure 0-15. The high-value areas of average annual growth rate were only distributed in some provinces, such as Gansu, Shaanxi and Hebei, followed by Jilin. Nevertheless, low-value areas of average annual growth rate were located in most regions in the south of the Yangtze River. While the lowest average annual growth rate of ski resorts with aerial lifts was located in Liaoning, which average annual growth rate was negative.

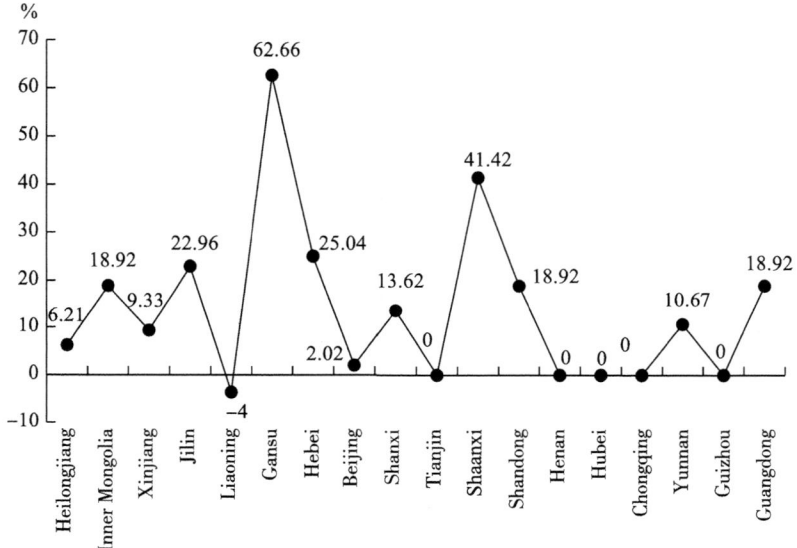

Figure 0-15 Growth Rate of Ski Resorts with Aerial Lift in China(2015-2019)

Part 1

2015 Report on Key Data of Ski Industry in China

Chapter 1　2015 Ski Resort

Compared with 2014, there was a 23.48% increase in domestic ski resorts in 2015. The total number of ski resorts in operation grew to 568. The number included 9 indoor ski halls, but excluded all types of outdoor and indoor snow play entertaining snow parks. Compared to 2014, there were 108 new ski resorts.

Ski equipment and facilities investment statistics was as follows: the number of aerial ski lifts totaled 198, the number of surface lift (ski t-bars, etc.) totaled 367, the number of magic carpets totaled 618; the total number of snowmaking machines was estimated to be about 4 thousand units (including both imported and domestically manufactured units), there were a total of 330 snow grooming machines, 300 of which were imported with the other 30 domestically manufactured. Ski rental totals were estimated at 350 thousand, snowboard rentals at 30 thousand, and ski suit rentals were estimated to total 100 thousand; imports for skis/boards tuning machines totaled 60 (including purchases for ski rental/repair shops, excluding purchases from ski factories).

I. Number & Distribution

For 1996-2015, the growth in the number of domestic ski resorts was detailed in Figure 1-1. The 1996-2011 data was inferred from the data suggested by the China Ski Association which combined with industry experience. The data for 2012 - 2015 information was extracted from *Chinese Ski Resort Encyclopedia*, subtracting the irrelevant information about other types of snow resorts.

In 2015, the number of ski resorts nationwide reached 568. Compared to 2014, there were 108 new resorts, an increase of 23.48%. Compared to 2010, there were 298 new resorts, an increase of 110.37%.

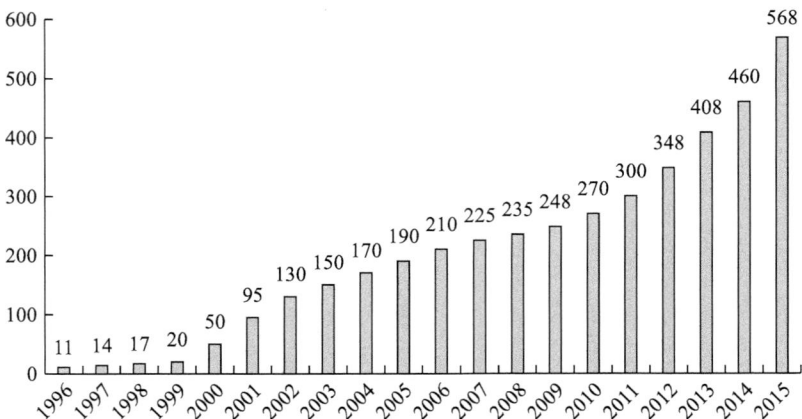

Figure 1-1 Number of Ski Resorts in China

568 ski resorts located in 25 provinces, autonomous regions and municipalities. The number of ski resorts in Heilongjiang was 120, ranking the first in China. See Figure 1-2.

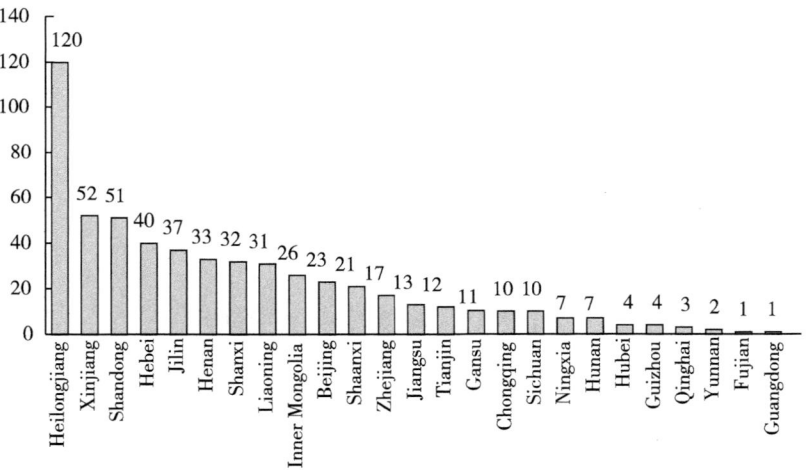

Figure 1-2 Distrubition of Ski Resorts in China (2015)

In order to facilitate a clearer understanding of the distribution of ski resorts in China, we divided the map into the northeast, north, northwest, east, central, southern and southwestern regions, as shown in Figure 1 – 3. Among them, the northeast region accounted for the largest number of ski resorts at 33.10%, followed by the North China region with 23.24%.

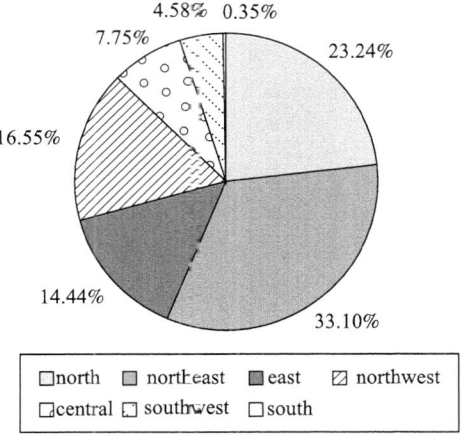

Figure 1-3 Distribution of the Number of Ski Resorts in China(2015)

Domestic changes in ski resort distribution was shown in Figures 1-4 and 1-5. By 2015, the total number of new ski resort was 108. Sorting by amount, the five provinces with the most growth were: Heilongjiang, Xinjiang, Shandong, Hebei and Jilin. Comparing 2014 to 2015, the individual province with the most growth was Shandong, with 22 new resorts, it was followed by Henan, Shanxi, Shaanxi, with a growth of 14, 11 and 9 resorts respectively, while Zhejiang, Jiangsu and Jilin each additional 7 ski resorts.

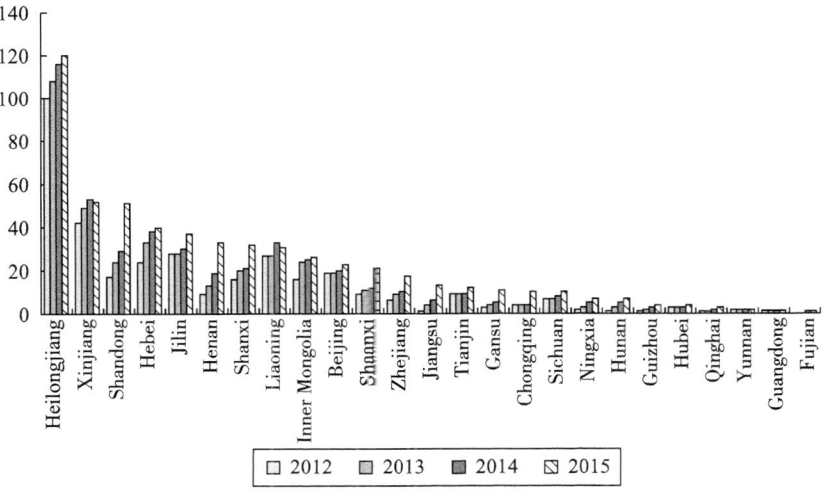

Figure 1-4 Changes in Ski Resort Distribution by Province(A)

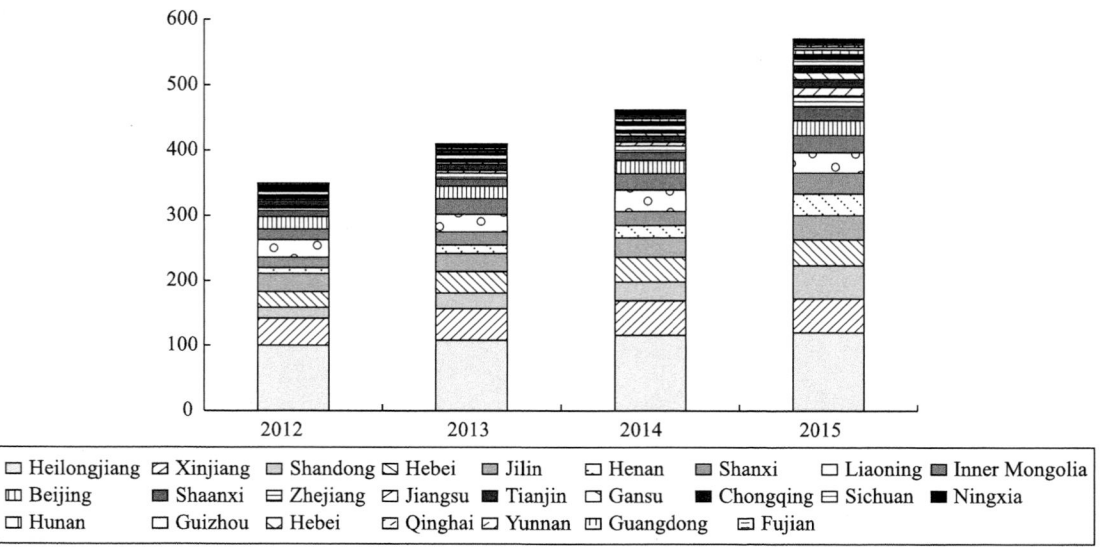

Figure 1-5   Changes in Ski Resort Distribution by Province (B)

In regards to the 7 regions, compared to 2014, the area with the greatest growth in ski resorts in 2015 was East China with 36 new resorts. It was followed by the North China region, with 20 new resorts. The standings were the same if we compare 2015 to 2012: East China was first, with 58 additional resorts, and the second was North China totaling 49 new resorts (shown in Figure 1-6).

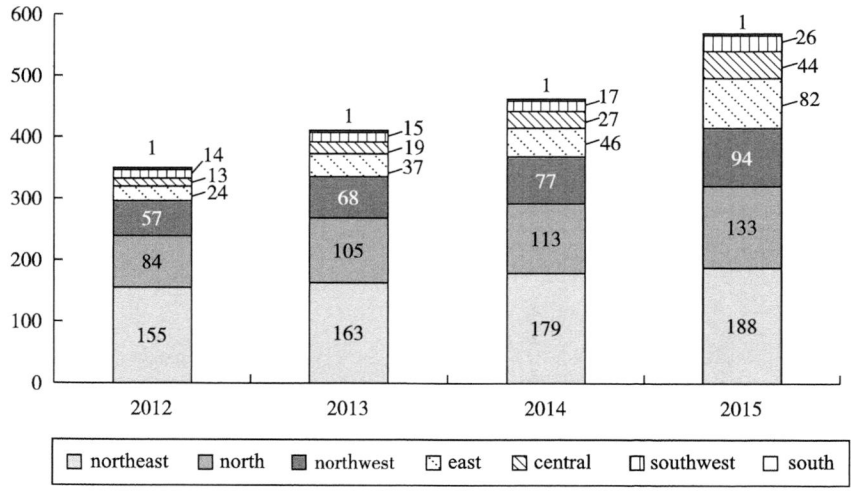

Figure 1-6   Changes in Ski Resort Distribution by Area

II. Classification Statistics

To more clearly show the status of the domestic ski situation, there are four factors to be considered: target audience, vertical drop, slope area, and the number of ski visits. Using these criteria, the statistics areas follows:

1. Classification by Target Group

Ski resorts can differ by the different types of customer they attract. Generally, it can be divided into three categories: travel/experience, educational, and destination resort. Detailed characteristics were shown in Table 1-1. The three categories broke down as follows: 75%, 22% and 3% respectively (shown schematically in Table 1-1).

Table 1-1 Classification of Ski Resorts (2015)

Type of Ski Resort	Per.	Target Group	Attributes	Resort Feature	Consumer Characteristics	Cases
Travel/experience ski resorts	75%	Sightseeing/experience guests	Tourist	Poor facilitate, only intermediate trails. Near scenic or cities	More than 90% one-time experience; residence time 2 hours	Snow World, Bird's Nest
Educational ski resorts	22%	Local/regional guests	Sportive, tourist	Little vertical drop, in suburban areas, all kinds of trails	Mainly road trip; residence time 3~4 hours	Nan shan Mountain, Jundu Mountain, Guaipo
Destination ski resorts	3%	Destination guests	Resort, sportive, tourist	Considerable scale trails, well accommodations and auxiliary facilities	Overnight visitors; residence time more than 1 day	Vanke Songhua Lake, Wanda Changbai Mountain, Beidahu, Yabuli, Wanlong, Genting

2. Classification by Vertical Drop

The total vertical drop of a ski resort is another available indicator for its resources scale. According to the development of vertical drop ski slopes, we can sort ski resorts in the following three categories: resorts with vertical drops of more than 300 meters, 19 resorts (see Table

1-2), resorts with drops between 100 and 300 meters, 103 resorts, and resorts with drops of less than 100 meters, 446 resorts. See Figure 1-7.

Table 1-2 List of Ski Resorts with Vertical Drop more tham 300 m (2015)

No.	Resorts	Vertical Drop/m	Top/m	Bottom/m	Province
1	Tianchi Snow	950	2600	1650	Jilin
2	Yabuli (High Mountain)	885	1360	475	Heilongjiang
3	Beidahu	870	1404	534	Jilin
4	Shangri-La	662	3980	3318	Yunnan
5	Vanke Songhua Lake	600	935	335	Jilin
6	Wanlong	580.3	2110.3	1530	Hebei
7	Xinjiang Silk Road	580	2440	1860	Xinjiang
8	Yabuli Sunlight	540	995	455	Heilongjiang
9	Thaiwoo	510	2062	1552	Hebei
10	Meilin Valley	480	1660	1180	Inner Mongolia
11	Genting	420	2100	1680	Hebei
12	Altay Jiangjun Mountain	405	1320	915	Xinjiang
13	Funiu Mountain	400	1931	1565	Henan
14	Tianqiaogou	392	878	486	Liaoning
15	Wanda Changbai Mountain	380	1200	820	Jilin
16	Duolemeidi	323	1963	1640	Hebei
17	Shijinglong	310	836	526	Beijing
18	Maoer Mountain	308	626	318	Heilongjiang
19	Changchengling	300	2060	1760	Hebei

As the above table shows, out of the 19 ski resorts with vertical dropped of greater than 300 meters, there are 5 in Hebei (all settled in Chongli County), 4 located in Jilin, 3 located in Heilongjiang, 2 in Xinjiang and 1 each in Inner Mongolia, Liaoning, Hebei, Yunnan and Beijing. It should be noted that the ski resort developing in Tianchi was the leader in vertical drops, but the facility depended on grooming machines and snowmobiles. Shijinglong resort (Yanqing, Beijing) got the largest vertical drop in Beijing with 310 meters.

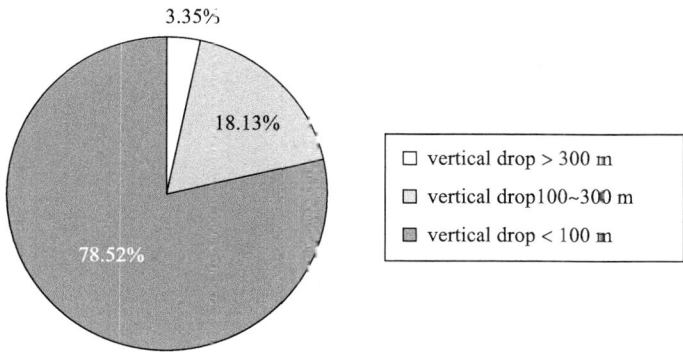

Figure 1-7   Classification of Ski Resorts by Vertical Drop(2015)

3. Classification by Slope Area

Ski area is another important dimension in measure the size of the ski resort. As of 2015, an interesting phenomenon was that "Three Wan" (in Chinese, indicating Vanke Songhua Lake, Wanda Changbai Mountain and Wanlong) was among the top three area ski resort in the country. Among them, the Vanke Songhua Lake was the only one ski resort which area exceeded 100 hectares, Wanda Changbai Mountain and Wanlong resorts' slopes were 96 and 97 hectares. See the statistics in Table 1 - 3. (Note: If you include Yabuli's three mountains in the slope area calculation, its area totaled to more than 100 hectares as well.)

Table 1-3   Number of Ski Resorts by Area of Slopes(2015)

Area of Slopes/hm²	Number of Ski Resorts
>100	1
50~100	7
30~50	5
10~30	20
5~10	50
<5	485
Total	568

4. Classification by Skier Visits

According to preliminary estimates, there were 12 domestic resorts which had reached or passed the 150 thousand visit milestone. From those 12, Wanda Changbai Mountain, Vanke Songhua Lake, Wanlong and Nanshan Mountain were 4 resorts whose visits had passed 200 thousand. And Wanda Changbai Mountain Ski Resort was projected to be the first resort in China to pass the 300 thousand milestone. During the last 3 seasons, there were 69 resorts that had more than 50 thousand but less than 150 thousand visits. And additionally there were 487 resorts with less than 50 thousand visits. Over half the resorts had less than 20 thousand visits (see Figure 1-8).

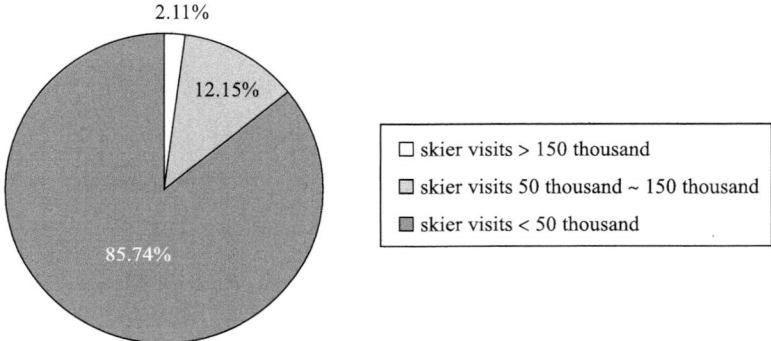

Figure 1-8 Number of Ski Resorts by Skier Visits (2015)

III. Facilities Statistics

1. Lift Facilities

Alpine skiing is inseparable from vertical lift. 20 years ago, the Chongli Saibei relied on Jeeps for transport due to a lack of lifts. Since then, domestic technologies has expanded to include towing, magic carpet, fixed grip aerial ropeway-cable, high-speed detachable towing aerial ropeway, the snowmobile and snow cat skiing (Tianchi Snow), and heli-skiing. With the development of the ski market, major changes in lift technology included:

· The increased demand for magic carpets in resorts. Originally used in beginner areas, domestically built magic carpets had exceeded 400 meters. Due to insufficient power and shrunken demand, magic carpets had become a tool used primarily for instruction purposes.

· High – speed detachable lifts were built mainly in resorts with over 300 meter vertical drop. All the new destination ski resorts which were built since 2012 had given up the fixed-grip lift.

According to the survey from all kinds of statistical data, as of 2015, there were total 198 aerial ropeways currently in service (including 10% missed estimate), which distributed in 122 ski resorts. And 367 vertical lift, 618 magic carpets.

(1) Aerial Lifts

Heilongjiang, Liaoning, Hebei, Beijing and Jilin were the country's top 5 in terms of numbers of aerial lifts. See Table 1-4.

Table 1-4　Distribution of Aerial Lifts in Ski Resorts (2015)

No.	Province	Number of Aerial Lifts	Number of Ski Resorts with Aerial Lift
1	Heilongjiang	38	22
2	Liaoning	29	22
3	Hebei	25	9
4	Beijing	24	12
5	Jilin	22	7
6	Xinjiang	10	7
7	Inner Mongolia	6	5
8	Sichuan	4	2
9	Henan	3	2
10	Hubei	3	2
11	Shandong	3	3
12	Yunnan	3	1
13	Shanxi	3	3
14	Chongqing	2	2
15	Tianjin	1	1
16	Guizhou	1	1
17	Shaanxi	1	1

Continued

No.	Province	Number of Aerial Lifts	Number of Ski Resorts with Aerial Lift
18	Gansu	1	1
	Missed Estimate (10%)	19	19
	Total	198	122

As of 2015, there were 26 detachable lifts in service. Jilin had 13, Hebei owned 9, and Heilongjiang had 4. Resorts distribution was shown in Table 1-5.

Table 1-5 Detachable Lifts in Ski Resorts (2015)

Ski Resort	Number of Detachable Ski Lifts
Vanke Songhua Lake	6
Wanda Changbai Mountain	5
Genting	3
Thaiwoo	3
Yabuli Sunlight	2
Beidahu	2
Wanlong	2
Duolemeidi	1
Maoer Mountain	1
Yabuli (High Mountain)	1
Total	26

According to statistics, there were 153 fixed-grip domestic lifts currently in operation (excluding 10% omissions). Nationally, total cable length amounted to 116938 meters, and the average length of each cableway was 764.30 meters. According to the calculations by industry professionals, estimated that currently, 30 new lifts were being added annually.

(2) Magic Carpets

According to the official website of the Electrical and Mechanical Road Wal and combining with the interviews of industry stakeholders, the total number of the magic carpets delivered since 2007 was 618, the cumulative length being 92062 meters and the average length of each magic carpet being 149 meters. In 2015, there were 164 new magic carpets added, with total length being

Part 1 2015 Report on Key Data of Ski Industry in China

over 20 thousand meters. Detailed data was shown in Table 1-6 and Figure 1-9. (Note: Before 2007, investment in magic carpets was negligible, and those data thus had been omitted.)

Table 1-6 New Magic Carpets Developed in Ski Resorts(2015)

Year	Number of New Magic Carpets	Length of New Added Magic Carpets/m	Average Length per Magic Carpet/m
2007	37	5131.58	139.29
2008	56	6292.59	113.27
2009	51	9030.23	176.50
2010	30	5381.82	177.60
2011	48	7547.54	158.76
2012	57	8666.67	153.33
2013	59	10285.51	173.10
2014	117	17941.00	153.15
2015	164	21785.07	133.02
Total	618	92062.01	148.91

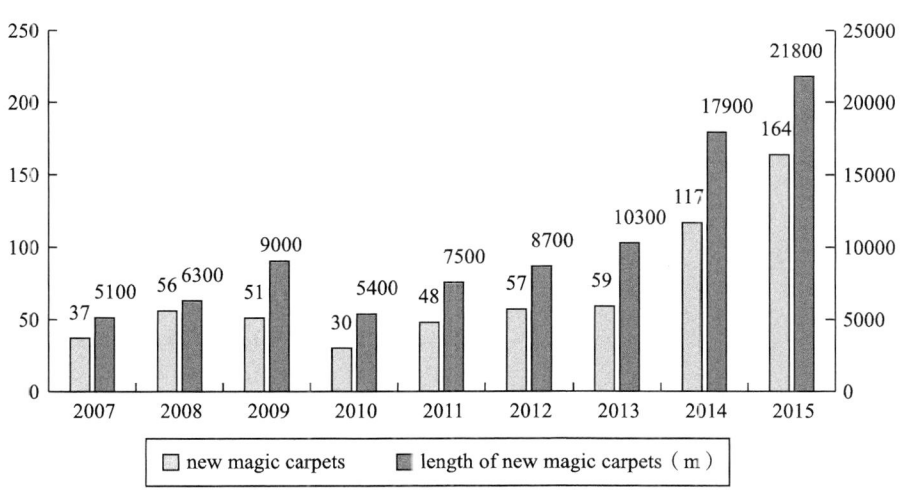

Figure 1-9 New Magic Carpets in Ski Resorts

Of the seven districts, North China occupied an absolute advantage in terms of magic carpet development in ski resorts, accounting for 36.98% of the national total, followed by the Northeast, accounting for 21.89%. See Figure 1-10.

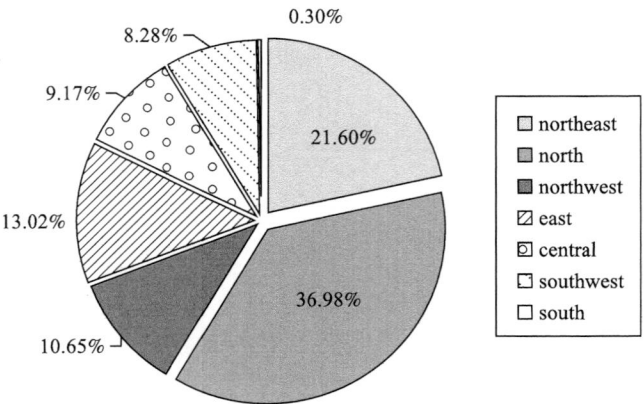

Figure 1-10　Distribution of Magic Carpets(2015)

2. Snowmaking & Grooming Facilities

According to statistical data, preliminary estimates of total domestic ski slopes' overall area was about 3080 hectares, 99% of which was man-made.

(1) Snowmaking System

According to the data which was provided by domestic industry leader Shuohuaji Co., Ltd., we can generally understand the basic applications of the snowmaking system in part of the resort. See Table 1-7.

Table 1-7　Snowmaking System Statistics

No.	Ski Resort	Area/hm²	Length/km	Year to Build
1	Vanke Songhua Lake	152	31	2014
2	Wanda Changbai Mountain	100	34	2010
3	Wanlong(1~5)	100	35	2004-2014
4	Genting	80	30	2010
5	Thaiwoo	72	26	2014
6	Yabuli Sunlight	55	16	2008
7	Beidahu	50	37	2005,2009
8	Xinjiang Silk Road	50	8	2009,2010

Continued

No.	Ski Resort	Area/hm²	Length/km	Year to Build
9	Fengguang Mountain	22	5.8	2008-2009
10	Fenghuang Mountain	20	5.8	2010
11	Tiaoqiaogou	20	6	2012
12	Changchengling(1~2)	16	5	2006,2013
13	Jilin Lianhua Mountain	14	6	2003
14	Shangri-La	12	5.5	2007
15	Qipan Mountain	10	3	2009
16	Daming Mountain	10	2	2010
17	Yulongwan	8.5	4.5	2012
18	Xiling Snow Mountain	8	8	2009
19	National Stadium(Bird's Nest)	5.7	0.8	2009
20	Beijing Olympic Park	2	/	2013
21	Beijing Hot Spring Leisure City	0.6	0.5	2009
	Total	850.8	270	

(2) Snowmaking Machines

According to estimates by major snow machine manufacturers, domestic snowmaking machines were around 4000 units with 3500 imported and 500 domestically manufactured. There was an increase of around 700 units in 2015.

(3) Grooming Machines

There were an estimated 330 grooming machines in China, 300 of which were imported and 30 of which were domestically built, accounting for 10%. Information provided by Italian company Prinoth, regarding the annual increase in grooming machines can be seen in Figure 1-11.

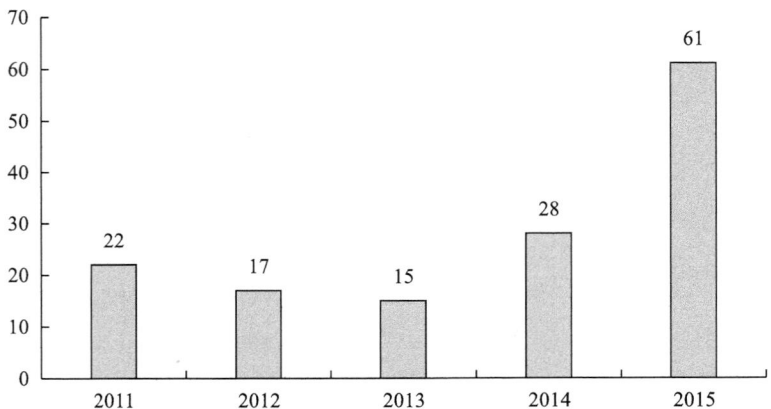

Figure 1-11 Annual Increase in New Grooming Machines

3. Rental Equipments

Using the information from major equipment providers, there was an estimated increase of 100 thousand sets of rental skis added to the market per year. In 2015, the total amount of new rental skis totaled 122700, a growth of 24.65% compared to the 2014 season. See Table 1-8 and Figure 1-12.

Table 1-8 Annual Increase in Rental Skis

Type	2014	2015	Growth Rate/%
Imported Rental Skis	30936	43200	39.64
Domestic Rental Skis	56000	63000	12.50
Second-Handed Rental Skis	11500	16500	43.48
Total	98436	122700	24.65

In 2015, the percentages of both new imported rentals and second-handed rentals were increased, while the percentage of domestic rentals was fell. See Figure 1-13.

Part 1 20-5 Report on Key Data of Ski Industry in China

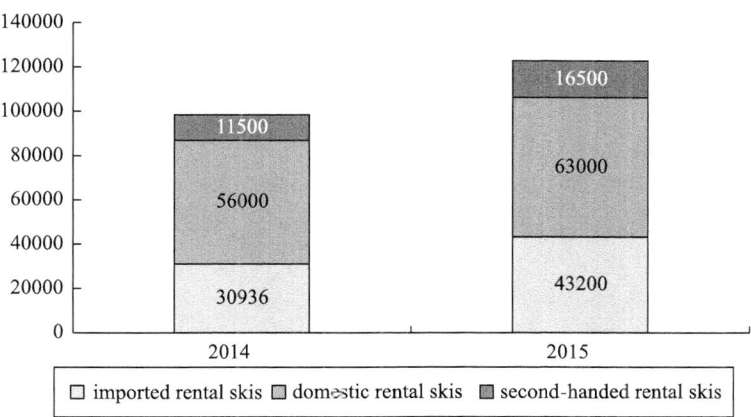

Figure 1-12 Annual Increase in Rental Skis

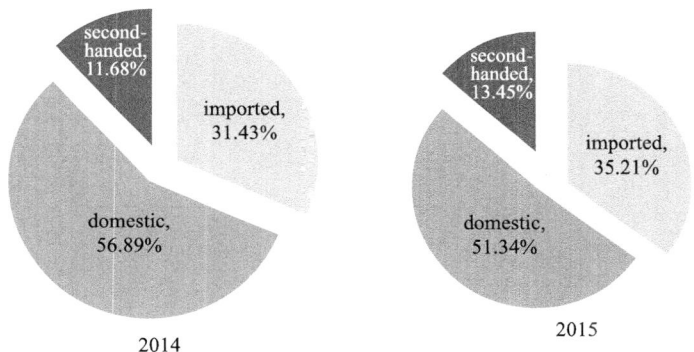

Figure 1-13 Comparison Diagram of Annual Increase in New Rental Skis

Because the demand for rental snowboards differ by resorts, there was a lack of conclusive data. Based on market trends, there was an estimated increase of 4000 rental boards per year. Similarly, the annual addition of ski suits was estimated to be around 30 thousand units.

IV. Human Resources Statistics

To facilitate the understanding of the human resources of domestic ski resorts, the Human Resources Research Group of this report chose the following main domestic resorts as samples to conduct research studies (hereinafter referred to assample resorts).

Table 1-9 List of Sample Resorts

Province	No.	Resort
Heilongjiang	1	Yabuli (High Mountain)
	2	Yabuli Sunlight
	3	Maoer Mountain
Jilin	4	Beidahu
	5	Wanda Changbai Mountain
	6	Vanke Songhua Lake
Liaoning	7	Northeast Asia
	8	Guaipo
Hebei	9	Wanlong
	10	Genting
	11	Changchengling
	12	Duolemeidi
	13	Thaiwoo
Beijing	14	Nanshan Mountain
	15	Jundu Mountain
Henan	16	Funiu Mountain
Shanxi	17	Meiyuannan Mountain
	18	Caiwei Manor
Sichuan	19	Xiling Snow Mountain
	20	Taiziling
Hubei	21	Shennongjia
Zhejiang	22	Daming Mountain
Chongqing	23	Jinfo Mountain
Shaanxi	24	Zhaojin
Gansu	25	Songmingyan
	26	Xinglong Mountain
Xinjiang	27	Silk Road
	28	Tianshan Mountain

According to the feedback of 28 samples resorts (seen on Table 1-10), senior managers of the resorts averaged 3.75 people, middle managers 7.68 people. The average number of coaches per resort was 27.36 people. There were 28 ski resorts with 110 employees who had been employed for 20 years or more, which on average, each resort owned less than 4.

Table 1-10 Core Employees of Sample Resorts (2015)

Type		>20 Years	10~20 Years	5~10 Years	Total	Average
Manager	Senior	14	58	33	105	3.75
	Middle	20	90	105	215	7.68
Technical Staff	Slope	16	44	59	119	4.25
	Lift	16	44	59	119	4.25
	Snowmaking	16	78	87	181	6.46
	Machine	5	24	52	81	2.89
	Stadium	2	11	37	50	1.79
	Ski Instructor	20	145	601	766	27.36
	Marketing	1	18	56	75	2.68
	IT	0	6	37	43	1.54
Total		110	518	1126	1754	62.64

Statistics showed that senior managers accounted for 6.0% of employees, middle managers accounted for 12.3%, and technical instructors and coaches accounted for 43.7% of employees in domestic resorts.

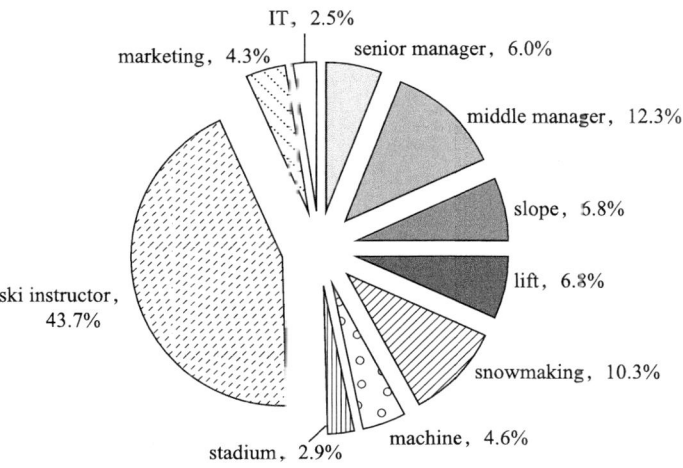

Figure 1-14 Core HR Distribution in Domestic Ski Resorts (2015)

V. Four Seasons Ski Resorts

1. Indoor Ski Resorts

As of 2015, there were 9 indoor ski resorts in operation. Three Bears in Changsha and Four Seasons Evergreen in Shijiazhuang were new indoor ski events in 2015. Furthermore, according to various types of public information, domestic projects and proposed projects are as follows:

· Wanda Series: Harbin, Guangzhou, Wuxi, Chengdu (building areas are 80000 m^2, 75000 m^2, 17500 m^2, 75000 m^2 respectively).

· Qiaobo Series: Nanjing, Guangdong (planning 10 resorts).

· AST Aoyue Series: Qiqihar, Zhuzhou Yunlong (planning 10 resorts).

· Zhonghong: Yumafang Fancy Resort.

· Wenzhou: Swan Castle.

· Chongqing: Xiannv Mountain (17000 m^2), Tianlai Valley (5700 m^2).

· Hunan: Changsha Dawang Mountain, Yueyang Dongdan.

· Shanghai, Wuhan, Handan, etc.

Table 1-11 Indoor Ski Resorts Operating in China

Name	Location	Open Year	Area/hm^2	Slopes	Longest Slope/m	Drag-Lift	Magic Carpet
Qiaobo Beijing	Shunyi, Beijing	2005	2	2	275	2	2
Qiaobo Shaoxing	Shaoxing, Zhejiang	2009	2	2	275	1	2
Alps Shenzhen	Shenzhen, Guangdong	2003	0.43	1	100	0	1
Funiu Mountain	Luoyang, Henan	2009	0.8	1	200	0	1
Ruixiang	Liyang, Hunan	2011	1.2	2	180	0	2
Dayong Mountain	Manchuri, Inner Mongolia	2005	1.2	1	200	0	1
Guanxiang	Fushun, Liaoning	2014	0.8	1	50	0	1
Three Bears	Changsha, Hunan	2015	1.26	1	170	0	2
Four Seasons Evergreen	Shijiazhuang, Hebei	2015	1.1	1	150	0	1

2. Dry Ski & Indoor Ski Training Bases

Information provided by Chengdu Peak Dry Snow chairman, demonstrating global dry snow distribution was shown in Figure 1-15. China ranked second in the world in terms of dry ski resorts.

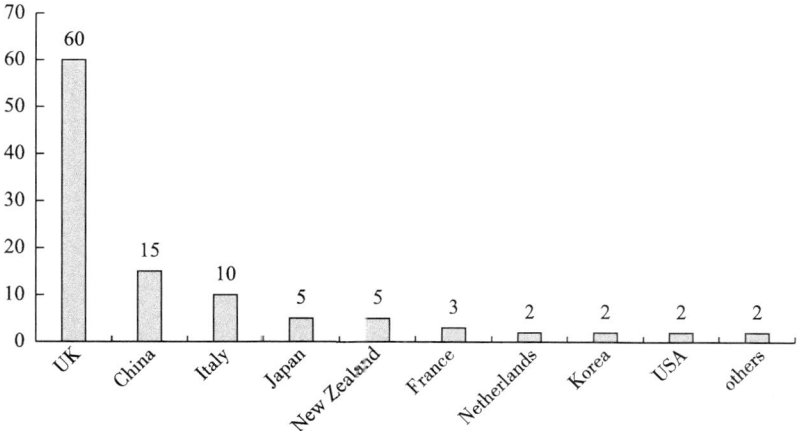

Figure 1-15 World Dry Ski Map(2015)

The distribution of established and proposed dry slopes in domestic was showed in Figure 1-16.

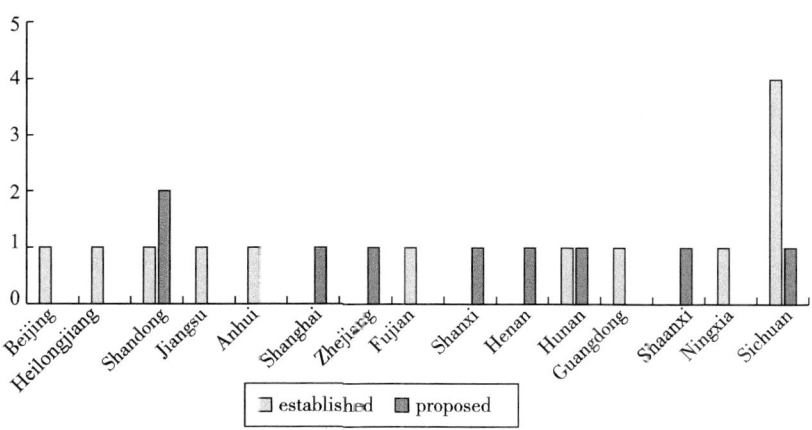

Figure 1-16 China Dry Slope Map(2015)

Except dry slopes, indoor ski training bases in Beijing and Shanghai had been built, including SKINOW and Sikaitaisi in Beijing, Zero Ski in Shanghai.

Chapter 2   2015 Skier

Ⅰ. Visits & Distribution

Analysis estimated 12. 5 million domestic visits in the 2014 – 2015 snow season, with indoor ski visitors data included in the 2014 annual data. Compared to the 2013 – 2014 snow season, total visits grew 21. 36%, and compared to 2009 – 2010 snow season total visits grew 98. 41%.

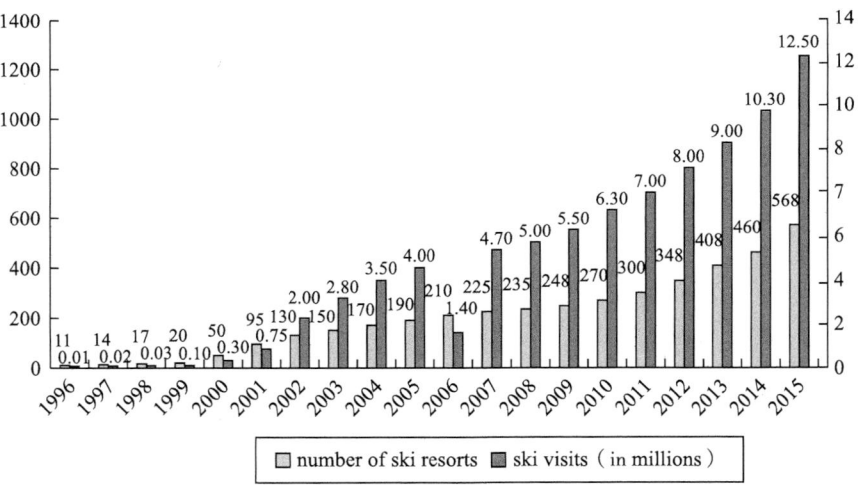

Figure 2-1   Comparison Diagram of Ski Resorts & Skier Visits in Domestic

According to the data provided by typical ski resorts in each region, Table 2-1 shows the distribution of total visits. During the 2014 – 2015 snow season, Beijing ski resort totaled 1. 69 million visits, the highest one in the country, followed by Heilongjiang, with 1. 49 million visits; they were followed by Jilin, having 0.96 million. Shandong and Hebei tied for fourth with 0.85 million visits each.

Table 2-1 Distribution of Skier Visits by Destination (2015)

No.	Province	Number of Resorts	Skier Visits (in Millions)
1	Beijing	23	16.90
2	Heilongjiang	120	14.90
3	Jilin	37	9.60
4	Shandong	51	8.50
5	Hebei	40	8.50
6	Xinjiang	52	7.70
7	Shanxi	32	7.20
8	Zhejiang	17	7.00
9	Liaoning	31	6.50
10	Inner Mongolia	26	5.90
11	Henan	33	5.80
12	Sichuan	10	4.20
13	Shaanxi	21	4.10
14	Tianjin	12	4.00
15	Jiangsu	13	2.90
16	Gansu	11	2.70
17	Hunan	7	2.50
18	Chongqing	10	2.10
19	Hubei	4	1.50
20	Ningxia	7	0.80
21	Guizhou	4	0.50
22	Qinghai	3	0.40
23	Yunnan	2	0.30
24	Fujian	1	0.20
25	Guangdong	1	0.20
Total		568	12.50

In terms of the seven districts, North China had the largest proportion of 34.01% of all domestic visits; followed by the northeast, it was accounting for 24.83%.

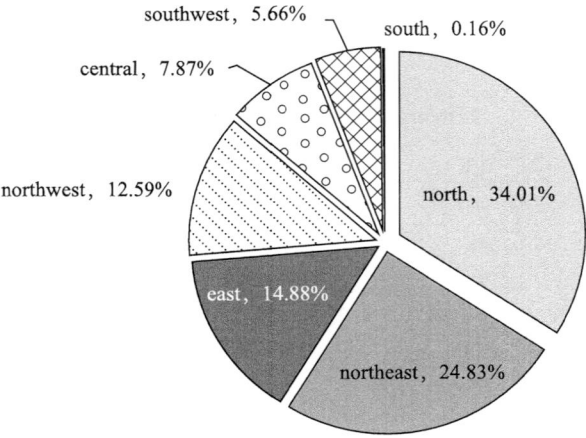

Figure 2-2 Distribution of Skier Visits by Region(2014-2015 Snow Season)

II. Characteristics

Demographic information is vital to understanding the current market, unfortunately there were not yet tools for reliable data collection on this subject. This report attempted to utilize ski groups existing on the country's high activity Tencent QQ platform to create sample group of skiers and tourists in order to conduct a preliminary analysis. While there has been no strong correlation proven among these groups studied. Table 2-2 showing the demographics of an average QQ ski group, male to female ratio was 63.88 : 36.12, and 45.36% were born after 1980, single persons accounted for 23.91%.

Table 2-2 Skier Characteristics on Social Media(2015)

District	Number of Samples	Male	Male/%	Born after 1980	Born after 1980/%	Single	Single/%
North	23540	14658	62.27	11092	47.12	5719	24.29
Northeast	22703	15711	69.20	9636	42.44	5676	25.00
East	6966	3975	57.06	3294	47.29	1754	25.18
Central	5563	3270	58.78	2478	44.54	636	11.43
Northwest	4643	2974	64.05	2133	45.94	1340	28.86

Part 1　2015 Report on Key Data of Ski Industry in China

Continued

District	Number of Samples	Male	Male/%	Born after 1980	Born after 1980/%	Single	Single/%
Southwest	1890	1185	62.70	989	52.33	482	25.50
South	410	208	50.72	189	46.10	104	25.37
Total	65715	41981	63.88	29811	45.36	15711	23.91

As seen in Figure 2-3, there was a correlation between QQ activity and interests in skiing (by district). The more skiing there was in a district, the higher amount of activity there was on social media regarding skiing in that region.

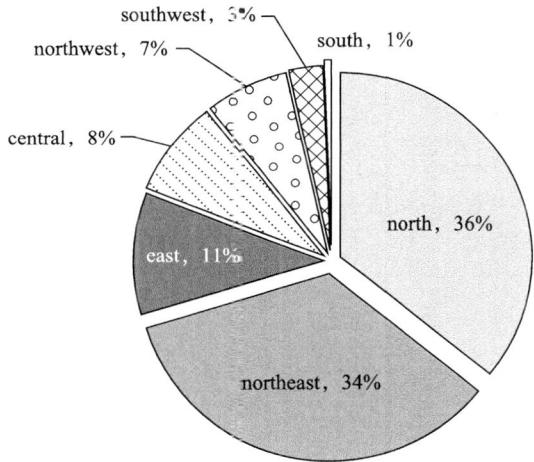

Figure 2-3　Distribution of Skiers on Sample Social Media (2015)

III. Ski Equipment Market

This report had collected the feedback information from the Chinese representatives from 9 different international companies. In 2014, the 9 brands combined had total retail sales of 10346 sets of skis. 2015 is projected to accomplish the sales of 13280, a growth rate of 28.36%. Taking into account other factors, annual retail ski sales is estimated to be about 20 thousand yearly.

An obvious trend was the difference in growth between the snowboard and the ski industries. According to information provided by 3 suppliers, snowboard amounted to 6063 in 2014. But 2015, snowboard sales are expected to be 8900, a growth rate of 46.79%. After estimating the same fashion, the annual retail sales of the board should be around 30 thousand, beating ski sale projections by 50%.

Chapter 3   Ski Competiton Development

I. The History of Ski Racing in Modern China

In 1957, China's First National Skiing Competition was held in Tonghua, Jilin. This event marked China's first steps to embracing the sport of skiing.

In 1959, Jilin held the First National Winter Games. In the early 1980s, Chinese ski industry modernized considerably.

In 1981, China formally joined the International Ski Federation (FIS), and became a full member. The establishment of the Chinese Ski Association (CSA) soon was followed.

Present, Heilongjiang, Jilin, Liaoning, Inner Mongolia, Xinjiang and other provinces have established facilities to carry out cross-country skiing, ski jumping, alpine skiing, freestyle skiing, snowboarding and other athletic types of skiing (shown in Table 3-1).

Table 3-1   Registered Teams and Athletes of Ski Events

Events		Registered Teams	Registered Athletes
Cross-Country Skiing		16	306
Ski Jumping		2	30
Alpine Skiing		10	94
Freestyle Skiing	Aerials	5	51
	Halfpipe	6	37
	Moguls	4	28

Continued

Events		Registered Teams	Registered Athletes
Snowboard	Parallel	9	81
	Halfpipe	9	56
Total		61	683

II. China's Participation in Previous Winter Olympic Games

China heavily involved in Winter Olympic and Asian Winter Games (shown in Table 3-2). The first Olympic medal was won at the 1998 Winter Olympic for Freestyle Skiing, Women's Aerials. The first gold medal for skiing was won at the 2006 Winter Olympic for Freestyle Skiing, Men's Aerials.

In 1980, Chinese delegation attended the 13th Winter Olympic for the first time. And until the Sochi Winter Olympic in 2014, China has continuously participated in 10 Winter Olympic games.

Table 3-2 Chinese Team in Skiing Events of Winter Olympic Games

Discipline	Event	1980 13th Lake Placid USA	1984 14th Sarajevo JUG	1988 15th Calgary CAN	1992 16th Albertville FRA	1994 17th Lillehammer NOR	1998 18th Nagano JAP	2002 19th Salt Lake City USA	2006 20th Torino ITA	2010 21st Vancouver CAN	2014 22nd Sochi RUS
Cross-Country Skiing	Men's Sprint						√	√	√	√	√
	Men's 10 km				√		√	√			
	Men's Individual	√	√	√				√	√	√	√
	Men's Skiathlon		√	√	√						
	Men's Mass Start				√				√		√
	Men's Relay		√				√	√	√		

Part 1 2015 Report on Key Data of Ski Industry in China

Continued

Discipline	Event	1980 13th Lake Placid USA	1984 14th Sarajevo JUG	1988 15th Calgary CAN	1992 16th Albertville FRA	1994 17th Lillehammer NOR	1998 18th Nagano JAP	2002 19th Salt Lake City USA	2006 20th Torino ITA	2010 21st Vancouver CAN	2014 22nd Sochi RUS
Cross-Country Skiing	Men's Pursuit				√				√		√
	Men's Team Sprint								√	√	√
	Women's Sprint								√	√	√
	Women's 5 km	√	√	√	√		√	√			
	Women's Individual	√	√	√			√	√	√	√	√
	Women's Skiathlon				√						
	Women's 20 km			√							
	Women's Mass Start				√				√		√
	Women's Relay		√				√	√	√		
	Women's Pursuit				√				√	√	√
	Women's Team Sprint							√	√	√	√
Alpine Skiing	Men's Giant Slalom	√	√						√	√	√
	Women's Giant Slalom	√	√		√				√	√	√
	Men's Slalom	√	√						√	√	√

Report on Key Data of *Ski* Industry in China(2015-2019)

Continued

Discipline	Event	1980 13th Lake Placid USA	1984 14th Sara-jevo JUG	1988 15th Calg-ary CAN	1992 16th Alber-tville FRA	1994 17th Lilleh-ammer NOR	1998 18th Nag-ano JAP	2002 19th Salt Lake City USA	2006 20th Torino ITA	2010 21st Vanc-ouver CAN	2014 22nd Sochi RUS
Alpine Skiing	Women's Slalom	√	√		√				√	√	√
	Women's Super-G				√						
Freestyle Skiing	Men's Aerials								√	√	√
	Women's Aerials					√		√	√	√	√
	Women's Moglus										√
Snowboard	Men's Halfpipe								√	√	√
	Women's Halfpipe							√	√	√	√
Ski Jumping	Men's Normal Hill Individual								√		
	Men's Large Hill Individual								√		
	Men's Team								√		

III. Important Ski Competitions in China

In 1959, the first National Winter Game was held as the highest level of national comprehensive winter games. It is held every four years and has been hosted for 12 sessions.

The major international events hosted by China included:

· Integrated games: in February 1996, Harbin, 3rd Asian Winter Games; in February 2007, Changchun, 7th Asian Winter Games; in February 2009, Harbin, 24th World University Winter Games.

· Individual competition: in March 2006, Changchun, Cross-Country Skiing Sprint World Cup Finals; in February 2007, Changchun, Cross-Country Skiing World Cup; from February 2003 to December 2015, continued hosting the Freestyle Skiing Aerials and Moguls World Cup; in February 2011, Snowboard Halfpipe Technique World Cup; from March 2004 to December 2015, continued hosting the FIS Alpine Skiing Point Race and Far East Cup.

IV. Competitive Ski Resorts in China

Before 1996, Chinese competitive ski resorts were primarily funded by the government, such as the first ski resort built in 1957 in Tonghua, Jilin and two other large scale resorts Yabuli and Beidahu, built in 1986 and 1995 respectively.

Direct government investment in ski resorts and the improvment of transportation, water facilities, electricity, telecommunications, environmental protection and other public infrastructure have greatly promoted the enthusiasm of private enterprises to invest in the skiing industry. After nearly 20 years of development, ski resorts in China are now setting competition, leisure, conference reception and other functions in one. Some larger ski resorts hosted international integrated or individual competitions, including: Yabuli, Beidahu, Wanlong, Genting, Wanda Changbai Mountain, Maoer Mountain, Duolemeidi, Wujimi, Jingyuetan, Xinjiang Silk Road, Altay Jiangjun Mountain, etc.

Part 2

2016 Report on Key Data of Ski Industry in China

Chapter 4　2016 Ski Resort

Ⅰ. Number & Distribution

According to the date from *Chinese Ski Resort Encyclopedia* and the statistical information from Carving research, subtracting the irrelevant information about other types of snow resorts, there were 646 ski resorts in total, including 78 new ski resorts opened in 2016, with an increase of 13.73%.

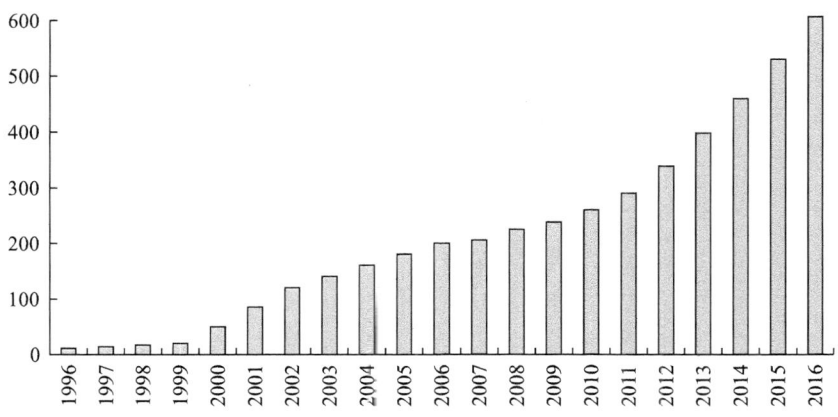

Figure 4-1　Number of Ski Resorts in China

646 ski resorts located in 27 provinces, autonomous regions and municipalities. The number of ski resorts in Heilongjiang was 122, ranking the largest one in China. See Figure 4 - 2, Table 4-1.

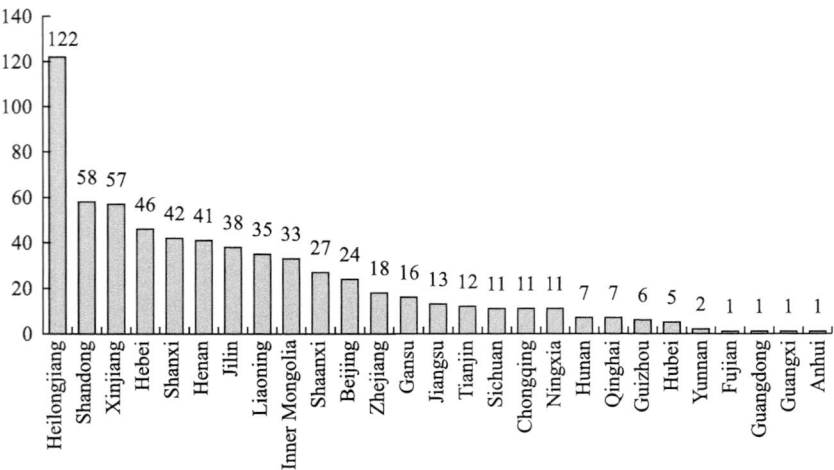

Figure 4-2 Distribution of Ski Resorts by Province(2016)

Table 4-1 Number of Ski Resorts by Province(2016)

No.	Province	Number of Ski Resorts	Number of Ski Resorts Cooperated with GOSKI Weather Forecast
1	Heilongjiang	122	37
2	Shandong	58	26
3	Xinjiang	57	33
4	Hebei	46	25
5	Shanxi	42	22
6	Henan	41	14
7	Jilin	38	26
8	Liaoning	35	26
9	Inner Mongolia	33	15
10	Shaanxi	27	13
11	Beijing	24	24
12	Zhejiang	18	7
13	Gansu	16	9
14	Jiangsu	13	5
15	Tianjin	12	7
16	Sichuan	11	8
17	Chongqing	11	5
18	Ningxia	11	5

Continued

No.	Province	Number of Ski Resorts	Number of Ski Resorts Cooperated with GOSKI Weather Forecast
19	Hunan	7	3
20	Qinghai	7	0
21	Guizhou	6	1
22	Hubei	5	3
23	Yunnan	2	2
24	Fujian	1	1
25	Guangdong	1	1
26	Guangxi	1	0
27	Anhui	1	0
	Total	646	318

Only Hong kong, Macao, Taiwan, Shanghai, Jiangxi, Tibet and Hainan have not established ski resorts yet among 34 provincial administrative regions It was understood that Shanghai, Jiangxi and Tibet have implemented new investment projects on ski resorts.

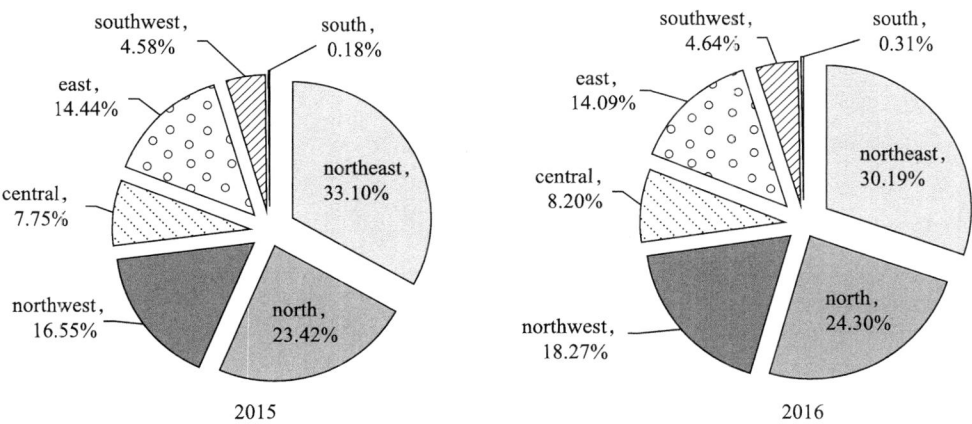

Figure 4-3 Distribution of Ski Resorts by Area

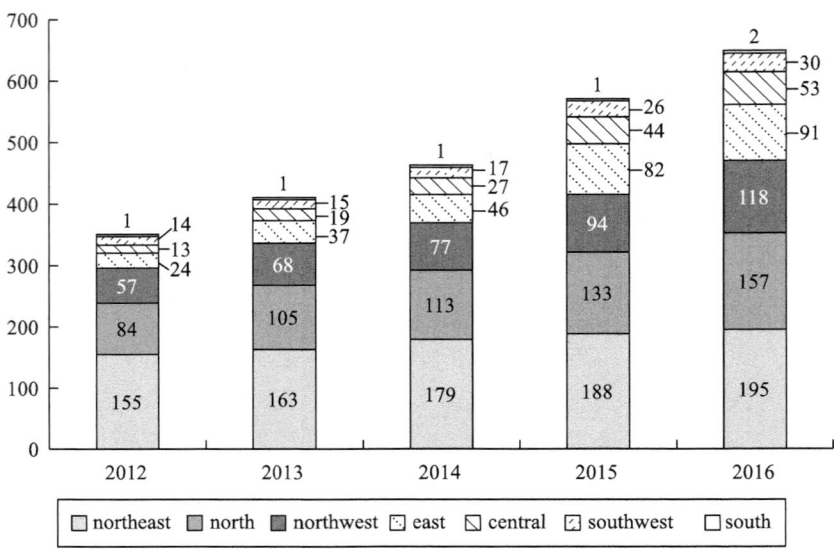

Figure 4-4 Number of Ski Resorts by Area

II. Classification Statistics

1. Classification by Target Group

Ski resorts can be differed by the different types of customer they attract. Generally, it can be divided into three categories: travel/experience, educational, and destination ski resort. Detailed characteristics were shown in Table 4-2. The three categories broke down as follows: 75%, 22% and 3% respectively.

Table 4-2 Classification of Ski Resorts by Target Group (2016)

Type	Per.	Target Group	Attributes	Resort Feature	Consumer Characteristics	Cases
Travel/ experience ski resorts	75%	Sightseeing/ experience guests	Tourist	Poor facilitate, only intermediate trails. Near scenic or cities	More than 90% one-time experience; stay 2 hours	Snow World, Bird's Nest

Part 2 2016 Report on Key Data of Ski Industry in China

Continued

Type	Per.	Target Group	Attributes	Resort Feature	Consumer Characteristics	Cases
Educational ski resorts	22%	Local/regional guests	Sportive, tourist	Little vertical drop, in suburban areas, all kinds of trails	Mainly road trip; stay 3~6 hours	Nanshan Mountain, Jundu Mountain, Vanke Shijinglong
Destination ski resorts	3%	Destination guests	Vacation, sportive, tourist	Considerable scale trails, well accommodations and auxiliary facilities	Overnight visitors; stay more than 1 day	Vanke Songhua Lake, Wanda Changbai Mountain, Beidahu, Yabuli, Wanlong, Genting, Thaiwoo

2. Classification by Vertical Drop

The total vertical drop of a ski resort is an available indicator for its resources scale. According to the development of vertical drop ski slopes, we can sort ski resorts in the following three categories: 19 resorts with vertical drop more than 300 meters, 120 resorts with drop between 100 and 300 meters, and 507 resorts with drop less than 100 meters. See Figure 4-5.

List of resorts with over 300 meters vertical drop was as Table 4-3, the same with 2015.

Table 4-3 List of Ski Resorts with Vertical Drop more than 300 m (2016)

No.	Resorts	Vertical Drop/m	Top/m	Bottom/m	Province
1	Tianchi Snow	950	2600	1650	Jilin
2	Yabuli(High Mountain)	885	1360	475	Heilongjiang
3	Beidahu	870	1404	534	Jilin
4	Shangri-La	662	3980	3318	Yunnan
5	Vanke Songhua Lake	600	935	335	Jilin
6	Wanlong	580.3	2110.3	1530	Hebei
7	Xinjiang Silk Road	580	2440	1860	Xinjiang
8	Yabuli Sunlight	540	995	455	Heilongjiang
9	Thaiwoo	510	2062	1552	Hebei
10	Meilin Valley	480	1660	1180	Inner Mongolia
11	Genting	420	2100	1680	Hebei
12	Altay Jiangjun Mountain	405	1320	915	Xinjiang

No.	Resorts	Vertical Drop/m	Top/m	Bottom/m	Province
13	Funiu Mountain	400	1931	1565	Henan
14	Tianqiaogou	392	878	486	Liaoning
15	Wanda Changbai Mountain	380	1200	820	Jilin
16	Duolemeidi	323	1963	1640	Hebei
17	Shijinglong	310	836	526	Beijing
18	Maoer Mountain	308	626	318	Heilongjiang
19	Changchengling	300	2060	1760	Hebei

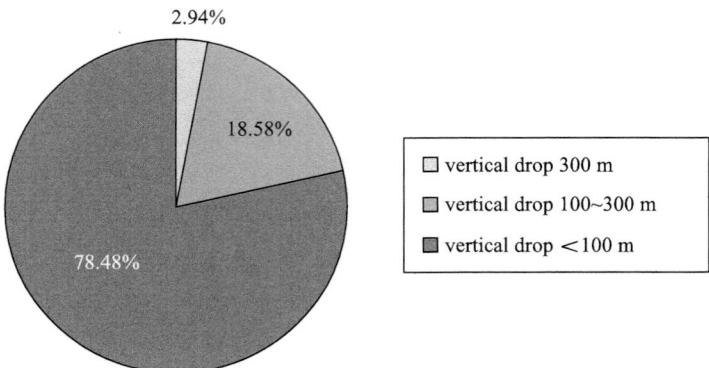

Figure 4-5   Classification of Ski Resorts by Vertical Drop (2016)

As Table 4-3 showed, out of the 19 ski resorts with vertical drop more than 300 meters, there were 5 in Hebei (all settled in Chongli), 4 located in Jilin, 3 located in Heilongjiang, 2 in Xinjiang, and 1 each in Inner Mongolia, Liaoning, Hebei, Yunnan and Beijing. It should be noted that the ski resort developing in Tianchi was the leader in vertical drop, but unfortunately the facility depended on grooming machines and snowmobiles. Shijinglong Ski Resort (Yanqing, Beijing) got the largest vertical drop in Beijing with 310 meters.

3. Classification by Slope Area

Ski area is another important dimension in measuring the size of the ski resort. In 2016, by large expansion, Beidahu and Wanlong, together with Vanke Songhua Lake, became the three biggest ski resorts in China, with area exceeded 100 hectares. See the statistics in Table 4-4.

Table 4-4　Number of Ski Resorts by Slope Area(2016)

Area of Slopes/hm²	Number of Ski Resorts	Ski Resort
>100	3	Vanke Songhua Lake, Beidahu, Wanlong
50~100	5	Yabuli, Wanda Changbai Mountain, Genting, etc.
30~50	7	Nanshan Mountain, Yakeshi, etc.
10~30	26	Vanke Shijinglong, etc.
5~10	87	
<5	518	
Total	646	

III. Facilities Statistics

1. Lift Facilities

(1) Aerial Lifts

As to the number of aerial lifts, Jilin totaled 17, the highest one in China, followed by Hebei with 13, and they were followed by Heilongjiang, having 6. (Note: in this statistics, only the lifts for skiing were considered, not for transport purposes.)

Table 4-5　Distribution of Aerial Lifts in Ski Resorts(2016)

No.	Province	Number of Aerial Lifts	Number of Ski Resorts with Aerial Lift
1	Heilongjiang	44	25
2	Hebei	30	10
3	Liaoning	29	22
4	Beijing	24	12
5	Jilin	26	8
6	Xinjiang	10	7
7	Inner Mongolia	6	5
8	Sichuan	4	2

Continued

No.	Province	Number of Aerial Lifts	Number of Ski Resorts with Aerial Lift
9	Henan	3	2
10	Hubei	3	2
11	Shandong	3	3
12	Yunnan	3	1
13	Shanxi	5	4
14	Chongqing	2	2
15	Tianjin	1	1
16	Guizhou	2	2
17	Shaanxi	1	1
18	Gansu	5	3
	Missed Estimate(10%)	25	25
	Total	226	137

Table 4-6 Rank of Detachable Lifts in Ski Resorts(2016)

Ski Resort	Number of Detachable Ski Lifts	Province
Vanke Songhua Lake	6	Jilin
Wanda Changbai Mountain	5	Jilin
Beidahu	4	Jilin
Wanlong	4	Hebei
Genting	3	Hebei
Thaiwoo	3	Hebei
Yabuli(High Mountain)	3	Heilongjiang
Yabuli Sunlight	2	Heilongjiang
Fulong	2	Hebei
Luneng Changbai Mountain	2	Jilin
Duolemeidi	1	Hebei
Maoer Mountain	1	Heilongjiang
Total	36	

(2) Magic Carpets

According to the official website of the Electrical and Mechanical Road Wal, there were 850 magic carpets in ski resorts in total, including the 232 new magic carpets in 2016. The total length was 128 km.

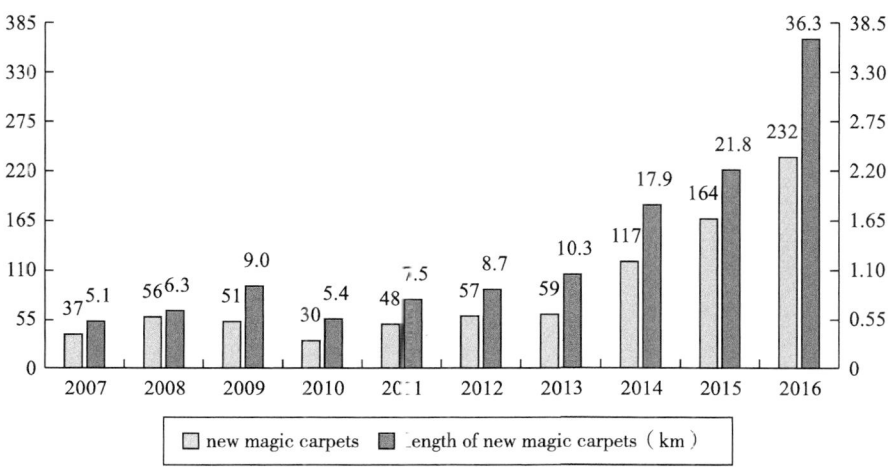

Figure 4-6　New Magic Carpets Developed in Ski Resorts

2. Snowmaking & Grooming Facilities

According to the estimation by major snow grooming machine manufacturers and research center of Carving Group, domestic grooming machines were around 80 units with 65 imported and 15 domestically manufactured.

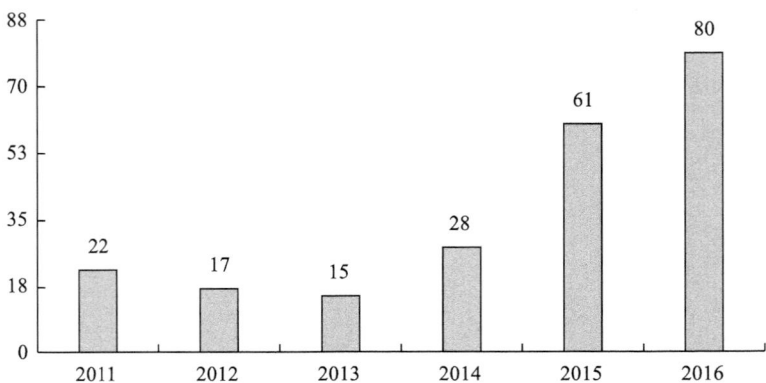

Figure 4-7 New Grooming Machines in Ski Resorts

There were about 5180 snowmaking machines in ski resorts in total, including 1180 new machines in 2016. And 15% of them were domestically manufactured.

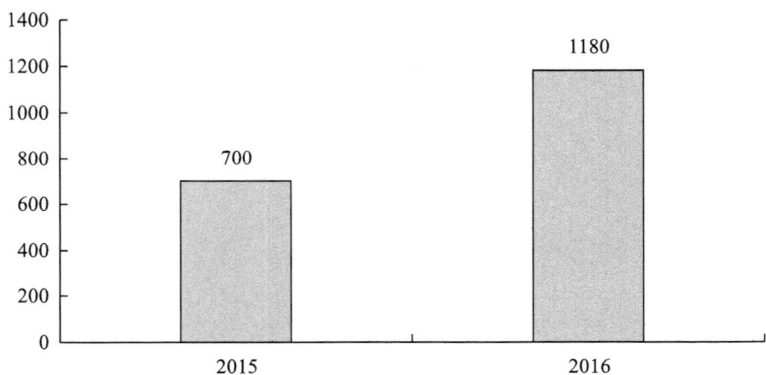

Figure 4-8 New Snowmaking Machines in Ski Resorts

3. Rental Equipments

Using the information from major equipment providers, in 2016, the total amount of new rental skis totaled 485 thousand pairs, a growth of 38.57% compared to 2015. The increase rate of imported board was higher than that of domestic board.

Part 2 2016 Report on Key Data of Ski Industry in China

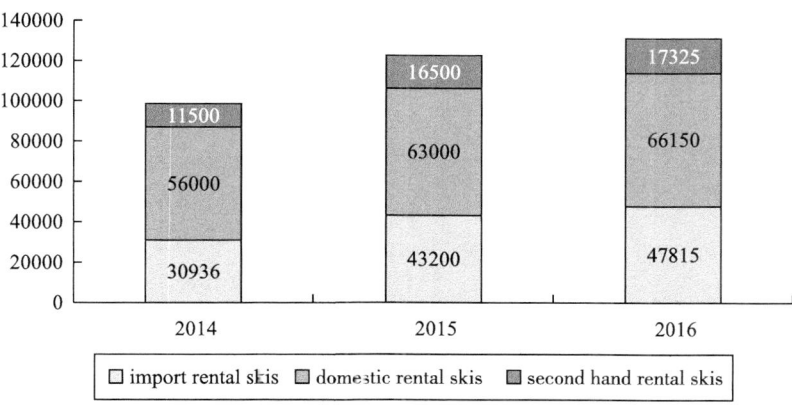

Figure 4-9 Annual Increase in Rental Skis

IV. Human Resources Statistics

According to the surveys provided by 100 ski resorts, the instructors engaged in ski teaching work in China were about 4810, and the average number of coaches per resort was 48. Among them, 63% were male coaches and 37% were female. Based on the teaching experience, the number of coachers with more than 5 years' experience accounted for 56%, and 44% coachers owned less than 5 years' experience. In addition, in terms of education structure, 50% of the ski instructors got high school or technical secondary education, 15% gained a junior college degree or above, and 35% had a below junior high school degree.

Table 4-7 Statistics of Ski Instructors (2016)

Indicator	Number	Percentage/%
Number of Sample Ski Resorts	100	/
Number of Ski Instructors	4810	/
Average Number of Ski Instructors per Ski Resort	48	/
Over 5 Years' Experience	2681	55.74
Below 5 Years' Experience	2129	44.26
Male	3042	63.24
Female	1768	36.76

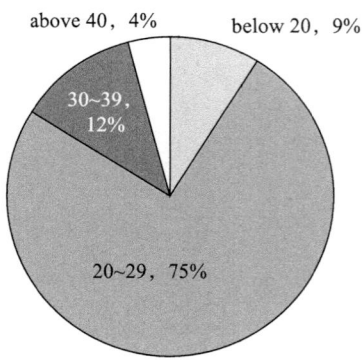

Figure 4-10　Statistics of Ski Instructors by Age (2016)

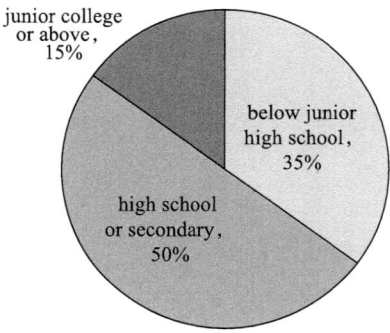

Figure 4-11　Statistics of Ski Instructors by Education Background (2016)

V. Four Seasons Ski Resorts

1. Indoor Ski Resorts

In recent two years, with the increasing number of indoor ski resorts, China has occupied the first place of indoor ski resorts. Wanda Harbin indoor ski resort will be open in June, 2017, which scale is much larger than Dubai's indoor ski resort. By then, the indoor ski resorts in China will be the first in the world in terms of number and scale. There is no doubt that with the development of the indoor ski resort, the overall market pattern will be changed and a steady stream of passengers will be provided.

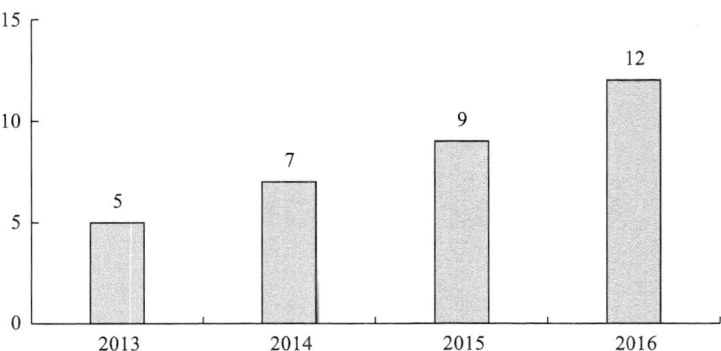

Figure 4-12　Indoor Ski Resorts Operating in China

2. Dry Ski

As an alternative of ski resorts, dry ski has developed rapidly in China in recent years. Based on the information provided by Peak Dry Snow, the main supplier of dry snow in China, the Peak dry ski resorts were totally 18 at the end of 2016 and another 5 were under construction.

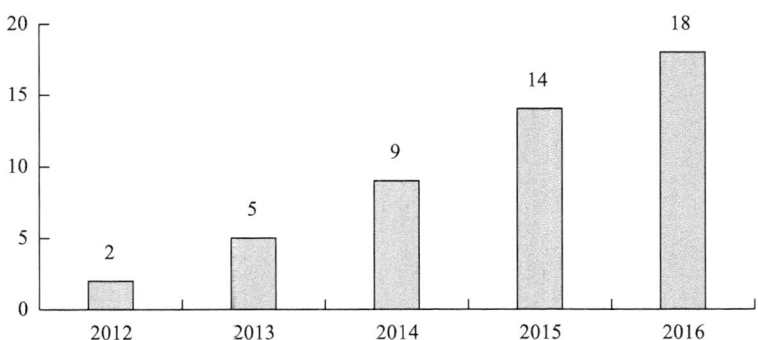

Figure 4-13　Number of Peak Dry Ski Resorts in Operation

3. Indoor Ski Simulator

Based on the information from the main supplier of indoor ski simulator, there were 25 simulated ski gymnasiums in China. Taking SKINOW Club as an example, LeSki Club had opened 3 indoor ski training centers in Beijing, which got 10 thousand skier visits in each one. There will be another 3 training places finished in 2017, totally 10 training centers in Beijing.

Chapter 5　2016 Skier

Ⅰ. Visits & Distribution

On ski market, one of the biggest questions we met is how many people have skied in China. Figure 5-1 showed a reasonable answer.

Analysis estimated that skiers were about 11.3 million in all 15.1 million skier visits in the 2016 snow season, with 1.33 times ski per capita. Compared with the 2015 snow season, the proportion of one-time visits decreased from 80% to 78%.

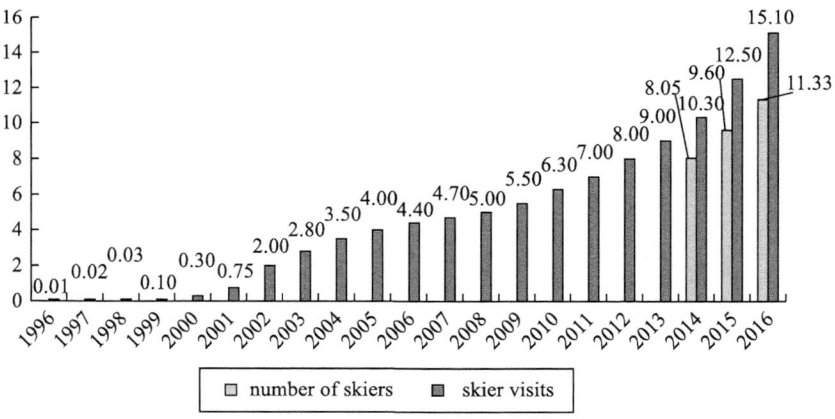

Figure 5-1　Skier Visits & Number (in Millions)

Table 5-1 showed the distribution of skier visits by destination. The skier visits growth of six provinces exceeded 200 thousand, including Hebei, Jilin, Xinjiang, Shanxi, Henan and Gansu.

Part 2 2016 Report on Key Data of Ski Industry in China

Table 5-1 Distribution of Skier Visits by Destination

Province	2015			2016		
	Rank	Number of Resorts	Skier Visits (in Thousands)	Rank	Number of Resorts	Skier Visits (in Thousands)
Beijing	1	23	1690	1	24	1710
Heilongjiang	2	120	1490	2	122	1580
Jilin	3	37	960	4	38	1180
Shandong	4	51	850	6	58	980
Hebei	5	40	850	3	46	1220
Xinjiang	6	52	770	5	57	990
Shanxi	7	32	720	7	42	960
Zhejiang	8	17	700	9	18	790
Liaoning	9	31	650	11	35	720
Inner Mongolia	10	26	590	10	33	760
Henan	11	33	580	8	41	820
Sichuan	12	10	420	13	11	500
Shaanxi	13	21	410	12	27	540
Tianjin	14	12	400	15	12	390
Jiangsu	15	13	290	16	13	290
Gansu	16	11	270	14	16	480
Hunan	17	7	250	17	7	270
Chongqing	18	10	210	18	11	240
Hubei	19	4	150	19	5	180
Ningxia	20	7	80	20	11	150
Guizhou	21	4	50	21	6	100
Qinghai	22	3	40	22	7	90
Yunnan	23	2	30	23	2	40
Fujian	24	1	20	24	1	30
Guangdong	25	1	20	25	1	30
Guangxi	26	0	0	26	1	30
Anhui	27	0	0	27	1	30
Total		568	12500		646	15100

Report on Key Data of Ski Industry in China (2015-2019)

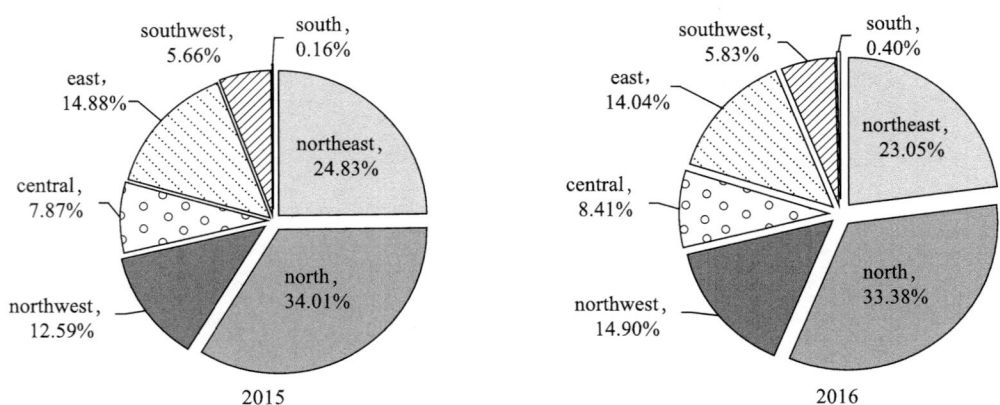

Figure 5-2 Distribution of Skier Visits by Area

II. Characteristics: Mobile Internet Data

It is the ultimate mission for us to draw a picture of Chinese skiers from different dimensions. This report attempted to utilize four active ski platform in order to conduct a preliminary analysis. The four mobile platforms are GOSKI, Ski+, HUAXUEZOO and LEDIAN Ski. Objectively, the users from these platforms are basically skiers who already have obtained some information and resources. Therefore, this section mainly reflected the characteristics of the skiers.

1. GOSKI Report

With links to snowboard, the GOSKI report reflected more characteristics of snowboarders. GOSKI users were mainly distributed in Beijing, Liaoning and Jilin, followed by Heilongjiang, Shandong and Xinjiang, other provinces only accounting for 23.64%. Furthermore, these members were male-based, with 57.49% snowboarder, 74% intermediate skiers and 63% IOS users. See Figure 5-3 and Figure 5-4.

From the GOSKI report, it was obviously that Vanke Songhua Lake was the most popular ski resort among the top ten favorite ski resorts for GOSKI users, followed by Wanlong, Beidahu. Burton was the most loved ski resorts brand, followed by NITRO and DC resorts. See Figure 5-5

Part 2 2016 Report on Key Data of Ski Industry in China

and Figure 5-6.

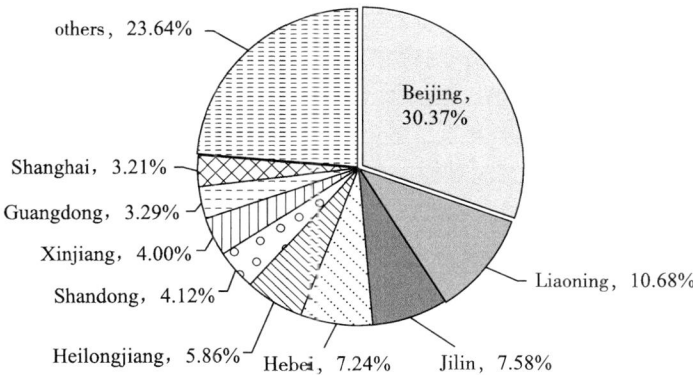

Figure 5-3 Distribution of GOSKI Users by Province (2016)

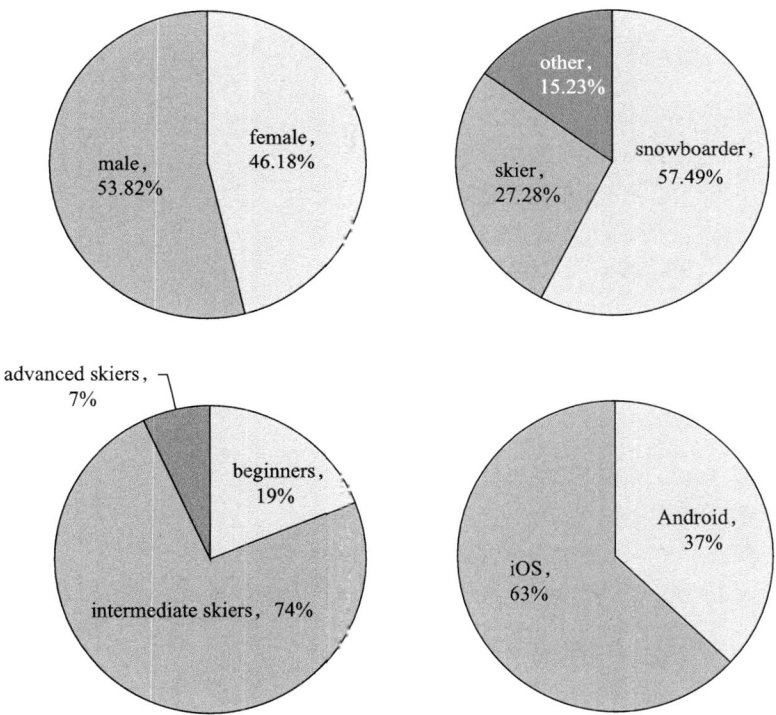

Figure 5-4 Characteristics of GOSKI Users (2016)

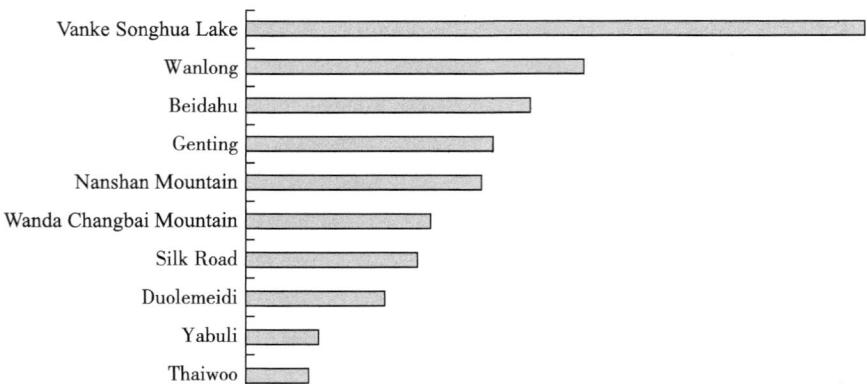

Figure 5-5　Top 10 Favorite Ski Resorts Label for GOSKI Users(2016)

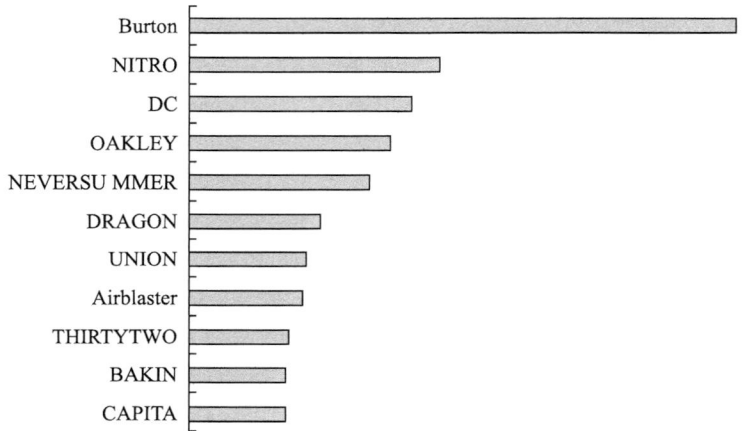

Figure 5-6　Top 10 Favorite Brands for GOSKI Users(2016)

2. Ski+ Report

The skiers using Ski+ software are enthusiasts, so it can be assumed that the Ski+ data mainly reflected the characteristics of ski enthusiasts.

During communication with Ski+ club, we found there were 481 ski clubs registered on this app. Since each member can only choose one club to register, the data study can effectively reflect the different characteristics of each skier.

In 2016, there were 348 ski resorts registered in Ski+, including 180 domestic ski resorts. The total number of users reached 179632, and their average skiing record per capita was 22.3 kilometers. Meanwhile, there were 481 registered ski clubs with 38021 registered users, with an average of 79 members per club.

In the basic information of ski resorts recorded by Ski+ in 2016, Vanke Songhua Lake ranked first, which recorded 4322 visits with a total mileage of 228687 kilometers, followed by Wanlong and Beidahu. In the basic information of ski clubs recorded by Ski+, the 1031 Ski Club took the top rank with 649 people recorded and a total mileage of 36058 kilometers.

Table 5-2 General Information of Ski+(2016)

Indicator	Number
Number of Ski+ Resorts Recorded in Total	348
Number of Ski+ Resorts Recorded in China	180
Number of Ski+ Resorts Recorded Aboard	168
Number of Users	179632
Users Recorded	53271
Ski+ Recorded Distance/km	1188729
Ski Distance Recorded on Average per User/km	22.3

Table 5-3 Top 20 Recorded Ski Resorts & Recorded Data from Ski+(2016)

Rank	Ski Resort	Number of Recorders	Total Ski Distance Recorded/km	Ski Distance per User/km	Ski Fall per User/m
1	Vanke Songhua Lake	4322	228687	53	11917
2	Wanlong	3463	209779	61	13688
3	Beidahu	1908	85229	45	10759
4	Thaiwoo	1847	84891	46	10042
5	Yabuli	1428	129996	91	19686
6	Fulong	1300	23758	18	3310
7	Genting	1278	94309	74	10217
9	Nanshan Mountain	1024	18128	18	2805
10	Wanda Changbai Mountain	977	28895	30	6040
10	Duolemeidi	953	33974	36	7249
11	Huaibei	951	15948	17	3171
12	Miaoxiang Mountain	769	14000	18	3544
13	Wanlong Bayi	675	13852	21	3181
14	Maoer Mountain	667	20921	31	7015
15	Changchengling	497	14308	29	5463

Continued

Rank	Ski Resort	Number of Recorders	Total Ski Distance Recorded/km	Ski Distance per User/km	Ski Fall per User/m
16	Guaipo	422	4157	10	2102
17	Yuyang	342	5993	18	3451
18	Jundu Mountain	337	3209	10	1552
19	Silk Road	331	15374	46	9628
20	Meilin Valley	319	10924	34	6124

Table 5-4 General Information of Members from Ski+(2016)

Indicator	Number
Number of Registered Ski Clubs	481
Number of Registered Ski Club Users	38021
Members per Club	79
Ski Distance Recorded by Ski Clubs/km	490826
Ski Distance per User Recorded by Ski Clubs/km	13

Table 5-5 Top 20 Recorded Ski Clubs from Ski+(2016)

Rank	Name of Ski Clubs	Number of Recorders	Total Ski Distance Recorded/km	Ski Distance per User/km	Ski Fall per User/m
1	1031	649	36058	56	25474
2	Xuankuzhilv	352	6369	18	11951
3	Guangdong	320	26904	84	34050
4	Xian Bingfeng	271	5794	21	8719
5	Changchun Jixian	266	5055	19	10306
6	Xuefeng	264	50186	190	58076
7	Yuanshan	257	23098	90	33429
8	Fengbao	247	6458	26	10211
9	Xuexian	229	5445	24	12148
10	Fenghuaxueyue	217	8775	40	17724
11	Xuewa	197	3297	17	9837
12	Tianjin Lingdu	186	8943	48	21589
13	Dianfeng 97	184	5843	32	14845
14	Chanxuedadui	182	4401	24	11489
15	678	178	5340	30	16465
16	Sstyle Xuefeng Outdoor	144	8128	56	30038
17	Monuo	106	10876	103	34877

Continued

Rank	Name of Ski Clubs	Number of Recorders	Total Ski Distance Recorded/km	Ski Distance per User/km	Ski Fall per User/m
18	Jilin Xuezhe	146	5625	39	26703
19	Panjin Rainbow	143	5075	35	18300
20	Veneer Snowboard	105	7282	69	28956

3. HUAXUEZOO Report

Beijing, Liaoning and Hebei were the main distribution areas for skiing visits with 33.67%, 16.76% and 10.67% customers, accounting for 61.10% of the whole travel source in China, which were followed by Heilongjiang, Jilin, Shanghai, Shandong, Tianjin and Shaanxi with 4.53%, 4.31%, 3.97%, 2.94%, 2.55% and 2.24% respectively. Furthermore, 18.36% ski visits were distributed in other regions, which had a large gap compared with Beijing, Liaoning and Hebei.

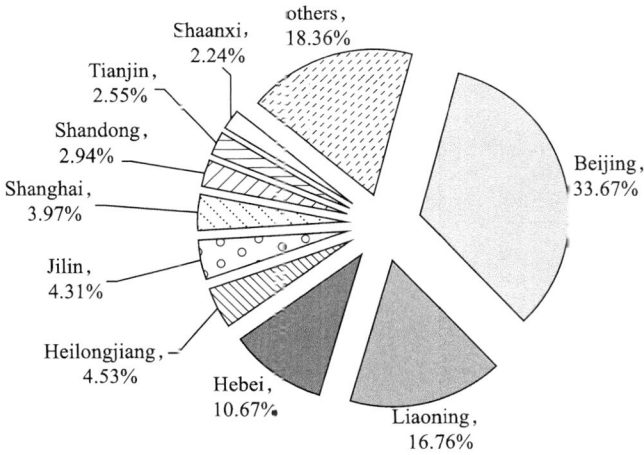

Figure 5-7 Distribution of HUAXUEZOO Users by Province(2016)

The transaction data of skiers based on 50 sample ski resorts was shown in Table 5-6. The online transaction volume of ski tickets, ski teaching, winter camp and hotel in 2016 increased significantly compared with 2015. From 2015 to 2016, the online transaction volume of ski tickets increased by 13 million yuan, the online transaction data of ski teaching increased by 3.38 million yuan, the online transaction data of winter camp increased by 1.77 million yuan, and the online transaction data of hotel increased by 4.18 million yuan.

Table 5-6　Online Sales Data of HUAXUEZOO (Based on 50 Sample Ski Resorts)

(million yuan)

Product	2015	2016
Tickets	3	16
Ski Lesson	0.31	3.69
Winter Camp	1.2	2.97
Hotel	0.46	4.64

The online sales data of ski tickets from 50 sample ski resorts was shown in Table 5-7. From 2015 to 2016, Beijing/Tianjin, Hebei and Northeast China's ski tickets online transaction data, including online transaction amount, per capita consumption amount and transaction number had obvious changes, the total amount of online trading and transaction times increased rapidly. Per capita consumption declined in Beijing/Tianjin and Hebei, and increased slightly in Northeast China. The online transaction volume in Beijing/Tianjin, Hebei and Northeast China increased by 1881754 yuan, 9996533 yuan and 2221265.5 yuan, respectively. The per capita consumption amount increased by -331 yuan, -268 yuan and 57.5 yuan, respectively. And the transaction number increased by 16420 times, 14696 times and 8076 times, respectively. In 2016, the total amount of online transactions, the amount of per capita consumption and the number of transactions in Northwest/Shandong were relatively small, which had a big gap compared with the other three regions.

Table 5-7　Online Sales Data of Ski Tickets Through HUAXUEZOO (Based on 50 Sample Ski Resorts)

Area	2015			2016		
	Total Online Sales/yuan	Per Capita Consumption/yuan	Consumption Time	Total Online Sales/yuan	Per Capita Consumption/yuan	Consumption Time
Beijing/Tianjin	98800	450	220	1980554	119	16640
Hebei	2269088	988	2297	12235621	720	16993
Northeast	317048	206.5	1539	2538313.5	264	9615
Northwest/Shandong	/	185282.3	49.3	3510	/	/

4. LEDIAN Report

According to the LEDIAN report, the proportion of Chinese skiers choosing to go skiing in Japan was 48%, followed by Europe, North America, New Zealand and Korea with 23%, 19%, 4% and 5% respectively, only 1% elsewhere.

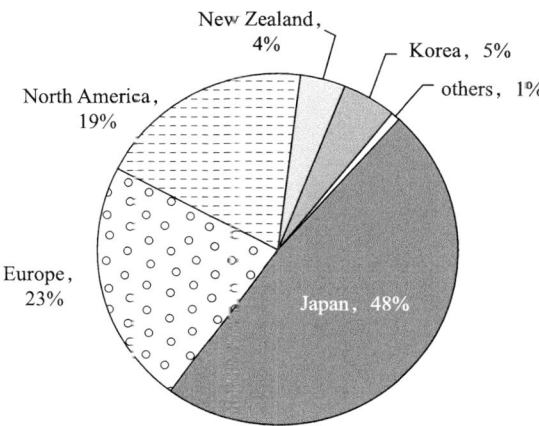

Figure 5-8   Proportion of Overseas Destinations Selected by Chinese Skiers (2016)

III. Ski Equipment Market

Ski equipment market is another important aspect reflecting skiers' characteristics. Because of the complex ski category and difficulty in obtaining information, limited information was collected. This part only provided some retail sales data for reference.

According to the data provided by different international brands, from 2014 to 2016, the retail sales of skis were much higher than snowboard, but the growth rate was lower than the snowboard. And the retail sales of skis and snowboard were increased by 4155 and 4764, with growth rates of 40.16% and 78.93% respectively.

From 2014 to 2015, the retail sales of skis were increased by 2935, a growth rate of 28.37%. And the sales of snowboard were increased by 2864 with a growth rate of 47.45%.

Report on Key Data of *Ski* Industry in China(2015-2019)

From 2015 to 2016, the retail sales of skis were increased by 1220, a growth rate of 9.19%. And the sales of snowboard were increased by 1900 with a growth rate of 21.35%. See Figure 5-9 and Figure 5-10.

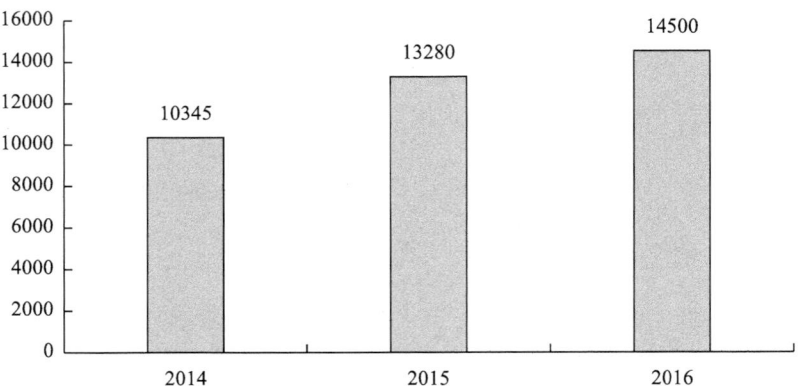

Figure 5-9　Skis Sales Based on 9 Main International Brands

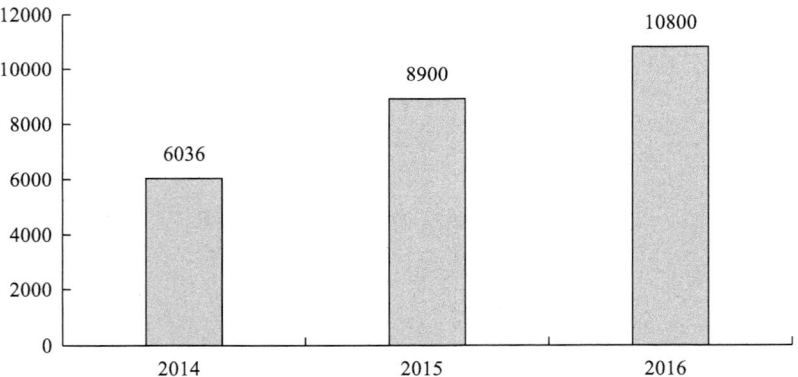

Figure 5-10　Snowboard Sales Based on 3 Main International Brands

Part 3

2017 Report on Key Data of Ski Industry in China

Chapter 6   2017 Ski Resort

I. Number & Distribution

1. Number & Distribution of Current Ski Resorts

In 2017, the number of ski resorts in China increased by 57 (including indoor resorts), with a total up to 703. That was a growth rate of 8.82%. Among those new 57 resorts, 20 had aerial lifts. At the end of 2017, there were 145 ski resorts with aerial lifts, out of 703 in total national wide.

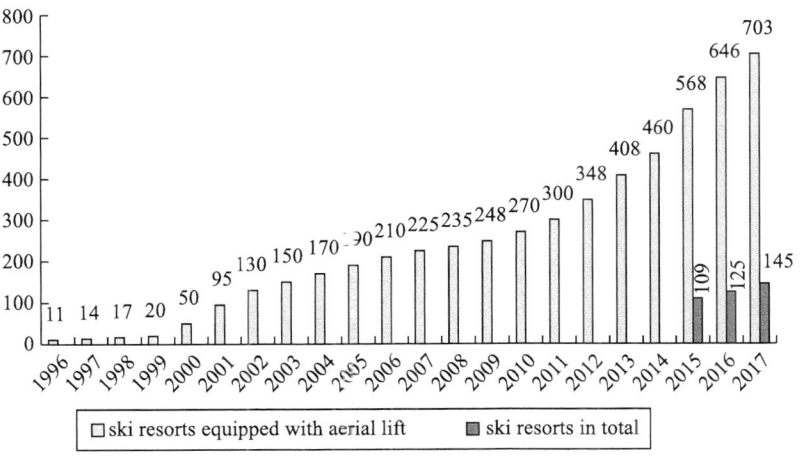

Figure 6-1　Number of Ski Resorts

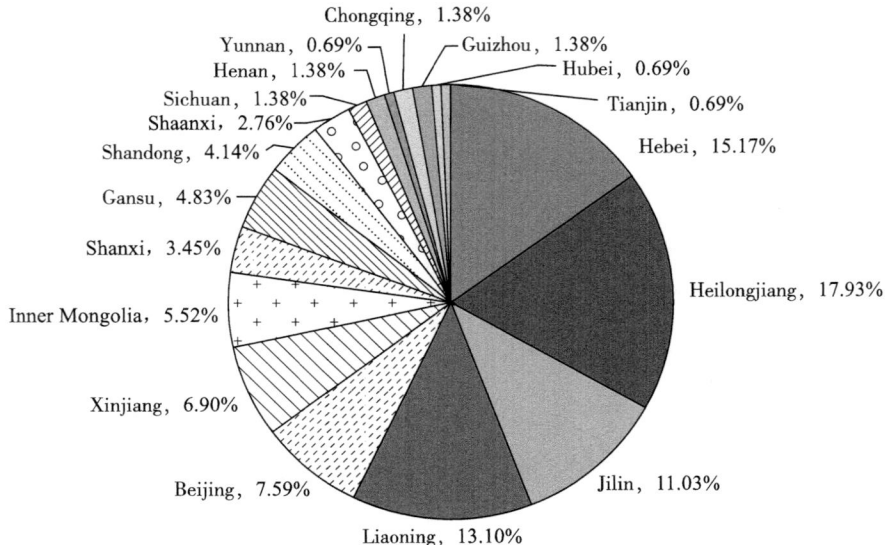

Figure 6-2 Distribution of Ski Resorts with Aerial Lift in China (2017)

703 ski resorts were distributed in 27 provinces, autonomous regions and municipalities, among which Heilongjiang took the top rank with a number of 124. See Table 6-1 for details.

Table 6-1 Distribution of Ski Resorts by Province

Rank	Province	Number of Ski Resorts in 2017	Number of Ski Resorts in 2016	Number of Newly Increased Ski Resorts in 2017
1	Heilongjiang	124	122	2
2	Shandong	61	58	3
3	Xinjiang	59	57	2
4	Hebei	58	46	12
5	Shanxi	45	42	3
6	Henan	42	41	1
7	Jilin	41	38	3
8	Liaoning	37	35	2
9	Inner Mongolia	37	33	4
10	Shaanxi	31	27	4
11	Beijing	24	24	0
12	Gansu	20	16	4
13	Zhejiang	18	18	0
14	Jiangsu	15	13	2

Continued

Rank	Province	Number of Ski Resorts in 2017	Number of Ski Resorts in 2016	Number of Newly Increased Ski Resorts in 2017
15	Chongqing	14	11	3
16	Tianjin	13	12	1
17	Ningxia	12	11	1
18	Sichuan	11	11	0
19	Guizhou	10	6	4
20	Hunan	8	7	1
21	Qinghai	7	7	0
22	Hubei	7	5	2
23	Anhui	3	1	2
24	Yunnan	2	2	0
25	Guangxi	2	1	1
26	Fujian	1	1	0
27	Guangdong	1	1	0
	Total	703	646	57

Only Hong Kong, Macao, Taiwan, Shanghai, Jiangxi, Tibet and Hainan have not established ski resorts yet among 34 provincial administrative regions, the same as last year. Hebei added 12 new ski resorts, the largest increase among all provinces.

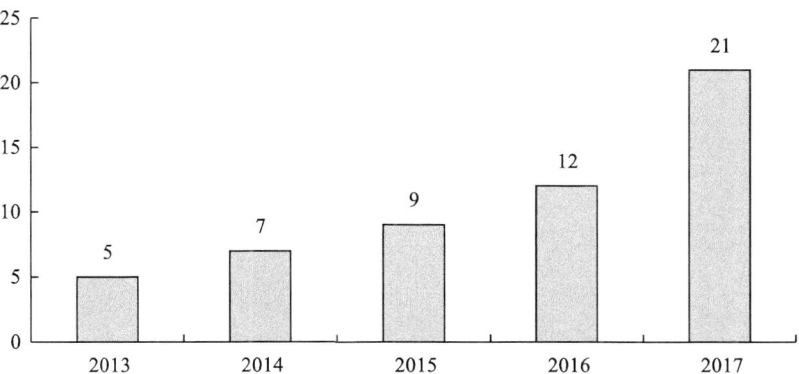

Figure 6-3 Indoor Ski Resorts Operated in China

As above mentioned, the number of ski resorts and skier visits included indoor ski resorts, while with the exclusion of artificial ski resorts like dry slopes and simulated ski gymnasiums, etc. There were 9 recently opened indoor ski resorts among the newly added 57 ski resorts. At the end of year 2017, the number of indoor ski resorts opened in China had reached 21.

In addition, based on the public information, there were 19 indoor ski resorts which had completed their planning and design and were in the process of construction, 11 among which will start operation in 2018, and others are to be in operation in 2019.

Among these operated indoor ski resorts, Harbin Wanda Yuxue Leyuan was the most representative one, which was officially in business on June 30th, 2017, and became the biggest indoor ski resort in the world. It made the achievement of having 200 thousand skier visits in 2017 alone.

Table 6-2 Operated Indoor Ski Resorts in 2017

No.	Province	Name of Indoor Resort	City	Opening Date
1	Guangdong	Alps Snow World	Shenzhen	2000.7
2	Inner Mongolia	Dayong Mountain	Manchuria	2005.12
3	Beijing	Qiaobo(Beijing)	Shunyi	2005.8
4	Zhejiang	Qiaobo(Shaoxing)	Shaoxing	2009.9
5	Henan	Funiu Mountain	Luoyang	2010.5
6	Hunan	Ruixiang Snow World	Liuyang	2011.10
7	Guangxi	Glacier Century Ski Resort	Laibin	2014.10
8	Hunan	Three Bear Ice Kingdoms	Changsha	2015.7
9	Hebei	Xibuchangqing	Shijiazhuang	2015.9
10	Zhejiang	Wencheng Swan Castle Ski Resort	Wenzhou	2015.10
11	Shaanxi	Qinlingsiji	Ankang	2016.4
12	Hebei	Four Seasons Ski Resort	Handan	2016.5
13	Chongqing	Xiannv Mountain	Chongqing	2016.7
14	Zhejiang	Qingtianleyuan	Lishui	2016.7
15	Hunan	Taohuaxueyuan	Changde	2017.2
16	Hebei	Qingqingsiji	Handan	2017.5
17	Heilongjiang	Harbin Wanda Yuxue Leyuan	Harbin	2017.6
18	Guizhou	Libo Ice World Theme Park	Libo	2017.8
19	Guizhou	Zunyisida Happy Valley	Zunyi	2017.9
20	Guizhou	Qiyuangu	Anshun	2017.10
21	Anhui	Ma'anshan Qidiqiaobo	Ma'anshan	2017.11

2. Number and Distribution of Ski Resort Planning and Design Projects

Table 6-3 summarized the planning and design projects of ski resorts signed by the major domestic planning and design institutes in the past two years, which also reflected the activity level of ski industry in Hebei. The number of projects in Hebei was 18, accounting for 28% of the total sample.

Table 6-3   Distribution of Major Planning and Design Projects in China (2016-2017)

No.	Province	Number of Projects
1	Hebei	18
2	Shanxi	5
3	Gansu	5
4	Inner Mongolia	5
5	Sichuan	3
6	Xinjiang	3
7	Jilin	3
8	Hubei	3
9	Hunan	2
10	Ningxia	2
11	Shaanxi	2
12	Beijing	2
13	Chongqing	2
14	Guizhou	2
15	Others	7
	Total	64

II. Classification Statistics

1. Classification by Target Group

If classified by target group, the domestic ski resorts were divided into three categories: travel/experience, educational and destination resort. The proportions of these three kinds were 75%, 22%

and 3% respectively.

Table 6-4 Classification of Ski Resorts by Target Group(2017)

Type of Ski Resort	Per.	Target Group	Attributes	Resort Feature	Consumer Characteristics	Cases
Travel/ experience ski resorts	75%	Sightseeing/ experience guests	Tourist	Poor facilitate, only intermediate trails. Near scenic or cities	More than 90% one-time experience; stay 2 hours	Snow World, Bird's Nest
Educational ski resorts	22%	Local / regional guests	Sportive, tourist	Little vertical drop, in suburban areas, all kinds of trails	Mainly road trip; stay 3~6 hours	Nanshan Mountain, Jundu Mountain, Vanke Shijinglong
Destination ski resorts	3%	Destination guests	Vacation, sportive, tourist	Considerable scale trails, well accommodations and auxiliary facilities	Overnight visitors; stay more than 1 day	Vanke Songhua Lake, Wanda Changbai Mountain, Beidahu, Yabuli, Wanlong, Fulong, Genting, Thaiwoo

Based on the above classification, the statistics of ski resorts with aerial lifts showed that: among those 145 ski resorts with aerial lifts, 17 of them were destination resorts, accounting for 11.7%; 107 were education ski resorts, accounting for 73.8%; and 21 of them were travel/experience ski resorts, accounting for 14.5%.

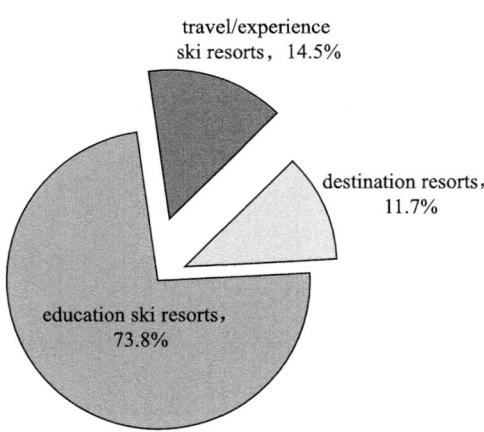

Figure 6-4 Classification of Ski Resorts by Target Group(2017)

2. Classification by Vertical Drop

The vertical drop of the ski resort is an important indicator for the resource scale of a ski resort. According to the actual vertical drop of the trails in the ski resorts, we can classify the domestic ski resorts to three categories: 24 ski resorts with more than 300 meters vertical drop-trails, 138 with vertical drop of 100~300 meters, and 543 with vertical drop of less than 100 meters. The proportion of the classified snow resorts according to the vertical drop was shown in Figure 6-5.

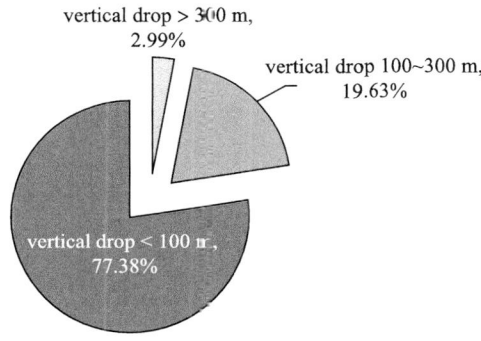

Figure 6-5 Classification of Ski Resorts by Vertical Drop(2017)

As shown in Table 6-5, among 22 ski resorts with a vertical drop of greater than 300 meters, there were 7 located in Hebei (all settled in Chongli), 4 located in Jilin, 3 in Heilongjiang, 3 in Xinjiang, 2 in Inner Mongolia, 1 each in Liaoning, Henan, Yunnan, Gansu and Beijing respectively.

Table 6-5 List of Ski Resorts with Vertical Drop more than 300 m(2017)

No.	Resorts	Vertical Drop/m	Province
1	Altay Yexue Park	1000+	Xinjiang
2	Tianchi Snow	900+	Jilin
3	Yabuli(High Mountain)	885	Heilongjiang
4	Beidahu	870	Jilin
5	Shangri-La	662	Yunnan
6	Vanke Songhua Lake	600	Jilin
7	Wanlong	580	Hebei
8	Xinjiang Silk Road	580	Xinjiang

Continued

No.	Resorts	Vertical Drop/m	Province
9	Yabuli Sunlight	540	Heilongjiang
10	Thaiwoo	510	Hebei
11	Fulong	480	Hebei
12	Meilin Valley	480	Inner Mongolia
13	Daihai	468	Inner Mongolia
14	Genting	420	Hebei
15	Jiangjun Mountain	405	Xinjiang
16	Funiu Mountain	400	Henan
17	Tianqiaogou	392	Liaoning
18	Wanda Changbai Mountain	380	Jilin
19	Duolemeidi	323	Hebei
20	Cuiyun Mountain Yinhe	315	Hebei
21	Vanke Shijinglong	310	Beijing
22	Maoer Mountain	308	Heilongjiang
23	Baolong Mountain Fenghuangling	304	Gansu
24	Changchengling	300	Hebei

The developed ski resorts with the first two vertical drop were all natural ski resorts without ropeways, which relied on mobile devices, such as snowmobile, groomer (snowcat) and helicopters to reach the peak of the mountain. The other 22 ski resorts all had cableways.

3. Classification by Slope Area

Area of slopes is another important indicator to measure the size of the ski area. In 2017, besides newly built ski resorts, the existing snow fields such as Beidahu, Miaoxiang Mountain in Changchun, Wanlong, Fulong and Genting in Chongli, had also stepped up the expansion of the resort.

At the end of 2017, there were 28 ski resorts with the area of slopes of more than 30 hectares, accounting for 3.98% of the total fields. The list of resorts was shown in Table 6-6.

Table 6-6　Number of Ski Resorts by Slopes Area(2017)

Area of Slopes/hm²	Number of Ski Resorts	Ski Resort
>100	6	Altay Yexue Leyuan, Tianchi Snow, Vanke Songhua Lake, Wanlong, Beidahu, Genting
50~100	7	Wanda Changbai Mountain, Thaiwoo, Fulong, Yabuli Sunlight, Yabuli (High Mountain), Taibai'ao Mountain, Silk Road
30~50	15	Jiangjun Mountain, Duolemeidi, Yulongwan, Nanshan Mountain, Langya Mountain, Baideng Mountain, Cuiyun Mountain Yinhe, Taziling, Funiu Mountain, Xiling, Wujin Mountain Lining, Qishan Mountain, Baolong Mountain Fenghuangling, Daihai, Yuyang
10~30	34	
5~10	105	
<5	536	
Total	703	

It is estimated that the total area of domestic ski slopes will be around 3500 hectares. Among them, the total number of 28 ski resorts listed in Table 6-6 will account for more than 40%. The total length of the domestic trails is more than 1000 km, and the total length of the trails of the 28 ski resorts will exceed 500 km.

III. Hardware Facilities

1. Lift Facilities

(1) Aerial Lifts

At the end of 2017, the total number of operating aerial lifts in domestic ski resorts was 236, distributed in 145 ski resorts. Hebei, Heilongjiang, Jilin listed on the top three with the number of 46, 39, 37 respectively. In the meantime, three provinces built 122 aerial lifts in total, accounting for 51.69% of all aerial lifts.

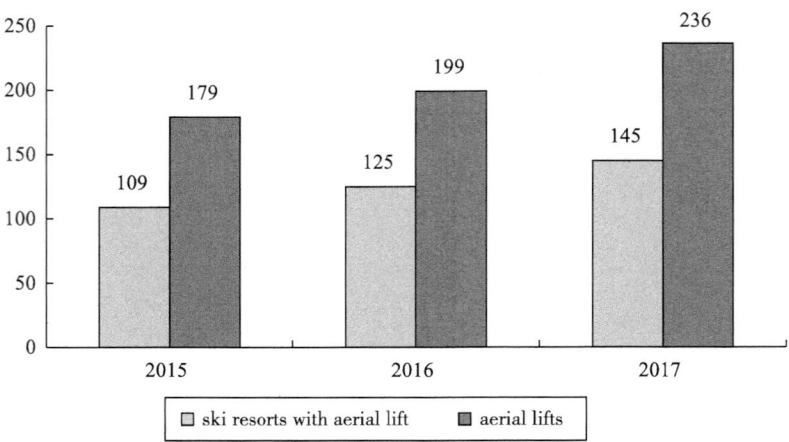

Figure 6-6 Aerial Lifts in Ski Resorts

Table 6-7 Distribution of Aerial Lifts in Ski Resorts (2017)

No.	Province	Number of Aerial Lifts	Number of Ski Resorts with Aerial Lift
1	Hebei	46	22
2	Heilongjiang	39	26
3	Jilin	37	16
4	Liaoning	28	19
5	Beijing	19	11
6	Xinjiang	16	10
7	Inner Mongolia	9	8
8	Shanxi	8	5
9	Gansu	8	7
10	Shandong	6	6
11	Shaanxi	5	4
12	Sichuan	3	2
13	Henan	3	2
14	Yunnan	3	1
15	Chongqing	2	2
16	Guizhou	2	2
17	Hubei	1	1
18	Tianjin	1	1
	Total	236	145

The number of detachable lifts reflected the scale and efficiency of ski resorts. In the past three years, the domestic detachable lifts developed rapidly, from 26 in 2015 to 48 in 2017, and the number of ski resorts with detached ropeways also increased from 10 to 18. See Figure 6-7.

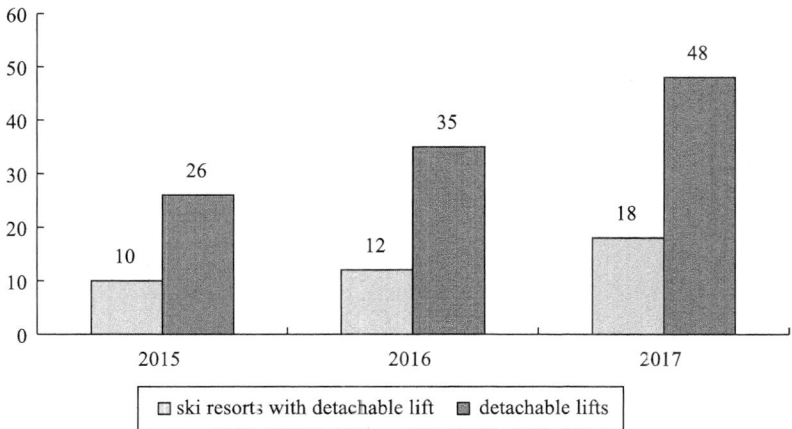

Figure 6-7 Detachable Lifts in Ski Resorts

Figure 6-8 showed the relationship between the number of imported and domestic detachable lifts in the past three years. Obviously, the development of domestic detachable was taking a high speed, increased from 2 in 2015 to 15 in 2017.

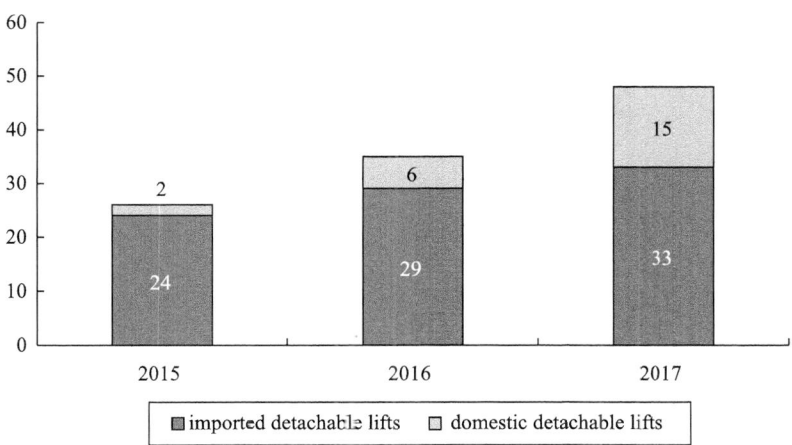

Figure 6-8 Number of Imported and Domestic Detachable Lifts

There were 48 detachable lifts in China totally. 18 detachable lifts located in Hebei, which were distributed in 6 ski resorts and all concentrated in Chongli, Zhangjiakou. 18 detachable lifts located in Jilin and distributed in 5 ski resorts. 6 detachable lifts were in Heilongjiang and distributed in 3 ski resorts. 2 were also built in each province including Shaanxi, Inner Mongolia and Xinjiang. (Notes: in this statistics, only the lifts for skiing were considered, not for transport purpose.)

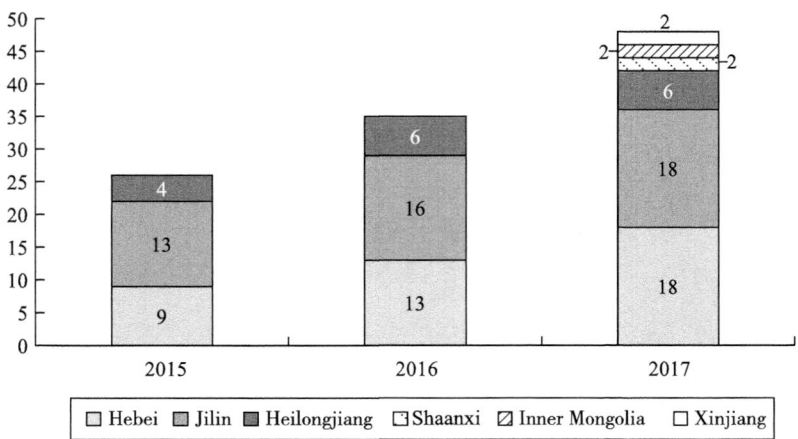

Figure 6-9 Distribution of Detachable Lifts by Province

Table 6-8 Rank of Detachable Lifts in China

No.	Resorts	Number	Province
1	Vanke Songhua Lake	6	Jilin
2	Wanda Changbai Mountain	5	Jilin
3	Wanlong	5	Hebei
4	Beidahu	4	Jilin
5	Genting	4	Hebei
6	Thaiwoo	3	Hebei
7	Fulong	3	Hebei
8	Yabuli(High Mountain)	3	Heilongjiang
9	Luneng Changbai Mountain	2	Jilin
10	Cuiyun Mountain Yinhe	2	Hebei
11	Yabuli Sunlight	2	Heilongjiang
12	Taibai'ao Mountain	2	Shaanxi

No.	Resorts	Number	Province
13	Daihai	2	Inner Mongolia
14	Miaoxiang Mountain	1	Jilin
15	Duolemeidi	1	Hebei
16	Maoer Mountain	1	Heilongjiang
17	Silk Road	1	Xinjiang
18	Jiangjun Mountain	1	Xinjiang
	Total	48	

(2) Magic Carpets

The data of magic carpets was from Daowo, Yahao and some other major domestic suppliers. Until 2017, there were totally 1076 magic carpets in operation in China, including the 226 new magic carpets in 2017. The total length was about 157 km.

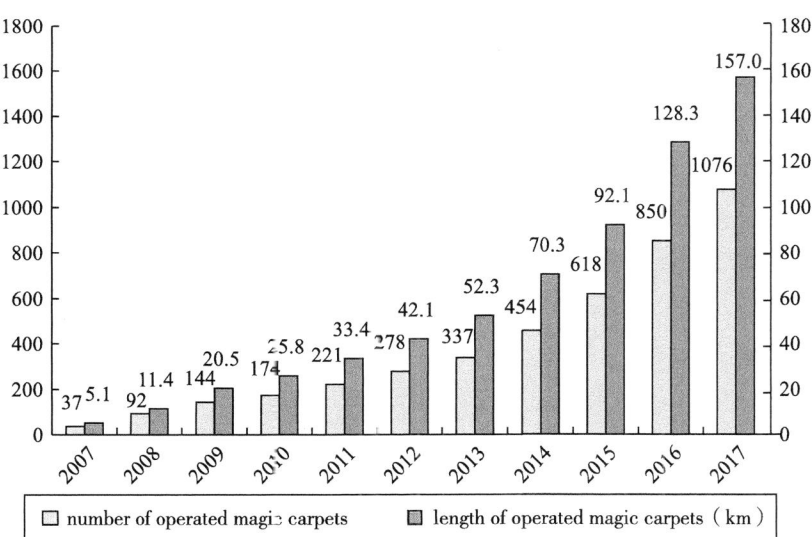

Figure 6-10 Number and Length of Operated Magic Carpets in Ski Resort

Report on Key Data of *Ski* Industry in China (2015-2019)

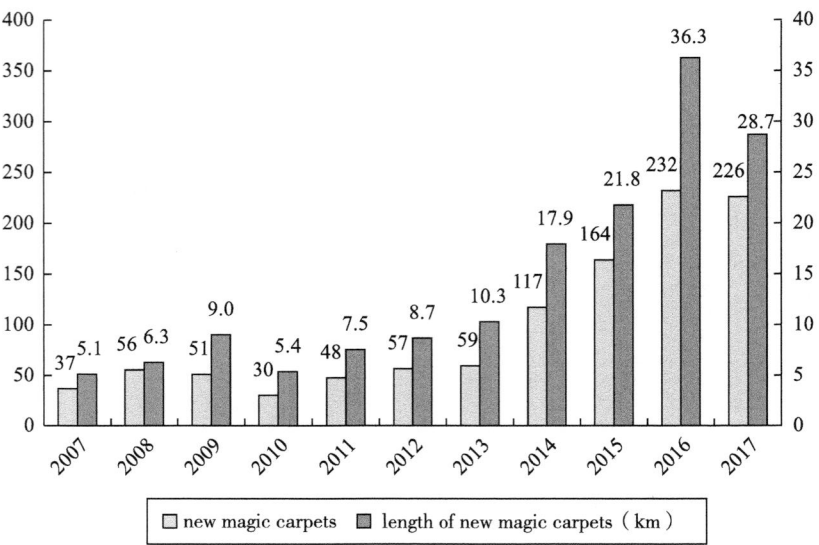

Figure 6-11 Number and Length of Newly Added Magic Carpet in Ski Resort

2. Grooming & Snowmaking Facilities

(1) Grooming Machines

According to the statistics, the total number of grooming machines in domestic ski resorts was about 485. In 2017, the number of new groomers in China was 75, slightly lower than the 80 in 2016. Among them, 48 new groomers were imported, a significant decline year on year. The data came from the main suppliers of grooming machines.

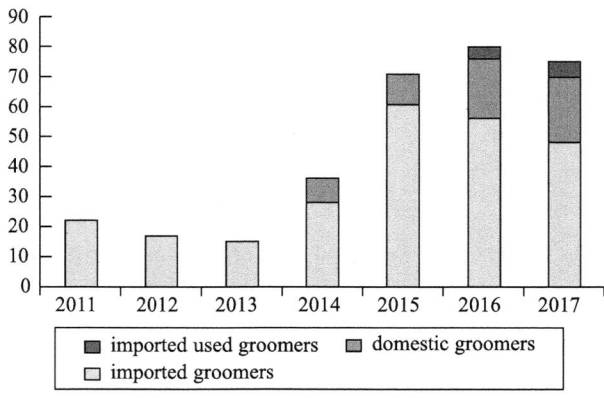

Figure 6-12 New Grooming Machines in Ski Resorts

Part 3 2017 Report on Key Data of Ski Industry in China

This report quoted the China Customs' data for the first time, which was related to the imported groomers. See Table 6-9. The data indicated that the main original places of imported groomers are Italy, Germany, Canada, USA, etc.

Table 6-9 Statistics of China's Imports (Grooming Machines)

Trading Partners	2011	2012	2013	2014	2015	2016	2017 (M1-M11)
World	22	24	23	31	68	68	58
Italy	12	18	10	18	28	28	25
Germany	2	3	6	7	16	20	24
Canada	1	1	2	4	12	11	6
USA	2	1	2	1	4	7	2
Others	5	1	3	1	8	2	1

Quote: China Customs, Beijing Longzhixun Information Consulting Company.

(2) Snowmaking Machines

In 2017, there were 1420 new snowmaking machines in China. The total number of snowmakers was about 6600. Among them, domestic machines accounted for about 15%.

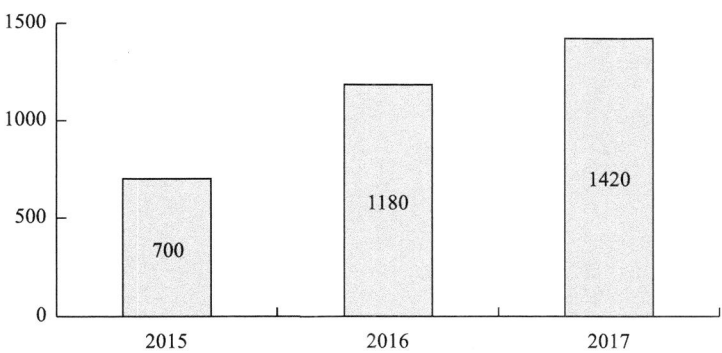

Figure 6-13 Newly Added Snowmaking Machines in Ski Resorts

3. Rental Equipments

Based on the import data from China Customs, the import quantities of bindings were growing with a high speed, and at the same time, the imports of each type of skis were in the significant decrease, which can also reflect the significant increase of domestic skis.

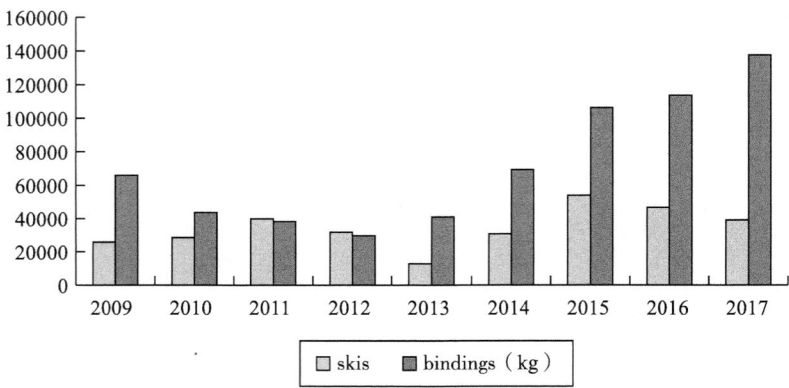

Figure 6-14 China Imports Statistics(Skis & Bindings)

Quote:China Customs,Beijing Longzhixun Information Consulting Company.

According to the information provided by main international ski suppliers, the international brands had a steadily development from the view of rental skis in ski resorts. In 2017, the number of imported rental skis, which were newly put into the market, was more than 50 thousand pairs, including a leasing project implemented by a famous big company in cooperation with the ski resorts. The whole number of rental skis in the market was more than 600 thousand pairs, and the average number in each resorts was close to 900 pairs.

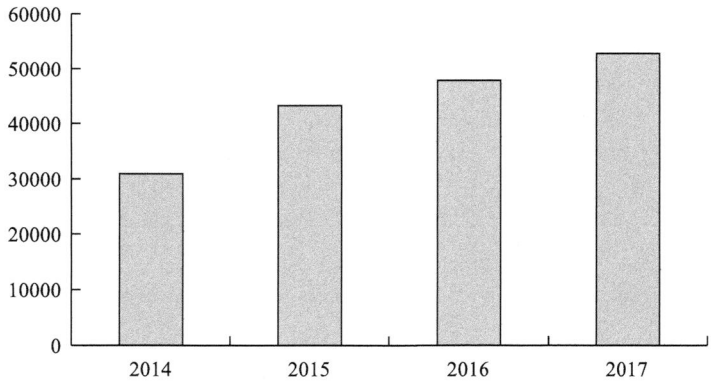

Figure 6-15 New Rental Skis in Ski Resorts

IV. Software Facilities

1. Information Management:iSNOW Snow and Ice Enterprise Cloud Service

The distribution of ski resorts with iSNOW Snow and Ice Enterprise Cloud Service was shown in Figure 6-16. Among them, 41% ski resorts were in North China, 23% ski resorts were in the northeast, 15% resorts were in the northwest, 13% resorts were in East China and 8% were in the southwest.

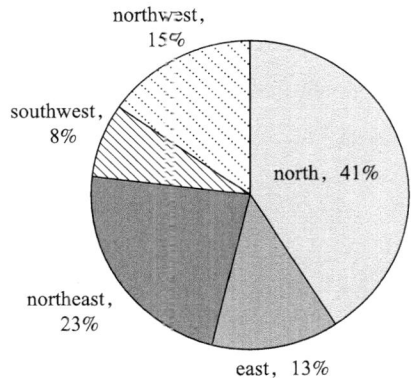

Figure 6-16 Distribution of iSNOW Snow and Ice Enterprise Cloud Service Ski Resorts(2017)

In 2017, the products of iSNOW Snow and Ice Enterprise Cloud Service mainly included snow tickets, coaches, training camps, hotels and others, among which 67% were snow tickets, and coaches, training camps and hotels were 14%, 5%, 5% respectively. In addition, it also contained 9% of other products.

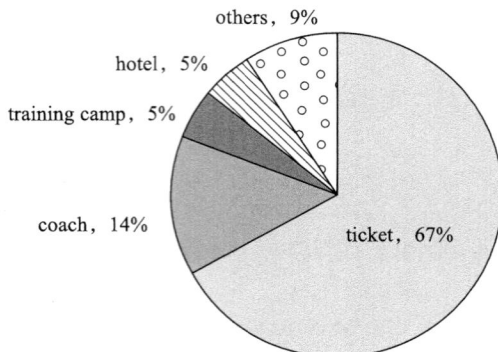

Figure 6-17　Proportion of iSNOW Snow and Ice Enterprise Cloud Service Products(2017)

Figure 6 – 18 showed the iSNOW Snow and Ice Enterprise Cloud Service in 2016 and 2017. There were significant changes in the two payment methods of mobile payment and cash plus card payment, and the proportion of mobile payment and cash plus card payment was basically equal in 2016. After 2016, mobile payment means rapidly increased to 73% of the total payment, occupying a dominant position. The cash plus card payment greatly decreased from 49% to 27%.

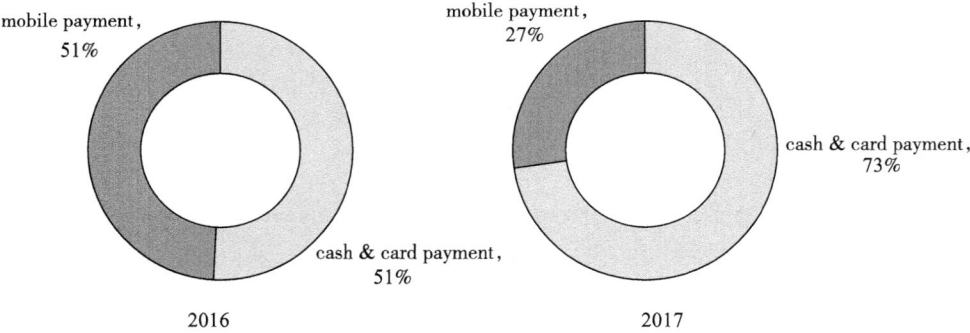

Figure 6-18　Condition of iSNOW Snow and Ice Enterprise Cloud Service

In 2017, compared with 2016, the change rate of online transaction of iSNOW Snow and Ice Enterprise Cloud Service was higher in all months except in April and September. In 2016, the maximum value of online trading of iSNOW Snow and Ice Enterprise Cloud Service appeared in November, and the minimum value appeared in May. In 2017, the maximum online transaction value of iSNOW Snow and Ice Enterprise Cloud Service appeared in December, which was much higher than 30 million yuan, while the minimum value appeared in April, which was less than 300 thousand yuan. See Figure 6-19.

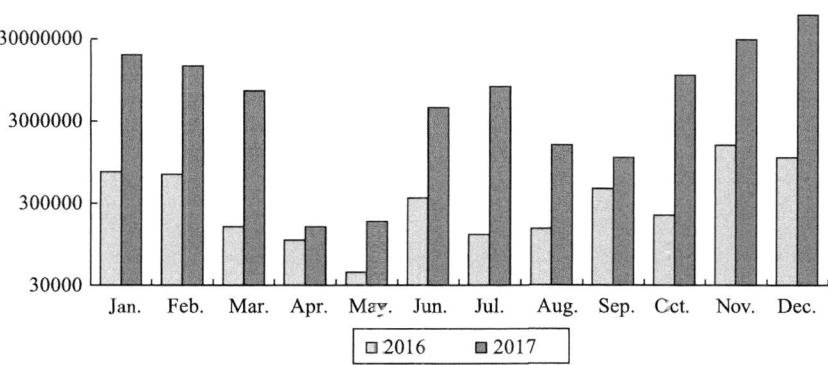

Figure 6-19 Trading Analysis on iSNOW Snow and Ice Enterprise Cloud Service

Figure 6-20 showed the comparison of customer flow of iSNOW Snow and Ice Enterprise Cloud Service from 2016 to 2017. There was a strong correlation between customer flow and online transaction. The greater the customer flow was, the higher the online transaction of enterprise cloud service would be. Otherwise the online trading would be lower. From October to the March of the next year, iSNOW Snow and Ice Enterprise Cloud Service customer flow was at its peak, from April to May, from August to September, passenger flow was small. In 2016, the maximum number of iSNOW cloud service customers appeared in December, with about 50 thousand people, and the minimum number appeared in September, with slightly more than 50 people. In 2017, the maximum number of iSNOW cloud service customers was in December, exceeding 5 million, and the minimum number appeared in April, which was below 500.

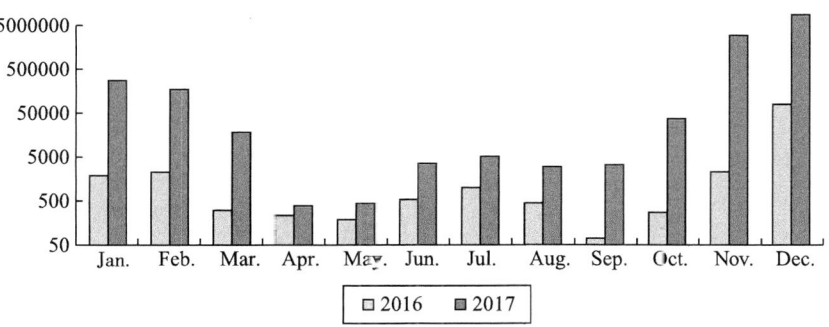

Figure 6-20 Comparison of Passenger Volume

2. Big Data Analysis and Services: Chongli Mobile Data Report[①]

The number of visitors to Chongli ski resorts varied greatly in different months, which main changing period was from June to September. The number of tourists increased rapidly in June and topped out at 1.19 million in August. After September, the number of tourists began to decline rapidly and then remained at a stable level. See Figure 6-21.

Among these tourists to Chongli, the ski visits from within Hebei were the main flow source and the proportion of visitors outside the province was relatively low. From January to November in 2017, the average proportion of tourists flowing into Chongli ski resorts from Hebei was 66.36%, which peaked at 75.20% in April and the lowest point was 57.32% in August. While the average proportion of ski visitors outside the province was 33.64%, which peaked at 42.68% in August and the lowest point was 24.80% in April. See Figure 6-22, Figure 6-23.

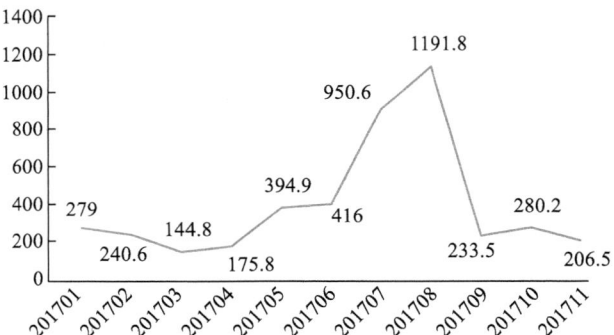

Figure 6-21 Analysis of Ski Visitors in Chongli (in Thousands)

---

① Authorized by the Chongli Government.

Part 3 2017 Report on Key Data of Ski Industry in China

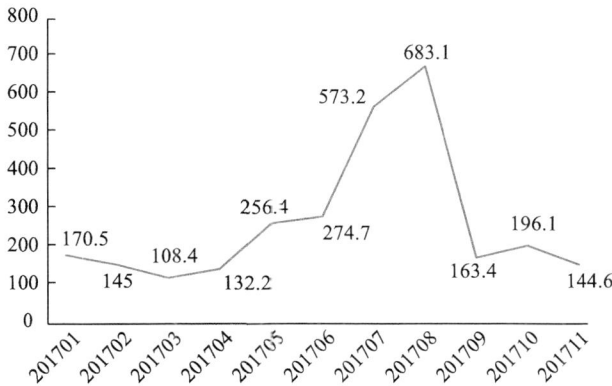

Figure 6-22 Analysis of Ski Visitor Flow from Hebei in Chongli (in Thousands)

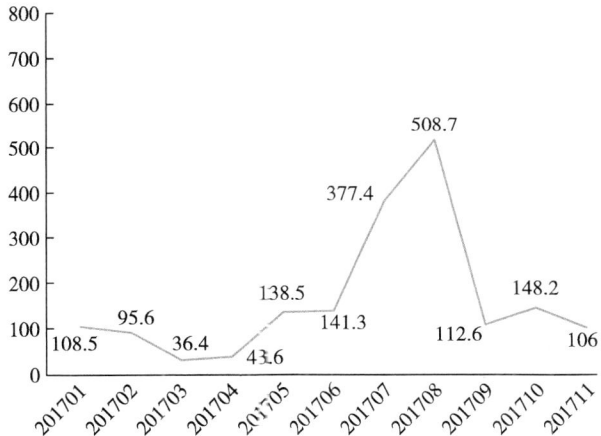

Figure 6-23 Analysis of Ski Visitors from Other Provinces in Chongli (in Thousands)

As shown in Figure 6-24, in April 2017, the tourists to Chongli mainly stayed for a short time and few lingered for more than three days. Meanwhile they were mostly concentrated in the surrounding areas. Among them, 67.65% tourists stayed for 1~2 days, 20.16% stayed for 3~9 days and 12.19% lingered for more than 10 days. As shown in Figure 6-25. Among those less than 30% visitors who stayed for Chongli more than 3 days, Hebei, Beijing, Tianjin and Inner Mongolia were the biggest sources of tourists, which Hebei and Beijing accounted for 70% and Tianjin, Inner Mongolia totaled 15%.

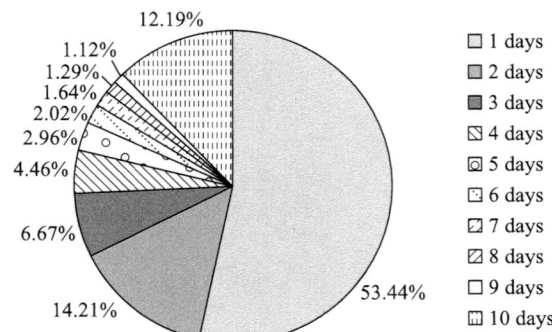

Figure 6-24　Distribution of Duration of Stay in April 2017

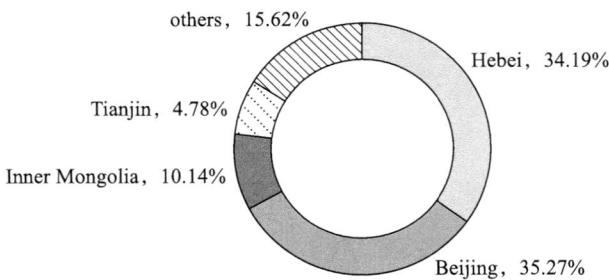

Figure 6-25　Distribution of Areas with Duration Above 3 Days in April 2017

Among these tourists to Chongli, 56.8% were male and 43.2% were female. From the perspective of age structure, young visitors who aged 20 ~ 40 and 40 ~ 60 were the main tourism sources, with 43.9% and 41.8% respectively. While the proportion of adolescents and elderly who aged 0 ~ 20 and over 60 was very low, only 14.3%. See Figure 6-26.

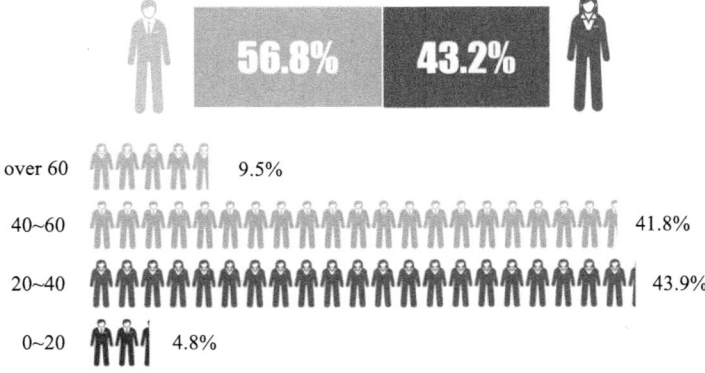

Figure 6-26　Gender and Age Structure of the Population Entering Chongli in April 2017

Table 6-10 showed the region distribution of tourists immersed in Chongli. Because of the short distance, the number of tourists was more prominent in Beijing, Inner Mongolia, Tianjin and Shanxi, which tourism immersion was much higher than other areas. Tourists from these areas can travel to and from within a short time. But the number of tourists from Liaoning, Shandong and other places was relatively small, having a large gap with Beijing and Inner Mongolia.

Table 6-10　Geographical Distribution of the People Entering Chongli in April 2017

Province	Amount
Beijing	148862
Inner Mongolia	32070
Tianjin	9890
Shanxi	9455
Liaoning	6816
Shandong	6812
Henan	5999
Shanghai	5249
Guangdong	4980
Jiangsu	4052

According to the analysis report based on big data, the transportation to Chongli was mainly self-driving and others, supported by railway and passenger transport. Because Beijing and Tianjin were closed to Chongli and their economic conditions and living standards were much higher, self-driving travel became a favorite choice for more and more people there. Besides, due to the short distance between Chongli and its surrounding counties, passenger transportation became an ideal option for residents and tour groups. Furthermore, for the visitors who lived far away, the railway became a preferred choice with the advantages of large carrying capacity, high punctuality rate and cheap price.

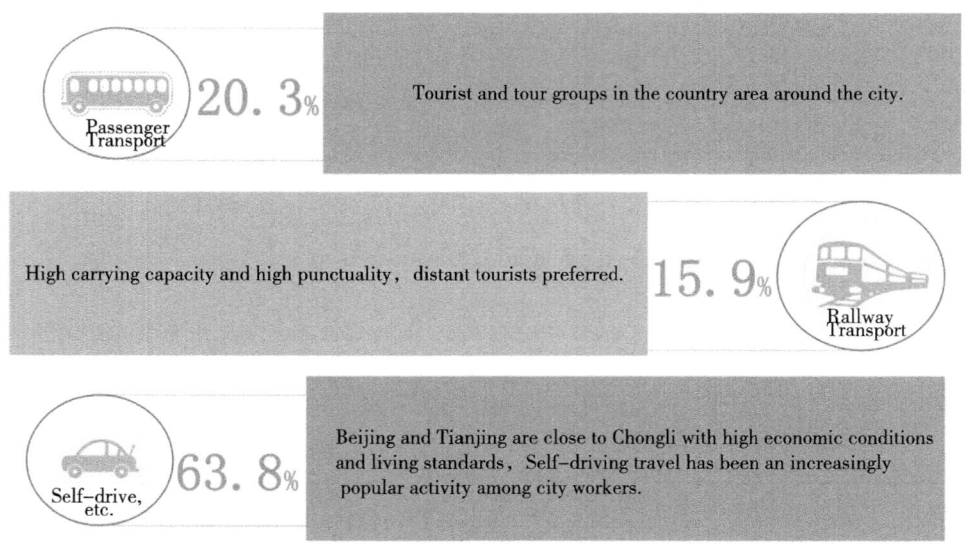

Figure 6-27 Chongli Mobile Data Report(2017)

3. Ski Instructor Training Certification[①]

Up to the end of 2017, the instructors engaged in ski teaching work in China were about 20 thousand, among which more than 9177 ski instructors holding ski social sports instructor certificate issued by General Administration of Sport of China and Ministry of Personnel, accounting for 46%.

In addition, obtaining all kinds of ski instructors association license of overseas became a trend, like USA PSIA、Canada CSIA、New Zealand NZSIA、UK、Austria and Japan, etc. In 2017, more than 900 people got ski instructor license issued by overseas entities, and it was 700 in 2016 and 300 in 2015 respectively.

---

① Data sorted out by Zhang Yan of Magic Ski School.

V. Four Seasons Ski Resorts

1. Dry Ski

As an alternative of ski, dry ski resort has a great development in recent years in China. Peak Dry Snow is a main supplier of China dry ski. According to the data provided by Peak Dry Snow, the operated Peak Dry Ski Resorts had reached 21 up to the end of 2017.

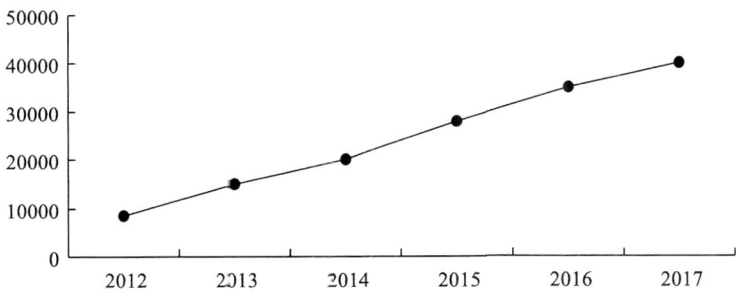

Figure 6-28   Annual Growth of Dry Skier Visits

Besides Peak Dry Snow, dry ski products of other brands all developed very fast. For example, Jisu Dry Ski had established 10 ski resorts in business, and another 5 were under construction.

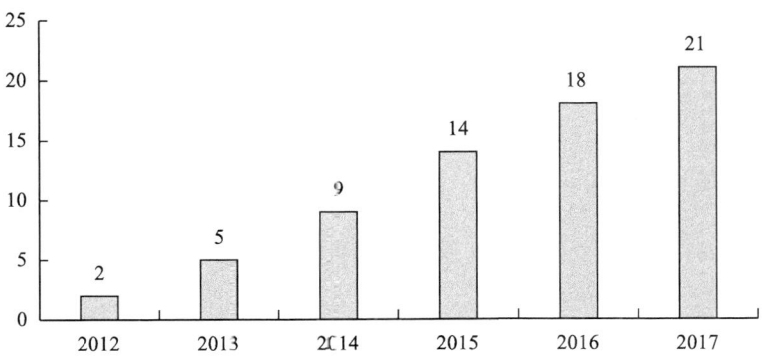

Figure 6-29   Number of Peak Dry Ski Resorts in Operation

2. Indoor Ski Simulator

Taking SKINOW as an example, LeSki Club opened 12 indoor ski training centers in Beijing with 28 simulative ski equipment in operation. It is estimated that there will be 140 thousand skier visits in full year. Meanwhile, SKINOW employed 59 ski instructors.

Chapter 7 2017 Skier

Ⅰ. Visits & Distribution

In 2017, how many people have skied in China? As research and calculation showed in this report, skiers were about 12.1 million in all 17.5 million skier visits, increasing 6.8% compared to 11.33 million in 2016. Among that, account for one-time experience people decreased from 77.8% in 2016 to 75.2%. In 2017, ski time per capita raised from 1.33 in 2016 to 1.45.

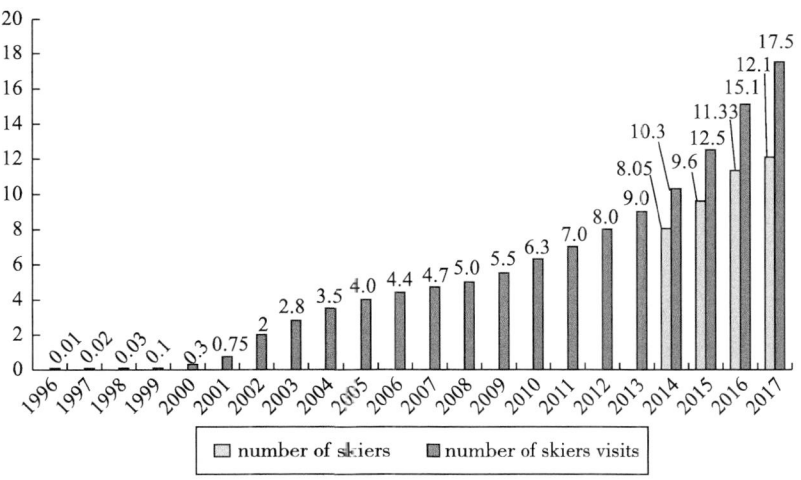

Figure 7-1 Skier Visits & Number (in Millions)

Rank of more than 100 thousand skier visits was Hebei, Heilongjiang, Jilin, Guizhou, Shanxi, Shaanxi, Zhejiang, Jiangsu. Among that, Hebei increased by 540 thousand due to the newly-increased 12 ski resorts; Heilongjiang increased by 380 thousand due to Harbin Wanda Yuxue Leyuan. Xinjiang decreased 130 thousand due to safeguard stability.

Table 7-1 Distribution of Skier Visits by Province

Province	2017			2016		
	Rank	Number of Ski Resorts	Skier Visits (in Thousands)	Rank	Number of Ski Resorts	Skier Visits (in Thousands)
Heilongjiang	1	124	1960	2	122	1580
Hebei	2	58	1760	3	46	1220
Beijing	3	24	1670	1	24	1710
Jilin	4	41	1470	4	38	1180
Shanxi	5	45	1100	7	42	960
Shandong	6	61	1040	6	58	980
Zhejiang	7	18	910	9	18	790
Henan	8	42	900	8	41	820
Xinjiang	9	59	860	5	57	990
Inner Mongolia	10	37	840	10	33	760
Liaoning	11	37	690	11	35	720
Shaanxi	12	31	680	12	27	540
Sichuan	13	11	580	13	11	500
Gansu	14	20	560	14	16	480
Tianjin	15	13	400	15	12	390
Jiangsu	16	15	390	16	13	290
Hunan	17	8	330	17	7	270
Chongqing	18	14	330	18	11	240
Guizhou	19	10	300	21	6	100
Hubei	20	7	210	19	5	180
Ningxia	21	12	180	20	11	150
Qinghai	22	7	100	22	7	90
Anhui	23	3	100	27	1	30
Guangxi	24	2	60	26	1	30
Yunnan	25	2	40	23	2	40
Fujian	26	1	30	24	1	30
Guangdong	27	1	30	25	1	30
Total		703	17500		646	15100

Ⅱ. Characteristics: Mobile Internet Data

It is the ultimate mission for us to draw a picture of Chinese skiers from different dimensions. The report continued to unite relatively active partners in the country, providing multi-dimensional analysis reports from their perspectives.

1. HUAXUEZOO Report

HUAXUEZOO, the brand of XUEZOO Technology Co., Ltd, was the earliest enterprise information services platform of vertical ice and snow in China. Since the establishment of HUAXUEZOO in 2014, it had become a companion for skiing and extreme sports enthusiasts. Here, you can share your interesting stories or experiences which were recorded in the form of pictures or videos with many ski friends, you can team up with friends or family to enjoy the most entertaining skiing experience. The indicators such as skiers' distribution, their self-portrait, ski equipment and reading volume in snowy season and non-snowy season were always carried out systematic analysis and application by HUAXUEZOO.

(1) Analysis on HUAXUEZOO Users Source by Province

The distribution of HUAXUEZOO users was shown in Figure 7-2. HUAXUEZOO users were mainly from Beijing, Hebei and Heilongjiang, accounting for more than 50% of skiers, followed by Henan, Liaoning, Jilin and other provinces with 44% users.

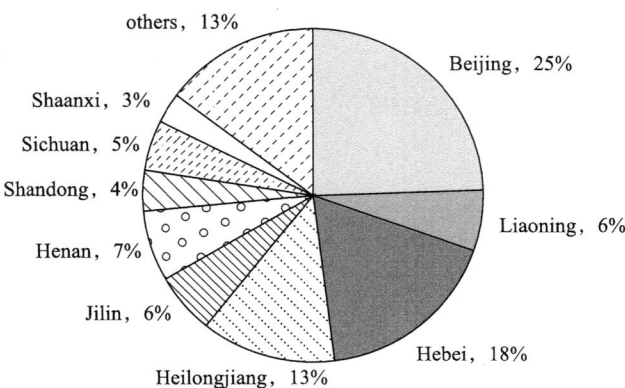

Figure 7-2   HUAXUEZOO Users Source by Province(2017)

(2) HUAXUEZOO Portrait and Analysis

According to the analysis of ski users' gender and terminal system, it was found that 53% users were male and 47% were female, and the ratio was approximately equal. From the perspective of users' terminal system, iPhone users became the hottest trend with 75% HUAXUEZOO users, much higher than the other terminal systems, followed by users of Android, Windows Phone 7 and other systems with 19%, 5% and 1% respectively.

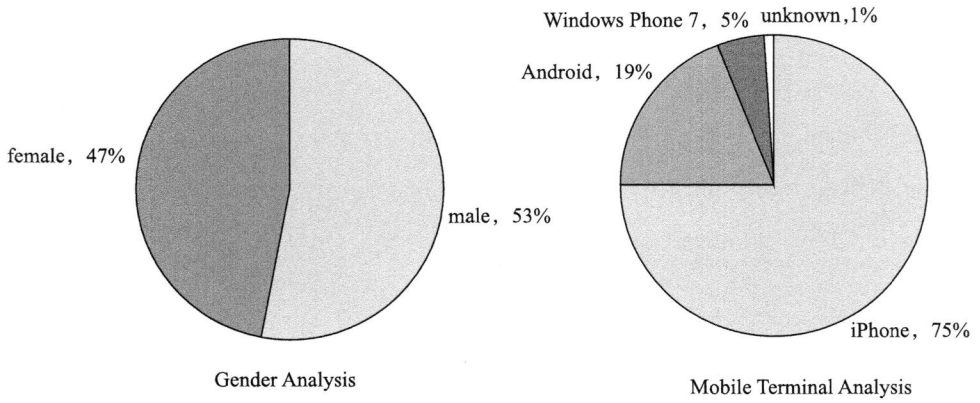

Figure 7-3   Gender and Terminal Analysis of HUAXUEZOO(2017)

(3) Analysis on HUAXUEZOO User Equipment

The proportion of skis and snowboard in the equipment of HUAXUEZOO skiers was quite different. 67% skiers used skis and only 33% used snowboard. Meanwhile, 74% HUAXUEZOO skiers used the rental equipment and 26% brought their own.

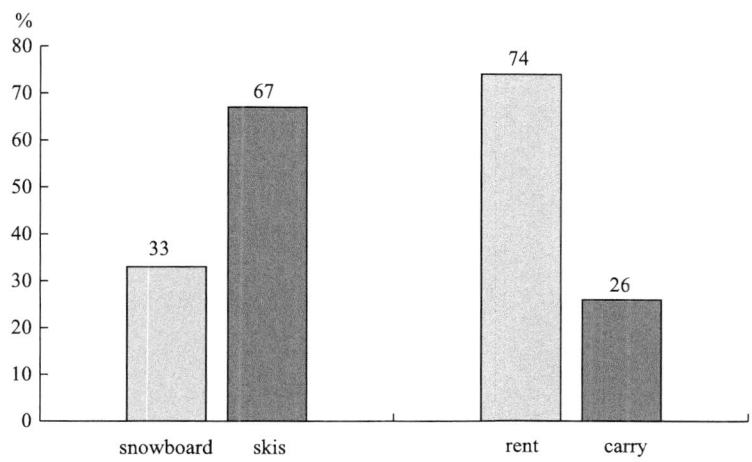

Figure 7-4　Analysis on HUAXUEZOO User Equipment(2017)

(4) Analysis HUAXUEZOO Reading Volume in Snowy Season and Non-Snowy Season

Based on the analysis of reading volume in snowy season and non-snowy season, it was found that the reading volumes in snowy season(January-April, October-December) was 7652661 times, accounted for 65.09%. And during the non-snowy season(April-October), the reading was 1937707 times with 34.91%, having obvious seasonal characteristics.

Table 7-2　Analysis on HUAXUEZOO Reading Volume in Snowy Season and Non-Snowy Season(2017)

Season	Reading Volume	Proportion/%
Snowy Season(Jan.-Apr., Oct.-Dec.)	7652661	65.09
Non-Snowy Season(Apr.-Oct.)	1937707	34.91

2. GOSKI Report

As the GOSKI team and resources had more links to snowboarder, the GOSKI report reflected more features of snowboarder.

Figure 7-5 showed the source of GOSKI users. GOSKI users were mainly distributed in Beijing, Liaoning, Jilin and Hebei, accounting for 66.79%. The ratio of male and female members was balanced. Furthermore, these users preferred to snowboard, accounting for 58.90%, followed by skis and others, with 24.90% and 16.20% respectively.

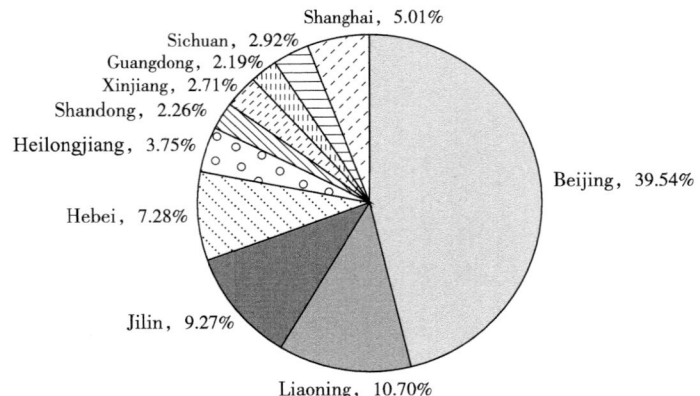

Figure 7-5　Source of GOSKI Users(2017)

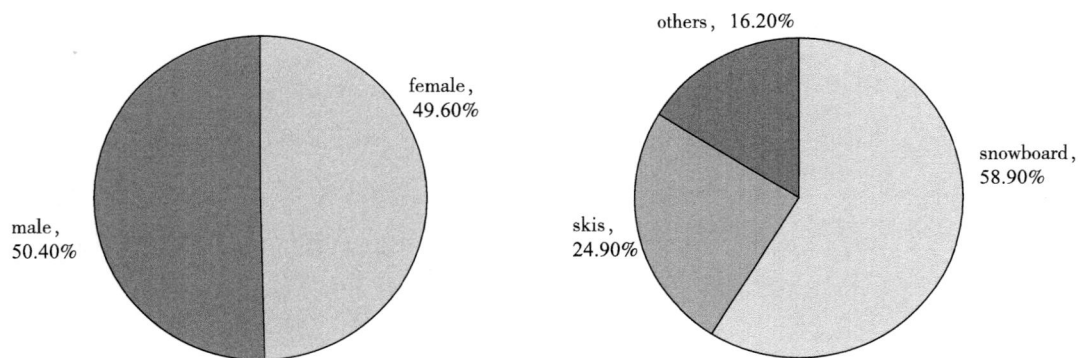

Figure 7-6　Characteristics of GOSKI Users(2017)

3. Ski+ Report

According to basic information provided by Ski+, there were totally 354 ski resorts in China and overseas, of which 62% were domestic resorts and 38% were abroad. The total number of Ski+ users was 373137, among them 96444 skiers recorded their movement tracks. Meanwhile, the cumulative trajectory of Ski+ users was 3448300 kilometers, 35 kilometers per capita.

Table 7-3　General Information of Ski+(2017)

Indicator	Number
Number of Ski Resorts Recorded in Total	354

Part 3 2017 Report on Key Data of Ski Industry in China

Continued

Indicator	Number
Number of Ski Resorts Recorded in China	219
Number of Ski Resorts Recorded Aboard	191
Number of Users	373137
Users Recorded	96444
Ski Distance Recorded / km	3448300
Ski Distance Recorded on Average per User / km	35

In 2017, the top 20 recorded ski resorts and their recorded data was shown in Table 7-4. As can be seen from the table, Wanlong Ski Resort took the top rank with a population of 8347 tourists and per capita mileage of 76.01 kilometers. Because the total mileage was 58056918 kilometers, Songhua Lake Resort was the second ski resorts with a population of 9353 visitors and 62.07 kilometers per capita. The one with the lowest total mileage was Mengdumei Ski Resort, with a population of 347 and total mileage of 19225.87 kilometers.

Table 7-4 Top 20 Recorded Ski Resorts & Recorded Data from Ski+(2017)

Rank	Ski Resorts	Number of Recorders	Total Ski Distance Recorded/km	Ski Distance per User/km	Ski Fall per User/m
1	Wanlong	8347	634493.84	76.01	15.69
2	Vanke Songhua Lake	9353	580569.18	62.07	13.4
3	Genting	5155	313796.49	60.87	10.53
4	Beidahu	4919	272470.24	55.39	12.65
5	Yabuli Sunlight	2877	269435.85	93.65	19.66
6	Thaiwoo	3825	176659.33	46.19	9.69
7	Wanda Changbai Mountain	3182	113471.25	35.66	7.11
9	Duolemeidi	2020	79504.12	39.36	7.58
10	Maoer Mountain	3101	79435.99	25.62	8.36
10	Fulong	1852	72315.56	39.05	4.2
11	Silk Road	968	53750.64	55.53	10.48
12	Nanshan Mountain	2316	49158.73	21.23	3.14
13	Miaoxiang Mountain	1670	39666.99	23.75	4.06
14	Yabuli	1042	35936.31	34.49	7.16
15	Meilin Valley	682	34781.77	51	8.63

Continued

Rank	Ski Resorts	Number of Recorders	Total Ski Distance Recorded/km	Ski Distance per User/km	Ski Fall per User/m
16	Changchengling	1171	34172.43	29.18	6.48
17	Huaibei	1764	33748.7	19.13	3.32
18	Wanlong Bayi	1269	30848.72	24.31	3.52
19	Tianqiaogou	633	19967.54	31.54	0.05
20	Mengdumei	347	19225.87	55.41	11.91

Based on the general information provided by GOSKI, in 2017, there were 872 ski clubs registered in GOSKI, including 48876 members totally. And on average, there were 56 members in each club. In addition, the total ski mileage of these clubs was 1624824 kilometers, with 29 kilometers per capita.

Table 7-5 General Information of Members from Ski+(2017)

Indicator	Number
Number of Registered Ski Clubs	872
Number of Registered Ski Club Users	48876
Members per Club	56
Ski Distance Recorded by Ski Clubs / km	1624824
Ski Distance per User Recorded by Ski Clubs / km	29

The trajectory of top 20 recorded ski clubs from GOSKI in 2017 was shown in Table 7-6. The 1031 Ski Club bore the brunt, recording a population of 637 members and a total mileage of 100606.27 kilometers. Due to its large number of recorded users, although its total mileage was the highest, the average mileage per capita of 1031 Ski Club was only 157.94 kilometers, with small ski fall. Rather, because of the fewer members and large total mileage, the average mileage per capita and ski fall of Yilong Ski Club were the largest.

Table 7-6　Top 20 Recorded Ski Clubs from Ski+(2017)

Rank	Name of Ski Clubs	Number of Recorders	Total Ski Distance Recorded/km	Ski Distance per User/km	Ski Fall per User/m
1	1031	637	100606.27	157.94	30.7
2	Xuefeng	263	96990.85	368.79	78.96
3	Guangdong	307	56911.24	185.38	37.94
4	Jilin Xuezhe	200	56515.9	282.58	36.04
5	Yuan Mountain	334	54223.75	162.35	50.08
6	Monuo	162	49912.31	308.1	60.03
7	Xingyu Outdoor	464	44719.04	96.38	18.09
8	Yilong	88	35179.31	399.76	81.14
9	Tianjin Lingdu	203	30614.47	150.81	28.21
10	Lingdu	165	26866.83	162.83	35.43
11	Fenghuaxueyue	174	24230.58	139.26	28.6
12	Sstyle Xuefeng Outdoor	176	23879.68	135.68	44
13	Daqing DCS	115	23608.01	205.29	27.72
14	Xuankuzhilv	205	22000.34	107.32	19.76
15	Changchun Jixian	291	19475.45	66.93	13.95
16	Panjin Rainbow	115	19401.62	168.71	24.57
17	Jiyingzhe	163	18572.41	113.94	31.11
18	Xi'an Bingfeng	219	17732.92	80.97	15.56
19	Veneer Snowboard	138	14595.64	105.77	36.5
20	678	86	14242.32	165.61	20.44

4. LEDIAN Report

According to the LEDIAN report, the number of Chinese skiers choosing to go skiing in Japan increased significantly, from 48% in 2016 to 55% in 2017. Closely after was Europe, in the ranking of European countries, Switzerland ranked obviously at the top, followed by France, Austria and Italy.

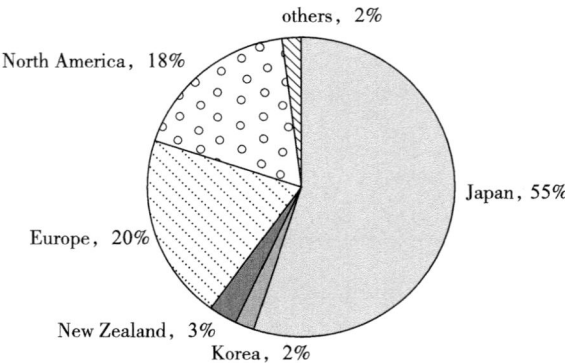

Figure 7-7　Proportion of Overseas Destinations Selected by Chinese Skiers(2017)

III. Ski Equipment Market

Although most manufacturers provided relevant data, unfortunately the description of ski equipment market was still the weakest part of this report. For most specialized channel like street stores, the ski equipment retail market has been in a platform stage without too much change. Two points needed to be focused: adolescent ski market has been overall launched which is worth of paying close attention; ski brand Wed'ze of DECATHLON has a strong growth tendency with the annual increase of 30%.

By the end of 2017, branches and camps of Magic Ski School increased from 3 to 10 with the growth rate of 230%. There were 220 full-time certified coaches and 80 part-time certified coaches with the annual increase of 160%. Teaching staff number was 3100 in 2015, 10900 in 2016 and 23000 in 2017 with the annual growth of 110%. Teaching income was 9 million yuan with the annual increase of 210%. Teaching repurchase rate was 67%. Teaching conversion rate was 32%, up to the standard of 3 or 4.

Part 4

2018 Report on Key Data of Ski Industry in China

Chapter 8 2018 Ski Resort

I. Number & Distribution

Besides the traditional outdoor and indoor snow fields, ski resorts include dry slopes and simulated ski gymnasiums, which have flourished development in recent years in China

1. Ski Resorts(Including Indoor Ski Resorts)

In 2018, the growth of ski resorts in China increased by 39(including indoor resorts), with a total up to 742. That was a growth rate of 5.55%. Among those 39 new resorts, 2 had aerial lifts. At the end of 2018, there were 149 ski resorts with aerial lifts, out of 703 in total national wide(besides two new added, another two ski resorts were opened with aerial lifts).

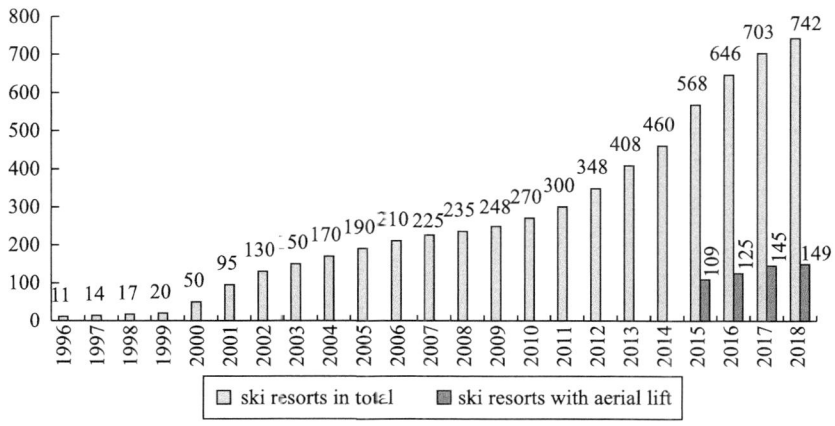

Figure 8-1 Number of Ski Resorts

742 Ski resorts were distributed in 28 provinces, autonomous regions and municipalities, Heilongjiang, Shandong, Xinjiang, Hebei and Shanxi listed on the top five. In 2018, Inner Mongolia took the top rank with the growth of ski resorts, followed by Shandong and Hubei. See Table 8-1 for details.

Table 8-1 Distribution of Ski Resorts by Province

No.	Province	2018	2017	2018 Growth
1	Heilongjiang	124	124	0
2	Shandong	65	61	4
3	Xinjiang	60	59	1
4	Hebei	59	58	1
5	Shanxi	48	45	3
6	Henan	43	42	1
7	Jilin	43	41	2
8	Inner Mongolia	42	37	5
9	Liaoning	38	37	1
10	Shaanxi	34	31	3
11	Beijing	24	24	0
12	Gansu	21	20	1
13	Zhejiang	19	18	1
14	Jiangsu	17	15	2
15	Chongqing	16	14	2
16	Tianjin	13	13	0
17	Ningxia	13	12	1
18	Sichuan	11	11	0
19	Hubei	11	7	4
20	Guizhou	10	10	0
21	Hunan	9	8	1
22	Qinghai	8	7	1
23	Yunnan	4	2	2
24	Anhui	3	3	0
25	Guangxi	2	2	0
26	Jiangxi	2	0	2

No.	Province	2018	2017	2018 Growth
27	Guangdong	2	1	1
28	Fujian	1	1	0
	Total	742	703	39

In 2018, there were 5 recently opened indoor ski resorts among the newly added 39 ski resorts. At the end of year 2018, the number of indoor ski resorts opened in China had reached 26. See Figure 8-2.

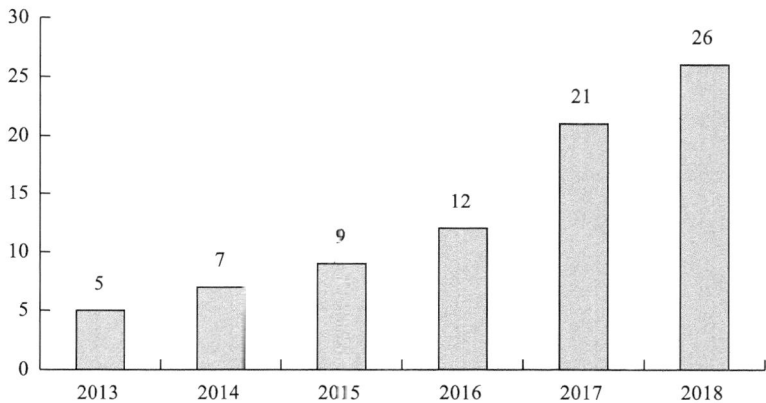

Figure 8-2　Statistics of Indoor Ski Resorts Operated in China

Table 8-2 summarized the planning and design projects of snow resorts signed by some major planning and design institutions in China in 2018, reflecting the relatively high level of activity in Hebei, Jilin and Xinjiang.

Table 8-2　Distribution of Major Planning and Design Projects in China(2018)

No.	Province	Amount
1	Hebei	7
2	Jilin	4
3	Xinjiang	3
4	Shanxi	2
5	Sichuan	2
6	Liaoning	2

No.	Province	Amount
7	Qinghai	1
8	Anhui	1
9	Shandong	1
10	Hubei	1
11	Heilongjiang	1
12	Fujian	1
Total		26

2. Dry Ski

As an alternative of ski, dry ski resort has a great development in recent years in China. At present, ski carpets used in China were mainly "enoki mushroom" dry snow blankets. According to the data provided by Peak Dry Snow, the operated Peak Dry Ski Resorts had reached more than 30 at the end of 2018.

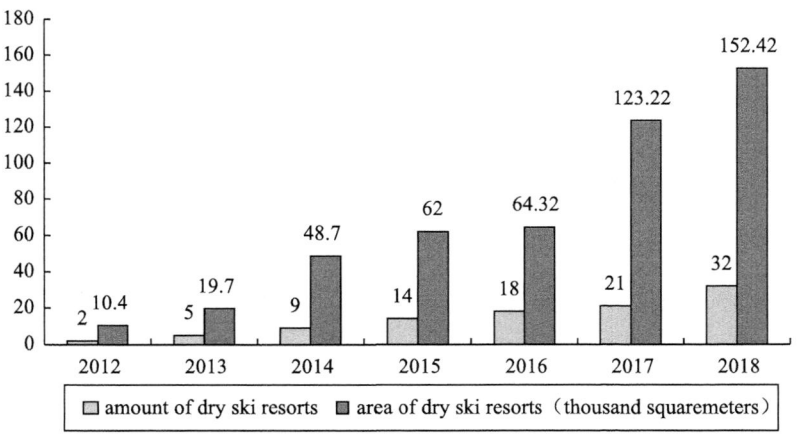

Figure 8-3 Number and Area of Dry Ski Resorts

In terms of the area of dry ski resorts, Shandong, Sichuan, Beijing, Hubei and Guangdong ranked the country's top five resorts at present.

3. Ski Simulator

In 2018, the ski simulator market showed a rapid growth in China as well. According to a report provided by Winter Wonderland, by of the end of 2018, it totaled 145 simulated ski gymnasiums in operation from 62 resorts in China. Beijing, Shanghai and Guangdong ranked the top three with 43.45%, 20% and 7.59% respectively.

II. Classification Statistics

1. Classification by Target Group

If classified by target group, the domestic ski resorts were divided into three categories: travel/experience, educational, and destination resort. The proportion of these three kinds was 75%, 22% and 3% respectively.

Table 8-3 Classification of Ski Resorts by Target Group (2018)

Type of Ski Resort	Per.	Target Group	Attributes	Resort Feature	Consumer Characteristics	Cases
Travel/experience ski resorts	75%	Sightseeing/experience guests	Tourist	Poor facilitate, only intermediate trails. Near scenic or cities	More than 90% one-time experience; stay 2 hours	Xiling Snow Mountain, Daming Mountain, Shennongjia
Educational ski resorts	22%	Local/regional guests	Sportive, tourist	Little vertical drop, in suburban areas, all kinds of trails	Mainly road trip; stay 3~6 hours	Nanshan Mountain, Jundu Mountain, Vanke Shijinglong, TOREAD Songding
Destination ski resorts	3%	Destination guests	Vacation, sportive, tourist	Considerable scale trails, well accommodations and auxiliary facilities	Overnight visitors; stay more than 1 day	Vanke Songhua Lake, Wanda Changbai Mountain, Beidahu, Yabuli, Wanlong, Thaiwoo, Fulong, Genting

Among those 149 ski resorts with aerial lifts, 19 of them were destination resorts, accounting for 12.75%; 108 were educational ski resorts, accounting for 72.48%; and 22 of them were travel/experience ski resorts, accounting for 14.77%. See Figure 8-4.

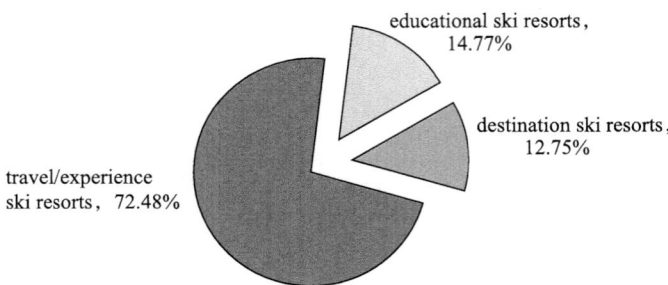

Figure 8-4　Classification of Ski Resorts by Target Group(2018)

2. Classification by Vertical Drop

The vertical drop of the ski resort is an important indicator for the resource scale of a ski resort. According to the actual vertical drop of the trails in the ski resorts, we can classify the domestic ski resorts to three categories: 26 ski resorts with more than 300 meters vertical drop-trails, accounting for 3.5%, 140 with vertical drop of 100~300 meters, accounting for 18.87%, and 543 with vertical drop of less than 100 meters, accounting for 77.63%. The proportion of the classified snow resorts according to the vertical drop was shown in Figure 8-5. Table 8-4 showed the top 10 ski resorts by vertical drop in the domestic.

Among these 26 ski resorts with more than 300meters vertical drop-trails, 7 resorts located in Hebei and all concentrated in Chongli, Zhangjiakou, Jilin and Xinjiang each had 4 ski resorts, Heilongjiang and Inner Mongolia each owed 3, and 1 was also built in each province including Liaoning, Henan, Yunnan, Gansu and Beijing.

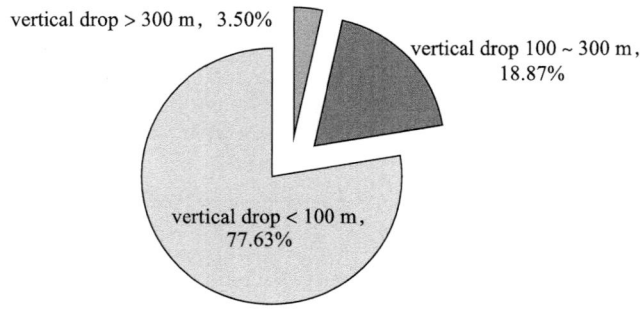

Figure 8-5　Classification of Ski Resorts by Vertical Drop(2018)

Table 8-4　Top 10 Ski Resorts by Vertical Drop(2018)

No.	Resorts	Vertical Drop/m	Province
1	Yabuli(High Mountain)	885	Heilongjiang
2	Beidahu	870	Jilin
3	Xinjiang Silk Road	700	Xinjiang
4	Shangri-La	662	Yunnan
5	Vanke Songhua Lake	600	Jilin
6	Wanlong	580	Hebei
7	Yabuli Sunlight	540	Heilongjiang
8	Thaiwoo	510	Hebei
9	Fulong	480	Hebei
10	Meilin Valley	480	Inner Mongolia

In addition, 3 wild ski resorts had been developed in China, which mainly relied on mobile devices, such as snowmobile, groomer (snowcat) and helicopters to reach the peak of the mountain. The three wild resorts were Xinjiang Altai Mountain Wild Snow Park, Jilin Changbai Mountain Tianchi Snow Field and Xinjiang Keketohai Ski Resort, which was newly developed in 2018 and planned to open cableways in 2019.

3. Classification by Slope Area

Area of slopes is another important indicator to measure the size of the ski area. In 2018, besides the newly built ski resorts, the Silk Road in Xinjiang stepped up the expansion of the resort. At the end of 2018, there were 29 ski resorts with the area of slopes of more than 30 hectares, accounting for 3.98% of the total fields. Among them, 26 ski resorts operated aerial lifts, accounting for 17.46%. See Table 8-5.

Table 8-5　Number of Ski Resorts by Slope Area(2018)

Area of Slopes/hm²	Number of Ski Resorts	Proportion/%	Ski Resorts with Aerial Lift	Proportion/%
>100	8	1.08	5	3.36
50~100	6	0.81	6	4.03
30~50	15	2.02	15	10.07

Continued

Area of Slopes/hm²	Number of Ski Resorts	Proportion/%	Ski Resorts with Aerial Lift	Proportion/%
10~30	35	4.72	35	23.49
5~10	106	14.29	88	59.06
<5	572	77.09	0	0
Total	742	100.00	149	100.00

The top 10 ski resorts by slope area were shown in Table 8-6, excluding the wild ones.

Table 8-6 Top 10 Ski Resorts by Slope Area (2018)

No.	Ski Resorts	Area of Slopes/hm²	Province
1	Vanke Songhua Lake	150	Jilin
2	Wanlong	140	Hebei
3	Beidahu	126	Jilin
4	Wanda Changbai Mountain	100	Jilin
4	Genting	100	Hebei
5	Thaiwoo	80	Hebei
6	Fulong	75	Hebei
7	Silk Road	170	Xinjiang
8	Yabuli Sunlight	50	Heilongjiang
8	Aoshan Mountain	50	Shaanxi

According to the estimation, the total area of domestic ski resorts was about 3500 hectares. Among them, there were 29 ski resorts with the area of slopes of more than 30 hectares, accounting for 40% of the total fields.

4. Classification by Business Days

According to the data provided by Meituan Tickets, the ski resorts within 80 business days accounted for 30% of the total fields. See Figure 8-6.

Part 4 2018 Report on Key Data of Ski Industry in China

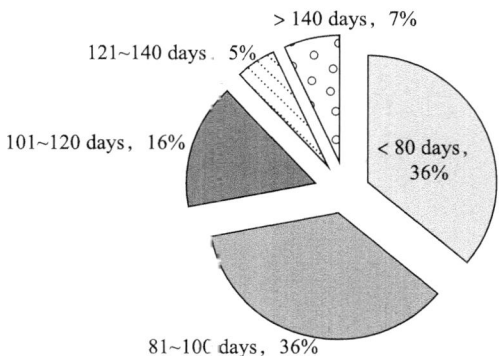

Figure 8-6 Classification of Ski Resorts by Business Days(2018)

5. Else

(1) Ski Night

At present, the ski resorts opened at night including Nanshan Mountain, Jundu Mountain, Wanlong Bayi, Beijing Lianhua Mountain, Wanda Changbai Mountain, Vanke Songhua Lake, Silk Road, Xiling Snow Mountain, Huaibei, Guaipo, Northeast Asia, Fulong, Miaoxiang Mountain, Jiangjun Mountain, Vanke Shijinglong, etc.

(2) Official Accounts on Wechat and Tmall Stores

According to the statistics, nearly more than 400 ski resorts had launched official accounts on Wechat, less than 20 resorts owing Tmall stores.

(3) Ticket Machines or Turnstiles

Tickets machines and turnstiles were more and more widely used in the ski resorts, such as Wanlong, Fulong, Thaiwoo, Cuiyun Mountain Yinhe, Vanke Songhua Lake, Beidahu, Duclemeidi, Guaipo, Wujin Mountain Lining, Nanshan Mountain and Aoshan Mountain.

III. Facilities Statistics

1. Lift Facilities

(1) Aerial Lifts

From 2015 to 2018, the total number of ski slopes and the ski resorts equipped with the aerial lifts were all increased. Moreover, the growth rate of aerial snow trails in the ski field was higher than that of the ski resorts with aerial ropeways. 149 ski resorts were equipped with the aerial lifts, increased by 36.70% in 2018 compared with 109 in 2015. The number of ski slopes was increased from 40 in 2015 to 71 in 2018, with a growth of 39.66%.

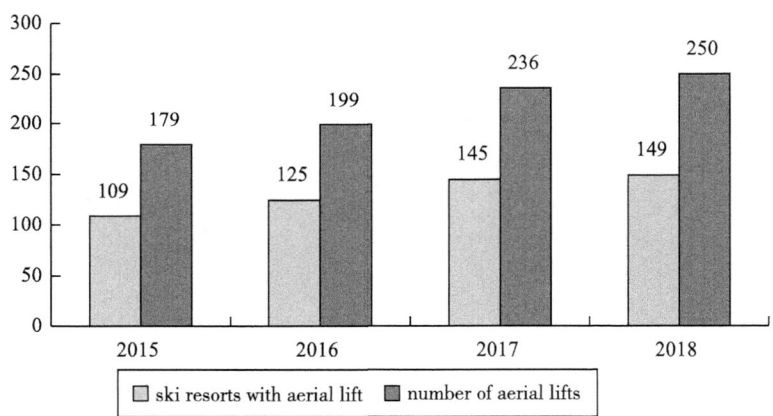

Figure 8-7　Aerial Lifts in Ski Resorts

The statistics proportion of ski resorts by the number of aerial lifts was shown in Table 8-7. 250 ropeways had been built and put into use in China, distributed in 149 ski resorts. Among these, there were 57 ropeways with 4 or more aerial lifts, distributed in 10 ski resorts, accounting for 22.80% of the total number of ropeways and 6.71% of the total number of ski resorts. And there were 36 ropeways with 4 aerial lifts, distributed in 12 ski resorts, accounting for 14.40% of the total number of ropeways and 8.05% of the total number of ski resorts respectively.

Besides, there were 60 ropeways with 2 aerial lifts, distributed in 30 ski resorts, accounting for 24.00% of the total number of ropeways and 20.13% of the total number of ski resorts. Furthermore, there were 97 ropeways owned one aerial lift, distributed in 97 ski resorts, accounting for 38.80% of the total number of ropeways and 65.1% of the total number of ski resorts respectively.

Table 8-7 Proportion of Ski Resorts by Number of Aerial Lifts (2018)

Classification	Number of Aerial Lifts	Percentage/%	Number of Ski Resorts	Percentage/%
⩾4	57	22.80	10	6.71
3	36	14.40	12	8.05
2	60	24.00	30	20.13
1	97	38.80	97	65.10
Total	250	100.00	149	100.00

At the end of 2018, the total number of operating aerial lifts in domestic ski resorts was 250, distributed in 149 ski resorts. Among them, Hebei, Heilongjiang, Jilin ranked top three, with 49, 39 and 37 aerial lifts respectively. In the meantime, three provinces built 125 aerial lifts in total, accounting for 51.69% of all aerial lifts. See Table 8-8.

Table 8-8 Distribution of Aerial Lifts in Ski Resorts (2018)

No.	Province	Number of Aerial Lifts	Number of Ski Resorts with Aerial Lift
1	Hebei	49	22
2	Heilongjiang	39	26
3	Jilin	37	16
4	Liaoning	23	19
5	Beijing	20	12
6	Xinjiang	19	10
7	Inner Mongolia	15	10
8	Shanxi	8	5
9	Gansu	8	7
10	Shandong	6	6
11	Shaanxi	5	4
12	Sichuan	3	2

Continued

No.	Province	Number of Aerial Lifts	Number of Ski Resorts with Aerial Lift
13	Henan	3	3
14	Yunnan	3	2
15	Chongqing	3	1
16	Guizhou	2	2
17	Hubei	1	1
18	Tianjin	1	1
	Total	250	149

The number of detachable lifts reflected the scale and efficiency of ski resorts. In the past three years, the domestic detachable lifts developed rapidly, from 26 in 2015 to 54 in 2018, and the number of ski resorts with detachable ropeways also increased from 10 to 19. See Figure 8-8.

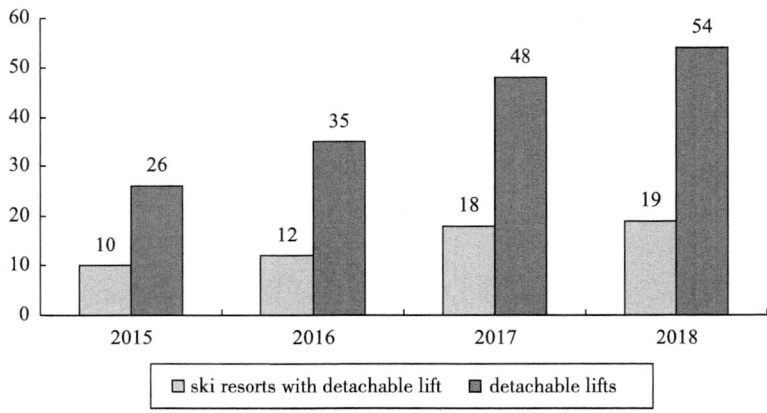

Figure 8-8 Detachable Lifts in Ski Resorts

Figure 8-9 showed the relationship between the number of imported and domestic detachable lifts in the past four years. Obviously, the development of domestic detachable lifts had been rapidly increased from 2 in 2015 to 18 in 2018.

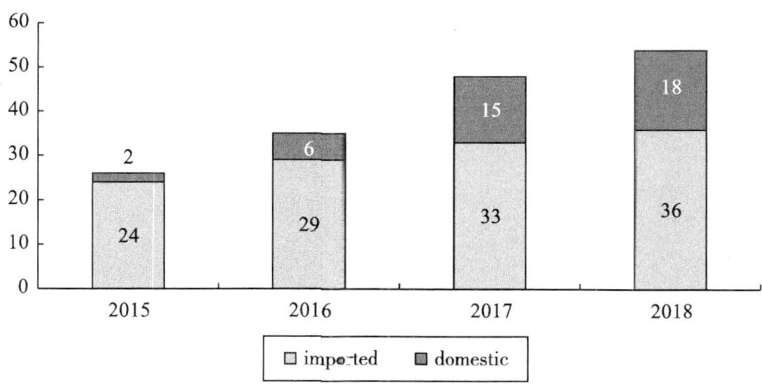

Figure 8-9　Number of Imported and Domestic Detachable Lifts

There were 54 detachable lifts in China totally. 21 detachable lifts located in Hebei, which were distributed in 7 ski resorts and all concentrated in Chongli, Zhangjiakou. 19 detachable lifts located in Jilin and distributed in 6 ski resorts. 6 detachable lifts were in Heilongjiang and distributed in 3 ski resorts. 4 detachable lifts were in Xinjiang and distributed in 2 ski resorts. 2 were also built in each province including Shaanxi and Inner Mongolia. (Notes: in this statistics, only the lifts for skiing were considered, not the lifts for transport purpose.)

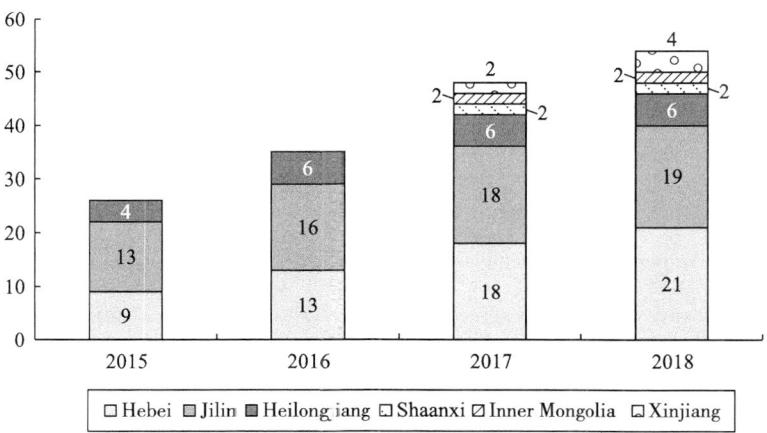

Figure 8-10　Distribution of Detachable Lifts by Province

Table 8-9 Rank of Ski Resorts According to the Number of Lifts (2018)

No.	Rank	Ski Resorts	Number	Province
1	1	Vanke Songhua Lake	6	Jilin
2	1	Wanlong	6	Hebei
3	3	Wanda Changbai Mountain	5	Jilin
4	3	Thaiwoo	5	Hebei
5	5	Beidahu	4	Jilin
6	5	Genting	4	Hebei
7	7	Silk Road	3	Xinjiang
8	7	Fulong	3	Hebei
9	7	Yabuli (High Mountain)	3	Heilongjiang
10	10	Aoshan Mountain	2	Shaanxi
11	10	Luneng Changbai Mountain	2	Jilin
12	10	Cuiyun Mountain Yinhe	2	Hebei
13	10	Yabuli Sunlight	2	Heilongjiang
14	10	Daihai	2	Inner Mongolia
15	15	Miaoxiang Mountain	1	Jilin
16	15	Duolemeidi	1	Hebei
17	15	Maoer Mountain	1	Heilongjiang
18	15	Lianhua Mountain	1	Jilin
19	15	Jiangjun Mountain	1	Xinjiang
		Total	54	

(2) Magic Carpets

The data of the magic carpets came from the main domestic suppliers such as Daowo and Yahao. By 2018, there were 1196 magic carpets in ski resorts in total, including the 120 new carpets in 2018. The total length was 176 kilometers. See Figure 8-11, Figure 8-12.

Part 4 2018 Report on Key Data of Ski Industry in China

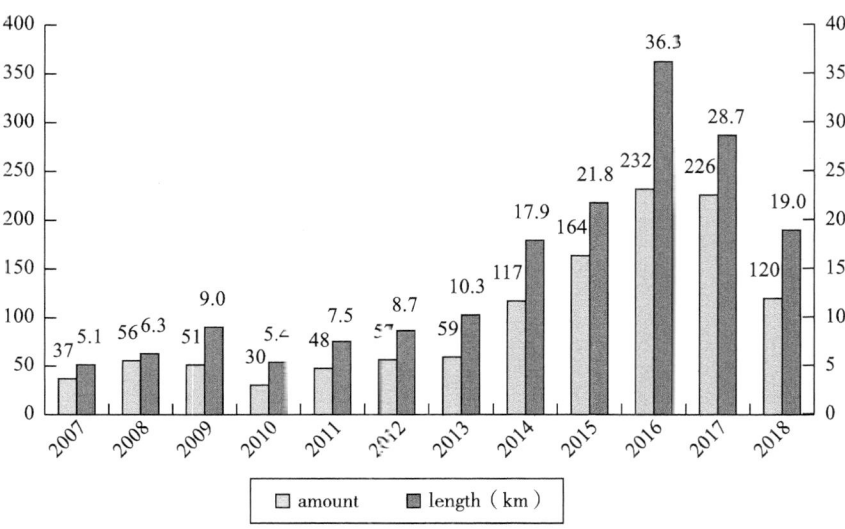

Figure 8-11 Number and Length of New Magic Carpets in Ski Resort

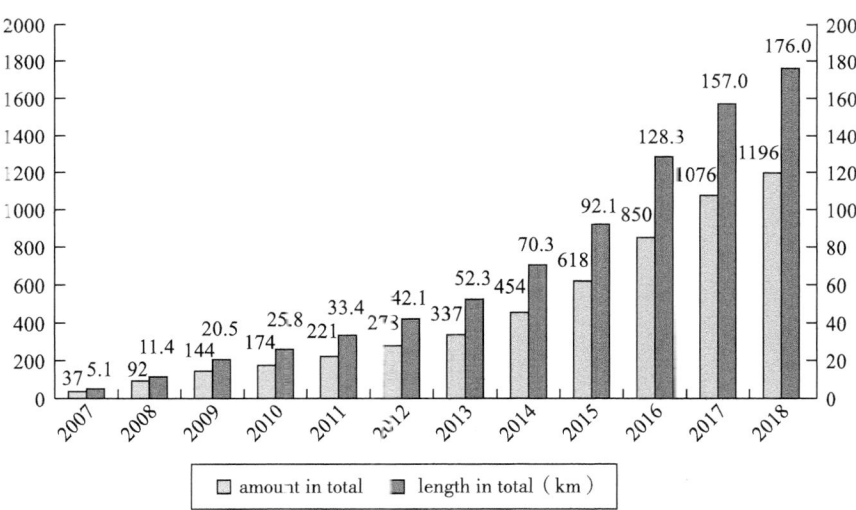

Figure 8-12 Number and Length of Operated Magic Carpets in Ski Resort

3. Grooming & Snowmaking Facilities

(1) Grooming Machines

According to the statistics, the total number of grooming machines in domestic ski resorts was about 541. In 2018, the number of new groomers in China was 56, slightly lower than the 75 in

2017. Among them, 36 new groomers were imported, a significant decline year on year. The data came from the main suppliers of grooming machines. See Figure 8-13.

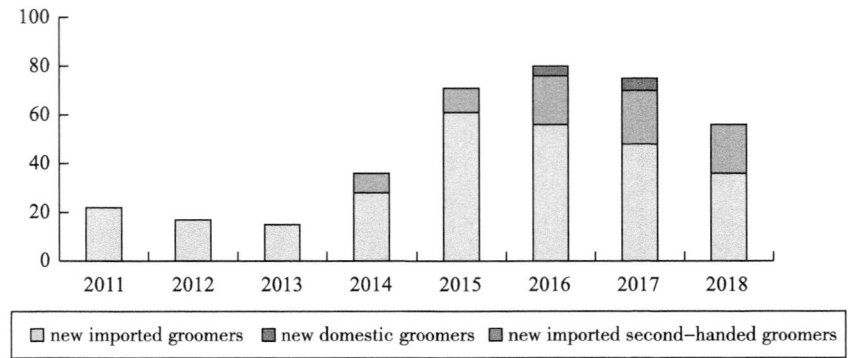

Figure 8-13   New Grooming Machines in Ski Resorts

From Table 8-10, the data from China Customs indicated that the main original places of imported groomers were Italy and Germany.

In 2018, a new phenomenon emerged in the snowmobile market, was the significant increase in the rental snowmobile business. It was estimated by insiders that the number of snowmobile vehicles had exceeded 30 at least.

Table 8-10   Statistics of China's Imports (Grooming Machines)

Trading Partners	2013	2014	2015	2016	2017	201711	201811	YOY of 2018/%
Total	23	31	68	68	60	58	52	-10.34
Italy	10	18	28	28	24	24	31	29.17
Germany	6	7	16	20	27	25	20	-20
China	0	0	0	0	0	0	1	/
Finland	1	1	0	0	0	0	0	/
Austria	0	0	1	0	0	0	0	/
Canada	2	4	12	11	6	6	0	-100
Japan	2	0	7	1	1	1	0	-100
Russia	0	0	0	1	0	0	0	/
USA	2	1	4	7	2	2	0	-100

Quote: China Customs, Beijing Longzhixun Information Consulting Company.

(2) Snowmaking Machines

In 2018, there were 810 new snowmaking machines in China, much lower than 1420 in 2017. By the end of 2018, the total number of snowmakers was about 7410. See Figure 8-14.

Similar to grooming machines, the rental snowmobile business of snowmakers was welcomed by markets, with the number of 60.

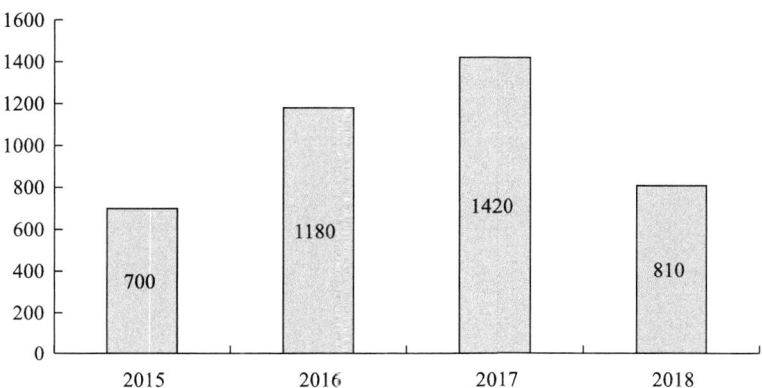

Figure 8-14　New Snowmaking Machines in Ski Resorts

4. Rental Equipments

Based on the import data from China Customs, after the high growth of import quantities of ski bindings in previous years, there was a sharp fall in 2018. At the same time, the imports of each type of skis were in the significant decrease, which can also reflect the significant increase of domestic skis. See Figure 8-15.

According to the information provided by main international ski suppliers, the international brands had an obvious decrease from the view of rental skis in ski resorts in 2018 (see Figure 8-16). The whole number of rental skis from the market was more than 600 thousand pairs, and the average number in each resort was close to 900 pairs.

Report on Key Data of Ski Industry in China (2015-2019)

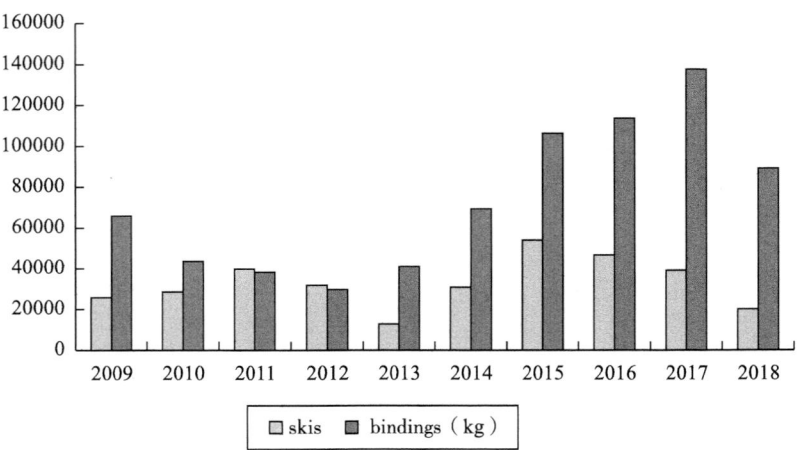

Figure 8-15 China Imports Statistics (Skis & Bindings)

Quote: China Customs, Beijing Longzhixun Information Consulting Company.

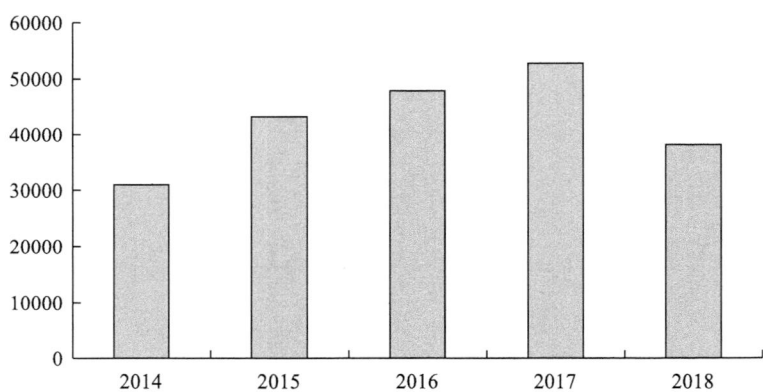

Figure 8-16 New Rental Skis in Ski Resorts

Chapter 9　2018 Skier

Ⅰ. Visits & Distribution

This report introduced the concept of total ski visits, taking the number of ski visits generated by dry slopes and simulated ski gymnasiums into account. By the end of 2018, the total ski visits in the domestic were 21.13 million. Among them, there were 19.7 million visits from ski resorts, including 0.85 million from dry slopes and 0.58 million from simulated ski gymnasiums.

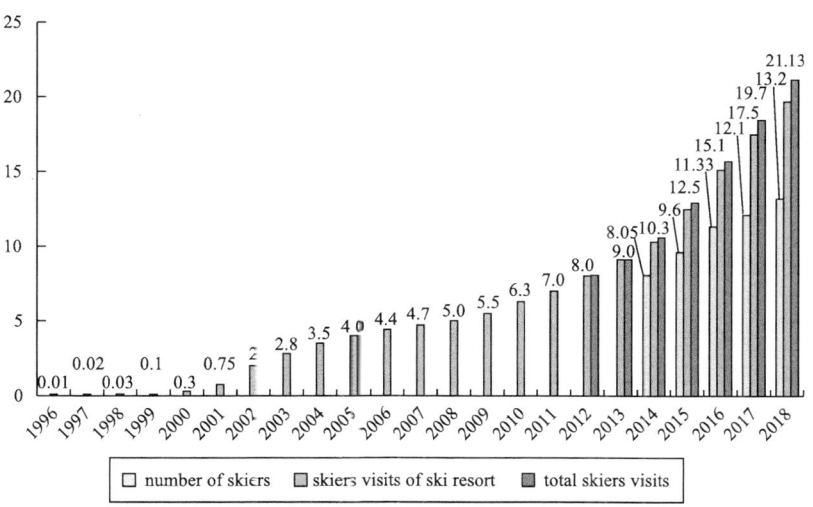

Figure 9-1　Skier Visits in Total, Skier Visits of Ski resorts & Skier Number (in Millions)

As research and calculation showed in this report, skier number was about 13.2 million visits, increasing 9.09% compared to 12.1 million in 2017. Among that, account for one-time ex-

· 297 ·

perience people increased from 75.2% in 2017 to 75.38%, basically the same as last year. In 2018, ski time per capita raised from 1.45 in 2017 to 1.49. See Figure 9-1.

From the list of ski visits, the business days of some ski resorts in Shandong and Jiangsu decreased significantly due to the climate change. Thanks to Rongchuang Ski Resort in Harbin, ski visits of Heilongjiang were up 12.76%. Among the 19.7 million ski visits, there were 1.66 million visits from indoor ski resorts.

Table 9-1 Distribution of Skier Visits by Province

Rank	Province	Number of Ski Resorts in 2017	2017 Skier Visits (in Millions)	Number of Ski Resorts in 2018	2018 Skier Visits (in Millions)	YOY/%
1	Heilongjiang	124	1.96	124	2.21	12.76
2	Hebei	58	1.76	59	2.10	19.32
3	Jilin	41	1.47	43	1.84	25.17
4	Beijing	24	1.67	24	1.76	5.39
5	Shanxi	45	1.10	48	1.16	5.00
6	Zhejiang	18	0.91	19	1.00	9.89
7	Inner Mongolia	37	0.84	42	0.98	16.43
8	Xinjiang	59	0.86	60	0.96	11.63
9	Shandong	61	1.04	65	0.94	-9.62
10	Henan	42	0.90	43	0.93	3.78
11	Shaanxi	31	0.68	34	0.82	20.59
12	Liaoning	37	0.69	38	0.73	5.80
13	Sichuan	11	0.58	11	0.72	24.14
14	Gansu	20	0.56	21	0.65	16.07
15	Tianjin	13	0.40	13	0.44	10.00
16	Chongqing	14	0.33	16	0.40	21.21
17	Hunan	8	0.33	9	0.39	19.09
18	Jiangsu	15	0.39	17	0.37	-5.64
19	Guizhou	10	0.30	10	0.33	10.00
20	Hubei	7	0.21	11	0.24	14.29
21	Ningxia	12	0.18	13	0.20	11.11
22	Qinghai	7	0.10	8	0.13	25.00
23	Anhui	3	0.10	3	0.10	0.00
24	Yunnan	2	0.04	4	0.08	100.00

Continued

Rank	Province	Number of Ski Resorts in 2017	2017 Skier Visits (in Millions)	Number of Ski Resorts in 2018	2018 Skier Visits (in Millions)	YOY/%
25	Guangdong	1	0.03	2	0.08	166.67
26	Guangxi	2	0.06	2	0.06	0.00
27	Jiangxi	0	0	2	0.05	/
28	Fujian	1	0.03	1	0.04	33.33
	Total	703	17.5	742	19.7	12.57

Based on the statistics report from Peak Dry Snow, a main supplier of dry ski in China, ski visits of dry ski resorts depended mainly on the location of resorts and the area of snow trails. Table 9-2 showed the distribution of ski visits of dry ski resorts in 2018.

Table 9-2 Distribution of Ski Visits of Dry Ski Resorts (2018)

Province	Annual Ski Visits	Province	Annual Ski Visits
Xinjiang	10000	Heilongjiang	37000
Sichuan	85000	Hebei	15000
Shanghai	5000	Guizhou	25000
Shaanxi	10000	Guangdong	135000
Shandong	105000	Gansu	35000
Liaoning	5000	Fujian	15000
Jiangsu	120000	Beijing	125000
Hunan	40000	Anhui	20000
Hubei	65000	Total	852000

According to the professional report provided by Mr. Cai Tianhui from Winter Wonderland, Figure 9-2 showed the distribution of 580 thousand ski visits which caused by simulated ski gymnasiums in 2018.

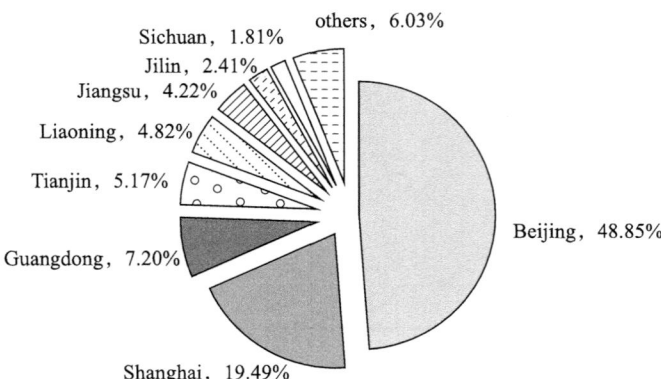

Figure 9-2 Distribution of Ski Visits Caused by Simulated Ski Gymnasiums(2018)

II. Characteristics

In this report, big data from Meituan Tickets presented the characteristics of Meituan ski consumers, which can basically reflect the overall profile of the ski market. Besides, there were many reports on the characteristics of ski enthusiasts provided by various Internet partners, such as GOSKI, Ski+, HUAXUEZOO. In addition, we can get the information of outbound skiers by U-tour.

1. Meituan Report

Provided by Meituan Tickets, the skiing consumers characteristics report took a more comprehensive assessment of ski consumer characteristics from 9 indicators, including gender and age, tourist source and destination, purchase frequency and repurchase interval, and ranking of ski visitors.

(1) Gender & Age

According to the skiing consumers' characteristics report provided by Meituan Tickets in 2018, 49% consumers were male and 51% were female, female member accounting for a relatively high proportion. From the perspective of age, ski consumers between the ages of 20~35 accounted for a larger proportion, reaching 73% and only 27% in other age groups.

Part 4 2018 Report on Key Data of Ski Industry in China

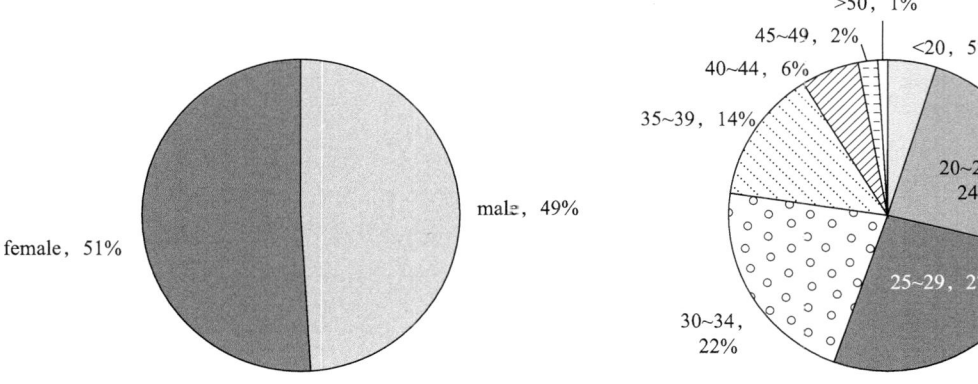

Figure 9-3 Proportion of Gender(2018)   Figure 9-4 Proportion of Age(2018)

(2) Tourism Source and Destination

The top 20 distribution statistics of tourist source and destination of dry ski resorts was shown in Table 9-3. Beijing ranked the first in terms of its largest tourist origin and destination, followed by Xi'an as tourist source and Shenyang as the destination. Hangzhou came last and its destination was Zhangjiakou.

Table 9-3 Distribution of Tourism Source and Destination of Dry Ski Resorts(2018)

Rank	Tourism Source	Destination
1	Beijing	Beijing
2	Xi'an	Shenyang
3	Shenyang	Xi'an
4	Tianjin	Tianjin
5	Urumchi	Urumchi
6	Dalian	Harbin
7	Jinan	Taiyuan
8	Qingdao	Dalian
9	Shenzhen	Jinan
10	Shanghai	Qingdao
11	Taiyuan	Jilin
12	Zhengzhou	Shijiazhuang
13	Lanzhou	Shenzhen
14	Shijiazhuang	Zhengzhou
15	Harbin	Lanzhou

Continued

Rank	Tourism Source	Destination
16	Chengdu	Liupanshui
17	Changchun	Changchun
18	Jilin	Yinchuan
19	Wuhan	Baoding
20	Hangzhou	Zhangjiakou

(3) Purchase Frequency and Repurchase Interval

Purchase frequency and repurchase interval were shown in Figure 9-5. Among them, 91% skiers experienced once, 7% members brought twice and only 2% customers repurchased three times or more. Meanwhile, 45% users would repurchase in one day, 29% users would repurchase in 2~10 days, 10% customers needed 11~30 days to repurchase, and the repurchase interval of 15% members were more than 31 days.

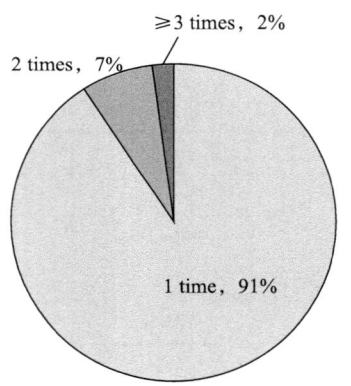
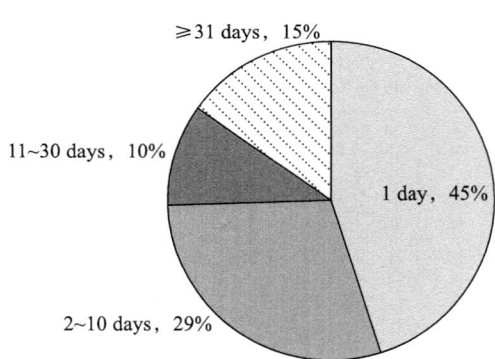

Figure 9-5　Purchase Frequency (2018)　　　　Figure 9-6　Repurchase Interval (2018)

(4) Rank of Ski Visitors

Based on the statistics of ski visits of dry ski resorts in 2017 and 2018, the rank had changed in two years, but to a lesser extent (except Guizhou and Guangdong). On the contrary, the year-on-year growth rate changed significantly in 2018. Especially in Guizhou, Guangdong, Chongqing and Jiangxi, the year-on-year growth rate was over 200%. And the largest growth rate was in Guizhou with 560%. Besides, the year-on-year growth rate of Jilin and Jiangsu declined rapidly in 2018, both at 14%.

Table 9-4　Ski Visits of Dry Ski Resorts by Province

Province	Rank in 2017	Rank in 2018	YOY of 2018/%
Beijing	1	1	5
Liaoning	2	2	-6
Shandong	4	3	12
Shaanxi	3	4	-5
Hebei	5	5	-6
Shanxi	7	6	-5
Tianjin	6	7	-6
Xinjiang	9	8	25
Jilin	8	9	-14
Heilongjiang	12	10	14
Henan	10	11	3
Gansu	11	12	-6
Zhejiang	13	13	16
Inner Mongolia	14	14	3
Guizhou	22	15	560
Sichuan	18	16	64
Guangdong	21	17	243
Ningxia	15	18	6
Hubei	16	19	6
Jiangsu	17	20	-14
Qinghai	20	21	25
Hunan	19	22	-2
Anhui	23	23	266
Chongqing	24	24	239
Jiangxi	25	25	221

(5) "Ski+X"

From the proportion of different categories of "ski+", attractions, hot spring, theme park took the top rank with 27.7%, 25.1% and 20.1%, which was followed by zoo, exhibition center and others with 7.9%, 7.3% and 11.8% respectively.

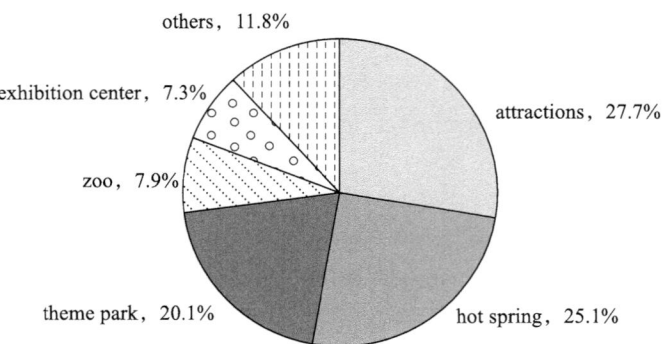

Figure 9-7 Proportion of "Ski+" Classification (2018)

(6) Customer Review

Among all customer reviews, the parent-child related reviews accounted for 8.2% and its average score was 3.6 points, which was lower than the average score of the total reviews of 3.7 points.

Table 9-5 Analysis on Customer Review (2018)

Review	Proportion/%	Average Score (out of 5)
Parent-Child Review	8.2	3.6
Total	100	3.7

(7) Change Trend of Passenger Flow in Snow Season

According to the analysis on the changing trends of passenger flow in the snow season in 2018, from January 1st to February 26th and from December 3rd to December 31st were the periods of larger passenger flow in the snow season. February 26th and December 3rd were two important node dates. During this period, the passenger flow reached the maximum on February 26th, with 18% of the annual passenger crowding, which was followed by the traffic on February 12nd with 12% of annual passengers. The minimum passenger flow was close to 0.

Part 4 2018 Report on Key Data of Ski Industry in China

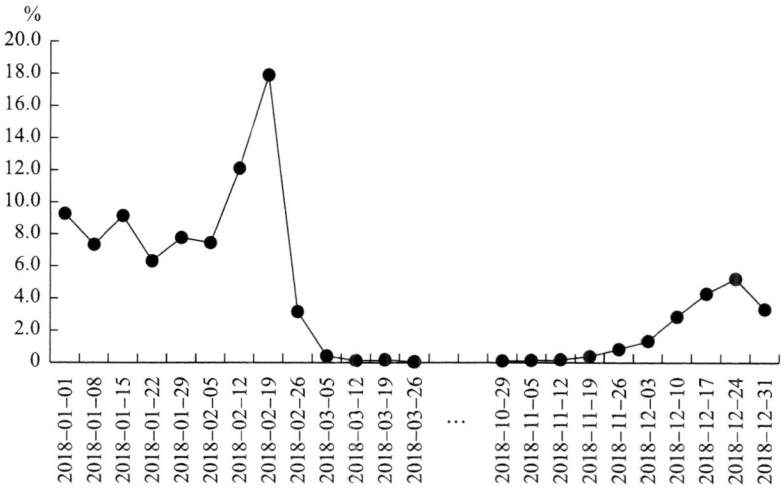

Figure 9-8 Change Trend of Passenger Flow in Snow Season (2018)

(8) Rank of Ski Visitors

As shown in Table 9-6, according to the rank of passengers in the ski resorts, it was found that the number of ski resorts and the number of tourists presented a mismatch. Shandong, owned the most ski resorts, ranked only the third in the number of ski visitors. And Heilongjiang, which had the second largest number of snow resorts, ranked the 11th in terms of passengers. On the contrary, some places such as Guangdong and Guizhou, ranked much higher in the number of skiers with fewer ski resorts.

Table 9-6 Rank of Ski Visitor (2018)

Province	Rank of Ski Resort Number	Rank of Ski Visitor Number
Shandong	1	3
Heilongjiang	2	11
Hebei	3	5
Liaoning	4	2
Beijing	5	1
Jilin	6	8
Henan	7	10
Inner Mongolia	8	14
Shanxi	9	6
Xinjiang	10	9

Continued

Province	Rank of Ski Resort Number	Rank of Ski Visitor Number
Shaanxi	11	4
Tianjin	12	7
Gansu	13	12
Jiangsu	14	20
Zhejiang	15	13
Ningxia	16	18
Hubei	17	19
Sichuan	18	16
Qinghai	19	21
Chongqing	20	24
Hunan	21	22
Guizhou	22	15
Anhui	23	23
Guangdong	24	17
Guangxi	25	27
Yunnan	26	26
Shanghai	27	28
Jiangxi	28	25
Fujian	29	29
Tibet	30	30

(9) Rank of per Capita Consumption

The rank of per capita consumption in ski resorts was shown in Table 9-7. Guangxi, Zhejiang and Guizhou occupied the top 3 respectively, while Shandong, Tianjin and Guangdong were comparatively lagged behind.

Table 9-7 Rank of per Capita Consumption in Ski Resorts (2018)

Province	Rank
Guangxi	1
Zhejiang	2
Guizhou	3
Hubei	4

Continued

Province	Rank
Sichuan	5
Anhui	6
Yunnan	7
Chongqing	8
Xinjiang	9
Jiangsu	10
Gansu	11
Hebei	12
Heilongjiang	13
Beijing	14
Ningxia	15
Shaanxi	16
Jilin	17
Qinghai	18
Liaoning	19
Shandong	20
Tianjin	21
Guangdong	22

2. Characteristic Report of Skiers

(1) Portrait and Analysis

Based on the characteristic report of skiers, the proportion of male and female was 64.33% and 35.67% respectively. The proportion of male users was much higher than that of female, which was unbalanced. See Figure 9-9.

Report on Key Data of *Ski* Industry in China(2015-2019)

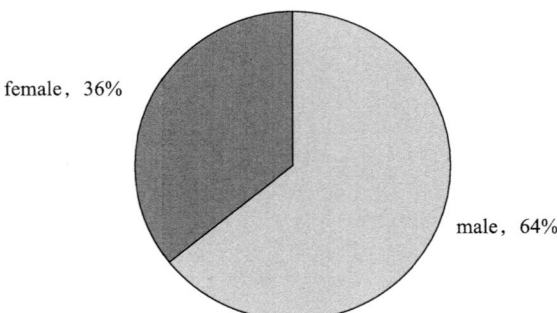

Figure 9-9　Proportion of Gender(2018)

(2) Analysis on the Age Structure

According to the characteristic report of skiers, most users were 20~30 and 30~40 years old, totally accounting for 79.3%. While the proportion of skiers aged 0~20, 40~50 and more than 50 years old was very small, only about 20.7%.

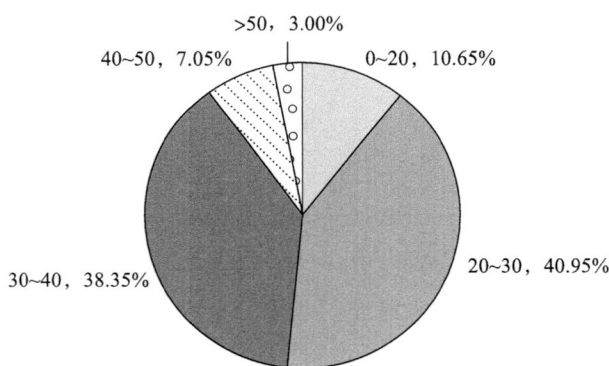

Figure 9-10　Proportion of Age(2018)

(3) Analysis of User Distribution

By analyzing the distribution of users, Beijing, Hebei and Jilin accounted for a large proportion, 31.11%, 16.01% and 11.17% respectively, followed by Heilongjiang, Liaoning, Shanghai and other places with a small proportion.

Part 4 2018 Report on Key Data of Ski Industry in China

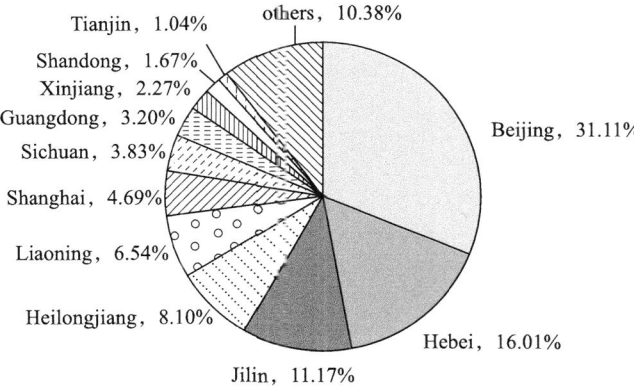

Figure 9-11 Users Distribution by Province(2018)

(4)Skiing Level

By analyzing the proportion of skiers' skiing level, it was found that there were few skiers with advanced skill in China, accounting for less than a quarter of all, and a great number of skiers were at the level of beginners. Among them, the beginners, intermediates and advanced skiers accounted for 44.67%, 33.33% and 22.00% respectively.

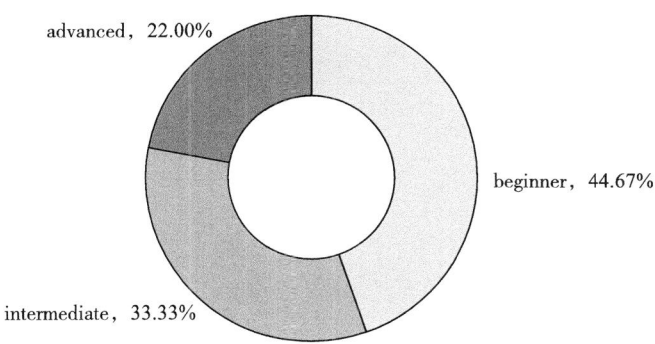

Figure 9-12 Proportion of Skiing Level(2018)

(5)Types of User Focus

There were great differences in content types among HUAXUEZOO, GOSKI and Ski+ members. HUAXUEZOO users mainly focused on the novelty, followed by equipment, hotspots and technology. The types that GOSKI users paid more attention to were mostly focused on ski friend activities, teaching and equipment. While the Ski+ members were interested in strategies, technology and characters.

· 309 ·

More than half of HUAXUEZOO members were interested in the novelty, less attention to the equipment, hotspots, technology and others, showing a trend of extreme differentiation. See Figure 9-13.

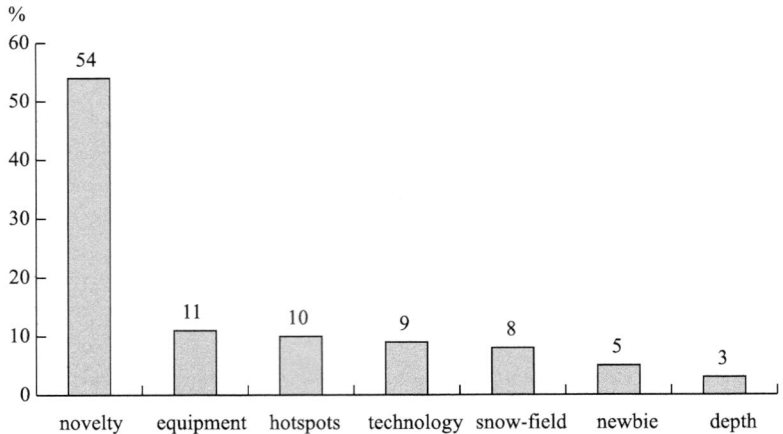

Figure 9-13　Types of User Focus from HUAXUEZOO(2018)

The types that GOSKI members concerned were ski friends' activities, teaching and strategies, et al. Unlike HUAXUEZOO, GOSKI members were interested in a variety of content which were evenly distributed. Among them, 20% users focused on their friends' activities, 19% interested in teaching and 16% focused on ski strategies, followed by excellent video, match news and tourism et al. See Figure 9-14.

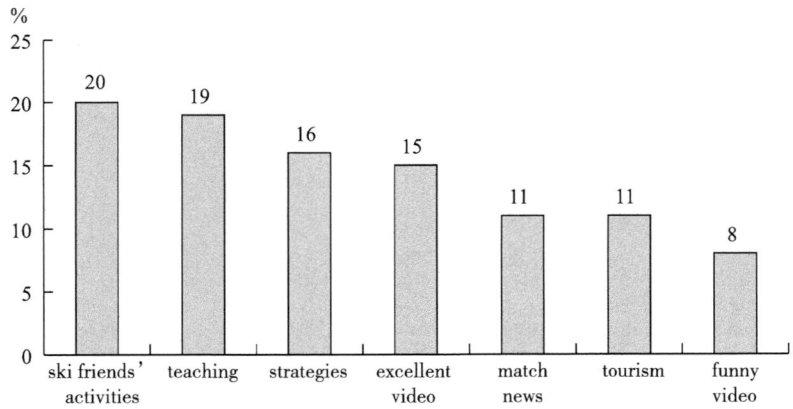

Figure 9-14　Types of User Focus from GOSKI(2018)

As to Ski+ users, 37.40% skiers concentrated on strategies, followed by technology, characters and activities, and fewer members focused on equipment and ski teaching. See Figure 9-15.

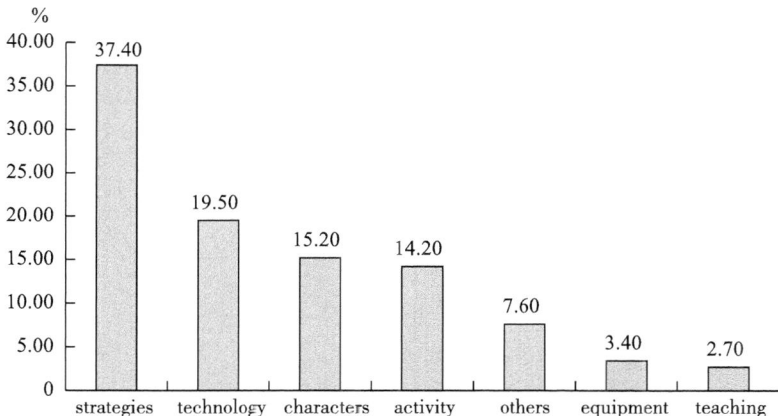

Figure 9-15   Types of User Focus from Ski+ (2018)

(6) Top 10 Recorded Ski Resorts

Recorded by HUAXUEZOO, the top 10 ski resorts in China with the most tracks were as following: Vanke Songhua Lake, Wanlong, Genting, Beidahu, Thaiwoo, Fulong, Wanda Changbai Mountain, Nanshan Mountain, Huaibei and Yabuli Sunlight.

Recorded by GOSKI, the top 10 ski resorts in China with the most tracks were as following: Wanlong, Genting, Fulong, Beidahu, Vanke Songhua Lake, Huaibei, Nanshan Mountain, Wanlong Bayi, Wanda Changbai Mountain and Thaiwoo.

Recorded by Ski+, the top 10 ski resorts in China with the most tracks were as following: Wanlong, Vanke Songhua Lake, Genting, Beidahu, Yabuli Sunlight, Thaiwoo, Fulong, Wanda Changbai Mountain, Cuiyun Mountain Yinhe and Huaibei.

(7) Top 10 Favored Ski Resorts

Recorded by HUAXUEZOO, the top 10 ski resorts with rave reviews were: Vanke Songhua Lake, Wanlong, Genting, Beidahu, Thaiwoo, Fulong, Wanda Changbai Mountain, Yabuli Sunlight, Cuiyun Mountain Yinhe and Silk Road.

Recorded by GOSKI, the top 10 ski resorts with rave reviews were as following: Wanlong, Wanda Changbai Mountain, Thaiwoo, Vanke Songhua Lake, Fulong, Nanshan Mountain,

Genting, Tianchi Snow, Beidahu and Yuyang.

Recorded by Ski+, the top 10 ski resorts with rave reviews were: Vanke Songhua Lake, Wanlong, Cuiyun Mountain Yinhe, Beidahu, Fulong, Wanda Changbai Mountain, Silk Road, Yabuli Sunlight, Thaiwoo and Genting.

3. Characteristics of Outbound Skiers

According to the report on outbound skiers' characteristics provided by U-tour, it was found that, firstly, the outbound skiing products, 6~8 days with 8000~12000 yuan per capita, were the most popular choices to customers. Secondly, the age range of the skiers was 25~40 and the ratio of male to female was 6 : 4. Thirdly, the gathered places of visitors were mainly concentrated in Beijing, Tianjin and Shanghai. Furthermore, more than 65% skiers chose Japan as their ski destination, which mainly concentrated in three destinations: Hokkaido Area, including Niseko, Furano, Rusutsu, Kiroro, Asahidake; Nagano Area, such as Hakuba, Shiga, Madarao; Northeast Area, Appi Kogen, Zao and Shizukuishi for example. Other destinations such as Three Valleys in French, Switzerland, Austria were all popular destinations, North America, New Zealand were all in the early stages of development.

III. Ski Equipment Market

This report collected retail data of snowboarders from DECATHLON, Burton, GOSKI, etc. In 2018, the total sales of snowboarders were about 38 thousand, with more than 25%, and the sales of snowboarders shoes were about 50 thousand pairs.

Compared to the snowboard market, the skis were in a sluggish market with 15 thousand annual sales, increasing by 5% year-on-year. The data was provided by DECATHLON, HEAD, ROSSIGNOL, ELAN, etc.

In 2018, online sales of ski equipment accounted for about one-third of the total. And there was a trend of continued growth.

Part 5

2019 Report on Key Data of Ski Industry in China

Chapter 10   2019 Ski Resorts and Ski Visits

Ski resorts and skier visits are the two cores of the entire ski industry, on which all business and activities of the ski industry are based. Therefore, the number of ski resorts and ski visits constitute the two core indicators of the ski industry. Based on the status quo of China, this report divided ski resorts into three categories: ski resorts (outdoor ski resorts and indoor ski resorts), dry slopes, and simulated ski gymnasiums.

I. Number of Ski Resorts, Ski Visits and Skiers

In 2019, the number of ski resorts increased by 3.77%, with 28 new ski resorts coming into operation, including 5 indoor ski resorts. Among these 28 resorts, 5 ski resorts were equipped with the aerial lifts. Besides, one resort in operation has built aerial lifts. Till the end of 2019, a total of 770 ski resorts were in operation, and 155 of them were equipped with the aerial lifts. The number of resorts equipped with aerial lifts increased by 4.03% in 2019 compared with 149 in 2018. The number of ski visits increased from 19.7 million in 2018 to 20.9 million in 2019, with a year-on-year growth of 6.09%. See Figure 10-1.

Report on Key Data of *Ski* Industry in China (2015-2019)

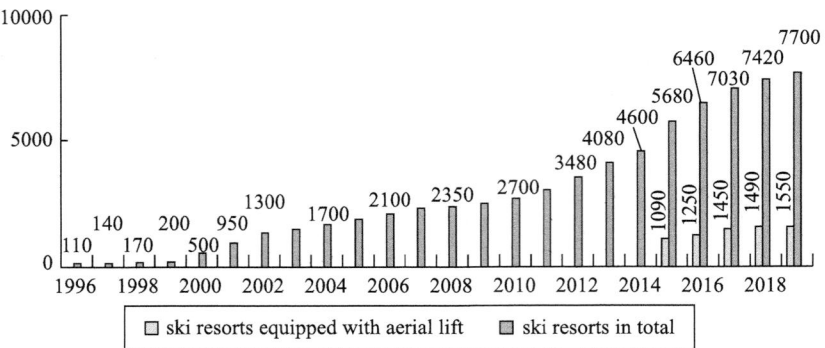

Figure 10-1 Number of Ski Resorts & Ski Visits (in Thousands)

Note: "ski resorts in total" and "ski visits" in this figure only took outdoor ski resorts and indoor ski resorts ski visits into account. The numbers of dry slopes and ski simulators were excluded.

With the 2022 Winter Olympic Games looming, various ski promotions were developing in depth, and the conversion rate of ski beginners has increased significantly. According to the anticipation of this report, the number of domestic skiers in 2019 was about 13.05 million, which was slightly lower than the 13.2 million in 2018. Among them, the proportion of one-time-only skiers dropped from 75.38% in 2018 to 72.04%, and the proportion of ski enthusiasts increased. In 2019, skiers go skiing in domestic ski resorts for 1.60 times per capita, which was higher than 1.49 times in 2018. See Figure 10-2.

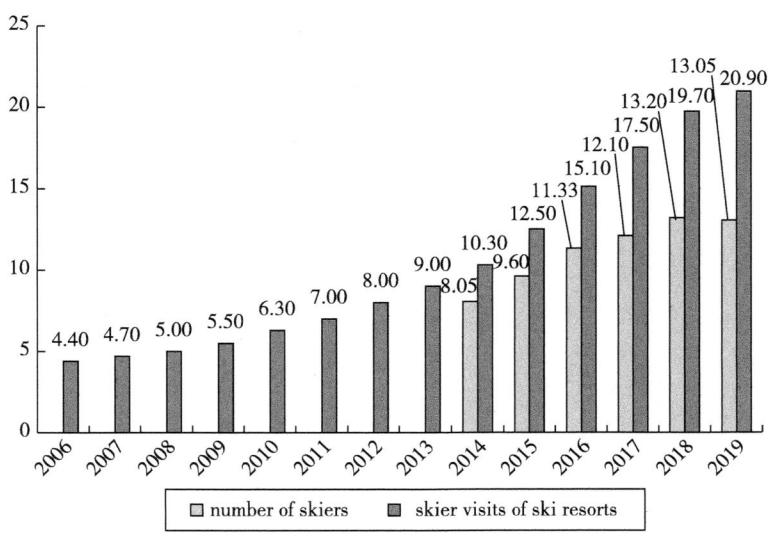

Figure 10-2 Number of Ski Visits & Skiers (in Millions)

II. Distribution of Ski Resorts and Ski Visits

There were 770 ski resorts distributed in 28 provinces, autonomous regions and municipalities. The top 5 provinces owned the most ski resorts were Heilongjiang, Shandong, Xinjiang, Hebei, and Shanxi. In 2019, Hubei and Xinjiang had the largest number of new ski resorts. See Table 10-1 for details.

Table 10-1　Number of Ski Resorts by Province

Rank	Province	2018	2019	2019 Growth
1	Heilongjiang	124	124	0
2	Shandong	65	67	2
3	Xinjiang	60	65	5
4	Hebei	59	61	2
5	Shanxi	48	49	1
6	Jilin	43	45	2
7	Henan	43	44	1
8	Inner Mongolia	42	42	0
9	Liaoning	38	38	0
10	Shaanxi	34	35	1
11	Beijing	24	25	1
12	Gansu	21	22	1
13	Zhejiang	19	20	1
14	Jiangsu	17	18	1
15	Chongqing	16	16	0
16	Hubei	11	16	5
17	Ningxia	13	14	1
18	Tianjin	13	13	0
19	Sichuan	11	12	1
20	Guizhou	10	10	0
21	Hunan	9	10	1
22	Qinghai	8	8	0
23	Yunnan	4	5	1

Continued

Rank	Province	2018	2019	2019 Growth
24	Anhui	3	3	0
25	Guangdong	2	3	1
26	Guangxi	2	2	0
27	Jiangxi	2	2	0
28	Fujian	1	1	0
	Total	742	770	28

The distribution of domestic ski visits in 2019 was shown in Table 10-2. The ski visits of Hebei, Jilin and Beijing increased a lot, surpassing Heilongjiang and becoming the top three. Moreover, the number of ski visits in Hebei and Jilin surpassed 2 million in 2019. At the same time, the domestic ski market was clearly differentiated in 2019. The number of ski visits in 13 provinces decreased. In addition, Sunac Snow World of Sunac Group, acquisition of Wanda Indoor Ski Resort, became a market hotspot, which all performed very well in Guangzhou, Wuxi, and Kunming.

Table 10-2 Distribution of Ski Visits by Province

Rank	Province	Total Ski Resorts in 2018	Ski Visits in 2018 (in Thousands)	Total Ski Resorts in 2019	Ski Visits in 2019 (in Thousands)	YOY/%
1	Hebei	59	2100	61	2430	15.71
2	Jilin	43	1840	45	2150	16.85
3	Beijing	24	1760	25	1890	7.39
4	Heilongjiang	124	2210	124	1860	-15.84
5	Xinjiang	60	960	65	1220	27.08
6	Zhejiang	19	1000	20	1110	11.00
7	Inner Mongolia	42	980	42	1010	3.06
8	Henan	43	930	44	960	3.23
9	Shanxi	48	1160	49	950	-18.10
10	Shandong	65	940	67	880	-6.38
11	Shaanxi	34	820	35	740	-9.76
12	Sichuan	11	720	12	680	-5.56
13	Liaoning	38	730	38	670	-8.22

Continued

Rank	Province	Total Ski Resorts in 2018	Ski Visits in 2018 (in Thousands)	Total Ski Resorts in 2019	Ski Visits in 2019 (in Thousands)	YOY/%
14	Guangdong	2	80	3	650	712.50
15	Gansu	21	650	22	600	-7.69
16	Jiangsu	17	370	18	540	45.95
17	Tianjin	13	440	13	460	4.55
18	Hubei	11	240	16	430	79.17
19	Chongqing	16	400	16	350	-12.50
20	Hunan	9	390	10	340	-12.82
21	Guizhou	10	330	10	320	-3.03
22	Ningxia	13	200	14	220	10.00
23	Qinghai	8	130	8	150	15.38
24	Anhui	3	100	3	120	20.00
25	Yunnan	4	80	5	90	12.50
26	Guangxi	2	60	2	50	-16.67
27	Jiangxi	2	50	2	40	-20.00
28	Fujian	1	40	1	20	-50.00
	Total	742	19700	770	20900	6.09

III. Classified Statistics of Ski Resorts

1. Indoor Ski Resorts

There were 5 indoor ski resorts in the 28 newly operating ski resorts. In China, totaled 31 indoor ski resorts came into operation till the end of 2019.

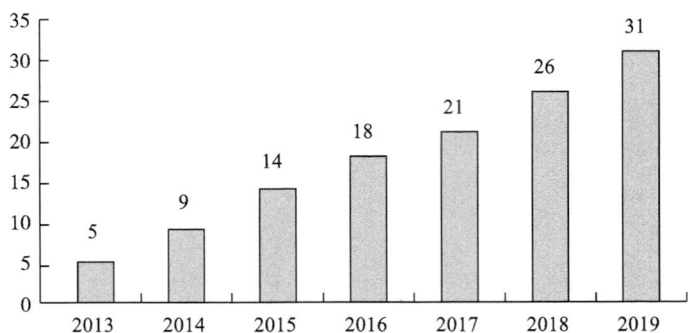

Figure 10-3 Number of Operated Indoor Ski Resorts in China

In 2019, the ski visits of all the 31 indoor ski resorts was 2.35 million in total. Among them, the most prominent was Guangzhou Sunac Snow World. With an area of 75 thousand square meters, Guangzhou Sunac Snow World was the second largest indoor ski resort in the world. From its opening on June 15th, 2019 to December 31st, 2019, Guangzhou Sunac Snow World had received a total of 550 thousand ski visits and was expected to become the largest ski visits of indoor ski resorts in the world. While at the same time, the performance of Harbin Sunac Snow World(formerly Harbin Wanda Entertainment Snow Park), the world's largest indoor ski resort, was not optimistic in 2019, with a significant drop of ski visits.

As can be seen from Table 10-3, ski visits in indoor ski resorts increased by 42% in 2019, which played a decisive role in the increase of ski visits in all ski resorts.

Table 10-3 Statistics of Ski Visits from Indoor Ski Resorts

Type	Number of Ski Resorts	Number of Ski Visits in 2019 (in Thousands)	Number of Ski Visits in 2018 (in Thousands)	Growth Rate/%
Indoor Ski Resort	31	2350	1660	42
Outdoor Ski Resort	739	18550	18040	3
Total	770	20900	19700	6

2. Destination Resorts

If classified by target group, the domestic ski resorts were divided into three categories: travel/experience, educational, and destination resorts. The proportions of these three kinds were

77%, 20% and 3% respectively. See Table 10-4.

Table 10-4 Classification of Ski Resorts by Target Group(2019)

Type of Ski Resort	Per.	Target Group	Attributes	Resort Feature	Consumer Characteristics	Cases
Travel/ experience ski resorts	77%	Sightseer	Touristic	Basic facilities equipped with only beginner trails, located in tourist attractions or suburb area	Over 90% are one-time-only visitors, average stay 2 hours	Xiling Snow Mountain, Daming Mountain, Langya Mountain
Educational ski resorts	20%	Tourists from neighboring areas	Athletic, touristic	Little vertical drop located in suburb areas, Equipped with all kinds of trails	Most are self-driving tourists from neighboringareas, average stay 3 to 4 hours	Nanshan Mountain, Jundu Mountain, Vanke Shijinglong, TOREAD Songding
Destination ski resorts	3%	Vocational tourist	Vacation/ leisure, athletic, touristic	Considerable vertical drop and land, well-equipped trails and auxiliary facilities such as accommodation	Visitors usually stay overnight, average stay one day	Vanke Songhua Lake, Wanda Changbai Mountain, Beidahu, Yabuli, Wanlong, Thaiwoo, Fulong, Genting

As for all the 770 ski resorts, about 20 of them were destination resorts and 8 of them were large-scaled destination resorts.

It can be seen from Table 10-5 that the growth of ski visits at destination ski pesorts was much larger than the growth at national ski resorts. Among them, the increase in ski visits at large destination ski resorts was much higher than that at medium destination ski resorts.

Table 10-5 Statistics of Ski Visits at Destination Ski Resorts(2019)

Type	Number of Ski Resorts	Ski Visits in 2019 (in Thousands)	Ski Visits in 2018 (in Thousands)	Growth Rate/%
Large Destination Ski Resorts	8	2560	1950	31
Medium Destination Ski Resorts	12	880	720	22
Total	770	20900	19700	6

3. Ski Resorts with Vertical Drop more than 300 Meters

The vertical drop of the ski resort is an important indicator for the resource scale of a ski resort. According to the actual vertical drop of the trails in the ski resorts, we can classify the domestic ski resorts to three categories: 26 ski resorts with more than 300 meters vertical drop-trails, accounting for 3.4%; 142 with vertical drop of 100~300 meters, taking up 18.44% and 602 ski resorts with vertical drop of less than 100 meters, making up 78.18%. As was shown in Figure 10-4:

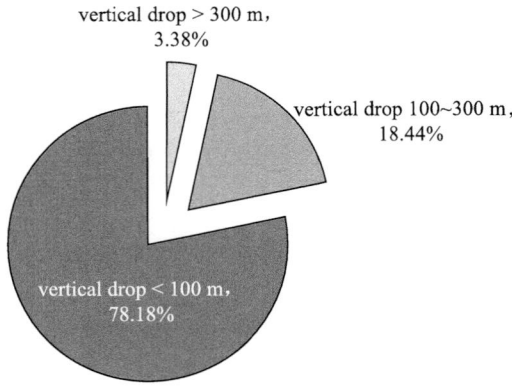

Figure 10-4　Classification of Ski Resorts by Vertical Drop(2019)

The newly built National Alpine Ski Center in Yanqing, Beijing is the main alpine ski resort for the Beijing Winter Olympics with a vertical drop of more than 900 meters, and it is currently the highest vertical drop of ski resorts with aerial ropeway in China. In addition, Heilongjiang Yabuli and Jilin Beidahu both have a vertical drop of more than 800 meters. They are the only two ski resorts in China that hosted the Asian Winter Games. In 2019, ski resorts with a vertical drop of more than 300 meters had 3.64 million visits, increasing by 17% compared to 2018, which was much higher than the growth rate of the total number of ski visits in all resorts.

Part 5　2019 Report on Key Data of Ski Industry in China

Table 10-6　Ski Visits in Ski Resorts with Vertical Drop more than 300 Meters(2019)

Type	Number of Ski Resorts	Ski Visits in 2019 (in Thousands)	Ski Visits in 2018 (in Thousands)	Growth Rate/%
Ski Resorts with Vertical Drop more than 300 Meters	26	3640	3120	17
Ski Resorts of All Kinds	770	20900	19700	6

4. Ski Resorts with Slope Area more than 30 Hectares

Area of slopes is another important indicator to measure the size of the ski area. By the end of 2019, there were 30 ski resorts with a total area of more than 30 hectares, accounting for 3.90%. As was shown in Table 10-7 for details.

Table 10-7　Number of Ski Resorts by Slope Area(2019)

Area of Slopes/hm²	Number of Ski Resorts	Proportion/%	Ski Visits in 2019 (in Thousands)	Ski Visits in 2018 (in Thousands)	Growth Rate/%
>100	8	1.04	4780	4150	16
50~100	7	0.91			
30~50	15	1.95			
10~30	37	4.81	/	/	/
5~10	126	16.36	/	/	/
<5	577	74.94	/	/	/
Total	770	100.00	2090	1970	6

5. Ski Resorts with Aerial Lift

In 2019, there were 155 ski resorts with aerial lift in China, increasing by 6 comparing the data of 2018. This report would increasingly focus on the ski resorts with aerial lift. As Table 10-8 showed, there were 8 ski resorts with 4 or more aerial lifts, which was coincided with the number of large destination ski resorts previously mentioned. In general, the more aerial lifts the ski resorts have, the larger increase in ski visits. There were 155 ski resorts with aerial ropeway, with a total of

· 323 ·

10.15 million ski visits, accounting for 48.56% of the total 20.9 million ski visits. There were 22 ski resorts with detachable lift, reached 3.54 million ski visits in 2019, up 20% year-on-year.

Table 10-8 Number of Ski Resorts with Aerial Lift (2019)

Type	Number of Ski Resorts	Ski Visits in 2019 (in Thousands)	Ski Visits in 2018 (in Thousands)	Growth Rate/%
> 4	8	2560	1950	31
> 3	23	3500	3000	17
> 2	57	6150	5350	15
≥ 1	155	10150	9040	12
Detachable Lifts	22	3540	2950	20
Total	770	20900	19700	6

6. Ski Resorts with Ski Visits more than 100 Thousand

Mr. Laurent, who is from Switzerland, has always focused on the ski resorts with more than one million ski visits in his *International Report on Snow & Mountain Tourism* over the years. It is increasingly practical significant to classify and screen ski resorts by the number of ski visits. In 2019, among the 770 ski resorts in China, the top three ski resorts in terms of ski visits were still the "Three WAN" (in Chinese) as dubbed before in this report, namely Vanke Songhua Lake, Wanda Changbai Mountain, and Wanlong ski resorts.

As a pilot study, the number of ski resorts with more than 100 thousand and 150 thousand ski visits in the whole year of 2019 was counted as in Table 10-9. It can be seen that, only 31 of the 770 ski resorts had more than 100 thousand ski visits, accounting for 4.03% of the total. But the 31 resorts received 6.09 million ski visits in total, 29.14% of the total. At the same time, it can be seen from the increase data that the ski resort with more ski visits had a greater year-on-year growth.

Table 10-9 Ski Resorts with more than 100 Thousand Ski Visits(2019)

Type	Number of Ski Resorts	Ski Visits in 2019 (in Thousands)	Ski Visits in 2018 (in Thousands)	Growth Rate/%
≥ 150 thousand	16	4510	3490	29
≥ 100 thousand	31	6090	4870	25
Total	770	2090	19700	6

IV. Dry Ski

According to the information provided by Peak Dry Snow①, by the end of 2019, the total number of dry ski resorts in China had reached 45. But 8 of them were closed for extended periods, and one was demolished.

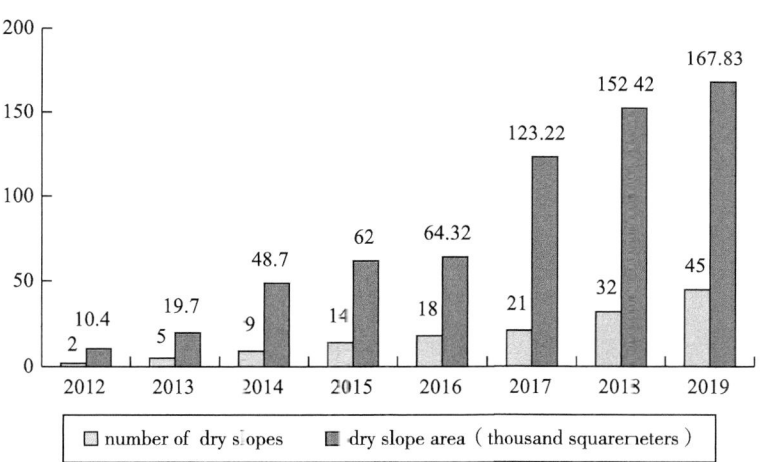

Figure 10-5 Dry Ski Resorts and Area in China

The distribution of dry slopes was shown in Figure 10-6. Currently, Sichuan, Beijing and Hebei were among the top three, accounting for more than 10%.

---

① The inventor and trademark owner of the World Enoki Mushroom Dry Snow(Peak Dry Snow) Jian Feng(Mr. Dry Slope) provided a complete and detailed report of the dry ski for this report. For further needs in the area of dry slopes, please contact Mr. Jian Feng: +86-13281197551.

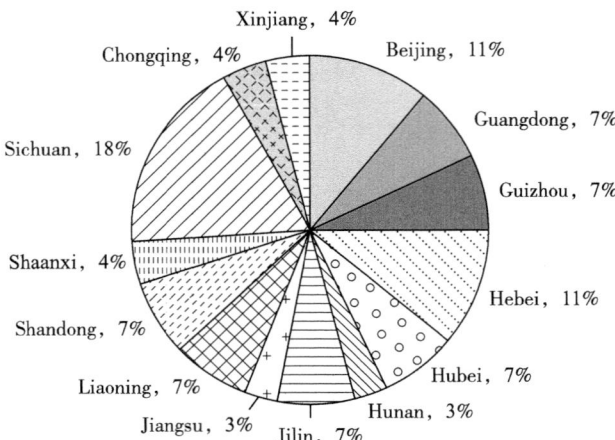

Figure 10-6 Dry Ski Resorts in Operation in China(2019)

Since the ski visits of snow tubing was included in the dry slopes statistics in 2018, it cannot be used as a reference for comparison. After excluding the data of the snow tubing in 2019, the number of ski visits generated in the dry slopes was 342300. As was shown in Figure 10-7.

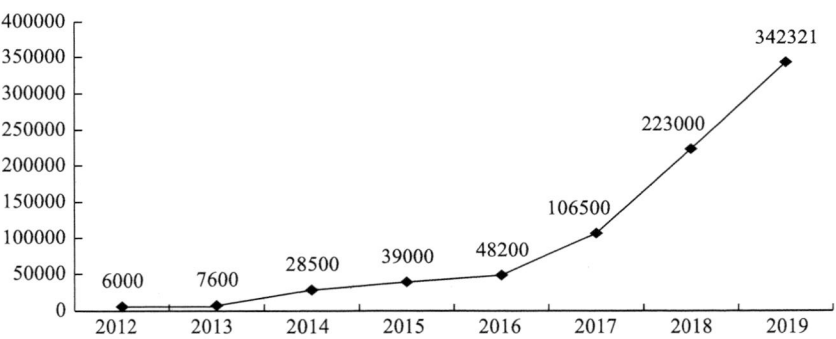

Figure 10-7 Ski Visits of Dry Slopes

V. Ski Simulator

In 2019, the ski simulator market continued to show accelerated growth. According to the information provided by SKINOW, by the end of 2019, the total number of stores in SKINOW had reached 96. According to the report provided by Winter Wonderland, by the end of 2019, there were 140 domestic simulated ski gymnasiums and 400 ski simulators of all kinds were in use. It was estimated by this report that the number of ski visits generated by the ski simulators in 2019 was around 780 thousand, up 34.48% from 580 thousand in 2018.

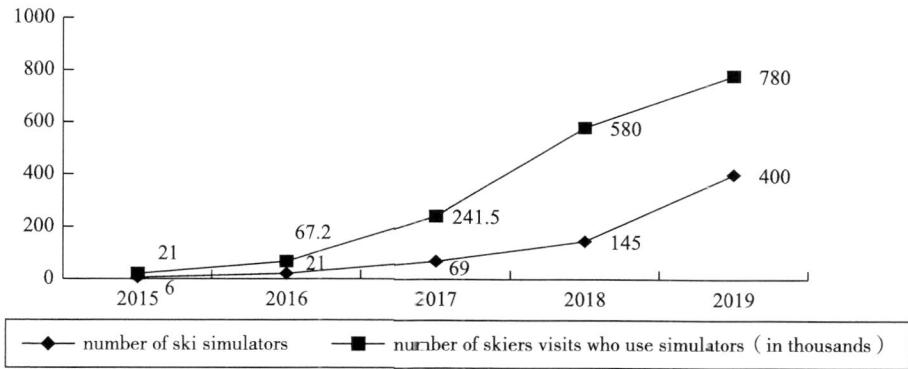

Figure 10-8 Numbers of Ski Simulators and Ski Visits

VI. Total Ski Visits

Based on the data from the ski resorts, dry slopes and ski simulators, the total number of ski visits in 2019 was 22.02 million.

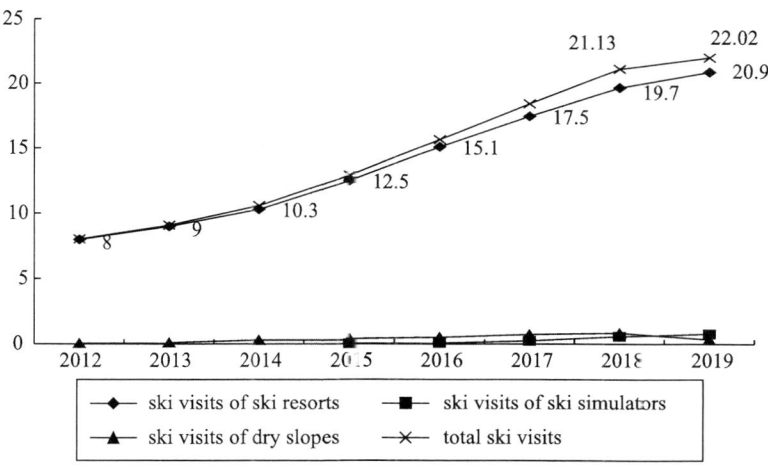

Figure 10-9 Total Ski Visits (in Millions)

Chapter 11 Facilities of Ski Resorts

I. Lifts Facilities

1. Aerial Lifts

By the end of 2019, the total number of operating aerial lifts in domestic ski resorts was 261, distributed in 155 ski resorts in 22 provinces across the country. Among them, Hebei, Heilongjiang, and Jilin ranked top three, with 49, 40, and 39 aerial lifts respectively. There were 128 aerial lifts in total had been built in these three provinces, accounting for 49% of the total aerial lifts in all the ski resorts in China.

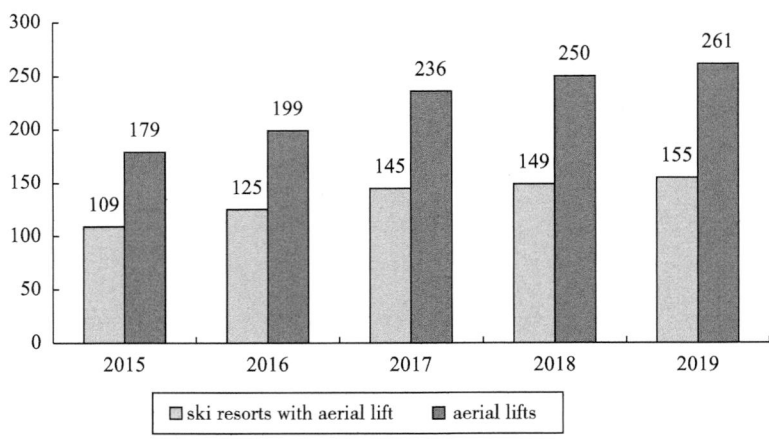

Figure 11-1 Aerial Lifts in Ski Resorts

Table 11-1 Distribution of Aerial Lifts in Ski Resorts (2019)

Rank	Province	Number of Aerial Lifts	Number of Ski Resorts with Aerial Lift
1	Hebei	49	22
2	Heilongjiang	40	28
3	Jilin	39	16
4	Liaoning	28	19
5	Beijing	23	13
6	Xinjiang	19	10
7	Inner Mongolia	17	10
8	Shanxi	8	5
9	Gansu	8	7
10	Shandong	6	6
11	Shaanxi	5	4
12	Sichuan	3	2
13	Henan	3	2
14	Yunnan	3	1
15	Chongqing	3	3
16	Guizhou	2	2
17	Hubei	2	2
18	Tianjin	1	1
19	Guangdong	1	1
20	Ningxia	1	1
	Total	261	155

The domestic detachable lifts developed rapidly, from 26 in 2015 to 60 in 2019, and the number of ski resorts with detachable lift also increased from 10 to 22.

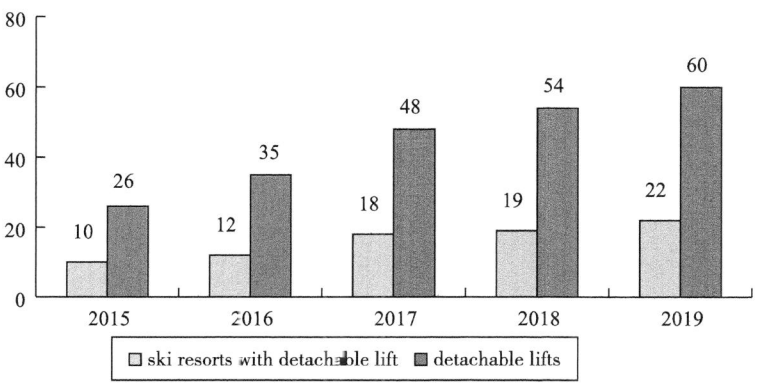

Figure 11-2 Detachable Lifts in Ski Resorts

Figure 11-3 summarized the relationship between the number of imported and domestic detachable lifts from 2015 to 2019. The number of domestically produced detachable lifts had been rapidly increased from 2 in 2015 to 20 in 2019.

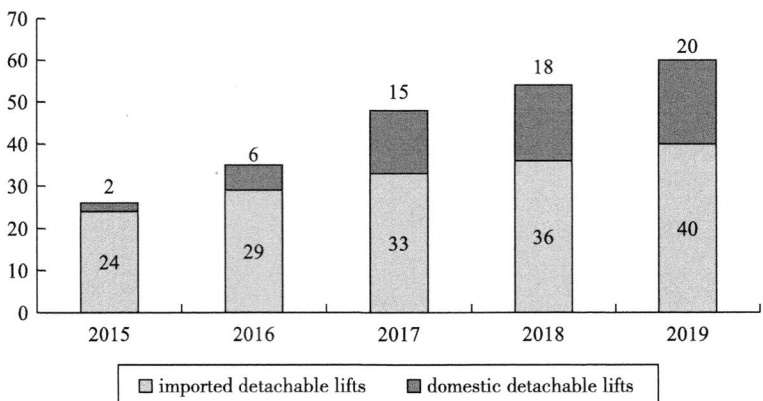

Figure 11-3　Number of Imported and Domestic Detachable Lifts

Among the 60 detachable lifts used in ski resorts, there were 21 in Hebei, distributed in 7 ski resorts which were concentrated in Chongli, Zhangjiakou; there were 19 in Jilin, distributed in 6 ski resorts; there were 7 in Heilongjiang, dividedly located in 3 ski resorts; there were 4 in Xinjiang, distributed in 2 ski resorts; Beijing and Inner Mongolia had 3 detachable lifts respectively; Shaanxi had 2 ski lifts and Hubei had 1 ski lift. (Note: This statistic was detachable lifts for skiing only, excluding non-skiing usage.)

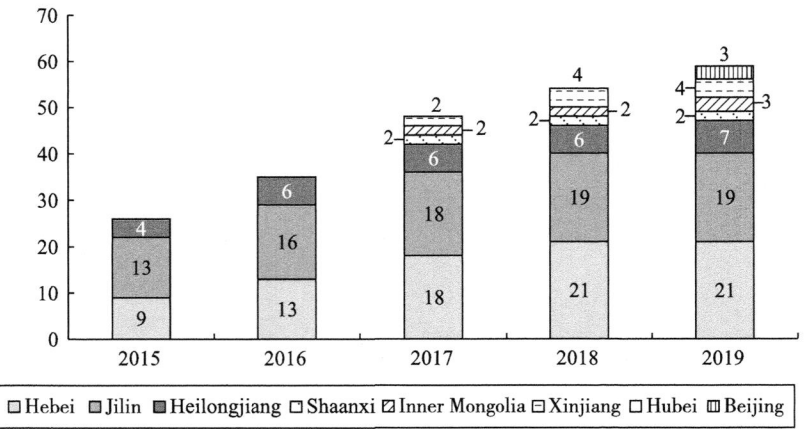

Figure 11-4　Distribution of Detachable Lifts in Ski Resorts by Province

Part 5 2019 Report on Key Data of Ski Industry in China

In 2019, among the ski resorts in China with detachable lifts, the National Alpine Ski Center located in Xiaohaituo, Yan Qing, Beijing deserved the most attentions. At present, the construction of 3 detachable lifts has been completed and put into competition operation. As the main venue for the Beijing Winter Olympic alpine skiing, the hardware facilities are unparalleled and will inevitably become a benchmark for domestic ski resorts.

Table 11-2 Rank of Ski Resorts According to the Number of Lifts (2019)

No.	Rank	Ski Resorts	Number	Province
1	1	Vanke Songhua Lake	6	Jilin
2	1	Wanlong	6	Hebei
3	3	Wanda Changbai Mountain	5	Jilin
4	3	Thaiwoo	5	Hebei
5	5	Beidahu	4	Jilin
6	5	Genting	4	Hebei
7	5	Yabuli (High Mountain)	4	Heilongjiang
8	8	National Alpine Ski Center (Yanqing Xiaohaituo)	3	Beijing
9	8	Silk Road	3	Xinjiang
10	8	Fulong	3	Hebei
11	11	Aoshan Mountain	2	Shaanxi
12	11	Luneng Changbai Mountain	2	Jilin
13	11	Cuiyun Mountain Yinhe	2	Hebei
14	11	Yabuli Sunlight	2	Heilongjiang
15	11	Liangcheng Daihai	2	Inner Mongolia
16	16	Miaoxiang Mountain	1	Jilin
17	16	Duolemeidi	1	Hebei
18	16	Maoer Mountain	1	Heilongjiang
19	16	Changchun Lianhua Mountain	1	Jilin
20	16	Jiangjun Mountain	1	Xinjiang
21	16	Meilin Valley	1	Inner Mongolia
22	16	Lvcongpo	1	Hubei
		Total	60	

2. Magic Carpets

To the biggest beginners skiing market in the world, magic carpets play a vital role in the development of the Chinese skiing market. In the past two years, with the decreasing of newly established outdoor ski resorts, the magic carpet market had fallen significantly as well. There were 21 thousand meters of new magic carpets in 2019, which was slightly higher than 2018.

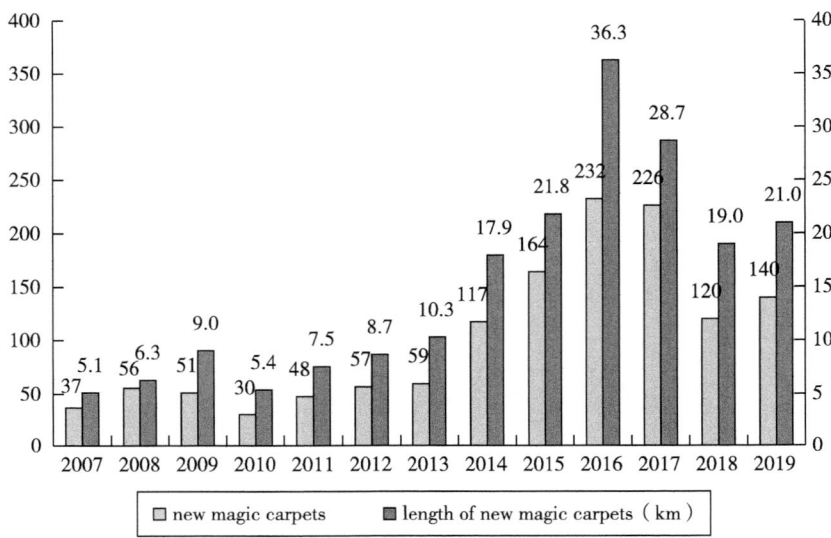

Figure 11-5　Number and Length of New Magic Carpets in Ski Resorts

The data of magic carpets was from the major magic carpets suppliers in China. As of 2019, there were 1336 magic carpets in operation in domestic ski resorts, including 140 new in 2019. The total length of all magic carpets was about 197 kilometers.

Part 5 2019 Report on Key Data of Ski Industry in China

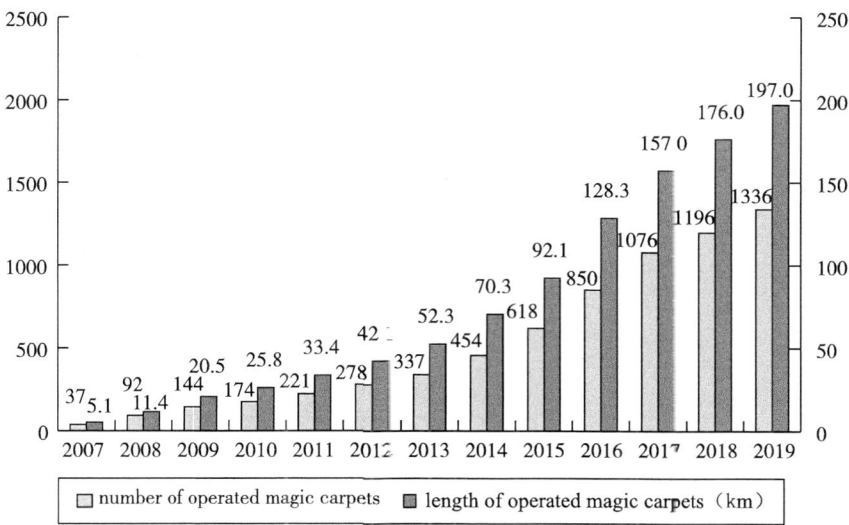

Figure 11-6 Number and Length of Operated Magic Carpets in Ski Resorts

II. Grooming & Snowmaking Facilities

Due to large orders from the Beijing Winter Olympic, the sale of grooming and snowmaking facilities had an apparent increase in 2019. Also, the recent climate changes caused great troubles in the snowmaking process and slope-maintenances. As a result, the managers had to purchase new snowmaking machines and improve existing grooming facilities.

1. Grooming Machines

According to statistics, there were about 629 grooming machines in all domestic ski resorts in China. In 2019, there were 88 new groomers in China, with 19 groomers from National Alpine Ski Center. This number was much higher than 56 in 2018. There were about 61 newly imported grooming machines and 27 domestic ones. Data was came from the major groomer production companies.

Report on Key Data of *Ski* Industry in China (2015-2019)

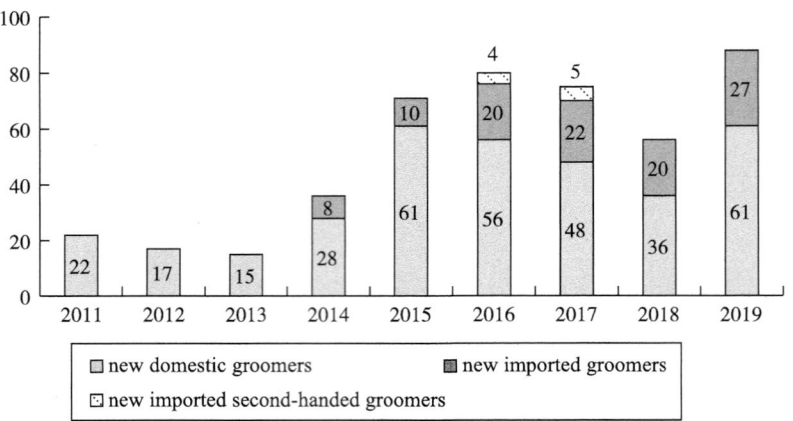

Figure 11-7 New Grooming Machines in Ski Resorts

2. Snowmaking Machines

In 2019, there were about 1149 new snowmaking machines in all domestic ski resorts (including Beijing Winter Olympic Stadiums), with 41.85% increase compared with 810 in 2018. As of the end of 2019, there were about 8559 snowmaking machines in total. ①

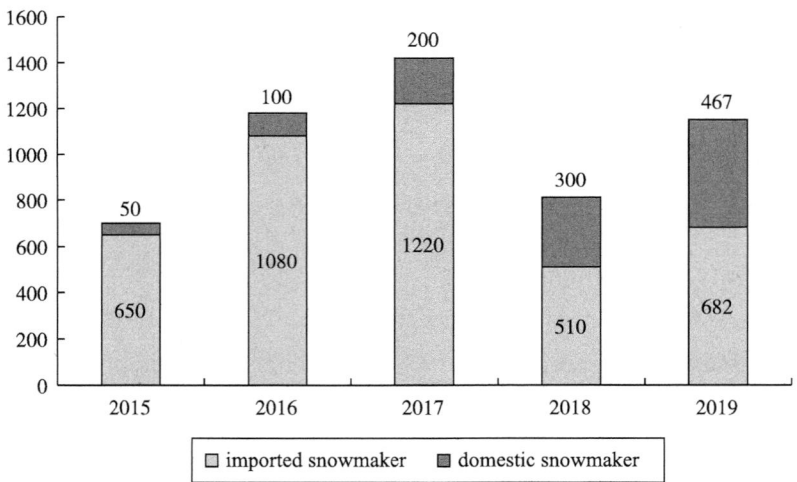

Figure 11-8 New Snowmaking Machines in Ski Resorts

---

① Data from major snowmaker suppliers.

III. Rental Skis

Currently, China does not have the ability to independently produce the ski bindings, so we used the customs import data on imported ski bindings to analyze the skis market. Also, the rental market of skis was much larger than retailing, showing a high relevance with the scale of imported ski bindings.

Based on the data provided by China Customs, it was found that after a sharp fall in 2018, the number of imported ski bindings rose rapidly from 92 ton to 119 ton, with a year-on-year increase of 29.35%. However, this number was still relatively lower compared with that in 2017 (137.45 ton).

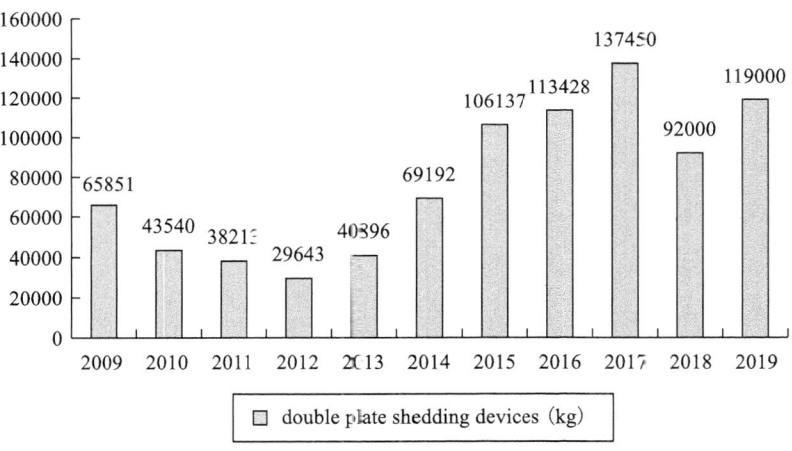

Figure 11-9 Statistics of China Imports (Ski Bindings)

Quote: China Customs, Beijing Longzhixun Information Consulting Co., Ltd.

It was a pity that as of the end of compiling this report, relevant data from the industry could not be obtained in time to estimate the performance of the rental skis bindings market in 2019. However, from what we had observed in previous years, the rapid increase on the imported ski bindings was a sign showing the prosperity of rental skis bindings market.

Chapter 12 Characteristics of Skiers

In order to write this report, besides large quantities of surveys we had made by our team, different online platforms like Ctrip Travel, Mafengwo Ski, HUAXUEZOO, Ski+, also submitted reports on the whole look of the characteristics of skiers. We hope you can see a preliminary picture of the skiers from this report.

I .Gender of Skiers

Maybe each single report did not tell you a clear picture, but there were interesting points came out after we collected and compared all the data.

Through comparison, we found that:

· The gender distribution of day-trip ski resorts was more balanced than destination ski resorts.

· The majority of ski enthusiasts were male from the report of iSNOW and Ski+.

· Two-thirds of users in Mafengwo Ski were female.

· The elementary indoor ski market had more female learners than males.

Table 12-1 Comprehensive Information on Gender Characteristics of Skiers(2019)

Indicator	Destination Ski Resorts	Day-Trip Ski Resorts	iSNOW	Ski+	Mafengwo Ski	Ski Simulator (SKINOW)	Indoor Ski Resorts (Sunac Snow World)
Male/%	57.70	52.80	58	68	32	55	44.37
Notes	Calculation based on the number of ski visits at each ski resort		Online users	Online users	Online users	Customers arrived	Skiing school students

II. Age of Skiers

From the comparison of the data provided in Table 12-2, we found that:

· The average age of skiers who go to destination ski resorts was higher than those who go to day-trip ski resorts.

· Skiers under 40 years old took up a proportion of 95% in SKINOW, which primarily provided ski teaching services. Among them, preschoolers accounted for 15%.

· 96% of skiers in iSNOW (mainly provided online services) were under 40 years old.

Table 12-2 Comprehensive Information on Age Characteristics of Skiers (2019) (%)

Age	Destination Ski Resorts	Day-Trip Ski Resorts	iSNOW	Ski Simulator (SKINOW)	Ctrip
Preschoolers (1~7)	3.74	4.21	/	15	/
7~20	10.74	17.06	6	19	22
20~30	27.69	34.59	51	26	25
30~40	33.66	28.19	39	35	30
40~50	18.38	12.02	3	4	15
Above 50	5.79	3.93	1	1	8

III. Other Characteristics

1. Ctrip Report (Extract)

Among all skiers, those who travel alone occupied the largest proportion (29.3%), followed by family travel and couple travel (respectively 27.5% and 22.8%). Those who travel with their friends or colleagues took up 20.4% (see Figure 12-1). In these years, there were growing numbers of tourists go skiing with their families. From the Ctrip orders, it was found that the youngest skiers traveled with parents were only 2.5 years old.Skiing became a popular activity among parent-child travel.

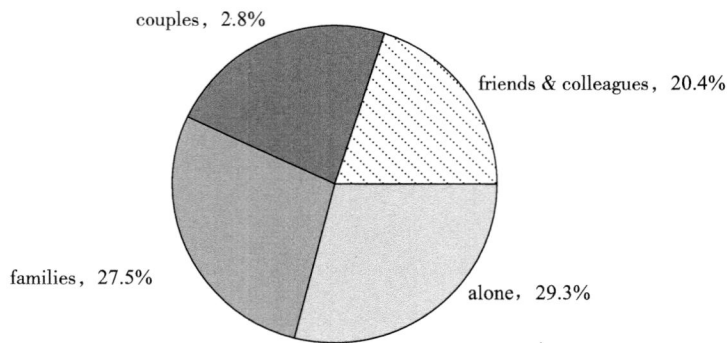

Figure 12-1　Distribution of Ski Partners(2019)

From the data provided by Ctrip, people from Shanghai had a strong passion on skiing, followed by those skiers from Guangzhou, Wuhan, Hangzhou, Suzhou, Nanjing, Fuzhou and Shenzhen.

According to Ctrip, average consumption on domestic skiing was 2398 yuan per capita, while average consumption on skiing abroad was 9893 yuan per capita.See Figure 12-2.

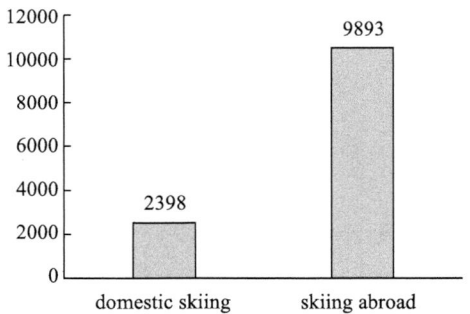

Figure 12-2　Average Consumption of Skiing(2019)

2.Mafengwo.com Report(Extract)

With the growing of ski members, skiing experiences shared by users in Mafengwo.com increased by 349.89% year-on-year, which was 1120.64% higher than that in 2017.

3.HAXUEZOO Report(Extract)

It was shown by HAXUEZOO that ski enthusiasts came from places all over China, while most of them were from Beijing, Hebei and Northeastern China (see Figure 12-3). According to the data of 2018-2019, online transactions grew rapidly, at the same time, mobile payment occupied a proportion of 82% (see Figure 12-4).

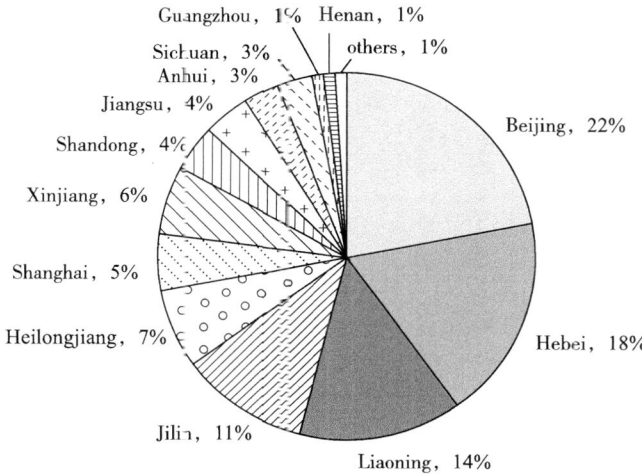

Figure 12-3　Users Analysis from HUAXUEZOO(2019)

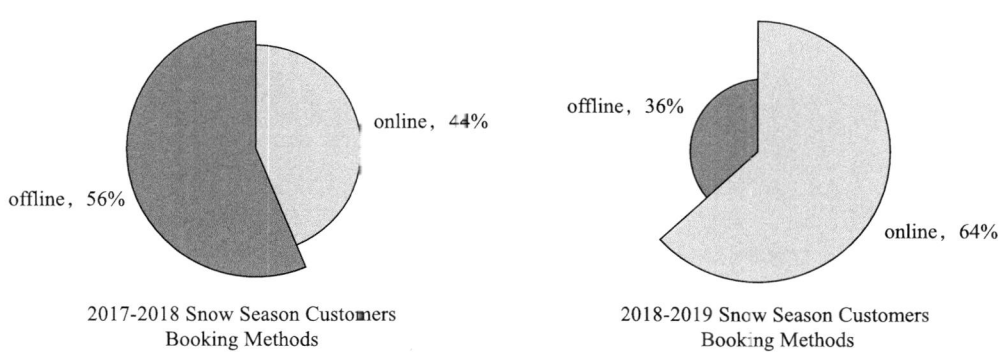

Figure 12-4　Comparisons of Customer Order

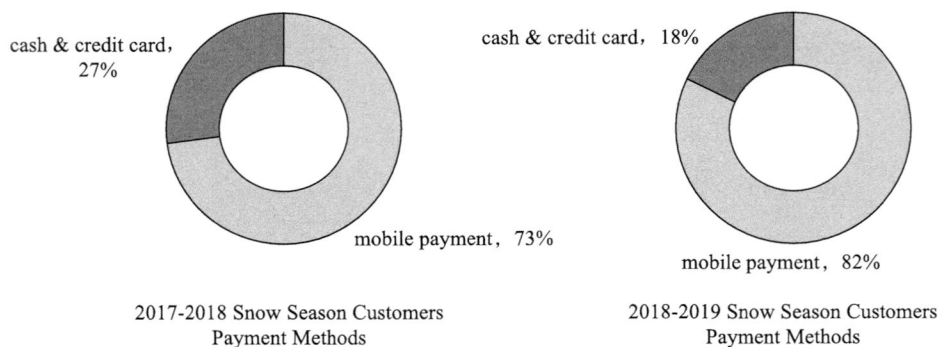

Figure 12-4 Comparisons of Customer Order (Continued)

4. Ski+ Report (Extract)

As of 2019, there were over 1172 clubs registered in Ski+, covering 126 cities and 29 regions (including 20 provinces, 4 municipalities, 4 autonomous regions and Hong Kong, Macao and Taiwan and other regions), and 13 clubs were in overseas.

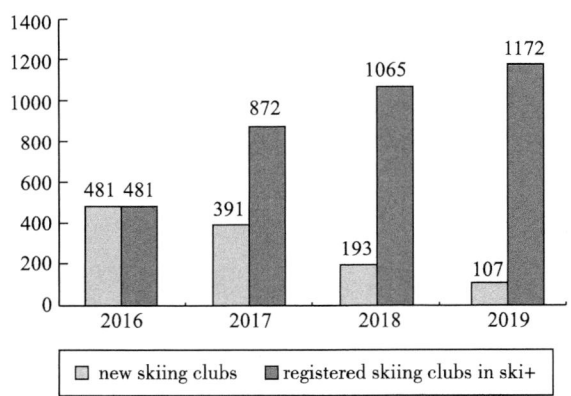

Figure 12-5 Number of Registered Skiing Clubs in Ski+

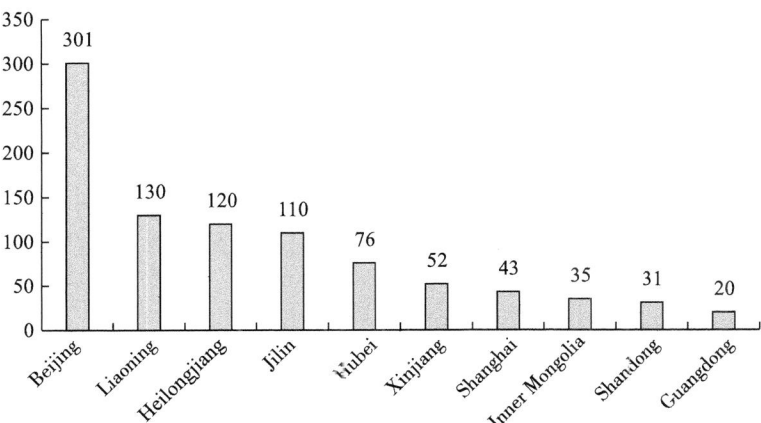

Figure 12-6　Top 10 Regional Clubs(2019)

Chapter 13　Ski Equipment Market

There was more positive news for the ski equipment market in 2019. Generally, the snowboard market entered a period of rapid growth, and the overall annual growth rate was expected to be between 25% and 30%. At the same time, there were also signs of recovery and the start-up of the skis market. The information of this chapter was mainly shared by French DECATHLON Wed'ze ski and GOSKI of Cold Mountain.

Ⅰ.China Market Report from DECATHLON Wed'ze Ski

In 2019, DECATHLON Wed'ze ski hit the shelves of 315 DECATHLON stores in China. The top three cities with the highest number of stores were Shanghai, Beijing and Guangzhou, and the top three cities of Wed'ze skiing brand sales were Beijing, Shanghai and Chengdu for five consecutive years. Wed'ze ski brand had achieved continuous growth for five consecutive years in China.

In terms of the sales of different categories of Wed'ze skiing brands, the sales of the snowboards were much higher than that of skis, and the growth rate of ski equipment for children's was higher than that for adults. Among them, in 2019, the year-on-year growth rate of children's snowboards and snowboard shoes was around 40%.

The sales of Wed'ze ski suits were the most outstanding. In 2019, the sales of adult and children ski suits series exceeded 1.5 million pieces.

The sales of Wed'ze ski helmets and wind goggles continued to grow rapidly in the past five years. In 2019, the annual sales of adult series and children series both achieved a growth rate of more than 100% compared with 2015.

II. Cold Mountain GOSKI Report

In 2019, 27 stores were opened by Cold Mountain. Sales were 75 million in 2017-2018 snow season, and increased to 90 million in 2018-2019 snow season, with an annual growth rate of 20%. And the per customer transaction was 2000 yuan.

The sales of the equipment for men and women accounted for 65% and 35% respectively.

Form the perspective of geographical distribution of sales, Beijing and Chongli took up 40% of the total sales, the Northeast China took up 30%, and the Yangtze River Delta region accounted for 5%.

In China, the sales of Oakley, a well-known eyewear brand, increased by more than 10 thousand every year, and the sales in the recent three snow seasons was 10 thousand, 20 thousand and 30 thousand respectively. It is expected to reach 60 thousand by the 2022-2023 snow season.

In China, the ski retail sales of Burton, a top snowboard brand, were 100 million yuan in the 2018-2019 snow season and 120 million yuan in the 2019-2020 snow season. The growth rate is expected to be between 30 to 50 percent a year for the next few years.

The market shared by Cold Mountain took up about 10% ~ 15% of the total core market[①], with an estimated market size of between 600 million to 900 million. In the next three years, with estimated annual growth rate of 30%, the 2019-2020 snow season will be 1 billion yuan, the 2020-2021 snow season will achieve 1.3 billion yuan, and the 2021-2022 snow season will reach 1.56 billion yuan.

According to SIA industry report in the United States, the snowboard retail industry in the U.S. ski market was about 800 million to 1 billion dollars, with the snowboard population of about 7.6 million, and the sales of the snowboard was about 450 thousand to 500 thousand pieces. So far, China accounted for about 10% of the U.S. market.

---

① Core market refers to professional brand market.